CLASSROOM ASSESSMENT

CANADIAN EDITION

CLASSROOM ASSESSMENT

Concepts and Applications

PETER W. AIRASIAN

Boston College

JOSEPH F. ENGEMANN

Brock University

TIFFANY L. GALLAGHER

Brock University

Toronto   Montréal   Boston   Burr Ridge, IL   Dubuque, IA   Madison, WI   New York
San Francisco   St. Louis   Bangkok   Bogotá   Caracas   Kuala Lumpur   Lisbon   London
Madrid   Mexico City   Milan   New Delhi   Santiago   Seoul   Singapore   Sydney   Taipei

Mc Graw Hill **McGraw-Hill Ryerson**

Classroom Assessment:
Concepts and Applications
Canadian Edition

ISBN-13: 978-0-07-095966-8
ISBN-10: 0-07-095966-8

1 2 3 4 5 6 7 8 9 10 TCP 0 9 8 7

Printed and bound in Canada

Care has been taken to trace ownership of copyright material contained in this text; however, the publisher will welcome any information that enables them to rectify any reference or credit for subsequent editions.

Editorial Director: Joanna Cotton
Sponsoring Editor: Karen Ritcey
Marketing Manager: Marc Trudel
Senior Developmental Editor: Denise Foote
Developmental Editor: Christine Gilbert
Editorial Associate: Marina Seguin
Supervising Editor: Graeme Powell
Copy Editor: Erin Moore
Senior Production Coordinator: Madeleine Harrington
Cover Design: Dianna Little
Interior Design: Valid Design & Layout
Page Layout: Jay·Tee Graphics
Printer: Transcontinental Printing Group

Library and Archives Canada Cataloguing in Publication

Airasian, Peter W.
        Classroom assessment : concepts and applications / Peter W.
Airasian, Joseph F. Engemann, Tiffany Gallagher. -- Canadian ed.

Includes bibliographical references and index.
ISBN-13: 978-0-07-095966-8
ISBN-10: 0-07-095966-8

  1. Educational tests and measurements. 2. Academic achievement.
3. Education--Evaluation. I. Gallagher, Tiffany L. II. Engemann, Joseph F. (Joseph Francis)
III. Title.
LB3054.C3A37 2006   371.27   C2006-902247-X

ABOUT THE AUTHORS

Peter W. Airasian is Professor of Education at Boston College, where he is Chair of the Department of Counseling, Developmental Psychology, and Research Methods. His main teaching responsibilities are instructing pre- and in-service teachers in classroom assessment. He received his PhD degree from the University of Chicago, with a concentration in assessment and evaluation. He is a former high school chemistry and biology teacher. He is coauthor of *Minimal Competency Testing* (1979), *School Effectiveness: A Reassessment of the Evidence* (1980), *The Effects of Standardized Testing* (1982), *Assessment in the Classroom* (1996), *Teacher Self-Evaluation Tool Kit* (2001), *Taxonomy for Learning, Teaching, & Assessing: A Revision of Bloom's Taxonomy of Educational Objectives* (2001), and *Educational Research: Competencies for Analysis and Applications* (2002), as well as many articles on classroom assessment and testing. He is past Chair of the American Educational Research Association's Special Interest Group on Classroom Assessment. Currently, he is studying the process classroom teachers use to assess themselves.

Joe Engemann has been with the Faculty of Education at Brock University since 1993, where he has served as a member of both the Department of Pre-service Education and the Department of Graduate and Undergraduate Studies. Before becoming a teacher educator, Joe taught elementary school for 17 years with the Lincoln County Catholic School Board. His research interests, along with classroom assessment and evaluation, include teacher induction and mentoring, literacy across the curriculum, and aboriginal science education. He is the past president of the Canadian Association of Teacher Education and acted as the Ontario Faculties of Education representative on the Science Teachers Association of Ontario Board of Directors. Joe received his B.Sc., B.Ed. and M.Ed. from Brock University and his PhD in science education from the State University of New York in Buffalo.

Tiffany L. Gallagher is a member of the Department of Pre-service Education of the Faculty of Education at Brock University. Recently, she completed her doctoral studies on the effects of tutoring students with learning difficulties and the associated experiences of their literacy tutors. Professionally, Tiffany was a teacher and administrator in private practice supplemental education for over a decade. In this capacity, she administered achievement and aptitude tests and interpreted the results for academic programming. Currently, she teaches courses in educational psychology and assessment and evaluation. She has also co-authored the text *Educational Psychology* (first and second Canadian editions). Tiffany's current research interests include literacy assessment, reading and writing strategy instruction, teachers with learning disabilities, and the role of the in-school resource teacher.

BRIEF CONTENTS

▶ CHAPTER 1
The Breadth of Classroom Assessment   1

▶ CHAPTER 2
Learning about Students: Diagnostic Assessment   19

▶ CHAPTER 3
Instructional Planning and Assessment   38

▶ CHAPTER 4
Assessing During Instruction: Formative Assessment   67

▶ CHAPTER 5
Preparing Selected and Constructed Response Tests   87

▶ CHAPTER 6
Administration of Selected and Constructed Response Tests   121

▶ CHAPTER 7
Performance Assessments   147

▶ CHAPTER 8
Grading   191

▶ CHAPTER 9
Large-Scale Assessment   237

▶ CHAPTER 10
Standardized Achievement Tests   261

▶ EPILOGUE
Summing Up Classroom Assessment   295

▶ APPENDIX A
Excerpted from the Principles for Fair Student Assessment
Practices for Education in Canada   301

▶ APPENDIX B
Taxonomy of Educational Objectives: Major Categories   304

▶ APPENDIX C
Statistical Applications for Classroom Assessment   305

CONTENTS

PREFACE *xvii*

▶ CHAPTER 1

The Breadth of Classroom Assessment *1*

Purposes of Classroom Assessment *3*
Diagnosing Students' Needs *3*
Providing Feedback and Evaluating Instruction *4*
Certifying Academic Learning *4*
Placing Students *4*

Types of Assessment *4*

Three General Ways to Collect Data: Paper-and-Pencil, Observation, and Oral Questioning *5*
Paper-and-Pencil Techniques *5*
Observation Techniques *6*
Oral Questioning Techniques *7*

Standardized and Nonstandardized Assessments *7*
Standardized Assessments *7*
Nonstandardized Assessments *8*
Technology and Assessment "PARE: Practical Assessment, Research, and Evaluation" *8*

Good Assessments: Valid and Reliable *8*
Validity *10*
Key Assessment Tools 1.1 "Key Aspects of Assessment Validity" *11*
Reliability *11*
Key Assessment Tools 1.2 "Key Aspects of Assessment Reliability" *12*

Ethical Issues and Responsibilities *13*

Ethical Issues and Assessment *14*
Fairness in Accommodating Special Needs *14*
Chapter Review *16*
OLC Chapter Review *16*
Questions for Discussion *17*
Activities *18*

▶ CHAPTER 2

Learning About Students: Diagnostic Assessment *19*

Gathering Information About Students *21*

Sources of Learning About Students *24*

Forming Student Descriptions *25*

Guidelines for Diagnostic Assessments *26*

Concerns About Ethics and Accuracy *29*

The General Problem *29*
The Issues of Validity and Reliability *30*
Chapter Case Study *31*
Key Assessment Tools 2.1 "Threats to the Validity and Reliability of Diagnostic Assessments" *33*
Chapter Review *34*
OLC Chapter Review *34*
Questions for Discussion *36*
Activities *36*

▶ CHAPTER 3

Instructional Planning and Assessment *38*

The Instructional Process *40*

Instructional Planning *41*

Student Characteristics *43*
Teacher Characteristics *44*
Instructional Resources *44*

Three Levels of Teaching Objectives *48*

Three Domains of Objectives *50*
 The Cognitive Domain 50
 The Affective Domain 52
 The Psychomotor Domain 53

Stating and Constructing Expectations or Learning Outcomes *54*
 Essential Elements of the Statement 54
 Forming Complete Statements 55
 Some Good Examples of Objectives 57
 Key Assessment Tools 3.1 "Criteria for Successful Objectives" 58
 Questions Often Asked about Educational Objectives 58

Improving the Tie Between Planning and Assessment *59*

Planning for Students with Exceptionalities *61*
 Chapter Review 64
 OLC Chapter Review 64
 Questions for Discussion 65
 Activities 66

▶ CHAPTER 4

Assessing During Instruction: Formative Assessment *67*

Assessment Tasks During Instruction *69*
 Indicators During Instruction 71
 Decision Making During Instruction 72
 Using Practical Knowledge 72
 Chapter Case Study 72

Guidelines for Formative Assessments *73*
 Student Self-Assessment 74

Questioning: Purposes, Types, and Strategies *75*
 Purposes of Questioning 75
 Questioning Strategies 78

Concerns About Accuracy 80

Problems That Affect Instructional Validity 80
Problems That Affect Instructional Reliability 81
Key Assessment Tools 4.1 "Validity and Reliability Problems of Instructional Assessment" 82

Accommodations and Formative Assessment 82

Technology and Assessment "Canadian Association of Second Language Teachers" 82
Chapter Review 83
Chapter OLC Review 83
Questions for Discussion 85
Activities 86

▶ CHAPTER 5

Preparing Selected and Constructed Response Tests 87

Summative Assessment 88

Selected and Constructed Response Test Items 90

Selected Response Items 90
Constructed Response Items 91
Comparing Selected and Constructed Response Items 93

Higher-Level Questions 94

Essay Questions 94
Interpretive Exercises 95

Guidelines for Writing and Critiquing Test Items 97

Cover Important Objectives 97
Write Clearly and Simply: Seven Rules 100
Review Items before Testing 108
Decisions in Planning a Test 109
Key Assessment Tools 5.1 "Writing Test Items" *109*
Assembling Tests 113
Key Assessment Tools 5.2 "Key Points to Consider in Judging Textbook Tests" *113*
Key Assessment Tools 5.3 "Common Problems in Developing or Selecting Tests to Assess Student Achievement" *114*
Technology and Assessment: "Journal of Technology, Learning and Assessment" *115*

Accommodations: Substitutions for Written Tests 115

Key Assessment Tools 5.4 "Guidelines for Assembling
a Test" 116
Chapter Review 118
OLC Chapter Review 118
Questions for Discussion 119
Activities 119

▶ CHAPTER 6
Administration of Selected and Constructed Response Tests 121

Preparing Students for Selected and Constructed Response Tests 122

Issues of Test Preparation 122
Review Before Testing 123
Key Assessment Tools 6.1 "'Do No Harm' Testing
Practices" 124
Ensure Familiarity with Question Formats 125
Scheduling the Test 125
Giving Students Information about the Test 127

Administering Tests 128

Physical Setting 128
Psychological Setting 128
Keeping Track of Time 129

Issues of Cheating 129

Types of Cheating on Tests 130
Deterring Cheating 130
Chapter Case Study 130

Scoring Selected and Constructed Response Tests 131

Scoring Selected Response Items 133
Scoring Short-Answer and Completion Items 133
Scoring Essay Items 134

Analyzing Item Validity 137

After-Test Analyses 138
After-Test Analyses of Multiple-Choice Items 139

Discussing Test Results with Students 141

Testing Students with Exceptionalities *141*

Technology and Assessment: "Accommodating Students with Exceptionalities During Testing" *143*

Chapter Review 144

OLC Chapter Review 144

Questions for Discussion 145

Activities 146

▶ CHAPTER 7

Performance Assessments *147*

The General Role of Performance Assessments *148*

Performance Assessment in Schools *149*

Performance-Oriented Subjects 150

Developing Performance Assessments *151*

Define the Purpose of Assessment 152

Identify Performance Criteria 152

Key Assessment Tools 7.1 "Examples of Performance Criteria" *153*

Provide a Setting to Elicit and Observe the Performance 158

Develop a Score to Describe the Performance 159

Anecdotal Records, Checklists, and Rating Scales *159*

Anecdotal Records 159

Checklists 160

Rating Scales 162

Rubrics *166*

Two Methods of Scoring 166

Devising Rubrics 168

Key Assessment Tools 7.2 "General Steps in Preparing and Using Rubrics" *170*

Technology and Assessment "Performance Assessment Resources" *171*

Involving Students in the Use of Rubrics 172

Portfolios *173*

Key Assessment Tools 7.3 "What Can Go Into a Portfolio" *174*

Purpose of Portfolios 175

Performance Criteria 176

Setting   177
Scoring   177

Validity and Reliability of Performance Assessments   *180*

Preparing Students   182
Validity   182
Reliability   184
Chapter Review   186
OLC Chapter Review   186
Questions for Discussion   189
Activities   189

▶ CHAPTER 8

Grading   *191*

Purposes and Difficulties of Grading   *193*

Why Grade?   193
The Difficulty of Grading   194
Grading in Cooperative Learning   196

Grading as Judgment   *197*

Chapter Case Study   197

Four Types of Comparison for Grading   *198*

Norm-Referenced Grading (Comparison with Other Students)   198
Criterion-Referenced Grading (Predefined Performance Standards)   199
Comparison to a Student's Own Ability   203
Comparison to a Student's Prior Performance   204

Deciding What to Grade   *205*

Academic Achievement   205
Affective Performances   206

Summarizing Varied Types of Assessment Information   *209*

What Should Be Included in a Grade?   212
Selecting Weights for Assessment Information   213
Combining Different Assessment Information   214
Technology and Assessment "Computerized Grading Systems"   215
Validity of the Information   215
Computing Overall Scores   216

Two Approaches to Assigning Grades 217

A Criterion-Referenced Example 217
A Norm-Referenced Example 219
Key Assessment Tools 8.1 "Steps in the Grading Process" 219
Report Cards 220
Key Assessment Tools 8.2 "Guidelines for Grading" 220

Grading Students with Exceptionalities 223

The Nature of the Challenge 223
Some Possible Strategies 227

Other Methods of Reporting Student Progress 229

Parent-Teacher Conferences 229
Additional Reporting Methods 231
Key Assessment Tools 8.3 "Parent-Teacher Conferences" 232
Chapter Review 233
OLC Chapter Review 233
Questions for Discussion 234
Activity 235

▶ CHAPTER 9

Large-Scale Assessment 237

Defining Large-Scale Assessment 239

Large-Scale Assessment in Canada 240

Provincial and Territorial Large-Scale Assessment Programs 240
National and International Assessment Programs 246

Implications of Large-Scale Assessment 248

The Impact on Teachers and Teaching 248
Problems and Limitations of Large-Scale Assessment 249
Reconsidering Large-Scale Assessment 250

Motivating Students and Teachers for Large-Scale Assessment 252

Staying Focused on Quality in the Classroom 252

Preparing Students for Large-Scale Assessments 253

Issues of Test Preparation 253
Provide Good Instruction 254

Key Assessment Tools 9.1 "'Do No Harm' Assessment
Practices" *255*
Review Before Testing 255
Ensure Familiarity with Question Formats 256
Scheduling the Test 256
Giving Students Information about the Assessment 257
Chapter Review 258
OLC Chapter Review 258
Questions for Discussion 259
Activities 260

▶ CHAPTER 10

Standardized Achievement Tests *261*

How Standardized Achievement Tests Are Created *265*

Test Construction   266

Administering the Test *270*

The Need for Consistent Administration   271

Interpreting Scores *271*

Percentile Rank Scores   272
Stanine Scores   273
Grade Equivalent Scores   273
Chapter Case Study   *275*

Examples of Standardized Tests *275*

Example 1: Practice Test   276
Example 2: Student Diagnostic Profile   276
Example 3: Overview of Standardized Tests   277
Example 4: Student List Report   277
Example 5: Student Performance Chart   277

The Validity of Standardized Achievement Tests *278*

Appropriate Coverage   278
Representative Norms   282
Conditions of Administration   286
Potential Misinterpretations   287
Technology and Assessment "Resources for
Standardized Tests"   *288*

Standardized Tests and Students with Exceptionalities *288*

Reporting Results to Parents *289*

In Conclusion *290*
  Chapter Review 291
  OLC Chapter Review 291
  Questions for Discussion 293
  Activities 294

▶ EPILOGUE

Summing Up Classroom Assessment *295*

Collecting Assessment Information *295*

Interpreting Assessment Information:
Five Guidelines *296*

Assessment: A Tool Used Wisely *300*

▶ APPENDIX A

Principles for Fair Student Assessment Practices for
Education in Canada *301*

▶ APPENDIX B

Taxonomy of Educational Objectives: Major
Categories *304*

▶ APPENDIX C

Statistical Applications for Classroom Assessment *305*

Glossary *314*

References *318*

Credits *324*

Subject Index *325*

PREFACE

A Conceptual and Applied Approach

This textbook represents the first Canadian edition of *Classroom Assessment: Concepts and Applications*. It is an adaptation of the highly successful American textbook of the same name written by Peter W. Airasian. We are very pleased to have been invited by McGraw-Hill Ryerson to author a textbook that will provide support for learning about assessment and evaluation within a Canadian context. This has not been an easy task, given the disparate nature of education across Canada, but we are confident that the essential theoretical and practical knowledge about assessment and evaluation has been provided for use in all Canadian jurisdictions.

The ability to construct and use classroom assessments is an essential educational skill for all teachers. Ongoing formal and informal classroom assessments provide teachers with the information they need to monitor and make decisions about their teaching and their students' learning. Increasingly, teachers must address not only their own classroom assessment, but also external sources such as large-scale provincial and territorial assessment and standardized tests. This textbook covers the broad range of assessments that confront teachers both in their classrooms and beyond. Each type of assessment is presented with attention to both concepts and application, so that students will understand the reasons and cautions that are inherent in the assessments they construct and interpret.

Classroom Assessment: Key Concepts and Applications provides a broad introductory overview of the critical terms, practices, and issues associated with assessment and evaluation. Chapter 1 introduces and defines key concepts such as *assessment, evaluation, measurement, validity*, and *reliability* and outlines the purposes for and types of assessment. Within this chapter, the reader is also introduced to the ethical issues and responsibilities associated with assessment of students. Chapter 2 focuses on *diagnostic assessment* by describing when it should be used, outlining what sources of data support it, and providing a set of guidelines that maximizes its potential for setting up the best possible learning situation. Chapter 3 deals with the relationship between instruction and assessment and evaluation. This chapter outlines the steps in *planning instruction* and delineates among the various levels of teaching objectives. Chapter 4 returns to the focus on types of assessment with a look at *formative assessment*. In this chapter, the reader is presented with the basics for developing the capacity to improve teaching and learning through assessment while instruction is taking place. Chapters 5 and 6 focus on *summative assessment* with an emphasis on the preparation and administration, respectively, of selected and constructed response tests. Many readers will find these two chapters exceptionally useful for much of the assessment that they plan to do. Chapter 7 describes *performance assessment* by providing the reader with information about how to develop such assessments and their strengths and weaknesses. As part of this chapter, the reader is also introduced to assessment using rubrics and portfolios. Chapter 8 centres on evaluation with a look at *grading* as a judgment process, which includes a comparison between norm- and criterion-referenced grading, and a presentation of strategies for conducting effective parent-teacher conferences. Chapter 9 focuses on *large-scale provincial and territorial assessment* and provides specific examples from across the Canadian landscape. Within this chapter the reader will gain familiarity with how large-scale assessments are constructed, their implications for teachers, and the problems associated with large-scale assessment. Finally, Chapter 10 provides information on the use, administration, interpretation, application, and reporting of *commercially available standardized achievement tests*.

Joseph F. Engemann
Tiffany L. Gallagher

Features of the Canadian Edition

This textbook includes the following features that make it especially useful for teachers at all levels of training and experience:

Length and Coverage: This text is concise but doesn't scrimp on coverage. The text has been condensed from 11 chapters to 10 following the length of a typical semester.

Realistic Assessment: The focus throughout is on the realities of classrooms and how assessments can serve these realities.

Canadian Content and Examples: Classroom Assessment: Key Concepts and Applications includes a number of Canadian examples, illustrations, and strategies for application, plus such practical concerns as organizing the classroom and interpreting assessment results.

Validity and Reliability: These central assessment concepts are introduced in the first chapter and then linked in later chapters to each specific type of assessment information. The validity and reliability issues of diagnostic, formative, summative, and performance assessment and standardized testing are identified. Practical strategies to improve validity and reliability of varied assessment approaches are presented in each chapter.

Practical Guidelines: A portion of each chapter focuses on practical guidelines to follow and common errors to avoid when using the type of assessment being presented.

Case Studies: Accessible through the Online Learning Centre (at www.mcgrawhill.com/college/airasian), these Canadian case studies bring chapter topics to life.

Key Assessment Tools: These boxes highlight practical resources and tools to use in the assessment process such as criteria for successful objectives and examples of performance criteria.

Technology and Assessment: These margin boxes present ways to use technology in assessment and point to added information online.

Students with Exceptionalities: The assessment of students with exceptionalities has been integrated into many chapters of this book.

Superior Service

*i*Learning Sales Specialist

Your Integrated Learning Sales Specialist is a McGraw-Hill Ryerson representative who has the experience, product knowledge, training, and support to help you assess and integrate any of the below-noted products, technology, and services into your course for optimum teaching and learning performance. Whether it's helping your students improve their grades, or putting your entire course online, your *i*Learning Sales Specialist is there to help you do it. Contact your local *i*Learning Sales Specialist today to learn how to maximize all of McGraw-Hill Ryerson's resources!

*i*Learning Services Program

McGraw-Hill Ryerson offers a unique *i*Learning Services package designed for Canadian faculty. Our mission is to equip providers of higher education with superior tools and resources required for excellence in teaching. For additional information visit www.mcgrawhill.ca/highereducation/iservices.

Instructor Resources

Instructor's Online Learning Centre The Online Learning Centre at www.mcgrawhill.ca/college/airasian includes a password-protected Web site for instructors. The site offers a downloadable Instructor's Manual and access to PageOut, the McGraw-Hill Ryerson Web site development centre.

Instructor's CD-ROM contains the Instructor's Manual, Computerized Assessment Bank, and Microsoft® PowerPoint® presentations.

➤ **Instructor's Manual** The Instructor's Manual contains such useful resources as chapter overviews, learning objectives, key terms, and instructional strategies.

➤ **Computerized Assessment Bank** Available in Windows format, this software provides you with the Assessment Bank in electronic form. The keyword search option lets you browse through the question bank for problems containing a specific word or phrase. Password protection is available for saved tests or for the entire database. Questions can be added, modified, or deleted.

➤ **Microsoft® PowerPoint® Presentations** This presentation system offers visual presentations that may be edited and manipulated to fit a particular course format. These slides contain useful outlines, summaries, and exhibits from the text.

Student Resources

Student Online Learning Centre This powerful electronic learning aid, located at www.mcgrawhill.ca/college/airasian, offers a wealth of materials, including quizzes, interactive exercises, learning objectives, case studies, Internet exercises, annotated Web links, bonus material, *Globe and Mail* news feeds, and much more.

Acknowledgements and Dedication

The Canadian edition would not have been possible without the support of the reviewers of this edition. For their helpful and perceptive feedback, our thanks go to the following colleagues:

John O. Anderson, University of Victoria
Laurie Carlson Berg, University of Regina
Robert Crocker, Memorial University
Laurie Hellsten, University of Saskatchewan
Liesel Knaack, University of Ontario Institute of Technology (UOIT)
J. Karen Reynolds, Lakehead University
Steven Van Zoost, Mount Saint Vincent University/Avon View High School

I would like to dedicate the Canadian edition to my wife, Lorraine, who has been an unwavering source of support and encouragement throughout all my professional endeavours.

Joseph F. Engemann

I would like to dedicate this Canadian edition to Blythe Marie (Williams) Law — great aunt and confidante, who lived every dream right alongside of me, but most importantly will always live in my heart.

Tiffany L. Gallagher

THE BREADTH OF CLASSROOM ASSESSMENT

M s. Racine has just completed a typical day with her Grade 6 students. As usual, she spends time after the students have left to complete some marking, review the success of the day's lessons, and begin planning for the next instructional day. Once again, she is struck by the variety and importance of the assessments that she has accomplished. Throughout the day she has diagnosed the academic needs of particular students, acquired summative assessment results, and is now planning to alter some of tomorrow's teaching based on formative assessment of some of the day's lessons. She realizes that her day has been filled with situations in which she has had to make decisions. Some of these decisions concerned individual students and some concerned the class as a whole. For her, the valuable learning about classroom assessment that she gained during pre-service education, from board-sponsored workshops, and from her own professional reading has always served her well.

Assessment is the process of collecting, synthesizing, and interpreting information to aid in decision making. Assessment is a necessary part of classroom life.

Classroom assessment is the process of collecting, synthesizing, and interpreting information to aid in classroom decision making. This book explores a broad range of assessment strategies for diagnosing students' needs, evaluating instruction, and determining academic progress. Chapter 1 lays out a general scheme of types of assessments and their uses that will be covered more deeply in later chapters. It explains how validity and reliability are the keys to effective assessment. It ends with some thoughts about ethical issues related to classroom assessment. (Visit the text OLC (www.mcgrawhill.ca/college/airasian) for a detailed description of each province's and territory's treatment of the terms *assessment* and *evaluation*.)

A test is a formal, systematic, usually paper-and-pencil procedure for gathering information.

When people hear the word assessment, they often think of the word "test." A **test** is a formal, systematic, often paper-and-pencil procedure used to gather information about students' performance. But while paper-and-pencil tests are one important tool for gathering assessment information, decisions about students' placement and progress can also be made using other information-gathering tools such as anecdotal record sheets, checklists, rating scales, and rubrics. Shortly, we'll say more about written tests, as well as techniques of observation and oral questioning. Later chapters will cover these options in greater detail.

Measurement is the process of quantifying or assigning a number to performance.

Measurement is the process of collecting data on student performance using an instrument that is associated with a numerical scale. The most common example of measurement in the classroom is when a teacher scores a quiz or test. Such measurement produces a numerical description of performance, such as 17 out of 20 or 85 percent, that is used to represent a student's performance.

Evaluation is the process of judging the quality or value of a performance or a course of action.

Once assessment information is collected, teachers use it to make decisions or judgments about students or instruction. **Evaluation** is the process of making judgments about what is good or desirable as in, for example, judging the quality of students' essays or the desirability of a particular instructional activity. Evaluation occurs after assessment data have been collected, synthesized, and interpreted because this is when the teacher is in a position to make informed judgments.

Imagine a teacher at the start of the year who wants to *assess* the math readiness of her students in order to decide where to start instruction. Notice that the reason for assessing is that a decision must be made. First, the teacher gives a grade-appropriate paper-and-pencil *test* of math readiness. The students' scores on the test provide a *measurement* of their math readiness. Of course, the teacher uses other forms of assessment to determine readiness. She talks to the students about math, watches them while they do math exercises, and checks prior grades and test scores in their school record files. The teacher then considers all of the assessment data she has collected. She *evaluates*, or makes a judgment about, the students' current state of readiness in math. Her final decision, based on her assessment and evaluation, is to recommend a review of last year's math before beginning this year's topics.

PURPOSES OF CLASSROOM ASSESSMENT

Teachers assess for many purposes because they are required to make many decisions. The remainder of this text focuses on assessment concerns and strategies for the following purposes: diagnosing students' needs, providing feedback and evaluating instruction, certifying academic learning, and placing students.

Diagnosing Students' Needs

Much of the assessment data that teachers gather are used to provide them with information about their students' academic, social, attitudinal, and behavioural characteristics so as to enhance communication and instruction. Assessment undertaken for these purposes is called **diagnostic assessment** and usually takes place at the beginning of the school year or before a unit of instruction. Having gathered this information, the teacher can sometimes carry out the remedial activities or make accommodations, but at other times the student must be referred for more specialized diagnosis and remediation outside the classroom. Examples of classroom diagnostic assessment might include the determination of the students' prior knowledge about the geographic regions of Canada, the students' learning style preferences, or the students' ability to use a search engine for research. Some students may require more formal diagnostic assessment using standardized achievement tests such as the *Canadian Test of Basic Skills* (*CTBS*; Nelson, 1998), the *Canadian Achievement Test* (*CAT-3*; Canadian Test Centre, 2001), or the *Gates-MacGinite Reading Tests* (*GMRT*; Nelson, 1992).

Providing Feedback and Evaluating Instruction

As teachers, we provide instruction so that our students will develop important skills and grow in knowledge. Maximal student learning requires teachers to continually gauge the success of their instruction and make the necessary modifications. Students must also know how well they are learning so that they, too, can take steps to improve. The use of observations and feedback intended to alter and improve students' learning while instruction is taking place is called **formative assessment**. Teachers gather formative assessment data by questioning students about the content of the lesson, checking assigned work, and reflecting on the lesson. These data should be used by the teacher to make decisions about whether new instruction may proceed, and, if not, how previous instruction might change in order to maximize student learning.

Certifying Academic Learning

The task of certifying students' learning at the end of instruction is termed **summative assessment**. Summative assessment data include such things as end-of-unit tests, examinations, projects, reports, and performances, which can be used to report on student learning and for making judgments about student learning. Much of our time, as teachers, is spent collecting information that we will use to make final judgments about students' academic learning.

Placing Students

Classroom teachers make decisions about the placements of their students. Whenever we divide students into reading or math groups, organize students into cooperative learning groups, or recommend that students be promoted to the next grade, assessments for placement purposes have taken place. These placements result from decisions that a teacher makes using information about the students from diagnostic, formative, or summative assessments.

TYPES OF ASSESSMENT

Assessments may be classified in various ways based on their characteristic differences: when the assessment takes place (diagnostic, formative, or summative), the type of expectations or learning outcomes being assessed (product or performance), the type of technique being used (paper-and-pencil, observation, or oral questioning), or whether the assessment is standardized or nonstandardized.

As indicated earlier in this chapter, teachers make decisions about when to assess based on the reason for assessment. If the teacher is interested in gathering data about students' knowledge or skills, prior to instruction, then she will perform a *diagnostic assessment*. Throughout a unit of study, teachers will conduct *formative assessment* that will provide evidence about how well the students are achieving. Formative assessment allows the teacher to adapt instruction to better accommodate the ongoing learning needs of the students, while the students can use the feedback from formative assessment to modify their efforts and strategies for learning. Finally, at the end of any instructional episode, whether a single lesson or a unit of study, teachers can use summative assessment to identify the level of students' learning and skill development.

Teachers also need to assess a variety of expectations or learning outcomes, some that are assessable through a *product* such as a test, lab report, or project that the student has produced. Other expectations or learning outcomes require a *performance assessment* while a student is actively engaged in a task such as giving a speech or using an instrument for data collection in science.

Assessment techniques and an explanation of the difference between standardized and nonstandardized assessment follow.

THREE GENERAL WAYS TO COLLECT DATA: PAPER-AND-PENCIL, OBSERVATION, AND ORAL QUESTIONING

Teachers rely on three primary methods to gather assessment information for classroom decisions: paper-and-pencil techniques, observation techniques, and oral questioning techniques.

In addition to the following sources, helpful supplementary information can be obtained from the students' previous teachers and parents. Teachers routinely consult previous teachers to corroborate or reinforce current observations. Parents frequently volunteer information and respond to teacher queries. While useful, each of these supplementary sources of information has its limitations and should be treated with caution when making decisions.

Teachers gather most of their assessment information using paper-and-pencil techniques, observation techniques, and oral questioning techniques.

Supplementary assessment information can be obtained from previous teachers and parents.

Paper-and-Pencil Techniques

Paper-and-pencil techniques refer to assessment methods in which students write down their responses to questions or problems. When students take a multiple-choice test, complete a written homework assignment, construct a written report, draw a picture, write an essay, or fill in a worksheet,

Paper-and-pencil assessments involve students writing down their responses to questions or problems.

There are two forms of paper-and-pencil assessment: selected response and constructed response.

Selected response techniques require students to select an answer from choices that are provided; constructed response techniques require students to construct a response to a question or problem.

they are providing paper-and-pencil evidence to the teacher. Paper-and-pencil assessment techniques are of two general forms: selected response and constructed response. Multiple choice, true-false, and matching items are called **selected response items**, because as the name implies, the student responds to each question by selecting an answer from choices provided. **Constructed response items** require the student to construct a response to a question. The length of the response can vary substantially. For example, an essay question necessitates the student's construction of a lengthy, detailed response, while a short answer or "fill-in-the-blank" question may only require a word or phrase. Complex constructed response items, such as book reports, journal entries, portfolios, science experiments, and class projects, are also commonly referred to as **performance assessments.** Notice that a selected response item provides the maximum degree of control for the question writer, since he or she specifies both the question and the answer choices. A constructed response item provides the question writer with control only over the item itself, since responsibility for constructing a response resides with the student. Paper-and-pencil assessment methods will be covered in detail in Chapter 5.

Observation Techniques

Observation techniques are applied to student activities and to student products.

Many important skills that students need to acquire are best observed while they are in the process of learning. Teachers may collect important assessment data as students make oral presentations, use specialized equipment such as a microscope, work in collaborative groups, or demonstrate the proper technique for completing specific tasks.

Some teacher observations are formal and planned in advance while others are informal and spontaneous.

Observation is a second major method classroom teachers use to collect assessment data. As the term suggests, **observation** involves watching or listening to students carry out some activity (observation of process) or judging a product a student has produced (observation of product). When students submit a science fair project, produce a still-life drawing, set up laboratory equipment, or complete a project, the teacher observes and judges the products they have produced.

Some observations are formal and planned in advance, as when teachers assess students as they read aloud in a reading group or present an oral report to the class. In such situations, the teacher wants to observe a particular set of student skills and behaviours. For example, in reading aloud, the teacher might be watching and listening for clear pronunciation of words, changing voice tone to emphasize important points, periodic looking up from the book while reading, and so forth. Because such observations are planned, the teacher has time to prepare the students and identify in advance the particular skills and behaviours that will be observed.

Other teacher observations are unplanned and informal, as when the teacher sees someone talking when they should be listening or observes the students fidgeting and looking out the window during a science lesson. Such spontaneous observations reflect momentary unplanned happenings that the teacher observes, mentally records, and interprets. Both formal and informal teacher observations are important information-gathering techniques in classrooms.

Oral Questioning Techniques

Asking oral questions is the third major method teachers use to collect assessment data. "Why do you think the author ended her story that way?" "Explain to me in your own words what an improper fraction is." "Who can summarize yesterday's discussion about the water cycle?" These are all teacher-type questions used to assess students during and at the end of a lesson. Questioning students is very useful during instruction, when it can be used to review a prior topic, brainstorm a new one, find out how the lesson is being understood by students, and engage a student who is not paying attention. The teacher can gather the information he or she wants without the intrusiveness of some form of paper-and-pencil assessment. Oral examinations are used in subject areas such as foreign language, speech, and vocal music. Strategies that can be used to increase the effectiveness of oral questioning can be found in Chapter 4.

Oral questioning provides a great deal of formal and informal information about students. Questioning is especially useful during instruction.

Paper-and-pencil, observation, and questioning techniques complement one another in the classroom. Imagine classroom decision making without being able to observe students' reactions, performances, answers to questions, and interactions. Now imagine what it would be like if no paper-and-pencil information could be obtained in classrooms, and imagine what it would be like if teachers could not ask oral questions of their students. Each type of information is needed to carry out the rich and meaningful assessments that occur in classrooms. As a result, it's important for teachers to master all of these evidence-gathering approaches.

The full range of data analysis methods is needed to gather all the information required for classroom assessment.

STANDARDIZED AND
NONSTANDARDIZED ASSESSMENTS

The information teachers collect and use in their classrooms comes from assessment procedures that are either standardized or nonstandardized. In both cases, most often they are administered in groups.

Standardized Assessments

Standardized assessment procedures are those administered, scored, and interpreted in the same way for all test takers, regardless of where or when they are assessed. Standardized assessments are intended to be administered to students in many different classrooms, but always under identical conditions of administration, scoring, and interpretation. The main reason for standardizing assessment procedures is to ensure that fair comparisons among students in different schools can be made.

Standardized assessments are intended to be administered, scored, and interpreted in the same way for all test takers.

Standardized tests that are commonly used across Canada include achievement tests such as the *Canadian Test of Basic Skills* (*CTBS*; Nelson, 1998) and the *Canadian Achievement Test* (*CAT-3*; Canadian Test Centre, 2001); psychoeducational assessments such as the *Wechsler Intelligence Scale for Children, 4th Edition* (*WISC-IV*; Harcourt Canada, 2003); and specific-area tests such as the *Gates-MacGinite Reading Tests, 3rd Edition* (*GMRT*; Nelson, 1992). Many provinces and territories, including Alberta, British Columbia, Manitoba, New Brunswick, Newfoundland, Nova Scotia, Ontario, Quebec, Saskatchewan, and the Yukon, have large-scale standardized assessments that measure the achievement of students in various grades for specific subjects (mathematics and science) or skills (reading and writing). Large-scale assessment and standardized assessment will be covered in more detail in Chapters 9 and 10 respectively.

Nonstandardized Assessments

Nonstandardized assessments are constructed for use in a single classroom with a single group of students. Most reflect the particular areas of instruction focused on in that single classroom. Teachers create tests, quizzes, checklists, rating scales, and rubrics in order to assess a narrow range of content and skills that is specific to expectations or learning outcomes outlined in curriculum documents. These assessments are usually written or constructed by the classroom teacher and may be modified for particular students depending on their learning styles or capabilities. Teachers also assess students informally through observations of their behaviour. These observations are usually recorded as anecdotal comments.

It is important to note that standardized assessments are not necessarily better than nonstandardized ones. Standardization is important when comparing students across many different classrooms and locations. If comparison beyond a single classroom is not desired, rigorous standardization is not needed, and indeed may be less appropriate for students in that classroom.

GOOD ASSESSMENTS: VALID AND RELIABLE

Whether assessment information helps teachers to make *good* decisions depends upon whether the assessment information collected is itself good. The key ideas are validity and reliability. We begin our examination into the characteristics of good assessment information with an example.

Mr. Ferris has just finished a three-week math unit on computing long division problems with remainders. During the unit, he taught his students the computational steps involved in doing long division problems and the concept of a remainder. He gave and reviewed both homework problems and examples from the text, and he administered a few quizzes. Now, at the end of the unit, Mr. Ferris wants to gather assessment information to find out whether his students have learned to do computational problems involving long division with remainders. He wants to gather this information to help him make a decision about how well his students have learned from his instruction so that he can assign a grade to each student.

To gather the information needed, Mr. Ferris decides to give a test containing items similar in content, format, and difficulty to those he has been teaching. From the millions of possible long division with remainder problems, Mr. Ferris selects 10 that are representative of his teaching. Note that if he picks 10 items that cover different content or are much harder, easier, or presented in a different format than what he taught in class, the results of the test will *not* provide good decision-making information. To assess how well his students learned from his instruction, his test items must be similar in content, format, and difficulty.

Mr. Ferris recognizes this potential pitfall and avoids it by writing 10 items that are similar in content, difficulty, and format to the items taught and practised in his classroom. He assembles the items into a test, administers the test during one class period, and scores the tests on a scale of 0 to 100. Mr. Ferris then has the assessment information he needs to make a decision about each student's grade.

Olivia and Justin each score 100 on the test and receive an A grade for the unit. Stuart scores 30 and receives a D grade. The grades are based upon Mr. Ferris' evaluation of the quality of their performance on the 10-item test. If Mr. Ferris is asked to interpret what Olivia's and Justin's A grades mean, he will likely say that "Olivia and Justin can do long division with remainder items very well." He will also likely say that Stuart's D is "indicative of his inability to do such items well."

In making these statements, Mr. Ferris illustrates the relationship between assessment data and resulting teacher decisions. He says Olivia and Justin "can do long division with remainder items very well." He does not say "Olivia and Justin can do the 10 items I included on my test very well." He judges and describes their performance in *general* terms rather than in terms of his specific 10-item test. Similarly, Stuart is judged in general rather than in test-specific terms. The logic that Mr. Ferris and all teachers use in making such judgments is that if a student can do well on the test items or performances that are actually assessed, the student is likely to do well on similar items and performances that are not assessed. If students do poorly on the 10 test items, it is likely that they also will do poorly on similar, unasked items.

Mr. Ferris' 10-item test illustrates a characteristic that is common to virtually all classroom assessments, regardless of whether they are formal or informal, paper-and-pencil, observational or oral, or standardized or nonstandardized. The essence of classroom assessment is to look at a *sample* of a student's performance and use that sample to make a generalization or prediction about the student's performance on similar, unobserved tasks.

Regardless of its other characteristics, the most important characteristics in determining the usefulness of assessment information are its validity and reliability.

The essence of classroom assessment is to look at a sample of a student's performance and to use that information to make a generalization or prediction about the student's performance in similar situations or on similar tasks.

What if the items on Mr. Ferris' test were not typical of his classroom instruction? What if the student has an "off day" or the teacher's impatience does not permit a student to show his or her "true" performance? If these things happen, then the decision made about the student is likely to be wrong and probably unfair.

Let's now consider a related, more scientifically precise term than fairness.

Validity

Validity is concerned with whether the information being gathered is relevant to the decision that needs to be made.

The single most important characteristic of good assessment is its ability to help the teacher make correct decisions. This characteristic is called **validity.** Assessment information is *valid* to the extent that it is *sufficient* and *appropriate* for making a given decision. Without validity, assessment data will not lead to correct decisions. When a teacher asks, as all teachers should, "Am I collecting the right information for the decision I want to make?" she is asking about the validity of her assessments (Linn, 1997). For any decision, some forms of evidence are more valid than others. For example, it was more valid for Mr. Ferris to determine his students' achievement by giving a test that contained items similar to those he had been teaching than it would have been for him to ask students to write an essay about their feelings towards math. Similarly, it is more valid to determine students' performance by observing their classroom work over a period of time than it is to base such judgments on the performance of their older siblings or the section of the city from which they come. These latter indicators are likely to be less valid for decision making than more direct classroom observation.

Validity (relevance to decision making) is just as applicable to informal teacher observations as it is to formally gathered paper-and-pencil information.

We shall have more to say about validity throughout this text. At this point it is sufficient to say three things about the validity of assessment information. First, validity is concerned with whether the information being gathered is really relevant and appropriate for making the desired decision. Second, validity is the most important characteristic that assessment information can possess because, without it, the assessment information is of no use. Third, concerns about validity pertain to all classroom assessment, not just to those involving formal, paper-and-pencil techniques. Key Assessment Tools 1.1 identifies key concerns in the validity of assessments.

One other note of caution about validity should be mentioned at this point. Decisions that may affect a student's education in a major way should not be made simply on the basis of one result, even if the validity of a single assessment seems strong. It is always prudent to assess the student's ability or performance through several different means in order to enhance the overall rightness of a major decision (Moss, 2003).

> **KEY ASSESSMENT TOOLS 1.1**
>
> ## Key Aspects of Assessment Validity
>
> 1. Validity is concerned with this general question: To what extent will this assessment information help me make an appropriate decision?
>
> 2. Validity refers to the decisions that are made from assessment information, not the assessment approach itself. It is not appropriate to say the assessment information is valid unless the decisions or groups for which it is valid are identified. Assessment information valid for one decision or group of students is not necessarily valid for other decisions or groups.
>
> 3. Validity is a matter of degree; it does not exist on an all-or-nothing basis. Think of assessment validity in terms of categories: highly valid, moderately valid, and invalid.
>
> 4. Validity is always determined by a judgment made by the test user.

Reliability

A second important characteristic of good assessment is its consistency, or **reliability.** Would the assessment results for this person or class be similar if they were gathered at some other time? If you weighed yourself on a scale, got off it, then weighed yourself again on the same scale, you would expect the two weights to be almost identical. If they weren't, you wouldn't trust the information provided by the scale. The information it provides to you is not reliable. Similarly, if assessment information does not produce stable, consistent information, a teacher should exercise caution in using that information to make a decision about a student or the class.

Reliability refers to the stability or consistency of assessment information, i.e., whether it is typical of a student's performance.

Recall that Mr. Ferris included 10 long division with remainder questions on his test, not just one, so that he would obtain reliable information about his students' achievement. He can have more confidence about students' learning by assessing them on 10 items than on only one or two.

Since any single assessment provides only a limited sample of a student's performance, no single assessment procedure or instrument can be expected to provide perfect, error-free information. All assessment information contains some unreliability or inconsistency due to such factors as ambiguous test items, interruptions during testing, differences in students' attention spans, clarity of assessment directions, students' luck in guessing items, mistakes in scoring (especially essay and observational assessments), and obtaining too small a sample to permit the student to show consistent, stable performance. Obviously, it is important to minimize this inconsistency. Key Assessment Tools 1.2 reviews key aspects of the reliability of assessment information.

All assessment information contains some error or inconsistency; thus validity and reliability are both a matter of degree and do not exist on an all-or-nothing basis.

One of the purposes of this text is to suggest methods that can help increase the amount of reliability in classroom assessments. If a teacher cannot rely upon the stability and consistency of the information gathered during an assessment, he or she must be careful not to base important deci-

KEY ASSESSMENT TOOLS 1.2

Key Aspects of Assessment Reliability

1. Reliability refers to the stability or consistency of assessment information and is concerned with this question: "How consistent or typical of the student's performance is the assessment information I have gathered?"

2. Reliability is not concerned with the appropriateness of the assessment information collected, only with its consistency, stability, or typicality. Appropriateness of assessment information is a validity concern.

3. Reliability does not exist on an all-or-nothing basis, but in degrees: high, moderate, or low. Some types of assessment information are more reliable than others.

4. Reliability is a necessary but insufficient condition for validity. An assessment that provides inconsistent, atypical results cannot be relied upon to provide information useful for decision making.

sions on that information. Thus, along with validity, which asks if the assessment information being gathered is relevant to the decision to be made, the classroom teacher must also be concerned with reliability, which asks if the information obtained is consistent and stable.

Consider the following assertion regarding the relationship between validity and reliability. "Valid assessment must be reliable, but reliable assessment need not be valid." The first half of the statement is fairly straightforward. Valid decisions are not possible if the assessment data on which the decisions are based are not consistent. So, to have a valid assessment, there must be reliable information.

As to the second part of the statement, imagine the following scenario. Suppose you ask a student in your class how many brothers and sisters he has. He says six, and you ask him again. He says six. You repeat the question several times, and each time the student indicates six brothers and sisters. You have assessed the number of his brothers and sisters with consistency; the assessment information you have gathered from him is reliable. Suppose you then use this reliable information to make a decision about what reading group to place the student in: the more brothers and sisters, the higher the placement. Since the number of brothers and sisters has little relevance to the student's reading performance, a decision based on this information, no matter how reliable it is, is not valid. In short, assessments can be reliable, but not necessarily valid. Figure 1.1 depicts the relationship between validity and reliability through the metaphor of shots at an archery target. Succeeding chapters will explore the relationship between validity and reliability in greater detail and offer suggestions for improving the validity and reliability of classroom assessment.

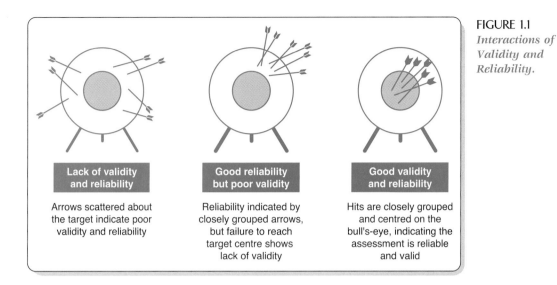

FIGURE 1.1
*Interactions of
Validity and
Reliability.*

**Lack of validity
and reliability**

Arrows scattered about
the target indicate poor
validity and reliability

**Good reliability
but poor validity**

Reliability indicated by
closely grouped arrows,
but failure to reach
target centre shows
lack of validity

**Good validity
and reliability**

Hits are closely grouped
and centred on the
bull's-eye, indicating the
assessment is reliable
and valid

FIGURE 1.1
*Interactions of
Validity and
Reliability.*

ETHICAL ISSUES AND RESPONSIBILITIES

Thus far we have presented a general technical introduction to classroom assessment. However, assessment is more than just a technical activity; it is a human activity that influences and affects many people, including students, parents, teachers, college and university admission counsellors, and employers. Think about the different kinds and purposes of assessment described in this chapter, and then think about all the ways people can be affected by them. This will give you a sense of the human side of assessment.

Teaching is a profession that has both a knowledge base and a moral base. Like other professionals who have knowledge and expertise their clients do not have and whose actions and judgments affect their clients in many ways, classroom teachers are responsible for conducting themselves in an ethical manner. This responsibility is particularly important in education, because students have no choice about whether they will or will not attend school. Also, compared to their teachers, students tend to be less experienced and more impressionable. Among the ethical standards that cut across all dimensions of teaching are the need to treat each student as an individual, to avoid physical or emotional abuse of students, to respect student diversity, to provide a balanced perspective on issues raised in instruction, and to provide the best instruction possible for all students.

Teachers' assessments have important long- and short-term consequences for students; thus teachers have an ethical responsibility to make decisions using the most valid and reliable information possible.

Ethical Issues and Assessment

It is the ethical responsibility of all teachers to ensure that assessment of students is fair and equitable. The criteria for determining fairness and equitability in student assessment have been outlined as principles and guidelines in *Principles for Fair Student Assessment Practices for Education in Canada* (Joint Advisory Committee, 1993). This document was produced through a collaborative effort among many recognized organizations within the Canadian educational community and has been supported by the Canadian Teachers Federation, the Canadian School Boards Association, and the Canadian Society for the Study of Education. It remains the nationally accepted framework for ensuring that all students are assessed and evaluated without prejudice and stereotyping.

Principles for Fair Student Assessment Practices for Education in Canada is divided into two sections: *Classroom Assessments* and *Assessments Produced External to the Classroom*. The classroom assessments section outlines principles and guidelines for:

➤ Developing and choosing methods for assessment
➤ Collecting assessment information
➤ Judging and scoring student performance
➤ Summarizing and interpreting results
➤ Reporting assessment findings

The section dealing with assessments produced external to the classroom provides recommendations for:

➤ Developing and selecting methods for assessment
➤ Collecting and interpreting assessment information
➤ Informing students being assessed
➤ Implementing mandated assessment program

Specific principles and guidelines for each of these interrelated thematic areas for both sections of the document are listed as part of Appendix A. (Note: Refer to the OLC (www.mcgrawhill.ca/college/airasian) for information on the *Standards for Teacher Competence in Educational Assessment of Students*, which is the American counterpart to the *Principles for Fair Student Assessment Practices for Education in Canada*.)

Fairness in Accommodating Special Needs

As part of their ethical responsibilities, teachers should be alert to indications of exceptionality that some students may have—and be ready to participate in an Individual Education Plan (IEP) to see that these students obtain needed help. Both law and general fairness to students with exceptionalities require six things in this regard (McMillan, 2000):

1. Proper training for those administering tests to determine exceptionality.
2. Assessment in the student's native language.
3. The identification of a student's specific needs, not just an overall judgment of ability.
4. Effective reflection of a student's ability or performance, in spite of any exceptionality.
5. The use of multiple scores or assessments before an IEP decision is reached.
6. A multidisciplinary assessment team for assessing an exceptionality.

This chapter has indicated that classrooms are complex environments calling for teacher decision making in many areas. Within such an environment, teachers are not expected to be correct in every decision they make. That would be an unrealistic standard to hold anyone to, especially in fluid, decision-rich classroom settings where uncertainty abounds. However, teachers should be expected and are morally bound to provide defensible assessment evidence to support classroom decisions and actions. This is the least that can be expected in an environment where teacher actions have such vital consequences for students.

CHAPTER REVIEW

CHAPTER REVIEW

Visit Chapter 1 of the Online Learning Centre at **www.mcgrawhill.ca/college/airasian** to take chapter quizzes, link to related Web sites, and read PowerWeb articles and news feed updates.

What is the difference between assessment and evaluation?

➤ Assessment is the process of collecting, synthesizing, and interpreting information about students and instruction to aid in classroom decision making.

➤ Evaluation is the process of judging the quality or value of a performance or a course of action.

What is a test?

➤ A test is a formal, systematic, often paper-and-pencil procedure used to gather information about students' performance.

What is measurement?

➤ Measurement is the process of collecting data on student performance using an instrument that is associated with a numerical scale.

What are the purposes for classroom assessment?

➤ Diagnosing students' needs;

➤ Providing feedback and evaluating instruction;

➤ Certifying academic learning; and

➤ Placing students.

What are the differences among diagnostic, formative, and summative assessment?

➤ Diagnostic assessment is assessment that takes place at the beginning of the school year or before a unit of instruction and provides teachers with information about their students' academic, social, attitudinal, and behavioural characteristics so as to enhance communication and instruction in the classroom.

➤ Formative assessment is assessment that occurs while instruction is taking place and includes observations and feedback intended to alter and improve students' learning and teachers' instructional practice.

➤ Summative assessment is assessment about students' learning at the end of instruction.

What is performance assessment?

➤ Performance assessment is assessment that occurs while students are actively engaged in a task.

What are the three primary methods by which teachers gather assessment data?

➤ The three primary methods by which teachers gather assessment data are paper-and-pencil techniques, observation techniques, and oral questioning techniques.

What is the difference between standardized and nonstandardized assessments?

➤ Standardized assessments are assessments that are administered, scored, and interpreted the same for all students taking the test, no matter when and where it is used.

➤ Nonstandardized assessments are assessments that teachers create in order to assess a narrow range of content and skills that is specific to expectations or learning outcomes outlined in curriculum documents.

What is the difference between validity and reliability?

➤ Validity is the extent to which assessment data is appropriate for making a decision about students and instruction.

➤ Reliability is the stability or consistency of assessment information.

What are the ethical standards that teachers are expected to follow?

➤ Treat each student as an individual;

➤ Avoid physically and emotionally abusing students;

➤ Respect student diversity;

➤ Provide a balanced perspective on issues raised in instruction; and

➤ Provide the best possible instruction for all students.

QUESTIONS FOR DISCUSSION

1. Do teachers' ethical responsibilities to their students change as students get older? If so, how? What ethical responsibilities remain constant across age levels?

2. In what ways can teachers improve their assessments so as to increase the assessments' validity and reliability?

3. What are your views on retention versus social promotion?

ACTIVITIES

1. Imagine that you are a first-year teacher. School starts in three weeks. Discuss in small groups what you must do to prepare for its start. Which of these preparations are related to classroom assessment?

2. Review one or more of your provincial or territorial curriculum documents for descriptions and examples of assessment.

3. Consider a typical day for a teacher at a particular grade level. Make a list of all the assessment tasks that this teacher might perform.

CHAPTER 2

LEARNING ABOUT STUDENTS: DIAGNOSTIC ASSESSMENT

CHAPTER OBJECTIVES

After reading this chapter, you will be able to:

➤ Define diagnostic assessment

➤ Appreciate the need to gather information about students

➤ Describe the sources of information for learning about their students

➤ Understand how student descriptions are formed

➤ Explain guidelines for diagnostic assessment

➤ Identify weaknesses in the validity and reliability of diagnostic assessment and suggest ways to overcome them

M s. Thomas is aware of how important the first days of the school year are for both teachers and students. These first days set the tone and lay the foundation for the rest of the year. Ms. Thomas regards these days as the one opportunity to make an initial impression. It is in these early days that a group of diverse individuals begins to come together to form a class. As a teacher of 12 years of experience, Ms. Thomas has been through the beginning of school many times before and uncertainties always accompany the start of a new school year. She knows that each new group of students has its own special mix of backgrounds, abilities, interests, needs, and personalities that make it unlike any other class that she has encountered.

Diagnostic assessment provides teachers with information about their students' academic, social, attitudinal, and behavioural characteristics so as to enhance communication and instruction in the classroom. Diagnostic assessment generally occurs at the beginning of the school year or before a unit of instruction.

This is a critical time in the school year to establish a learning environment that will support students' academic growth—this learning context needs to be maintained across the entire school year. Assessment plays a key role in establishing and maintaining a conducive learning environment at each juncture in the academic year. In particular, **diagnostic assessment** provides teachers with information about their students' academic, social, attitudinal, and behavioural characteristics so as to enhance communication and instruction in the classroom. Diagnostic assessment generally occurs at the beginning of the school year or before a unit of instruction.

In this chapter we will explore the nature of diagnostic assessment, sources of diagnostic assessment data, and evaluation of these data in the classroom. Chapter 10 includes a discussion with respect to the use of diagnostic tests to identify students with exceptionalities. The goal of diagnostic assessment in the classroom is for teachers to answer questions such as the following about their students:

➤ What prior knowledge and experience do the students bring to the class?

➤ Do students possess any misconceptions?

➤ How much review will be necessary before a new curriculum can be introduced?

➤ Which students will need support, modifications, or accommodations to begin new curriculum?

➤ Which students possess the skills to begin a new curriculum?

➤ What instructional approaches and strategies will be most effective?

If you were a teacher, what other questions would you add to this list and why? Answers to these questions identify the pertinent aspects of diagnostic assessment. The data collected through diagnostic assessment are evaluated and can be used to inform your decisions about what, where, when, how, and why to teach a given unit of instruction.

GATHERING INFORMATION ABOUT STUDENTS

In the first days of the school year, teachers try to learn about each individual student and the class as a whole in order to establish a classroom environment that is characterized by productive learning. The academic and socioeconomic backgrounds of students, as well as their mix of personalities, learning styles, languages, special needs, and interests, differ from classroom to classroom (Katz, Earl, & Olson, 2001). Consequently, because of such differences, planning, delivering instruction, and evaluating are context-bound activities; that is, the ways in which teachers plan, teach, assess, and evaluate are dependent upon the varied characteristics of their students. This means that a teacher must know about the characteristics of his or her students. Consider that resource teachers and guidance counsellors may be a source of information regarding the learning needs of some of the students that they have on their caseload. These teachers are likely to have data on students that may augment the information that you as the classroom teacher are gathering about your students. The teacher's role in the classroom involves a series of judgments or decisions about students, curricula, instruction, and learning. The teacher is both a participant and an observer in the classroom. Classroom teachers must provide good and defensible grounds for their decisions and actions.

Life in classrooms is a series of judgments or decisions about students, curricula, instruction, and learning.

Teachers need assessment tools to effectively record student performance. Maintaining these assessment records is essential for providing accurate documentation of what students know. Ultimately, these records will inform classroom instruction and contribute to a repertoire of assessments. Manitoba's Ministry of Education and Youth has developed a publication, *Independent Together—Supporting the Multilevel Learning Community* (Manitoba Education and Youth, 2003), which highlights best practices in classroom assessment and offers suggestions to teachers for gathering and monitoring information about students. Table 2.1 features an example of an assessment tool called "Focused Observation Form," which is particularly useful for diagnostic and formative assessment. This example, as well as blank master copies, is available for teachers to download at Manitoba's Ministry of Education and Youth Web site at www.edu.gov.mb.ca/ks4/cur/multilevel/index.html.

Table 2.2 describes two teachers' classrooms. Imagine that these classrooms are at the same grade level. Notice that all of the characteristics listed in the table are ones over which the teacher normally has very little control. How might these various characteristics influence the way the two teachers gather information about their students as a function of diagnostic assessment? Which characteristics seem most advantageous to a teacher, and which seem disadvantageous? Thinking about these questions should give you some sense of how approaches to teaching are always dependent on both the students and the classroom factors.

Teaching is a context-bound activity involving the characteristics of students and classroom factors.

TABLE 2.1 Focused Observation Form (Example)

Learning Experience / Targeted Learning Outcomes	Criteria	Met (M)	Not Yet Met (NY)
Reading Comprehension—Before-During-After Reading (B-D-A): GLO 2: 2.1.2; 2.1.4; 2.2.2	• Make predictions and inferences.		
	• Reread to make sense.		
	• Make connections to self and other texts.		
	•		

Observation Date(s)/ Assessments Student Names	Sept. 18/03 Independent silent reading	Sept. 19/03 Shared reading: (B-D-A) Text: *Did You Hear Wind Sing Your Name?*	Sept. 24/03 Strategic lesson: B-D-A Text: *Water Dance*	Sept. 26/03 Reading conference: Own choice	Sept. 29/03 Strategic lesson: Repeated readings— To read smoothly from beginning to end. Text: *Welcome to the Green House*
Student A	Reading *Harriet the Spy* (ch. 5-6)	B- "The colours make me think it will be about seasons."	B- "I wonder if there will be changes. Each illustration shows a change in the weather."	Text: *Harriet the Spy* "Can I read the last chapter because I want to read another book by this author?"	
Student B		A- "I heard the wind when I was camping."		Text: *I Have a Question, Grandma* "This was an easy read because I visit my Grandma and I know all the words."	Partnered with "D"
Student C	Book Bag: • two *National Geographic: Reading Expeditions* • two comic books Flipping pages; talking to classmate.	No response	B- "It looks like a lake and some water." D- "It is about water." A- "It's water."	*Civilizations Past to Present: Greece* Talks about the illustrations—"I like the war stories."	Partnered with "Teacher" — "I think this will be about a jungle. It is about life in the jungle" Text too difficult, so did read aloud.
Student D	Read *What Is a Scientist?* and *For the Love of Our Earth.*	D- "Now I think the author will use patterns like colours and questions."	B- "I see the word dance. I think it will feel like water moving." A- "I like the author's pattern *I am...* This reminds me of *Did You Hear Wind Sing Your Name?*"	Text: *Earthquack!* "This is a challenge read." crumbling—"cr- crums," "crums," rereads sentence, "Is it crumbling?"	Partnered with "B"

Student Literature Cited

Belleveau, C. *I Have a Question, Grandma.* Don Mills, ON: Pearson Education, 1998.

De Coteau, Orie S. *Did You Hear Wind Sing Your Name? An Oneida Song of Spring.* Greenvale, NY: MONDO Publishing, 1997.

Fitzhugh, L. *Harriet the Spy.* New York, NY: Harper Collins Publishers, 1964.

Hallinan, P.K. *For the Love of Our Earth.* Nashville, TN: Ideals Publishing Corporation, 1992.

Lehn, B. *What Is a Scientist?* Brookfield, CT: The Millbrook Press, Inc., 1998.

Locker, T. *Water Dance.* San Diego, CA: Harcourt Brace and Company, 1997.

Palatini, M. *Earthquack!* Toronto, ON: Simon and Schuster Books for Young Readers, 2002.

Supples, K. *Civilizations Past to Present: Greece.* Washington, DC: National Geographic School Publishing, 2000.

Yolen, J. *Welcome to the Green House.* Toronto, ON: Scholastic Inc., 1993.

SOURCE: Independent Together—Supporting the Multilevel Learning Community, Manitoba Education and Youth (2003), www.edu.gov.mb.ca/ks4/cur/multilevel/blms/blm_5a.doc.

TABLE 2.2 Comparison of Two Classroom Contexts	
Classroom A	**Classroom B**
30 students	16 students
Students abilities clustering at three disparate levels	Fairly homogeneous student abilities
Several students with speech difficulties and physical challenges	A few students who crave attention while a few seem extremely shy
Range of socioeconomic backgrounds	Uniformly middle class
Parent pressures for multicultural learning	Parent pressures for high grades
Balanced gender mix	Predominantly boys
Separate art and music programs in another class	No separate art or music
Spacious, quiet room	Small room with noise from class next door
Nearly all students together for several years	Most students meeting each other for the first time
Individual student desks	Tables and chairs
Educational assistant available	No educational assistant

All teachers strive to learn about their students, although teachers will gather different information depending on the different levels of education. At the elementary level, most students spend five to six hours a day in the same classroom with the same teacher and classmates. Often, instruction is carried out in small groups, which challenges teachers to gather information about their students' academic capabilities and general learning skills. A shift toward gathering information that is focused on intellectual-cognitive achievement tends to occur with teachers of early adolescents in middle-school (Hargreaves, Earl, & Ryan, 1996). There are also widely used informal methods of gathering information about early adolescents based on their performances and daily work that enhance the quality of teacher diagnosis and integrate assessment with the learning process (Hargreaves, Earl, & Ryan, 1996). At the secondary level, students generally rotate among teachers. As a consequence, secondary-level teachers tend to focus on academic characteristics, subject matter, study skills, and interest. Teachers strive to gather information that will help them to hone the content and method of their instruction.

Diagnostic assessment is becoming more difficult for teachers. North American teachers increasingly face learners varied in ability, class, race, culture, and language. Issues of poverty, exceptionalities, violence, abuse, teen pregnancy, and drugs confront many of our students and impact their school performance and success (Wiseman, Cooner, & Knight, 1999). How-

The information about students that a teacher collects prior to instruction forms perceptions and expectations that will influence the way the teacher plans for, interacts with, and manages students and instruction.

ever, in spite of this difficult reality, teachers are expected to know and teach all their students. The information about students that a teacher collects prior to instruction forms perceptions and expectations that will influence the way the teacher plans for, interacts with, and manages students and instruction. Some important student characteristics may not manifest themselves in the first few days of school; issues such as poverty, violence, abuse, and pregnancy may not be immediately apparent to a teacher, while issues of culture, language, and physical challenges probably will be.

SOURCES OF LEARNING ABOUT STUDENTS

The information teachers use to learn about their students can come from both formal and informal sources. Teachers use a variety of information including personal observations, official school records, comments from other teachers, and formal assessments to assess their students prior to instruction. In addition to these, Table 2.3 lists some common sources and kinds of information that teachers seek.

Thus, teachers are constantly listening and watching for information about their students. Sometimes their attention is drawn to things that

TABLE 2.3 Sources and Kinds of Information for Diagnostic Assessment

What Students Say	What Students Do	What Students Write
Informal oral reports	Pretests	Pretests
Interviews	Homework assignments	Journals
Class discussion	In-class tasks	Surveys
Peer interaction	Group work	Reflections
	Peer tutoring	In-class tasks
	Observations	
Potential Information	**Potential Information**	**Potential Information**
Attention	Attention	Academic skills
Oral fluency	Work habits	Organizational abilities
Vocabulary	Ability to follow directions	Prior experience
Anxiety	Academic skills	Prior knowledge
Participation	Cooperation	
Prior knowledge	Study skills	
Prior experience	Prior knowledge	
	Prior experience	

seem, on the surface, to have little to do with the main task of the school: the way students dress, their posture and body language, student discussions in the hallways and cafeterias, and who they "hang around" with. By such means, most teachers have gathered information and can provide fairly detailed descriptions of student characteristics.

Two facts about this source and kind of information deserve attention. First, much of it comes from informal observations. Most teachers do not rely heavily on tests or other assessments when initially determining student characteristics. If they seek diagnostic information, they often go to the official school record folders or administer subject matter pretests. Second, because this initial information is obtained largely by means of informal observations, teachers are exposed to only a small sample of each student's behaviour.

Another problem concerns the amount of information teachers obtain to learn about a student or class. Since teachers can observe any given student only part of the time, it is inevitable that their observations will be incomplete and limited. Personal communications are varied, often brief, and focused on a large number of students, thus increasing the possibility that insufficient information will be obtained to provide reliable interpretations about student characteristics. Teachers need to recognize the potential problems of selective memory and insufficient information.

Teachers rely heavily on informal observations when initially assessing their students.

FORMING STUDENT DESCRIPTIONS

Based on the information gathered and synthesized, teachers form general descriptions of their students. These descriptions rely on informal and formal information and convey a perception about many dimensions of student behaviour and background. The following is a Grade 6 teacher's description of one of her students that was written during the first term of the school year:

> Sanjay has had a positive beginning to the school year. He generally participates in class and group activities. He follows routines and instructions with some reminders. He has shown development in the area of time management and organization. In particular, Sanjay comes to class with all necessary materials and usually completes homework on time and with care. Sanjay is encouraged to continue to persevere with his good efforts and to set attainable goals.

This example of a student description includes both academic and nonacademic factors. Notice also that the description provides praise and encouragement for the student to continue with his purposeful efforts. Teachers become adept at quickly forming impressions about all of the students in their classes. Diagnostic assessments play a role in the development of these impressions. Assessments produce a set of perceptions and expectations that influence the manner in which the teacher plans for, instructs, interacts with, and evaluates the students throughout the school year (Shulha, 1999). Conversely, perceptions and expectations influence assessment.

Canadian researcher, Lyn Shulha (1999) analyzed the behaviour and dialogue of pre-service teachers in order to document the complexity of thinking that contributed to their assessment practices. She found that for pre-service teachers, the task of assessment was influenced by grading policies, perceptions of the appropriateness of the assessment tools, and their expectations of their students. These teachers also recognized that making assessment decisions is dependent on an appreciation for the contexts within which learning takes place. Consequently, student assessment is credited with being a complex task based on several interconnected influential factors: education system, teacher, student, learning environment, and the principles of measurement.

Diagnostic assessments produce a set of perceptions and expectations that influence the manner in which the teacher plans for, instructs, interacts with, and evaluates the students throughout the school year.

Diagnostic assessments involve the natural tendency to observe and make judgments about students on the basis of what is seen and heard about them in everyday classroom interactions. Spontaneous, informal observations provide information about student behaviour and performance. These student observations attend to a broad range of cognitive, affective, and psychomotor characteristics. Teachers synthesize their observations in idiosyncratic ways to form a generalized perception of students. Most often, these perceptions are unwritten and selectively communicated. Initial perceptions are usually very stable from the beginning to the end of the school year. These impressions facilitate gaining knowledge about their students so that teachers may interact with them on a personal and relatable level. Diagnostic assessment observations and descriptions provide a frame of reference within which social interaction and meaningful instruction can take place.

GUIDELINES FOR DIAGNOSTIC ASSESSMENTS

Following are some guidelines that should be considered when administering diagnostic assessments. Teachers should do everything possible to gather accurate information and to revise judgments when initial impressions prove to be wrong. Bear in mind the following:

1. *Be aware of diagnostic assessment and its effects on students.* Diagnostic assessment is such a natural part of the beginning of the school year or instructional unit that many teachers are unaware that they are doing it. They do not recognize the dangers of forming incorrect impressions of students. As a first step, then, it is important for teachers to be aware of this type of assessment and to be sensitive to the consequences of making incorrect judgments based on incomplete or invalid observations.

2. *Treat initial impressions as hypotheses to be confirmed or corrected by subsequent observations and information.* First impressions should be considered tentative hypotheses that need to be confirmed or disproved by subsequent observation and information. Teachers should refrain from judging and labelling students on the basis of hearsay, a single brief observation, or a student's race, culture, gender, or language. They should also gather their own evidence about students and confirm first impressions with subsequent observations and information. They should not be afraid to change an incorrect first impression.

Teachers should treat initial impressions as hypotheses to be confirmed or corrected by later information.

One way to make your observations more thorough, and less likely to be unconsciously selective, is to pick one student characteristic per day and structure classroom activities to encourage all students in the class to demonstrate that characteristic.

3. *Use direct indicators to gather information about student characteristics.* To learn about students, teachers must interpret the student observations they gather. Some observations require less interpretation than others. The closer the behaviour observed is to the student characteristic a teacher wishes to describe, the more valid the resulting information is and the more confident the teacher can be about the student's true characteristic. For example, actually listening to a student read aloud provides more direct and valid evidence about a student's oral reading than the reading grades the student got from a prior teacher or the student's reported interest in reading.

When making assessments, teachers should try to use information that requires minimum interpretation.

In diagnostic assessments, teacher-student interactions are often brief, and the tendency is for the teacher to focus on superficial, indirect characteristics such as facial expression, helpfulness, mood, or general appearance. Teachers then read into these superficial observations complex traits and personality factors like motivation, self-concept, trustworthiness, self-control, and interest. Such indirect generalizations are likely to be invalid. Thus, teachers should focus evidence gathering on direct behaviours and indicators.

4. *Supplement informal observations with more formal, structured activities.* There is no rule that demands that only informal observations be used to assess students. In fact, complete reliance on informal observations means that the teacher does not have a variety of information sources. Effective teachers recognize this limitation and supplement their informal observations with more structured activities. For example, they:

Because informal observations involve spontaneous behaviour that may not be repeated, teachers should supplement their informal observations with more structured activities.

➤ Administer textbook review or diagnostic pretests to assess students' entering levels.

➤ Require students to keep a journal during the first week of school or write an essay on What I Did Last Summer to assess students' experiences, writing skills, and thought processes.

➤ Carry out group discussions or group projects to assess how students interact and work in groups.

➤ Let students read aloud to determine reading fluency.

➤ Play classroom games based on spelling words, math facts, geographical knowledge, or current events to assess general knowledge, interest, and competitiveness.

➤ Use games related to listening skills to assess students' abilities to follow directions and process auditory information.

➤ Employ more formal observational instruments.

Formal assessments that require students to perform the same behaviour permit comparison against benchmark standards.

Some school systems collect samples of students' work into what are called **portfolios.** These portfolios may accompany the students as they progress from grade to grade and provide a new teacher with concrete examples of a student's work. (Portfolios and other formal methods of assessing student performance are described more fully later.) Formal assessments provide information about students' interests, styles, and academic performance that is not always obtainable from informal observations. Formal assessments also often require all students to perform the same behaviour and thereby permit comparisons of desired characteristics against benchmark standards.

Reliable assessments usually require multiple observations in order to identify typical student behaviour.

5. *Observe long enough to be fairly certain of the student's typical behaviour.* Reliable information is that which represents the *typical* behaviour of a student. To obtain reliable data, the teacher must look for *patterns* of behaviour, not single, one-time behaviours. The greater the consequences that an assessment is likely to have for students, the more the teacher should strive to gather multiple sources of reliable information.

Whenever possible, teachers should base their decisions on different kinds of information that support one another.

6. *Determine whether different kinds of information confirm each other.* Teachers can have more confidence in their student perceptions if they are based upon two or more kinds of supporting evidence. For example, are test scores supported by classroom performance? Are classroom observations of a student's needs consistent with those identified by last year's teacher and the student's parents? Do classroom behaviour patterns persist in the lunchroom and on the playground?

These guidelines suggest the use of multiple sources of information to corroborate the teacher's perception of a student. However, note that it is better if the present teacher forms his or her own impressions of the student *before* obtaining corroborative information from other sources. By doing this, the teacher avoids letting his or her perceptions be influenced or prejudiced by the perceptions of others.

CONCERNS ABOUT ETHICS AND ACCURACY

Because diagnostic assessments form the basis for many important judgments made throughout the school year, teachers have an ethical responsibility to make them as valid and reliable as possible. However, an assessment process that is based upon quickly obtained, often incomplete evidence has the potential to produce incorrect, invalid, and unreliable decisions about students.

The General Problem

There are four realities that contribute to the general problem about ethics and accuracy of diagnostic assessment. First, teachers' initial impressions of their students tend to remain stable over time. Once a teacher forms an impression of a student, that impression often remains, and teachers will act to maintain these impressions, even in the face of contradictory evidence. Second, classroom teachers are fairly accurate in their beginning-of-the-year predictions of students' academic performance as measured by test scores, although, even the most accurate teacher is not correct about every student. However, teachers are less accurate when evaluating students' personalities, interests, emotions, motivation, self-concepts, and social adjustment. Overall, teachers' perceptions of these affective characteristics are less accurate than their academic perceptions, at least at the start of the school year.

Because initial diagnostic assessments have important consequences for students, teachers have an ethical responsibility to make them as valid and reliable as possible.

Third, diagnostic assessments not only influence the way teachers perceive, treat, and make decisions about students, they may be transmitted to students. Teachers often unknowingly and unintentionally communicate their impressions with comments that tell students and the class a great deal about their perceptions: "Oh Robert, can't you even remember what we just talked about?" "All right, Sarah, will you tell the rest of the class the answer it can't seem to come up with?" "Didn't Mohammed read that paragraph with a lot of expression?" Sometimes perceptions are conveyed indirectly, as when a teacher waits patiently for one student to think through a problem but allows another only a few seconds; expresses encouragement and assurance to one student but says "at least try" to another; encourages one to "think" but another to "take a guess." Tone of voice, physical proximity, gestures, seating arrangements, and other signals all tell students how they are perceived in the classroom.

Teachers often communicate their impressions to students in unintended ways, and students may live up to these teacher perceptions.

Fourth, teachers' perceptions and expectations may even create a **self-fulfilling prophecy,** in which the expectations for a student lead the teacher to interact with that student in a particular manner (Trouilloud, Sarrazin, Martinek, & Guillet, 2002). The student, in turn, observes the way the teacher interacts with him or her and begins to behave in the way or at the level the teacher expects, whether or not the original expectation is correct. Needless to say, it is the teacher's ethical responsibility to avoid this situation by making the expectations as fair and accurate as possible for all students, and not using them to demean or embarrass a student.

Thus far, we have seen that diagnostic assessments are largely based upon information that is gathered as impressions, that teachers form these assessments relatively quickly, that they use them to "know" students, and that they remain fairly stable once formed. Diagnostic assessments determine perceptions and expectations, which in turn influence teachers' interactions with students. Because assessments can be so influential in setting expectations, influencing teacher-student interactions, and affecting students' performance and self-perceptions, it is important to examine more closely the dangers inherent in that process and the strategies teachers can use to improve their initial assessments.

The Issues of Validity and Reliability

In the previous section we noted the ethical responsibility for teachers to make diagnostic assessments valid and reliable. Recall from Chapter 1 that the two main criteria for good assessments are validity and reliability. Validity is concerned with the collection of *appropriate* evidence; that is, evidence that is related to the student characteristic(s) under consideration. Reliability pertains to collecting *enough* high quality evidence to be relatively certain that the student's *optimal* performance is being observed. Validity and reliability work hand in hand to ensure that the perceptions formed in assessment are appropriate and fair, leading to good decisions about students.

Threats to Validity

Observer prejudgment can stem from prior knowledge, first impressions, or personal prejudices, and often interferes with fair and valid assessments.

There are two main issues that occur during assessment that diminish the validity of the information teachers gather: prejudgment and logical error. **Prejudgment** occurs when a teacher's prior knowledge, first impressions, or personal prejudices and beliefs interfere with the ability to make a fair and valid assessment of a student. All of us have personal prejudices, beliefs, and preferences. We have interests, ideas, and expectations that differentiate us from others. However, when these likes, dislikes, beliefs, and prejudices interfere with our ability to make fair student assessments, there is a real problem.

Prejudgment may be the result of one of three sources. The first source is *prior information,* information a teacher obtains before meeting a student. Information passed from teacher to teacher or the performance of prior siblings often influences and prejudices a teacher's perceptions, even before the student enters the teacher's classroom. This may contribute to statements such as, "Oh, you're Sarah's brother! I'm expecting you to do as well as she did when she was in my class."

The second source is *initial impressions,* which tend to influence subsequent impressions. If the teacher judges a student upon how he is dressed on the first day of school or how she behaved in the cafeteria last year, the teacher may unconsciously let this initial impression dictate subsequent observations and interpretations of the student's characteristics.

The third source of prejudgment includes teachers' *personal theories and beliefs* about particular kinds of students, which often lead to stereotyped perceptions. Wilson and Martinussen (1999) sought to determine whether Canadian pre-service teachers' perceptions and expectations influenced their assessment of achievement. Indeed, early expectations based on socioeconomic status and differential growth patterns contributed to final reported grades. The pre-service teachers held high expectations for the students from high socioeconomic backgrounds. Consequently, these teachers disregarded disconfirming information for those struggling students for whom they held high expectations. Information about the lack of progress was ignored. When teachers think "this student is from downtown, and kids from downtown are poor learners and discipline problems," or "girls do poorly in math," or "everyone knows that students of that culture have no interest in school," they are expressing their personal theories or stereotypes of what they think certain students are like and how they learn. Being labelled with such stereotypes without a fair chance to show true characteristics can preclude students' learning opportunities.

Teachers should be careful not to interpret cultural differences as cultural deficits.

This is especially so with regard to teachers' racial, cultural, exceptionality, and language prejudices or stereotypes. When making diagnostic assessments, teachers who are not familiar with students' cultures and languages often interpret what are really cultural *differences* as cultural *deficits* (Ladson-Billings, 1994; Delpit, 1995). As well, teachers' stereotypes or personal beliefs can produce invalid diagnostic assessments of students who are different from the teacher. Teachers must strive to recognize their personal beliefs and stereotypes and judge each individual student on the basis of how he or she actually performs in class. Each student is entitled to be judged on his or her own merits, not on the basis of stereotypes and personal beliefs. This is a teacher's ethical responsibility.

Teachers should recognize that prejudgments and stereotyping can invalidate diagnostic assessments. At the beginning of a new school year, some teachers choose to ignore any preconceived notions about a student's behaviour, work habits, and social skills generated by comments from the student's previous teachers. These teachers believe that a student may have a negative experience with one teacher, but a positive experience with another teacher. Consequently, these teachers prefer to make their own judgments about students as they consider the real and consequential dangers of prejudgment.

Logical error occurs when teachers focus on the wrong indicators to assess desired student characteristics, thereby invalidating their judgments. It is tempting to read a great deal into a single observation, especially at the start of the year when teachers want to quickly characterize

CHAPTER CASE STUDY

Visit the text OLC to read the case of Anita Underwood, who describes her initial observations and assessments of her students.

www.mcgrawhill.ca/college/airasian

each student in order to organize their classes. It would be convenient, for example, to read a whole series of inferences about motivation, attention span, interest in the subject, self-concept, and initiative from a student's eager hand raising. Maybe all the interpretations will prove to be correct, but it is dangerous not to recognize the difference between what is directly observed and interpretations made from an observation. When observation of one characteristic (hand raising) is used to make inferences about other, unobserved characteristics (motivation, interest), the potential for logical errors and invalid assessment is great.

Teachers should be careful not to mislabel students based on observations that do not justify the label.

The labels teachers use to describe their students represent their interpretations of observed behaviours. Teachers do not directly observe characteristics such as motivation, intelligence, leadership, self-confidence, aggressiveness, anxiety, shyness, and intolerance. Rather, teachers observe a student behaving in some way, interpret what the behaviour signifies, and give the behaviour a label. In most cases, it is the label given to the behaviour that attaches to the student, not the specific behaviour that prompted the label. Teachers remember that a student is a bully, self-confident, aggressive, aloof, motivated, or shy, but they rarely remember the specific observations that led them to label the student in that way. Because teachers' labels "stick" to students, it is important that the observations leading to a label are valid indicators of that label.

Threats to Reliability

While validity is concerned with collecting information that is appropriate for determining a student's characteristics, reliability is concerned with collecting enough high quality evidence to be sure that it represents typical student behaviour. Formal or informal, teachers' assessments are based upon samples of their students' behaviour. These samples are used to determine students' more general behaviour patterns. Thus, an important issue in teacher assessment is how well the observed samples represent students' general or typical behaviour patterns. Reliable information captures consistent and stable student characteristics.

Teachers should be careful not to form a permanent perception of students based on one or two observations that may not be typical behaviour.

The nature of diagnostic assessment creates special reliability issues. As noted earlier, the spontaneity of many teacher-student interactions limit what teachers are able to see and what students demonstrate. Also, the time available to observe students often is brief, since attention must be distributed among many students and classroom activities. In short, the few initial samples of behaviour that are observed under these circumstances may not provide reliable indicators of students' typical behaviour.

Teachers recognize this problem and related issues. Teachers' first impressions of a student are often salient. As well, teachers trust their ability to make early and valid assessments of their students' skills and learning potential (Wilson, 1990). Yet, students usually do not present their typical classroom behaviour during the first few days of school. Some students are intimidated and uncomfortable, while others are testing the teacher's

KEY ASSESSMENT TOOLS 2.1

Threats to the Validity and Reliability of Diagnostic Assessments

Validity Threats

I. Observer prejudgments prevent teachers from making an objective assessment of the students.

    a. Prior information passed from teacher to teacher, siblings, or nonclassroom experiences

    b. First impressions that influence subsequent impressions

    c. Personal theories or attitudes that influence subsequent observation (e.g., girls can't do math)

II. Logical errors that cause teachers to judge students based on the wrong characteristics (e.g., observe attention and judge learning; observe clothes and judge ability).

Reliability Threats

I. Inadequate behaviour sampling in which too few observations prevent learning about students' typical behaviour and characteristics.

    a. Decisions about a student on a single piece of information.

    b. Behaviours observed in one setting (e.g., the playground) and behaviour assumed to be the same in another setting (e.g., the classroom).

tolerance limits. The implications are such that teachers must be sure to observe sufficient samples of students' behaviour before they solidify their initial perceptions and rely on these impressions for decision making. Key Assessment Tools 2.1 is a review and summary of the threats to validity and reliability.

CHAPTER REVIEW

CHAPTER REVIEW

Visit Chapter 2 of the Online Learning Centre at **www.mcgrawhill.ca/ college/airasian** to take chapter quizzes, link to related Web sites, read PowerWeb articles and news feed updates, and access study tools, including the case study referenced in this chapter.

What is diagnostic assessment?

➤ Diagnostic assessment provides teachers with information about their students' academic, social, attitudinal, and behavioural characteristics so as to enhance communication and instruction in the classroom.

➤ Diagnostic assessment generally occurs at the beginning of the school year or before a unit of instruction.

Why do teachers gather information about students?

➤ The teacher must know about the characteristics of his or her students as this determines the ways in which teachers plan, teach, assess, and evaluate.

➤ Teachers seek to gather information that will help them to hone the content and method of their instruction.

What are the sources of learning about students?

➤ Prior to instruction, teachers collect personal observations, official school records, comments from other teachers, and formal assessments as sources of learning about students.

➤ Teachers also glean information from what students say (e.g., class discussions), what students do (e.g., group work), and what students write (e.g., journals).

How do teachers form student descriptions?

➤ Student descriptions rely on informal and formal information and convey a perception about many dimensions of student behaviour and background.

➤ Spontaneous, informal observations provide information about student behaviour and performance.

What are the six guidelines for diagnostic assessment?

➤ Be aware of the effects of diagnostic assessment

➤ Treat initial impressions as hypotheses

➤ Use direct indicators to gather information about students

➤ Supplement informal observations with formal activities

➤ Observe for a period of time

➤ Determine whether kinds of information are confirming

What are the four issues that contribute to concerns about ethics and accuracy of diagnostic assessment?

➤ Teachers' initial impressions are stable

➤ Teachers' perceptions of affective characteristics are not always accurate

➤ Teachers unintentionally communicate impressions

➤ Teachers' perceptions create a self-fulfilling prophecy

What is a self-fulfilling prophecy?

➤ A self-fulfilling prophecy occurs when the teachers' expectations for a student lead the teacher to interact with that student in a particular manner. The student observes the way the teacher interacts with him or her and begins to behave in the way or at the level the teacher expects.

What are the threats to validity of diagnostic assessment?

➤ Two main problems affect the validity of diagnostic assessments: prejudgment and logical error.

What is prejudgment?

➤ Prejudgment occurs when a teacher's prior knowledge, first impressions, or personal prejudices and beliefs interfere with the ability to make a fair and valid assessment of a student.

➤ Prejudgment may result from prior information, initial impressions, or personal theories and beliefs.

What is logical error?

➤ Logical error occurs when teachers focus on the wrong indicators to assess desired student characteristics, thereby invalidating their judgments.

What are the threats to reliability of diagnostic assessment?

➤ In diagnostic assessment, observed samples of behaviour must capture student characteristics consistently across several settings.

➤ Teachers must be sure to observe sufficient samples of students' behaviour before they solidify their initial perceptions and rely on these impressions for decision making.

QUESTIONS FOR DISCUSSION

1. What are the advantages and disadvantages of examining a student's school (cumulative) record folder before the start of the year? Under what circumstances would you examine a student's record folder?

2. How much must teachers really know about a student's home and family background? What home and background information is absolutely essential for teachers to know? Why? What information does a teacher have no right to know about a student's home or background?

3. Why do teachers rely so heavily on informal observation when sizing up students? Should teachers use such observations to label students?

4. What are some of the potential biases that might be present if you solicit comments from other teachers as a source of diagnostic information about students?

5. Formal assessments are a source of learning about students. What should you as a teacher consider when you are reviewing formal assessment data for the purposes of learning about your students?

6. Consider what will be your course of action if you collect some diagnostic information about a student through observing the student in your class and this information is contradictory to information contained in the student's official school records. Which information will you consider to be most accurate?

ACTIVITIES

1. Table 2.2 shows the resources available in two different classrooms. In small groups, compare the two classrooms. How do the resources in each classroom influence planning and instructing students? Give specific examples.

2. Interview a classroom teacher. Find out the answers to questions like the following: What information does the teacher have about students before the first day of school? What are the sources of that information? How much does the teacher rely upon the comments of other teachers when getting to know a new class? If the teacher could know only two specific characteristics of each student at the end of the first day of school, what would these be? Why? What information is most useful for managing students in the classroom? Add three questions of your own to this list. Why did you select those three questions?

3. Refer to Table 2.3, "Sources and Kinds of Information for Diagnostic Assessment." Choose one source of information from "What Students Say" and the "Potential Information" that is derived from this source and hypothesize a conclusion that can be drawn from this source and kind of information. Then choose one source of information from "What Stu-

dents Do" and the "Potential Information" that is derived from this source and hypothesize a conclusion that can be drawn from this source and kind of information. Finally, choose one source of information from "What Students Write" and the "Potential Information" that is derived from this source and hypothesize a conclusion that can be drawn from this source and kind of information.

4. Review the six guidelines for diagnostic assessment that were presented in this chapter. Choose two of the six guidelines and write a diagnostic assessment goal statement that you will strive to fulfill.

CHAPTER 3

INSTRUCTIONAL PLANNING AND ASSESSMENT

CHAPTER OBJECTIVES

After reading this chapter, you will be able to:

➤ Define curriculum, instruction, achievement, and ability

➤ Cite the basic steps comprising the instructional process

➤ State the main considerations in planning instruction

➤ Outline the three levels of teaching objectives

➤ Describe instruction and assessment in terms of the cognitive, affective, and psychomotor domains of behaviour

➤ Construct effective learning expectations or outcomes

➤ Outline instructional planning ideas for accommodating students with exceptionalities

A udra is preparing for her practice teaching placement in a school located in Kuujjuaq, an Inuit community near Ungava Bay in Quebec. As a person born and raised in this community, Audra is eager to provide the best possible learning experiences for her Aboriginal students. She realizes the importance of the instructional process, including planning for instruction, delivering the planned instruction, and assessing how well her students achieve the outcomes that she will include in her plans. Undaunted by the complexity of the task ahead, Audra begins to collect and organize the resources and documents that she will need, looking forward to the meaningful instruction and assessment that she will provide for her eager students.

The purpose of schools is to educate students, but what does it mean to educate? Under what circumstances can a teacher claim credit for helping to educate a student? To **educate** means to help students change and to help them learn and do new things. When teachers have helped students to read, identify parts of speech in a sentence, use the scientific method, or write a cohesive paragraph, they have educated these students. Many experts describe education as a process intended to help students change in important and desirable ways. This view leads to a fundamental question all teachers have to ask themselves: what do I want my students to know or be able to do following instruction that they did not know or do at the start of instruction? Education is the process of fostering these important and desired student changes.

Education is the process of helping to change students' knowledge and behaviour in desired ways.

It is important to point out, however, that this view of education is not the only possible one. Thoughtful critics often suggest that education conceived solely as a process of preplanned student behaviour change can lead to a preoccupation with narrow expectations or learning outcomes and afford the student virtually no role in the creation of his or her educational program. Critics recognize the importance of a teacher's ability to artistically build upon a student's prior experience and to seek multiple, not necessarily predefined, outcomes from instruction. But despite the merits of alternative views, education for most teachers is conceived, practised, and assessed with the primary function of helping to change learners in desired ways.

A **curriculum** describes the skills, performances, knowledge, and attitudes students are expected to learn in school. The curriculum contains expectations or learning outcomes, which are statements of desired student learning, and descriptions of the methods and materials that will be used to help students attain this. The methods and processes actually used to change students' behaviour are called **instruction.** Lectures, discussions, worksheets, cooperative projects, and homework are but a few of the instructional techniques used to help students learn.

Students undergo many changes during their school years, and many sources beside the school contribute to these changes: maturation, peer groups, family, reading, and TV, among others. The term **achievement** is used to describe school-based learning, while terms like **ability** and

Achievement refers to school-based learning, while ability and aptitude refer to broader learning acquired mostly through nonschool sources such as parents and peer groups.

aptitude are used to describe broader learning that stems from nonschool sources. Since the focus of schooling is to help students develop particular behaviours, understandings, and processes, almost all of the formal tests that students take in school are intended to assess their achievement. The Friday spelling test, the unit test on chemical equations, the math test on the Pythagorean theorem, the delivery of an oral speech, the autobiography, and midterm and final examinations all should focus on assessing student achievement—that is, what they have learned of the things that were taught in school.

The central concept in this chapter is that planning and assessment should be driven by a clear knowledge of expectations or learning outcomes about what students will learn and master. Some have called this a backward approach to planning, inasmuch as it starts by defining the intended results (Wiggins & McTighe, 1998). Indeed it is; and in this case "backwardness" is a virtue.

THE INSTRUCTIONAL PROCESS

The instructional process involves three interdependent steps: planning, delivering, and assessing.

The instructional process comprises three basic steps. The first is *planning instruction,* which includes identifying specific expectations or learning outcomes, selecting materials to foster these expectations or outcomes, and organizing learning experiences into a coherent, reinforcing sequence. The second step involves *delivering the planned instruction* to students, that is, teaching them. The third step involves *assessing how well students learn or achieve the expectations or outcomes.* Notice that to carry out the instructional process the three steps should be aligned with one another. That is, the planned instruction should be logically related to the actual instruction and the assessments should relate to the plans and instruction.

Figure 3.1 shows these three steps and the relationships among them. Notice that the diagram is presented as a triangle rather than as a straight line. This indicates that the three steps are interrelated in a more complicated way than a simple one-two-three sequence. For example, in planning

FIGURE 3.1

Steps in the Instructional Process.

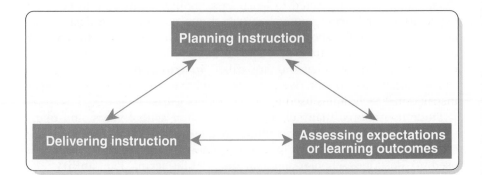

instruction (step 1), the teacher considers the characteristics of students and the resources and materials available to help attain desired changes (step 2). Similarly, the information gained at the time of student assessment (step 3) is useful in assessing the appropriateness of the learning experiences provided students (step 2) and the suitability of intended expectations or learning outcomes (step 1). Thus, the three steps are interdependent pieces in the instructional process that can be aligned in different orders.

All three steps in the instructional process involve teacher decision making and assessment. Obviously step 3, assessing expectations or learning outcomes, involves the collection and synthesis of formal information about how well students are learning or have learned. But the other two steps in the instructional process are also dependent upon a teacher's assessment activities. For example, a teacher's planning decisions incorporate information about student readiness, appropriate methods, available instructional resources, materials, student culture, language, and other important characteristics obtained from diagnostic assessments. Similarly, during instruction the teacher employs formative assessment to obtain information to help make decisions about lesson pace, reinforcement, interest, and comprehension. Remember that formative assessment includes observations and feedback intended to alter and improve students' learning while instruction is taking place. Thus, the entire instructional process, not just the formal assessment step, depends upon decisions that rely on assessment evidence of various kinds.

All three steps in the instructional process involve assessment and teacher decision making.

The processes of planning and providing instruction are important activities for classroom teachers. Not only do they occupy a substantial amount of their time, but teachers define their teaching rewards in terms of their students' instructional successes. Teachers like to work with students, make a difference in their lives, and experience the joy of a student "getting it." Teachers feel rewarded when they know that their instruction has reached their students. Since the classroom is where pride in teaching is forged, it is not surprising to find that teachers guard their classroom instructional time jealously. They want few interruptions to distract them from teaching their students.

Teachers define their own success and rewards in terms of their students' learning.

INSTRUCTIONAL PLANNING

The true rewards of teaching are identified in terms of the impact that the teachers' instruction and mentoring has upon students. Pride in teaching does not come from collecting lunch money, planning field trips, meeting the morning bus, and the thousand other semiadministrative tasks teachers perform. It comes from teachers' knowledge that they have taught students to do, think, or perform some things they otherwise would have been unable to do, think, or perform.

Teachers plan in order to modify the curriculum to fit the unique characteristics of their students and resources. To plan, teachers reflect on and integrate information about their students, the subject matter to be taught, the curriculum they are following, their own teaching experience, the resources available for instruction, the classroom environment, and other factors. Their reflection and integration of these factors leads to an instructional lesson plan. The plan helps teachers allocate instructional time, select appropriate activities, link individual lessons to the overall unit or curriculum, sequence activities to be presented to students, set the pace of instruction, select the homework to be assigned, and identify techniques to assess student learning.

Planning helps teachers in five basic ways:

1. By helping them feel comfortable about instruction and giving them a sense of understanding and ownership over the teaching they plan.
2. By establishing a sense of purpose and subject matter focus.
3. By affording the chance to review and become familiar with the subject matter before actually beginning to teach it.
4. By ensuring that there are ways in place to get instruction started, activities to pursue, and a framework to follow during the actual delivery of instruction.
5. By linking daily lessons to broader integrative goals, units, or curriculum topics.

Classrooms are complex environments that are informal rather than formal, ad hoc rather than linear, ambiguous rather than certain, process-oriented rather than product-oriented, and people-dominated rather than concept-dominated. The realities and strains of the classroom call for order and direction, especially when teachers are carrying out formal instruction. In such a world, some form of planning and organization is needed.

Planning instruction is a context-dependent activity that includes consideration of students, teacher, and instructional materials. A lesson that fails to take into account the needs and prior knowledge of the students or that poorly matches lesson aims to lesson instruction is doomed to failure. Similarly, a lesson that does not take into account the context in which it will be taught can also lead to difficulty.

Teachers have a great deal of control over many classroom features associated with instructional planning. For example, most teachers have control over the physical arrangement of the classroom, the rules and routines students must follow, the interactions with students, the kind of instruction planned and the nature of its delivery, and the methods used to assess and grade students. However, there are important features that teachers do not control. For example, most teachers have little control over the number and characteristics of the students in their classes, the size of their classroom, the quality of their instructional resources, and the Ministry/Department curriculum guidelines. In planning, teachers must arrange the factors they do control to compensate for the factors they do not.

TABLE 3.1 Comparison of Two Classroom Contexts	
Classroom A	**Classroom B**
22 students	34 students
Range of student abilities	Mainly low-ability students
Strong student self-control	Poor student self-control
Good prerequisite skills	Range of prerequisite skills
Intense parental interest	Moderate parental interest
10-year-old textbooks	New textbooks
Poor computer access	Excellent computer access
Small classroom size	Large classroom size
Individual student desks	Students sit at four-person tables
Little colleague support	Strong colleague support

Table 3.1 compares two teachers' classroom situations. Imagine that these classrooms are at the same grade level. Suppose the teachers are each planning a lesson on the same topic. Teachers normally would have little control over these characteristics of their classrooms. How might these different classroom characteristics influence the ways these two teachers plan instruction? What features are especially influential in determining teaching plans? Which characteristics would be advantageous to a teacher and which ones might be disadvantageous? Do you think the teachers would construct identical instructional plans? In what ways might they differ? The following discussion examines in more detail how student and teacher characteristics as well as instructional resources can affect instructional planning.

Student Characteristics

Initial and extremely important considerations when planning instruction are the present status and needs of the students. What are they developmentally ready to learn? What topics have they mastered thus far in the subject area? How complex are the instructional materials they can handle? How well do they work in groups? What exceptionalities do they have and how are they accommodated? What is the range of students' culture and language in a given classroom? What are their learning styles? The answers to these questions provide needed and valuable information about what and how to teach. Note that teachers obtain much of the information to answer these questions from their diagnostic assessments.

At the start of the school year, most teachers begin instruction by reviewing subject matter concepts and skills normally mastered in the prior grade or course. The information gained in such a review provides the most direct evidence about students' readiness and needs. It is especially important to assess readiness and needs in those subjects that are sequentially organized, such as mathematics and language arts. The structure of these subjects is such that concepts and ideas build upon one another. For example, in order to do long division problems correctly, a student must be able to use the processes of addition, subtraction, regrouping, and multiplication. Thus, it would make little sense for a teacher whose students did not understand regrouping and multiplication to teach only long division, even though it might be a specific curriculum expectation or learning outcome.

It is obvious that student characteristics such as exceptionality, readiness, independence, and self-control should be taken into account in planning instructional activities. To ignore these factors would be irrational. However, it is very important to recognize that much of the needed information comes to teachers from their diagnostic assessments. Consequently, it is crucial that teachers strive to make these assessments as valid and reliable as possible.

Teacher Characteristics

When planning instruction, teachers should take their own characteristics and knowledge into account along with their students' characteristics and the time and resources available.

Most beginning teachers do not take their own characteristics into account when planning instruction. However, subject matter knowledge, personality, and physical limitations are important factors in planning and delivering instruction. It is impossible for teachers to know everything about all the topics they teach. Nor can they be expected to keep abreast of all advances in subject matter knowledge or pedagogy. Consequently, the topics teachers choose to cover, the accuracy and up-to-dateness of their topical coverage, and their teaching methods all are influenced by their own knowledge limitations. Moreover, teachers' personalities often lead them to favour certain instructional techniques over others. While individual preferences are to be expected among teachers, it is important to understand that when carried to the extreme, they can result in an overly narrow repertoire of teaching methods. This has the potential to limit learning opportunities for those students who could learn better from other instructional techniques. Finally, since teaching is a rigorous, fatiguing activity, teachers should consider their own physical limitations when planning instruction. This caution is especially appropriate for beginning teachers, whose enthusiasm and lack of experience often lead them to overestimate what they can physically accomplish in the classroom.

Instructional Resources

The instructional resources available to a teacher influence not only the nature of instruction but also how effectively the expectations or learning outcomes can be met. The term *resources* is used here in its broadest sense to include available supplies, equipment, space, educational assistants or volunteers, textbooks, and time. Each of these resources influences the nature of instruction and therefore the student achievements that can be pursued.

A Grade 2 teacher may wish to have his or her students construct felt pictures of book covers, but is unable to because the school cannot afford to provide the felt. A biology teacher may wish his or her class to learn about the internal organs of a frog by having each student perform a frog dissection. However, if the school has no biology laboratory and no dissecting equipment, the teacher must forgo this expectation or learning outcome. In these and other ways, material resources matter.

Educational assistants or volunteers who read to students, work with small groups, or serve as tutors during a unit on the computer can free the classroom teacher to plan and pursue enrichment activities that might not have been possible otherwise. Resources of all kinds are important to consider when planning instruction.

Another resource that greatly influences what is planned, taught, and learned in classrooms is the textbook. More than any other single resource, the textbook determines instructional plans in many classrooms. A large part of students' learning time and a large part of the teacher's instructional time are focused on textbook use.

The teacher's edition of most textbooks contains many resources to help teachers plan, deliver, and assess instruction. However, teachers should not abdicate their planning, teaching, and assessment decision-making responsibilities, which require a teacher to carefully assess the adequacy of the textbook objectives and other materials in terms of student needs and resources. Two recent critics of textbooks assert that many textbooks are too long and at the same time superficial and poorly organized for constructing effective classroom objectives (Daniels & Zemelman, 2004). They note that another potential limitation is to base instructional objectives solely on a textbook; this tends to steer students toward accepting one authority and one point of view.

To slavishly follow the lessons in a textbook is to abdicate instructional decision making.

Teachers should screen textbook objectives using three criteria: (1) Are the objectives and text materials clearly stated? (2) Are the objectives and text materials suitable for students in this particular classroom? (3) Do the objectives and text materials exhaust the expectations or learning outcomes and activities to which these students should be exposed? The following are considerations for each of these three criteria.

The first criterion examines the way objectives and instructional plans are stated. Do objectives and instructional plans contain a clear description of the process and content knowledge the students will learn and the instructional activities that enhance learning? Most, though not all, textbook objectives do provide a clear description of the desired process and content knowledge. In the event that the textbook author's objectives are vague and ambiguous, the teacher must define these terms, recognizing that his or her definition may differ from the author's and thus may not be reflected in the instructional suggestions and materials that accompany the textbook.

The second criterion examines appropriateness for particular students. When teachers develop their own plans, they take into account the status, needs, and readiness of the students. Textbook authors, however, can only state a single set of objectives and plans. Often these objectives and plans are more suitable for some students than for others. Consequently, teachers must ask, "Do my students have the prerequisites needed to master the textbook objectives? Can they be taught these objectives in a reasonable amount of time? Will the lesson activities interest them? Do the lesson activities pertain to all the important expectations or learning outcomes in the unit?"

The final criterion examines completeness. Do the textbook objectives exhaust the important expectations or learning outcomes students should learn? Lesson plans in textbooks tend to emphasize structured didactic methods in which the teacher either tells the students things or elicits brief replies to teacher questions. Lessons using such objectives are easier to devise and present than divergent, complex ones. Relatively few textbook objectives call for synthesis or analysis of ideas, themes, or topics. Although teachers commonly omit topics from a textbook when teaching, they rarely introduce new topics that are not in the textbook. If teachers wish to include or emphasize higher-level objectives in their instruction, they may be forced to break this pattern and introduce additional objectives that round out student learning.

If the textbook material appears useful after all three of these criteria have been applied, then a teacher may use the textbook to help focus instruction and assess student learning. Table 3.2 summarizes the advantages and disadvantages of textbook objectives and instructional plans.

TABLE 3.2 Advantages and Disadvantages of Textbook Objectives and Instructional Plans	
Advantages	**Disadvantages**
Convenient, readily available objectives and plans	Designed for teachers and students in general, not necessarily for a given teacher or class
Can save valuable time in planning	Heavy emphasis on lower-level objectives and activities
Provide an intergrated set of objectives, plans, and assessments	Lesson activities tend to be didactic and teacher-led
May contain ancillary materials for planning, instructing, and assessing	If accepted uncritically, can lead to inappropriate instruction for students

TABLE 3.3	Areas to Consider When Planning Instruction	
Student Characteristics	**Teacher Characteristics**	**Instructional Resources**
Prior knowledge	Content knowledge	Ministry/Department curriculum expectations/ learning outcomes
Prerequisite skills and knowledge	Instructional method preferences	Time
Work habits, socialization	Assessment preferences	Textbook materials
Special learning needs	Physical limitations	Technology
Learning styles		Collegial and administrative support
Cultural/language differences		Other resources (space, educational assistants, equipment)
Exceptionalities		

A final important, though often overlooked, resource that greatly influences teacher planning is time. Because there is never enough time to teach students all the important skills and concepts in a subject area, teachers must carefully match their instructional time to the curriculum expectations or learning outcomes. Each teacher's decisions about what content to stress or omit is based in part on the instructional time available. When a teacher skips a concept, unit, or chapter in a textbook, the teacher is saying, "All other things being equal, I prefer to spend my limited instructional time focusing on other topics and skills that are more important."

While teachers make decisions about the allocation of instructional time daily, it is often in the last few weeks of the school year that these decisions become most apparent. The end of the school year always seems to arrive before all the planned topics can be taught. At this point, explicit decisions about how to allocate scarce time are made: "We must cover subtraction of fractions before the end of the year, but we can omit rate, time, and distance word problems." "If I don't finish parts of speech this year, next year's teacher will be upset. I'll take the time from the poetry unit to work on parts of speech." Time is a limited resource that has important consequences for planning instruction. Table 3.3 summarizes student, teacher, and instructional resources and considerations.

THREE LEVELS OF TEACHING OBJECTIVES

In our everyday activities, objectives help us focus on what's important; they remind us of what we want to accomplish. Instructional objectives describe the kinds of content and processes teachers hope their students will learn from instruction. Canadian provinces and territories use the terms *expectations* or *learning outcomes* instead of objectives. Whatever they are called, objectives are important in developing lesson plans. Teachers need to be aware of these objectives and support their students to meet them. Similarly, if teachers don't identify their objectives, instruction and assessment will be purposeless.

Objectives are particularly crucial in teaching because teaching is an intentional and normative act. Teaching is intentional because teachers teach for a purpose; they want students to learn something as a result of teaching. Teaching is also normative because what teachers teach is viewed by them as being worthwhile for their students to learn. In fact, it would be unethical for teachers to teach things that they did not believe were beneficial to students.

Because teaching is both intentional and normative, it always is based on expectations or learning outcomes. Normative teaching is concerned with selecting expectations or learning outcomes that are worthwhile for students to learn. Intentional teaching is concerned with issues of how teachers will teach these expectations or learning outcomes—what learning environments they will create and what methods they will use to help students learn the intended expectations or learning outcomes. Although expectations or learning outcomes may sometimes be implicit and fuzzy, it is best that they be explicit, clear, and measurable.

Expectations or learning outcomes can range from very general to very specific. Compare the following two expectations or learning outcomes: "The student can add three one-digit numbers," and "The student will become mathematically literate." Clearly the former is more specific than the latter. Notice how different instructional time, learning activities, and range of assessments would be needed for the two expectations or learning outcomes. Because objectives vary widely in specificity, a more limited framework for discussing objectives is commonly used. Three levels of abstraction represent degrees of objective specificity: global, educational, and instructional (Krathwohl & Payne, 1971). Note that regardless of the type or specificity of an objective, its focus should always be on *student* learning and performance.

There are three general levels of objectives: global, educational, and instructional, ranging from most broad to least broad.

Global objectives, often called "goals," are broad, complex student learning outcomes that require substantial time and instruction to accomplish. They are very general, encompassing a large number of more specific objectives. Examples include:

➤ The student will become a lifelong learner.
➤ The student will become mathematically literate.

➤ Students will learn to use their minds well, so that they may be prepared for responsible citizenship, further learning, and productive employment.

Because they are broadly inclusive, global objectives are rarely used in classroom assessment unless they are broken down into more narrow objectives. Global objectives mainly provide a rallying cry that reflects what is important in education policy. The breadth encompassed in global objectives makes them difficult for teachers to use in planning classroom instruction. Narrower objectives are needed to meet classroom needs.

Educational objectives represent a middle level of abstraction. Here are several examples:

➤ The student can interpret different types of social data.
➤ The student can correctly solve addition problems containing two digits.
➤ The student distinguishes between facts and hypotheses.

Educational objectives are more specific than global objectives. They are sufficiently narrow to help teachers plan and focus teaching, and sufficiently broad to indicate the richness of the objective and to suggest a range of possible student outcomes associated with the objective.

Instructional objectives are the least abstract and most specific type of objective. Examples of instructional objectives include:

➤ The student can correctly punctuate sentences.
➤ Given five problems requiring the student to find the lowest common denominator of a fraction, the student can solve at least four of five.
➤ The student can list the names of the Canadian provinces and territories.

Instructional objectives focus teaching on relatively narrow topics of learning in a content area. These concrete objectives are used in planning daily lessons.

Table 3.4 illustrates the difference in degree of breadth among the three types of objectives and compares their purposes, scopes, and time frames. The distinctions among these three levels of objectives are far more than semantic. The level at which an objective is stated influences its use in planning, instructing, and assessing. For example, the perspectives of teachers planning instruction and assessment for a global objective such as "The student will become mathematically literate" are quite different from those of teachers planning instruction and assessment for an instructional objective such as "The student will write common fractions in their lowest terms." Thus, the level at which an objective is stated—global, educational, or instructional—has an impact on the manner in which processes such as planning, instructing, and assessing will be structured and carried out.

TABLE 3.4	Comparing the Three Levels of Teaching Objectives		
Level of Objective	Global	Educational	Instructional
Scope	Broad	Intermediate	Narrow
Time to accomplish	One or more years	Weeks or months	Hours or days
Function	Provide vision	Develop curriculum, plan instruction, define suitable assessments	Plan teaching activities, learning experiences, and assessment exercises
Examples of breadth	The student will acquire competency of worldwide geography	The student will gain knowledge of devices and symbols in maps and charts	Given a map or chart, the student will correctly define six of the eight representational devices and symbols on it
	The student will be aware of the role of different levels of government in Canada	The student will interpret various types of social data	The student can interpret bar graphs describing population density
	The student will know how to repair a variety of home problems	The student will use appropriate procedures to find solutions to electrical problems in the home	Given a home repair problem dealing with a malfunctioning lamp, the student will repair it

THREE DOMAINS OF OBJECTIVES

Classroom assessments cover cognitive, affective, and psychomotor behaviours.

By this point it should be clear that objectives are logically and closely tied to instruction and assessment. In addition to differing in terms of level, classroom objectives (and their related instruction and assessments) differ in terms of three general types of human behaviour: the cognitive, affective, and psychomotor domains.

The Cognitive Domain

Cognitive assessments involve intellectual activities such as memorizing, interpreting, applying, problem solving, reasoning, analyzing, and thinking critically.

The most commonly taught and assessed educational objectives are those in the cognitive domain. The **cognitive domain** includes intellectual activities such as memorizing, interpreting, applying, problem solving, reasoning, analyzing, and thinking critically. Virtually all the tests that students take in school are intended to measure one or more of these cognitive activities. Teachers' instruction is usually focused on helping students attain cognitive mastery of some content or subject area. A weekly spelling test, a unit test in history, a worksheet on proper use of *lie* and *lay,* an essay on supply and demand, and an oral recitation of a poem all require cognitive behaviours. The School Achievement Indicators Program (SAIP), the written part of a provincial or territorial driver's licence, an ability test, and standardized achievement tests such as the *Canadian Achievement Test (CAT-3),* the *Woodcock Reading Mastery Tests (WRMT-R),* or the *Gates-MacGinite Reading Tests, 2nd Edition (GMRT-2)* are all intended to assess students' cognitive behaviours.

Bloom's Taxonomy

The many cognitive processes have been organized into six general categories. This organization is presented in the *Taxonomy of Educational Objectives: Book 1, Cognitive Domain* (Bloom et al., 1956). Commonly referred to as Bloom's Taxonomy, or the Cognitive Taxonomy, it is widely used by teachers to describe and state cognitive objectives.

A taxonomy is a system of classification. Bloom's cognitive taxonomy is organized into six levels, with each successive level representing a more complex type of cognitive process. Starting with the simplest and moving to the most complex, the six cognitive taxonomic processes are knowledge, comprehension, application, analysis, synthesis, and evaluation (see Table 3.5). It is important to note that in Bloom's Taxonomy "knowledge" refers only to memorizing and remembering information. It does not include other kinds of cognitive processes. The table provides some action verbs indicative of each cognitive process of Bloom's Taxonomy, and the general description of each process. Table 3.5 also lists sample objectives derived from Bloom's Taxonomy.

In recent years, besides Bloom's Taxonomy, other systems of cognitive-related objectives have been developed (Anderson et al., 2001; Marzano, Pickering, & McTighe, 1993). Although these taxonomies have extended the reach of objectives, Bloom's taxonomy remains the most used in assessment.

Although cognitive taxonomies can differ in the particular levels or categories they include, their most important function is to remind teachers of the distinction between higher- and lower-level thinking behaviours. In general, any cognitive behaviour that involves more than rote memorization or recall is considered to be a **higher-level cognitive behaviour**. Thus, the knowledge level of Bloom's Taxonomy represents **lower-level cognitive behaviour**, since the focus is upon memorization and recall. All succeeding levels in these taxonomies represent higher-level behaviours that call for students to carry out thinking and reasoning processes more complex than memorization. There is a growing emphasis in classroom instruction and assessment to focus upon teaching students higher-order thinking skills that go beyond rote memorization.

Lower-level cognitive behaviours involve rote memorization and recall; cognitive behaviours that involve more than rote memorization or recall are termed higher-level cognitive behaviours.

TABLE 3.5	Types of Cognitive Processes Identified in Bloom's Taxonomy		
1. Knowledge	Memorizing facts	Remember, recall, identify, recognize	The students can identify the correct punctuation marks in a writing assignment.
2. Comprehension	Explaining in one's own words	Translate, rephrase, restate, interpret, describe, explain	The students can translate French sentences into English.
3. Application	Solving new problems	Apply, execute, solve, implement	The students can add previously unseen proper fractions.
4. Analysis	Breaking into parts and identifying relatioships	Break down, categorize, distinguish, compare	The students can categorize paintings by their historical periods.
5. Synthesis	Combining elements into a whole	Integrate, organize, relate, combine, construct, design	The students can integrate the information from a science experiment into a lab report.
6. Evaluation	Judging quality or worth	Judge, assess, value, appraise	The students can judge the quality of various persuasive essays.

The Affective Domain

Affective assessments involve feelings, attitudes, interests, preferences, values, and emotions.

Teachers rarely make formal affective assessments but are constantly making them informally.

A second behaviourial domain is the affective domain. The **affective domain** involves feelings, attitudes, interests, preferences, values, and emotions. Emotional stability, motivation, trustworthiness, self-control, and personality are all examples of affective characteristics. Although affective behaviours are rarely assessed formally in schools and classrooms, teachers constantly assess affective behaviours informally. Teachers need to know who can be trusted to work unsupervised and who cannot, who can maintain self-control when the teacher has to leave the classroom and who cannot, who needs to be encouraged to speak in class and who does not, who is interested in science but not in social studies, and who needs to be prodded to start class work and who does not. Most classroom teachers can describe their students' affective characteristics based on their informal observations and interactions with the students.

In contrast to the cognitive domain, there is no single, widely accepted taxonomy of affective behaviours, although the taxonomy prepared by Krathwohl, Bloom, and Masia (1964) is the most commonly referred to and used. In general, affective taxonomies are all based upon the degree of a person's involvement in an activity or idea. The lower levels of affective taxonomies contain low-involvement behaviours such as paying attention, while the higher levels contain high-involvement behaviour characterized by strong interest, commitment, and valuing.

The Psychomotor Domain

A third behavioural domain is the psychomotor domain. The **psychomotor domain** includes physical and manipulative activities. Shooting a basketball, setting up laboratory equipment, building a bookcase, word processing, holding a pencil, buttoning a jacket, brushing teeth, and playing a musical instrument are examples of activities that involve psychomotor behaviours. Although psychomotor behaviours are present and important at all levels of schooling, they are especially stressed in the preschool and elementary grades, where tasks like holding a pencil, opening a locker, and buttoning or zippering clothing are important to master. (How would you like to button the jackets of 24 students?) Similarly, with certain special-needs students, a major part of education involves so-called "self-help" skills such as getting dressed, attending to personal hygiene, and preparing food, all of which are psychomotor accomplishments.

Psychomotor assessments involve physical and manipulative behaviours.

There are a number of psychomotor behaviour domain taxonomies (Hannah & Michaels, 1977; Harrow, 1972). Like the affective domain, however, no single taxonomy has become widely accepted and used by the majority of teachers and schools. The organization of psychomotor taxonomies typically ranges from a student showing a readiness to perform a psychomotor task, to the student using trial and error to learn a task, to the student actually carrying out the task on his or her own.

Psychomotor assessments are particularly important with very young or some students with exceptionalities.

As noted previously, diagnostic assessments encompass the cognitive, affective, and psychomotor domains because teachers are interested in knowing about their students' intellectual, attitudinal, and physical characteristics. Notice, however, that different assessment approaches characterize the different behaviour domains. For example, the cognitive domain is most likely to be assessed using paper-and-pencil tests or various kinds of oral questioning. Behaviours in the affective domain are most likely to be assessed by observation or questionnaires: for example, which subject do you prefer, English or chemistry? Do you believe that teachers should be accountable for their students' learning? Psychomotor behaviours are generally assessed by observing students carrying out the desired physical activity.

STATING AND CONSTRUCTING EXPECTATIONS OR LEARNING OUTCOMES

There are many ways to state expectations or learning outcomes, but not all of them convey clearly what students are to learn from instruction. Ensuring clarity requires being aware of what makes an expectation or learning outcome statement complete.

Essential Elements of the Statement

Consider the following three expectations or learning outcomes:

1. Students will learn to use their minds well, so that they may be prepared for responsible citizenship, further learning, and productive employment.
2. The student can read French poetry.
3. The student can correctly punctuate sentences.

Although they represent a global, educational, and instructional objective, respectively, these objectives have common characteristics. First, all are stated in terms of what the student is to learn from instruction. Objectives describe *student learning,* not teacher learning or the activities teacher or students engage in during instruction. Second, each objective contains two parts: some content for students to learn and a process to show their learning. The content in the three objectives above are, respectively, "citizenship," "French poetry," and "sentences." The cognitive processes are "develop," "read," and "punctuate." Another way to think about an objective's content and process is in terms of nouns and verbs. The content is the noun and the process is the verb. Thus, at a minimum, an objective is stated in terms of the content (noun) and process (verb) the student is expected to learn. Third, notice that the nouns and verbs differ from one objective to another because different subject matter, grade levels, and teaching styles require different objectives.

Objectives such as those shown above are widely used to guide teachers' planning, instruction, and assessment. For example, the objective "The students can categorize paintings by their historical periods" is focused on analysis (categorize) by identifying relationships. Or, the objective "The student can explain in his or her own words the meaning of a second-year-level French paragraph" is focused on comprehension (explain). Note that the verbs in the objectives we have examined (e.g., summarize, add, remember, categorize, explain) are *not* labelled using Bloom's generic taxonomy names (e.g., knowledge, comprehension, analysis). Instead, they are described using narrower, more specific verbs. These more specific and observable cognitive verbs are preferred over the generic taxonomy names because they more clearly indicate the particular process (verb) the students will be expected to carry out.

Forming Complete Statements

Examine the sample objectives in Table 3.6 and consider their usefulness in helping a teacher plan and guide instruction and assessment. Remember, the intent of an objective is to clearly identify what students are to learn in order to (1) communicate to others the purpose of instruction, (2) help teachers select appropriate instructional methods and materials, and (3) help plan assessments that will indicate whether or not students have learned what they were taught.

In Table 3.6, objectives 1, 2, and 3 all have the same deficiency. Each describes a body of content that will be covered in instruction, but each omits information about what the students will be expected to do with that content. Will they be expected to identify causes of the war, match generals to battles, cite strengths and weaknesses of the two sides, or explain in their own words why the Battle of the Plains of Abraham was the turning point of the war? What should students know or understand about Canadian government and the laws of motion? Without including information about what students are to know or do about the Seven Years' War, Canadian government, or laws of motion, it is hard to select appropriate instructional materials, activities, and assessment techniques. For example, it will make a difference in instruction and assessment if students have to match generals to battles (teach recall and assess with a matching item) or explain in their own words why the Battle of the Plains of Abraham was the turning point of the war (teach interpretation and assess with an open-ended question). Clarity and consistency between what is taught and what is assessed is necessary for valid assessment results.

TABLE 3.6 Sample Statements of Poor Educational Objectives
1. The Seven Years' War
2. Canadian government
3. The laws of motion
4. Analyze
5. Understand
6. Appreciate
7. Worthy use of leisure time
8. Pursue lifelong learning
9. Become a good citizen

Objectives 4, 5, and 6—analyze, understand, and appreciate—provide no reference to content matter. These statements prompt the question: analyze, understand, and appreciate what? Just as a content description by itself lacks clarity because it does not include a desired student performance, so too does a behaviour by itself lack clarity if there is no reference to a targeted body of content.

There is an additional problem in objectives 4, 5, and 6. Words like *analyze, understand,* and *appreciate* are themselves nonspecific. They can be interpreted in many different ways and hence do not clearly convey what students will learn. For example, one teacher might interpret the objective "understanding the basic features of a society" to mean the students will be able to explain the features in their own words. Another teacher might interpret the same objective to mean the students will give a real-life example of the social features studied. A third teacher might want students to distinguish between correct and incorrect applications of features. Although each teacher taught "understanding the basic features of society," each would teach and assess completely different outcomes. Such misunderstandings can be avoided if teachers describe their educational objectives in terms of the actual behaviours they expect their students to perform after instruction. For example, students can explain features in their own words, give real-life examples of the features, or distinguish correct from incorrect applications of the features. This level of specificity distinguishes clearly the different interpretations of *understand.*

Well-written educational objectives should clearly specify what students are to learn and how they are to demonstrate that learning.

In stating educational objectives, it is better to clearly describe the behaviour the student will perform than to use more general, ambiguous terms that are open to many different interpretations. Thus, it is better to say *explains* the importance of conserving natural resources than to say *realizes* the importance of conserving natural resources; better to say *translates* French sentences into English than to say *understands* French sentences; better to say can *differentiate* subjects and predicates than to say *knows* about subjects and predicates; better to say *states* three differences between good and bad art than to say *appreciates* art. In each example, the first statement describes a student behaviour that can be observed, instructed, and assessed, while the second uses less clear, unobservable, and ambiguous terms. Clear descriptions foster alignment among objectives, instruction, and assessment, thus producing valid assessment results.

Objectives 7, 8, and 9 are too general and complicated to be achieved by students in a single subject area or grade level. They are, as noted previously, goals. Not only do these outcomes take years to develop, but their generality provides the classroom teacher with little guidance regarding the activities and materials that could be used to attain them. Broad goals such as these must be narrowed by the classroom teacher before they can be used to instruct and assess students.

Some Good Examples of Objectives

In summary thus far, the basic requirements for well-stated educational objectives are that they (1) describe a student behaviour that should result from instruction; (2) state the behaviour in terms that can be observed and assessed; and (3) indicate the content on which the behaviour will be performed. A simple model for preparing educational objectives is "the students can" (observable behaviour) (content). Here are examples of appropriately stated educational objectives.

➤ The students can list three causes of the Seven Years' War.
➤ The students can solve word problems requiring the sum of two numbers.
➤ The students can write a correctly formatted and punctuated business letter.
➤ The students can translate a French paragraph into English.
➤ The students can count to 20 aloud.
➤ The students can list three differences between the climates of Canada and Mexico.
➤ The students can write balanced chemical equations.
➤ The students can state the main idea of short stories.
➤ The students can explain the water cycle in their own words.

Notice how these objectives help focus the intended student learning and thus help the teacher identify suitable instructional activities, materials, and assessments.

Other information can be added to elaborate an objective. For example, some teachers wish to include information in their objectives about the conditions of student performance and about how well the student must perform the objective in order to master it. Such extended objectives would be written as follows:

➤ Given 10 word problems requiring the sum of two numbers, the students can solve at least eight correctly.
➤ Given a diagram of the water cycle, the students can explain in their own words what the water cycle is with fewer than two errors.
➤ Given a French paragraph of less than 20 lines and a dictionary, the students can translate the paragraph into English in 5 minutes with fewer than six errors.

Extended objectives provide more details about the conditions under which the behaviour must be performed and the level of performance the student must show. Extended objectives take more time to prepare than their simpler counterparts and are sometimes difficult to state prior to the

Extended objectives provide additional details about the conditions under which students must demonstrate their learning and the level of performance they must show.

> **KEY ASSESSMENT TOOLS 3.1**
>
> **Criteria for Successful Objectives**
>
> **1.** Be sure the objectives have clear answers.
> **2.** Be sure the objectives represent important aspects of a lesson or chapter.
> **3.** Be sure the objectives center on a verb that specifies student performance.
> **4.** Be sure that the objective can be fulfilled in a reasonable amount of time.

start of instruction. Consequently, the simpler model suffices in most instructional situations. Key Assessment Tools 3.1 is a brief reminder of criteria for successful objectives.

Questions Often Asked about Educational Objectives

1. *Is it necessary to write down objectives?* Beginning teachers and students in a teaching practicum usually are required to write lesson objectives. Even if you are an experienced teacher, listing your objectives reminds you to focus on what students are expected to get out of instruction, not just what your teaching activities will be. Annual assessment of existing objectives is an important part of any teacher's classroom assessment responsibilities, because each year students and curricula change.

2. *What are higher-level objectives?* Cognitive behaviours can be divided into lower-level ones such as memorizing and remembering and higher-level ones requiring more complex thinking behaviours. Higher-level behaviours, or higher-order thinking skills (HOTS), include activities such as analyzing information, applying information and rules to solve new problems, comparing and contrasting objects or ideas, and synthesizing disparate pieces of information into a single, organized idea. In the following examples, the lower-level objective calls only for memorization, while the higher-level objective calls for a more complex behaviour.

Higher-level objectives include cognitive activities such as analysis, application, synthesis, and evaluation. These take longer to teach and evaluate than lower-level objectives involving rote memorization.

Lower level: The student can write a definition of each vocabulary word.

Higher level: The student can write sentences using each vocabulary word correctly.

Lower level: The student can match quotes from a short story to the characters who said them.

Higher level: The student can contrast the motives of the protagonist and the antagonist in a short story.

Lower level: The student can write the formula for the Pythagorean theorem.

Higher level: The student can use the Pythagorean theorem to solve new word problems involving the length of ladders needed by the fire department.

All teachers should be aware of the difference between lower- and higher-level thinking skills and should strive to incorporate some higher-level objectives in their plans and instruction.

3. *How many objectives should I state in a subject area?* The answer to this question depends in part upon the time frame being considered and the specificity of the objectives: the longer the period of instruction and the more specific the objectives, the more objectives that can be stated with expectation for students to attain. In general, there may be many instructional objectives and fewer educational objectives. Also, higher-level objectives usually take longer to teach and learn, so fewer of them can be taught in a given instructional period; it takes longer to teach students to interpret graphs than to memorize a formula. Teachers who have hundreds of objectives for the year's instruction either are expecting too much of themselves and their students or are stating their objectives too narrowly. On the other hand, teachers who have only five objectives for the school year are either underestimating their students or stating their objectives much too broadly.

4. *Are there any cautions I should keep in mind regarding objectives?* Objectives are usually stated before instruction actually begins and are meant to guide both instruction and assessment. However, objectives are not meant to be followed slavishly when circumstances suggest the need for adjustments. Because objectives are written before instruction starts and because it is difficult to anticipate the flow of classroom activities during instruction, teachers must exercise discretion regarding how closely they will follow the objectives they stated prior to the start of actual instruction.

Because educational objectives are written before instruction begins, teachers must be ready to deviate from them when necessary.

IMPROVING THE TIE BETWEEN PLANNING AND ASSESSMENT

In planning instruction, there are a few common guidelines that teachers can follow to strengthen the effectiveness of their planning.

1. *Perform complete diagnostic assessments of students' needs and characteristics.* Because the purpose of instruction is to help students

do things they were unable to do before instruction, planning responsive lessons requires that the needs and characteristics of students be
taken into consideration. Knowledge of students' readiness, abilities,
and attention spans helps the classroom teacher determine how long
lessons should be, whether they should involve whole-class or small-
group activities, and whether they should be teacher-led or student-
directed. The more valid and reliable student and class diagnostic
assessments are, the more appropriate the lesson plans are likely to
be.

2. *Use diagnostic assessment information when planning.* A teacher
   may have done an exceptional job with the diagnostic assessment of
   students, but if the teacher does not use that information when planning lessons, it is useless. Planning involves fitting instruction to student needs and characteristics, and it is the teacher's responsibility to
   plan accordingly.

3. *Do not rely entirely and uncritically on textbooks and their accompanying aids when planning.* The teacher's edition of textbooks can
   provide much of the information needed to plan, carry out, and
   assess instruction, but usually not all. It is important to match the
   suitability of textbook plans and assessments with student characteristics and needs. Teacher's guides should be assessed, adapted, and
   supplemented to provide the best possible instruction to each
   teacher's class.

4. *Include a combination of lower-level and higher-level objectives.* The
   instructional activities offered in most teacher's editions are heavily
   weighted toward whole-class practices such as recitation, teacher
   presentation, and seatwork. Such practices normally emphasize
   lower-level objectives. It is important, therefore, that lesson plans
   and activities (whether textbook or teacher-made) include *both* lower-
   and higher-level objectives.

5. *Include a wide range of instructional activities and strategies to fit
   your students' instructional needs.* Teachers who use the same strategy (e.g., lecture, seatwork, or board work) every day with little
   change or variety create two problems. First, they risk boring students and reducing their motivation to attend to the repetitive activity. Second, by limiting their teaching repertoire to a single or very
   few strategies, they may not be reaching students whose learning
   styles, needs, or language backgrounds are best suited to some other
   method (e.g., small-group instruction, learning games, hands-on
   materials). It is important to include varied teaching strategies and
   activities in lesson plans.

6. *Match educational objectives with teaching strategies and planned
   assessments.* Objectives describe the desired results of instruction.
   Teaching strategies and activities represent the means to achieve
   those results. Assessment is a measure of the success of the objectives
   and instruction. To reach the desired ends, the means must be rele-

Means: Read a short story silently.
End: The students can summarize a short story in their own words.

Means: Show a film about computers.
End: The students can differentiate between computer hardware and software.

Means: Discuss the organization of the periodic table.
End: The students can place an element in its periodic group when given a description of the element's properties.

FIGURE 3.2
Examples of Instructional Means and Ends.

vant and appropriate. Without student ends clearly in mind, it is difficult to judge the adequacy of an instructional plan or the quality of an assessment. Figure 3.2 shows the relationship between statements of ends (objectives) and statements of means (teaching activities).

7. *Recognize one's own knowledge and pedagogical limitations and preferences.* Teachers assess many things when planning instruction, but they often neglect an assessment of themselves. Content knowledge limitations may lead a teacher to omit an important topic, teach it in a perfunctory or superficial manner, or provide students with incorrect information. Likewise, preferences for one or two teaching methods may deprive students of exposure to other methods or activities that would enhance their learning. When a teacher's knowledge limitations and pedagogical preferences outweigh student considerations in determining what is or is not done in classrooms, serious questions must be raised about the adequacy of the teacher's instructional plans.

8. *Include assessment strategies in instructional plans.* The object of planning and conducting instruction is to help students learn new content and behaviours. Consequently, lesson plans should include some formal measure or measures to determine whether students have learned the desired objectives and to identify areas of misunderstanding or confusion. While informal assessments about student enthusiasm and participation can be useful, they are not substitutes for more formal assessments such as follow-up seatwork, homework, quizzes, or oral questioning.

PLANNING FOR STUDENTS WITH EXCEPTIONALITIES

Initially it may seem odd to introduce student exceptionalities and accommodations in a chapter focused on objectives and planning instruction. On reflection, however, it is not really odd at all. Student exceptionalities and, particularly, student accommodations are very important aspects that must be addressed in a teacher's instructional planning.

According to the Canadian Charter of Rights and Freedoms (1982), every Canadian has the right to equal treatment under the law without discrimination based on race, national or ethnic origin, colour, religion, sex, age, or mental or physical disability. By extension, all Canadian provinces and territories have developed policies and procedures that guarantee *all* students access to equitable educational opportunities without discrimination based on a designation as "exceptional."

From an analysis of special education services across Canada, Dworet and Bennett (2002) found that similarities exist that "include the use of individual education plans (IEPs), a collaborative approach to problem-solving, and an emphasis on inclusion" (p. 22). Therefore, regardless of location, each exceptional student in Canada will receive an IEP outlining the strengths and needs of the student and the program and instructional modifications that are necessary to support the student's learning opportunities. The IEP will include information about the student's present level of educational performance, annual goals and short-term objectives, prescribed educational services, degree of inclusion in regular education programs, and assessment criteria for determining achievement of the goals and objectives of the plan.

The requirement for inclusionary practices and fair and appropriate educational opportunities for exceptional children has placed greater responsibility and challenge on the classroom teacher. If a student is identified as exceptional, a committee, which includes the teacher, will decide on how and what the student will be taught and assessed. Using the IEP, the teacher must modify objectives, instructional strategies, and assessment methods to best suit the student's needs and learning style. The following lists provide some instructional planning ideas for accommodating students with exceptionalities.

Accommodations when planning content:

➤ If students have fallen behind in the curriculum, teach what is most generalizable.
➤ Teach learning strategies along with teaching content.
➤ Select content based on student interest; for example, allow students to read the sports page to practise reading skills.

Accommodations when planning objectives:

➤ Pretest before teaching to make sure the objectives are appropriate for the students.
➤ Determine whether an objective can be altered for some students; for example, can students who have poor writing skills demonstrate their knowledge orally?

Accommodations when deciding on instructional methods:

➤ Recognize that students with some learning and behavioural exception-alities often need very explicit directions.
➤ Evaluate the level of structure students need to be successful; do not assume that all students learn best with unstructured approaches.
➤ If students have fallen behind in the curriculum, use time-efficient methods.
➤ Be sure students have the necessary skills to be successful with the instructional method being used.

Accommodations when planning the lesson:

➤ Provide directions, procedures, and rules; describe them orally and in writing.
➤ Follow up by asking questions or by having students repeat or para-phrase what they are to do.
➤ Repeat key words often, using the same wording.
➤ Ask for frequent active responses.
➤ Break up information: teach a couple of steps, practise, teach a few more steps, practise. Keep reminding students of the whole task. Stop often to summarize.
➤ Point to steps on a written list as they are demonstrated.

CHAPTER REVIEW

What purpose does a curriculum serve?

➤ A curriculum describes the skills, performances, knowledge, and attitudes students are expected to learn in school.

What is instruction?

➤ Instruction is the set of methods and processes used to change students' behaviour.

What is the difference between achievement and aptitude or ability?

➤ Achievement refers to school-based learning, while ability or aptitude refer to broader learning acquired mostly through nonschool sources such as parents and peer groups.

Describe the three steps of the instructional process.

➤ Planning instruction, which includes identifying specific expectations or learning outcomes, selecting materials to foster these outcomes, and organizing learning experiences into a coherent, reinforcing sequence.

➤ Delivering the planned instruction to students (i.e., teaching them).

➤ Assessing students, which involves the collection and synthesis of formal information about how well students are learning or have learned the expectations or learning outcomes.

What are the three general levels of teaching objectives?

➤ The three general levels of teaching objectives are global objectives, educational objectives, and instructional objectives.

What are the three domains of human behaviour for which educational objectives can be written?

➤ The cognitive domain, which includes knowledge, comprehension, application, analysis, synthesis, and evaluation.

➤ The affective domain, which involves feelings, attitudes, interests, preferences, values, and emotions.

➤ The psychomotor domain, which includes physical and manipulative activities.

What is Bloom's Taxonomy?

➤ Bloom's Taxonomy is a system of cognitive processes organized into six levels, with each successive level representing a more complex type of cognitive process.

➤ Starting with the simplest and moving to the most complex, the six cognitive taxonomic processes are knowledge, comprehension, application, analysis, synthesis, and evaluation.

What are some essential elements of a well-written teaching objective?

➤ It is stated in terms of what the student is to learn from instruction.

➤ It contains two parts: some content for students to learn and a process to show their learning.

What are some important guidelines to follow when planning instruction?

➤ Perform complete diagnostic assessments of students' needs and characteristics.

➤ Use diagnostic assessment information when planning.

➤ Do not rely entirely and uncritically on textbooks and their accompanying aids when planning.

➤ Include a combination of lower-level and higher-level expectations or learning outcomes.

➤ Include a wide range of instructional activities and strategies to fit your students' instructional needs.

➤ Match educational expectations or learning outcomes with teaching strategies, activities, and planned assessments.

➤ Recognize one's own knowledge and pedagogical limitations and planned preferences.

➤ Include assessment strategies in instructional plans.

QUESTIONS FOR DISCUSSION

1. What student characteristics are most important to take into account when planning instruction? How realistic is it to expect a teacher to plan instruction that takes into account the important needs of all the students?

2. Which subject areas are the most difficult to plan for? Why?

3. What would be the characteristics of a class that would be easy to plan for? What would be the characteristics of a difficult-to-plan-for group?

4. Why do you think that many teachers describe stating expectations or learning outcomes as "backward planning"? Is "backward planning" useful? Why or why not?

5. What differentiates a well-stated expectation or learning outcome from one that is poorly stated?

6. What are the most common exceptionalities that students have? How might they influence planning, instruction, and assessment?

7. A teacher's skill at instructional planning has been linked to his or her students' academic success. Explain why this is the case? What other teacher characteristics may be correlated with student achievement?

ACTIVITIES

1. Ask a teacher to show and discuss with you a lesson plan that he or she has used. Report on the teacher's expectations or learning outcomes and how the plan took various resources and conditions into account, as well as how closely the plan was actually followed when the lesson was taught.

2. In a small group, choose an imaginary student with a certain exceptionality in a certain grade. To each student in the group assign the role of teacher, parent, a school administrator, and possibly a learning resource teacher within the school. Describe the types of accommodations that a person in each role would emphasis in an IEP for that student.

CHAPTER 4

ASSESSING DURING INSTRUCTION: FORMATIVE ASSESSMENT

After reading this chapter, you will be able to:

➤ Define formative assessment

➤ Describe the sources of information for formative assessment

➤ Outline how formative assessment data guides instruction

➤ Interpret and judge the value of the data collected through formative assessment

➤ Explain the purposes, types, and guidelines for oral questioning

➤ Explain the role of student self-assessment in formative assessment

➤ Identify weaknesses in the validity and reliability of formative assessment and suggest ways to overcome them

As a beginning secondary math teacher, Mitch often relies on the practice of assessing his students' progress during the learning process. During his daily lessons, Mitch frequently pauses to verbally question students for their comprehension and he intently listens to their responses for misconceptions. As students complete seat work practice, Mitch continuously moves around the classroom ready to assist any students who may be having difficulty. In this way, Mitch identifies which students need his individual attention and this helps him to form and guide subsequent instruction.

The assessment activities that teachers carry out prior to instruction are different from those carried out during instruction as Table 4.1 shows. Recall that assessment that takes place at the beginning of the school year or before a unit of instruction is called **diagnostic assessment**. Teachers gather these assessment data for information about their students' academic, social, attitudinal, and behavioural characteristics so as to enhance communication and instruction. This chapter instead will focus on assessment that occurs *during* instruction for the purpose of evaluating its effectiveness.

Formative assessment refers to those assessments made during instruction that indicate how well the lesson is going.

The process of collecting data to improve students' learning while instruction is taking place is called **formative assessment**. Teachers gather formative assessment data by picking up on student cues such as attention, questioning students about the content of the lesson, checking assigned work, assigning quizzes or open book tests, and reflecting on the lesson. These data are used by the teacher to make decisions about whether new instruction may proceed, and, if not, how previous instruction might change in order to improve student learning—formative assessment is a guide during the learning process. It is also important to note that students' self-assessment is also a form of formative assessment that is

	Diagnostic	Formative
	TABLE 4.1 Comparison of Diagnostic and Formative Assessment	
Purpose	To determine the ways in which teachers plan, teach, assess, and evaluate	To monitor and guide instruction and learning while it is still in progress
Time of assessment	Beginning of instruction	During instruction
Type of assessment technique	Observations, school records, discussions, quizzes, comments	Observations, questions seatwork, quizzes, homework
Use of assessment information	Hone the content and method of instruction	Improve and change instruction and learning while it is still going on

used to support students to focus during the learning process (this form will be discussed later in this chapter). In this way, formative assessment is contexualized in the instructional process and comprises an integral part of both teaching and learning (Bell & Cowie, 2001).

Canadian researcher, Lorna Earl reminds teachers that formative assessment might be indistinguishable from instruction since it occurs frequently as part of classroom activity. Formative assessment may be formal or informal, it may occur with an individual or a group, and it does not always contribute to students' final grades (Earl & Cousins, 1996). It is important to note that it is the *purpose* of assessment, not necessarily the *method*, which distinguishes formative assessment from the other types of assessment. For example, a paper-and-pencil test or a teacher's observation of students' performance, are commonly used to collect data to improve students' learning while instruction is taking place. As well, a paper-and-pencil test or a teacher's observation of students' performance, can also be used as assessment tools at the end of a classroom process, activity, unit, or course to assess the outcomes of instruction. This latter purpose is for summative assessment; Chapter 5 will further discuss summative assessment.

Black and Wiliam (1998) report that properly implemented formative assessment has the potential to enhance student performance more than most known educational interventions. Furthermore, low-achieving students, including students with exceptionalities, are most significantly supported by the use of formative assessment. However, high-quality formative assessment is not used in many classrooms simply because most teachers lack the knowledge of formative assessment techniques. This chapter will describe how to carry out formative assessment in order to improve student learning.

ASSESSMENT TASKS DURING INSTRUCTION

Once instruction begins, teachers carry on two tasks: they deliver the instruction that they have planned and they constantly assess the progress and success of their instruction in order to modify it if necessary. For many reasons, things do not always go as planned. Interruptions, misjudgments about student readiness and attention, shifts in student interest, and various events (e.g., fire drills, assemblies) can alter planned instruction. As a result, the teacher must constantly gauge the learning of the class to make decisions about what to do next. Thus, once the teacher initiates instruction, he or she engages in an ongoing process of assessing its progress and deciding about students' reactions to it.

Note that when planning instruction, the focus is on student characteristics, readiness, subject matter objectives, and learning activities. Once instruction actually begins, the focus shifts to more action-oriented concerns, especially on how students are reacting to the instructional process.

Consequently, during instruction, teachers collect formative assessment data to help monitor factors such as:

➤ Interest level of individual students and the class as a whole
➤ Apparent or potential behaviour problems
➤ Appropriateness of the instructional technique or activity being used
➤ Adequacy of a student's answer
➤ Pace of instruction
➤ Implications of students' questions
➤ Transitions from one activity to another
➤ Suitability of examples used to explain concepts
➤ Degree of students' comprehension
➤ Appropriateness of ending the lesson

Such monitoring, of course, is a complicated task, since instruction, assessment, and decision making are taking place almost simultaneously. Many decisions are required during instruction. In fact, these instructional decisions are informed by assessments that teachers make as part of the instructional process. In this way, the instructional process could be considered an ongoing formative assessment (Boston, 2002).

Figure 4.1 illustrates this process of ongoing formative assessment. Once *teaching* begins, the teacher continually *assesses* its progress by observing student reactions and asking them questions. On the basis of these reactions and responses, the teacher makes a *decision* about how instruction is going. If the teacher decides that the lesson is progressing satisfactorily, he or she continues teaching as planned (path A). If the teacher senses a problem, such as lack of student understanding or interest, the planned instructional activity should be *revised* to alleviate the problem and another teach-

FIGURE 4.1
Process of Formative Assessment.

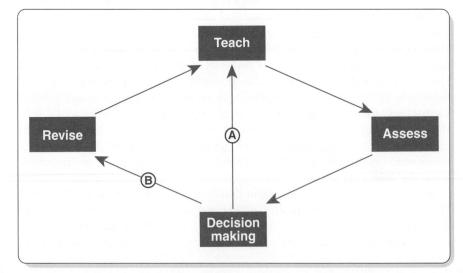

ing activity or strategy initiated (path B). This cycle is repeated many times in the course of a single lesson.

Canadian researcher, Bernard Mohan, has documented how teachers can enhance their instructional effectiveness by evaluating the process by which their students contemplate responses. Ultimately, students' learning can be enhanced as a function of teacher feedback. Teachers can provide their students with reasons why certain responses may not be plausible and then guide their students to reject erroneous responses and accept correct responses. In this way, teachers engage in a "two-level" assessment process as they explain why a response is incorrect and how to obtain a solution (Leung & Mohan, 2004). Black and Wiliam (1998) concur that students need the opportunity to express their understanding, engage in classroom dialogue that explores understanding, and receive feedback that includes guidance on how to improve.

Indicators During Instruction

As a teacher, what are the indicators you might consider assessing during instruction? Given the pace and complexity of instructional activities, teachers often rely on informal indicators to monitor their instruction (Green & Mantz, 2002). They rely on behavioural cues from the students, such as eye contact and facial expressions or body language, rather than on more formal paper-and-pencil assessments. The latter may break the flow of the lesson and student involvement with a distinct change in activities.

Other indicators that teachers use to judge the success of their instruction are based on their perceptions of classroom dynamics. These include students' participation in discussions, their eagerness to raise their hands to answer questions, or the noise level in the classroom. Over time, teachers establish levels of tolerance that indicate what is normal class or student behaviour. These tolerance levels vary from teacher to teacher. Part of the process of "reading" the class during instruction involves knowing when students are exhibiting behaviours that are out-of-tolerance and call for a response from the teacher. Some students demonstrate a lack of instructional engagement by daydreaming, fidgeting, talking to their neighbour, or frequenting the washroom.

Responding to a variety of immediate classroom needs allows teachers little time to reflect on what they are doing. Many teachers have the sense that they automatically assess many environmental cues during instruction. Teachers should take care to supplement informal assessments with formal feedback such as review exercises, worksheets, and homework. When considering which indicators to assess during instruction, a teacher must remember to keep instruction flowing smoothly so as to keep students engaged in the learning process.

Decision Making During Instruction

How do we as teachers go through a decision-making process during instruction? Teachers begin by thinking about the adequacy of their teaching. Teachers' thoughts are often concerned with the effect of instruction on students; that is, how much they are attending to and benefiting from instruction. For example, when determining how much students are benefiting from instruction, teachers consider the implications of providing students with more examples of a concept, how to alter a learning strategy, how to devise a worksheet to reinforce an idea, and when to review a lesson. Likewise, when there is a transition point in the lesson from one activity to another, when the teacher anticipates a problem in teaching a concept, when there is insufficient time to complete planned activities, or when there is a shortage of materials, the teacher must make a decision about the nature of subsequent instruction.

Using Practical Knowledge

Most of the observations, interpretations, and decisions that occur during instruction are made on the basis of the teacher's practical knowledge of the students. **Practical knowledge** comprises those beliefs, insights, perceptions, and habits that enable teachers to teach. Practical knowledge, in contrast to theoretical knowledge, is time-bound and situation-specific. It is relevant to a particular class and to particular individuals in the class. It changes from year to year as the characteristics of students and the class change. Examples of practical knowledge include classroom management techniques for small versus large group instruction, or visual versus auditory learning strategies. Each class has its own personality, strengths, weaknesses, and challenges, and every year the teacher must rely on diagnostic assessments to help build up a new store of practical knowledge about the new class. Throughout the school year, teachers call on their practical knowledge about their students to decide on a course of action. Teachers have a store of practical knowledge that fits students and the class as a whole to enable them to continue to carry out instruction.

To summarize this section, the direction, flow, and pace of instruction are dictated by the dynamic of the classroom at any given time. The teacher's assessment task during instruction is to monitor the progress and success of the instruction. In most classrooms, monitoring boils down to assessing the appropriateness of the instructional procedures and the students' reaction to them. Decisions that teachers make during instruction are prompted by (1) unusual student behaviour that requires a response or reaction from the teacher and (2) typical issues that arise during instruction, such as responding to a student's question, deciding who to call on next, and deciding whether to move on to the next topic. The assessment information that teachers gather when they monitor their instruction comes mostly from informal observations of the students. These cues, plus

CHAPTER CASE
STUDY

Visit the OLC to read
the case of Frank Oakley
who reflects on his
teaching and refines his
methods to meet the
needs of his students.

www.mcgrawhill.ca/
college/airasian

the teacher's knowledge of the class, support the assessments and decisions that teachers make during classroom instruction. Assessments of abnormal behaviour help to maintain whatever level of tolerance the teacher intends to allow. Above all, ongoing assessment is rooted in a teacher's practical knowledge of the class.

GUIDELINES FOR FORMATIVE ASSESSMENTS

Successful formative assessment depends upon a teacher's "feel" for the instructional process. This "feel" is dependent in large measure upon the teacher's informal assessments and practical knowledge of the students' typical behaviour. It permits the teacher to anticipate instructional problems, select the correct instructional procedure from the many options available, and utilize a few valid indicators to determine how instruction is going. Teachers will always have to rely in part upon their "feel" for the classroom situation when gathering assessment information and making decisions during instruction. However, this does not mean that the process cannot be made more valid and reliable, so that decision making is improved and student learning enhanced. The following list contains some guidelines that should be considered during the formative assessment process:

Effective teachers will always be those who develop a feel for how things are going, moment by moment in the classroom.

1. *Include a broad sample of students when assessing instruction.* Avoid calling on only those higher-achieving students whose behaviours or answers are likely to reinforce your perception of instructional success. Directing attention only at the few students who always know the answer might cause you to lose touch with the class as a whole. As teachers, we should make an effort to sample a wide range of students in the class. Unless information about the progress and success of instruction has been gathered from a representative sample of students, then formative assessment may be unreliable.

2. *Supplement informal assessment information with more formal information about student learning.* To obtain a complete and more reliable picture of instructional success, teachers should supplement their informal observations with formal types of evidence such as seatwork, homework assignments, and review exercises. Each of these is a valuable source of information that can tell the teacher something about how well students have mastered lesson objectives. These sources should be examined to identify misunderstandings and problem areas.

3. *Gather formative assessment information from both lower- and higher-level instructional activities.* As discussed earlier, teachers evaluate themselves in terms of student involvement and attention during instruction. Do not be tempted to focus only on the objectives of lower-level instructional activities that are more easily attained by your students than those from higher-level instructional activities.

4. *Take the time to gather sufficient corroborative evidence that supports the decision-making process.* Despite the rapidity of classroom events, you should attempt to collect multiple sources of formative assessment data over the course of time. These data may include observations, oral questions, seatwork, homework, quizzes, or open book tests. Furthermore, these formative assessment data should be collected through a variety of techniques such as the teacher taking observational notes, posing questions to students, checking seatwork or homework, or testing students. Additionally, the students can make oral presentations, or self-assess their progress.

As well, the Joint Committee on Standards for Educational Evaluation (2003) has published a set of guidelines for assessing classroom evaluation practices called *The Student Evaluation Standards: How to Improve Evaluations of Students*. This text discusses such topics as where in the instructional process assessments should occur, how assessment information should be used to direct student learning, and what kinds of questions teachers should pose to their students. These guidelines have been approved by several professional societies including the Canadian Evaluation Society and the Canadian Society for the Study of Education.

Student Self-Assessment

Formative assessment is also used as a method to support the students' focus during the learning process. This may be accomplished through students' self-assessment as this purpose can provide insights into how they are interpreting their own learning. Earl and Katz (2000) believe that students themselves are in the best position to describe their own beliefs and understandings. With this orientation, teachers should attempt to identify and develop sources of competence in their students, but allow the students to evaluate their own progress and competency. One way that students can take responsibility for their own learning and progress is by becoming effective questioners (Chappuis & Stiggins, 2002). Learners should be empowered to ask reflective questions and consider efficient learning strategies (Earl & Cousins, 1996). Yet, the skill of self-assessment does not necessarily come naturally to all students. Teachers should model and encourage students to use three basic self-assessment questions: "Where am I going? Where am I now? How do I close the gap?" Teachers should show students samples of anonymous work and teach them how to ask and answer questions about the attributes of good performance. Prior to a test, students should be encouraged to create their own sets of questions for practice. Finally, teachers should display learning objectives in the classroom and ask students to rephrase them. Overall, teachers should model questions that focus students on the learning process rather than on approval or disapproval.

QUESTIONING: PURPOSES, TYPES, AND STRATEGIES

Conducting assessment during instruction is a craft. As teachers we need to be savvy enough to determine if students are learning the desired objectives. One means of gathering information about instructional effectiveness is oral questioning. Oral questions are a popular formative assessment technique for classroom teachers, with some teachers asking as many as 300 to 400 questions a day (Morgan & Saxton, 1991; Christensen, 1991). Except for lecturing, questioning is the most dominant teaching strategy at all levels of education and, together with discussion, comprises the most common form of student-teacher interaction.

Purposes of Questioning

Questions also facilitate learning by stimulating thinking and inquiry and keep students involved in the lesson. Questioning can require students to go beyond factual recall of information and engage in higher order thinking that involves the application, analysis, synthesis, and evaluation of knowledge (Chin, 2004). The following are common reasons that teachers use questions during instruction:

1. *To promote attention.* Questioning is a way to keep students' attention during a lesson, a way to engage them actively in the process of learning.

2. *To promote deeper processing.* Questioning lets students verbalize their thoughts and ideas, thereby promoting the thinking and reasoning that lead to deeper processing of information.

3. *To promote learning from peers.* Questioning allows students to hear their peers' interpretations and explanations of ideas, processes, and issues. Often, other students explain things in ways that are more in tune with the minds of their peers.

4. *To provide reinforcement.* Questioning is used by teachers to reinforce important points and ideas. The questions teachers ask cue students regarding what and how they should be learning.

5. *To provide pace and control.* Questions that require brief, correct responses keep students engaged in learning and require them to pay continuous attention. Questions that are more general and open-ended slow the pace of instruction so students can reflect upon and frame their answers and explanations.

6. *To provide diagnostic information.* Questions provide the teacher with information about students and class learning. Teachers' questions can supplement their informal observations of student learning

Teachers ask questions in order to reinforce important points, to diagnose problems, to keep students' attention, and to promote deeper processing of information.

in the least disruptive way. Also, for group or cooperative learning activities, questioning of group members after completion of their task is a useful way to assess the success of the group.

Types of Questions

Convergent questions are those that have a single correct answer, whereas divergent questions may have several appropriate answers.

There are higher- and lower-level questions and convergent and divergent questions. **Convergent questions** have a single correct answer: What is the capital of Brazil? Who is credited with the discovery of radium? How many corners does a cube have? **Divergent questions** may have many appropriate answers: What are the benefits of a good education? Describe some differences between the Japanese and French systems of government. What kinds of jobs do people in your neighbourhood have? Divergent questions tend to demand more thought than convergent questions, although it should be recognized that both types are important to use during instruction (Wiggins & McTighe, 1998).

Christensen (1991) has developed the following typology of questions that shows the breadth of information that can be obtained from varying types of questions:

➤ Open-ended questions	What is your reaction to this poem?
➤ Diagnostic questions	What is the nature of the problem in this short story?
➤ Information questions	What was the last province/territory in Canada to join Confederation?
➤ Challenge questions	What evidence is there to support your conclusion?
➤ Action questions	How can we go about solving the problem of high school dropouts?
➤ Sequence questions	Given limited resources, what are the two most important steps to take?
➤ Prediction questions	What do you think would happen if the government shut down for three months?
➤ Extension questions	What are the implications of your conclusion that grades should be abolished in schools?
➤ Generalization questions	Based on your study of classroom assessment, how would you sum up the general concept of validity?

Lower-level, factual questions generally begin with words such as who, what, and when, whereas higher-level questions begin with action words such as explain, predict, distinguish, and solve.

Questions also can be categorized by whether they require higher or lower levels of thinking. Lower-level thinking, requiring recall or memorization, resides in the lowest category of Bloom's Taxonomy (see Table 4.2). **Lower-level questions** generally begin with words such as, "who," "when," "what," and "how many." Such questions focus on factual information that the student is expected to remember and produce when questioned.

TABLE 4.2 Examples of Questions for the Levels of Bloom's Cognitive Taxonomy	
Knowledge (remembering)	What is the definition of a noun?
	How many planets are in our solar system?
	In what year did Confederation occur?
Comprehension (understanding)	Summarize the story in your own words.
	Explain what $E = MC^2$ means.
	Paraphrase the author's intent.
Application (using information to solve new problems)	What is a real-world example of that principle?
	Predict what would happen if the steps in the process were reversed.
	How could the Pythagorean theorem be used to measure the height of a tree?
Analysis (reasoning, breaking apart)	Which of these statements are facts and which are opinions?
	How did the main character change after her scary nightmare?
	Explain the unstated assumption that underlies this argument.
Synthesis (constructing, integrating)	What do all these pictures have in common?
	Describe a generalization that follows from these data.
	State a conclusion supported by these facts.
Evaluation (judging)	What was the most important moment in the story and why?
	What is your opinion of the school policy for grades and extracurricular participation?

Higher-level thinking requires students to perform processes such as understanding conceptual knowledge and applying procedural knowledge. **Higher-level questions** typically start with words such as, "explain," "predict," "relate," "distinguish," "solve," "contrast," "judge," and "produce." Questions such as these pose tasks that require students to think and to go beyond factual recall.

The questions teachers ask should match the learning objectives. Although most teachers want their students to attain both lower- and higher-level outcomes from instruction, they tend to focus instruction and classroom questions on lower-level questions. Only about 10 to 20 percent of teachers' classroom questions are higher level. Students are not frequently asked to explain ideas in their own words, apply knowledge in unfamiliar situations, analyze components of an idea or story, synthesize different pieces of information into a general statement or conclusion, or judge the pros and cons of particular courses of action.

Four factors explain this emphasis on lower-level questions. First, memory-focused questions tend to be utilized heavily in lesson plans. Second, lower-level questions are the easiest for students to answer, because they usually have already been taught. Focusing questions at lower levels gives students the best chance to reply correctly, and thus promotes a feeling of instructional success among teachers. Third, teachers themselves are most likely to know the answers to lower-level questions, so they feel more confident in asking such questions. Finally, lower-level questions are much easier to create than higher-level questions. While Bloom's Taxonomy provides a useful model to classify lower- and higher-level questions, it is less important to ask questions at specific taxonomic levels than it is to focus generally on asking a range of questions that stimulate both memory and reflection.

Questioning Strategies

The following strategies can be used to increase the effectiveness of oral questioning:

1. *Ask questions that are related to the objectives of instruction.* Teachers' questions communicate what topics are important and the ways these topics should be learned, so there should be consistency among objectives, instruction, and questioning. This consistency is especially important when higher-level objectives are stressed. It is useful to prepare a few higher-level questions before instruction begins and then incorporate them into the lesson plan.

2. *Avoid global, overly general questions.* Do not ask, "Does everyone understand this?" because many students will be too embarrassed to admit they do not and others will think they understand what has been taught when in reality they do not. Ask questions that probe students' comprehension of what is being taught. Similarly, avoid questions that can be answered with a simple yes or no unless the students are also expected to explain their answers.

3. *Involve the entire class in the questioning process.* Do not call on the same students time after time. Occasionally call on nonvolunteers in order to keep everyone attentive. Arranging students into a circle or a U and asking questions in a variety of ways in order to adapt them to students' varying ability levels increases student participation. Finally, support the response efforts of weak students and encourage everyone who tries.

4. *Be aware of patterns in the way questions are distributed among students.* Some teachers call on high-achieving students more frequently than low achievers, on girls more than boys, or on those in the front rows more than those in the back. Other teachers do the

opposite. Be sensitive to such questioning patterns and strive to give all students an equal opportunity to respond.

5. *Allow sufficient "wait time" after asking a question.* This permits students to think about and frame a response. Students need time to process their thoughts, especially to a higher-level question. Remember, silence after a question is good because it means the students are thinking. Three to five seconds is a suitable "wait time" that permits most students to think about an answer to the question. Giving students time to think also leads to improved answers.

6. *State questions clearly and directly to avoid confusion.* Avoid vague questions or prompts like "What about the story?" or "Talk to me about this experiment." If students are to think in desired ways, the teacher must be able to state questions in ways that focus and produce that type of thinking. Clarity focuses thinking and improves the quality of answers. Again, preparing key questions before teaching a lesson is a useful practice.

7. *Probe student responses with follow-up questions.* Probes such as "Why?" "Explain how you arrived at that conclusion," and "Can you give me another example?" indicate to students that the "whys" or logic behind a response are as important as the response itself and will encourage them to articulate their reasoning.

8. *Remember that instructional questioning is a social process that occurs in a public setting.* Consequently, all students should be treated with encouragement and respect. Incorrect, incomplete, or even unreasonable answers should not evoke demeaning, sarcastic, or angry teacher responses.

9. *Allow private questioning time for students who are shy or have difficulty engaging in the questioning process.* If possible, allow private questioning time for these students, perhaps during seatwork or study time. Then, as they become more confident in their private responses, gradually work them into public discussions, first with small groups and then with the whole class.

10. *Recognize that good questioning also involves good listening and responding.* In addition to framing good questions, it is important to be both a good listener and responder to students' answers to questions. Good listening means hearing the meaning and implications of students' responses. Good responding means following up a student's answers with comments that will benefit the student.

11. *Be sensitive to how questioning is viewed by different cultures.* Sage advice is offered by the Saskatoon Public School Division (2004), "Teachers should also understand that asking and responding to questions is viewed differently within different cultures. The teacher must be sensitive to the cultural needs of students and aware of the effects of his or her own cultural perspective on questioning."

12. *Consult online resources on questioning techniques.* Find links to these sites on our OLC at www.mcgrawhill.ca/college/airasian.

CONCERNS ABOUT ACCURACY

Because there is little time for teachers to reflect on what is observed or to collect additional information during instruction, they must make decisions and act on the basis of incomplete and uncertain evidence. Even so, many teachers are quite successful in overcoming these difficulties and do carry out thorough formative assessments. In spite of the success of some teachers, however, it would be naive and inappropriate to overlook problems of accuracy associated with formative assessment.

Problems That Affect Instructional Validity

Validity relates to collecting evidence that will help teachers correctly interpret observed student performance and make appropriate decisions about students' attention, comprehension, and learning as well as the pace and suitability of the instructional activities. As mentioned previously, during instruction, teachers assess these areas mainly by observing student attentiveness and by the verbal reactions and responses of their students. An important validity question is, do these student indicators provide the information teachers need to make appropriate decisions about instructional success? Two potential threats to validity are (1) the lack of objectivity by teachers when judging their own instruction and (2) the incompleteness of the evidence used to make decisions about instruction and student learning.

Objectivity of the Teacher as an Observer

Because teachers have a stake in the success of their instruction, there is the danger that they will look only for positive student reactions.

Being a participant in the instructional process can make it difficult for the teacher to be a dispassionate, detached observer who can make unbiased judgments about his or her own instruction. Teachers have a stake in the success of instruction with a strong personal and professional investment in the instructional process. Because teachers rely heavily on their observations to assess instruction, it can be asked whether teachers see only what they want to see—that is, only those things that will give them reinforcement. If so, the evidence they use to assess their instruction is potentially invalid.

Teachers sometimes ask easy, low-level questions in order to get correct answers that make them feel good about their instruction.

Evidence of invalid assessments of instruction is not hard to find. For example, the types of questions teachers ask can influence their sense of personal effectiveness. Simple, factual questions are likely to produce more correct student responses than open-ended, complex ones. Concentration on lower-level rote skills and information, rather than on higher-level skills and processes, can ensure more student participation. Teacher comments, such as "This topic is too hard for my students, so I'll skip over it," may be a realistic appraisal of student readiness or they may simply be a way for teachers to avoid instructional challenges. In short, the desire to achieve teaching satisfaction may bias teachers' observations and produce invalid conclusions about the success of instruction.

Incompleteness of Instructional Indicators

The primary indicators that teachers use to monitor instruction are those that are most readily available, most quickly surveyed, and least intrusive: reactions from students such as facial expressions, posture, participation, questions, and attending. Using such indicators, teachers "read" a student or the class and judge the success of instruction. But the real criterion of teachers' instructional success is *student achievement.* Although the *process* of instruction—its flow, pace, and student reactions—is important and should be assessed, it does not provide direct evidence of student learning. It deals only with intermediate events that may or may not lead to a more important outcome, namely, learning.

Being attentive and involved in instruction is desirable, but does not necessarily mean that learning is taking place. Thus, valid assessment of instruction should include appropriate information about both student involvement and student learning. If it does not or if it focuses only on student interest and facial expressions, judgments about the ultimate goal—how well students are learning—may be invalid.

Instructional assessment should focus on student learning as well as student involvement.

Problems That Affect Instructional Reliability

Reliability is concerned with the stability or consistency of the assessment data that are collected. However, one of the features of teaching is the fast-changing nature of instruction. If the message a teacher gets from his or her observations changes each time new evidence is gathered, the teacher should not rely upon that evidence to help in decision making. Since teachers obtain most of their information about the success of instruction by observing their students, the greater the number of observations, the more reliable the information.

Often because of seating arrangements or an unconscious inattention to certain students, teachers tend to use an overly narrow sample of students when assessing the success of instruction. This inadequate sampling, of course, reduces the reliability of their assessment. It must be understood, however, that problems of narrow sampling during instruction result as much from the rapidity of classroom events as from the teacher's inattention to particular students.

Instructional assessment that involves feedback from a broad range of students is more reliable than assessments based on the reactions of one or two students.

Key Assessment Tools 4.1 summarizes validity and reliability problems in instructional assessment.

> ### KEY ASSESSMENT TOOLS 4.1
> ### Validity and Reliability Problems of Instructional Assessment
>
> **Validity Problems**
> 1. Lack of objectivity by the classroom teacher
> 2. Concentrating instruction on objectives and assessments that will provide the teacher maximum reinforcement but which narrow instruction for students
> 3. Focusing on instructional process indicators (e.g., facial expressions, posture, or participation) without also considering instructional outcome indicators (e.g., student learning)
>
> **Reliability Problems**
> 1. Fast pace of classroom activities and decision making inhibit the collection of corroborative evidence
> 2. Focusing on a limited number of students to obtain information about the process of instruction and student learning

ACCOMMODATIONS AND FORMATIVE ASSESSMENT

As we stressed in Chapter 3, an important aspect of planning and delivering instruction is accommodating students with exceptionalities. This also holds true for the assessment of instructional effectiveness for these students. Based on the knowledge gained from diagnostic assessments and the teaching of initial lessons, teachers should begin to identify needs and appropriate accommodations for students. Consider the following accommodations before assessing whether students with exceptionalities are getting the most out of instruction:

For students who have difficulty maintaining attention:

➤ State the student's name before asking questions
➤ Ask questions in a variety of different ways

For students who have difficulty comprehending:

➤ State questions orally and in writing
➤ Modify seatwork and homework assignments

For students with a vision impairment:

➤ Record material
➤ Orally read directions and questions

For students with a hearing impairment:

➤ Speak slowly when questioning
➤ Use written rather than oral directions

TECHNOLOGY AND ASSESSMENT

www.caslt.org/research/assessment.htm

The Canadian Association of Second Language Teachers has collaborated with a number of teachers across Canada to offer a resource containing formative assessment instruments including performance charts, rating scales, observation forms, questions, and surveys.

Find a link to this site and others on our OLC at

www.mcgrawhill.ca/college/airasian.

Through planning and implementing accommodations for students who need them, teachers provide students with exceptionalities with opportunities to learn most effectively, thus improving the validity of instruction and assessment.

CHAPTER REVIEW

What is formative assessment?

➤ Formative assessment is the process of collecting data to improve students' learning while instruction is taking place.

What types of data are gathered for formative assessment?

➤ Teachers gather formative assessment data by picking up on student cues such as attention, questioning students about the content of the lesson, checking assigned work, and reflecting on the lesson.

➤ These data are used by the teacher to make decisions about whether new instruction may proceed, and, if not, how previous instruction might change in order to improve student learning.

Why do teachers collect formative assessment data?

➤ Formative assessment data help monitor factors such as interest levels of students, potential behaviour problems, appropriateness of instructional techniques, adequacy of students' answers, pace of instruction, implications of students' questions, transitions from one activity to another, suitability of examples, degree of students' comprehension, and appropriateness of ending the lesson.

➤ Formative assessment has the potential to enhance student performance more than most known educational interventions.

What is the process of formative assessment?

➤ Teaching begins and the teacher continuously assesses its progress by observing student reactions and asking them questions. The teacher makes a decision about how instruction is going and may then continue to teach as planned or revise the teaching activity.

What are the factors teachers consider assessing during instruction?

➤ Teachers often rely on informal indicators to monitor their instruction such as behavioural cues from the students, eye contact, facial expressions or body language, rather than on more formal paper-and-pencil assessments.

➤ Other indicators are based on their perceptions of classroom dynamics.

CHAPTER REVIEW

Visit Chapter 4 of the Online Learning Centre at **www.mcgrawhill.ca/ college/airasian** to take chapter quizzes, link to related Web sites, and read PowerWeb articles and news feed updates, and access study tools, including the case study referenced in this chapter.

What is practical knowledge and how do teachers use it?

➤ Practical knowledge comprises those beliefs, insights, perceptions, and habits that enable teachers to teach.

➤ Teachers have a store of practical knowledge that fits students to enable them to continue to carry out instruction.

➤ Throughout the school year, teachers call on their practical knowledge about their students to decide on a course of action.

What are the six purposes for using questioning during instruction?

➤ To promote attention

➤ To promote deeper processing

➤ To promote learning from peers

➤ To provide reinforcement

➤ To provide pace and control

➤ To provide diagnostic information

What are the different types of questions?

➤ There are convergent questions that prompt for one single correct answer and divergent questions that prompt for many appropriate answers.

➤ Lower-level questions focus on factual information and higher-level questions require students to perform processes such as applying procedural knowledge.

What strategies can teachers use to improve their effectiveness of oral questioning?

➤ Relate questions to instructional objectives

➤ Avoid overly general questions

➤ Involve the entire class in questioning

➤ Distribute questions among students

➤ Allow "wait time" after asking a question

➤ State questions clearly and directly

➤ Probe responses with follow-up questions

➤ Treat students with encouragement and respect

➤ Allow private questioning for some students

➤ Be a good listener

➤ Be sensitive to cultural differences

What are some guidelines to enhance the validity and reliability of formative assessment?

➤ Include a broad sample of students when assessing instruction.

➤ Supplement informal assessment information with more formal information about student learning.

➤ Gather formative assessment information from both lower- and higher-level instructional activities.

➤ Take the time to gather sufficient corroborative evidence that supports the decision-making process.

QUESTIONS FOR DISCUSSION

1. What challenges do you see during instruction in the need to both monitor your students' learning and maintain classroom management? How are the two activities connected?

2. In what situations should a teacher change instruction in response to student interest and attentiveness, and in what situations should a teacher not change instruction?

3. Under what circumstances would you call on a shy student who never raises a hand for oral questions?

4. How often do you anticipate a need to formatively assess your students? What methods are you most likely to employ? How will you strive to employ a variety of formative assessment strategies?

5. Consider a student who does not complete seatwork or return homework to you on a regular basis. What other types of formative assessment data might you attempt to collect to evaluate this student's progress?

ACTIVITIES

1. Complete the following checklist for students to use to assess their own class participation. Use the following framework and provide more explanation of the participation criteria. The first one has been done for you.

STUDENT SELF-ASSESSMENT OF PARTICIPATION

Participation Criteria	(provide explanation)	YES	NO
Flexibility in roles	I accept alternate roles within the class/group		
Active involvement			
Cooperation			
Preparation			
Communication			
Collaboration			

2. Devise a worksheet to take classroom observational notes. Consider how you track individual students as well as groups of students. Decide how you will identify the focus or purpose of the observational notes.

3. Throughout the next 24 hours, try to notice what questions you tend to ask or not ask of those around you. In writing, summarize how well your current question-asking skills are likely to serve in the classroom. What might you do to improve them?

4. Interview a teacher about how he or she knows when a lesson is going well or poorly. Ask the teacher to recall a recent lesson and ask what his or her main thoughts were during the lesson.

CHAPTER 5

PREPARING SELECTED AND CONSTRUCTED RESPONSE TESTS

CHAPTER OBJECTIVES

After reading this chapter, you will be able to:

➤ Define summative assessment, selected response test items, constructed response test items, item stem, distractors, and specific determiners

➤ Compare the purpose for and other aspects of diagnostic, formative, and summative assessments

➤ Write fair and accurate selected response and constructed response test items

➤ Compare the advantages and disadvantages of different types of selected response and constructed response test items

➤ List guidelines for constructing or selecting interpretive exercises

➤ Cite guidelines for writing and critiquing test items

➤ Describe decisions required in planning a test

➤ State guidelines for assembling a test

I n preparation for her first year of teaching Grade 5, Rita is planning a science unit on weather. As part of this preparation, Rita is developing an assessment plan for this unit that will include different ways of assessing her students' knowledge and understanding of concepts related to weather. Rita has included an end-of-unit test as one of the methods of assessment to be included in her plan. She is committed to constructing a test that will measure her students' higher-level thinking skills as well as their knowledge of concepts related to weather. In order to accomplish this, Rita plans to make use of a variety of different types of test items including multiple-choice, true-false, matching, short-answer, completion, essay, and interpretive exercise questions. She is hopeful that this test will be both interesting to her students and a valid measure of their knowledge about weather and their ability to employ higher-level thinking skills.

At most grade levels, tests are the most commonly used procedure for gathering evidence about student learning. These tests may be constructed by teachers, textbook publishers, Ministries or Departments of Education, or standardized test publishers. In terms of student evaluation and the reporting of grades, the value of effective instruction can be undone if the actual test questions are poorly constructed, unclear, or subjectively scored. Such problems do not give students a fair chance to show what they have learned and, consequently, do not provide a valid basis for decision making. No matter whether one is concerned with teacher-made, textbook, Ministry- or Department-mandated, or standardized tests, it is important that teachers be able to differentiate between well-constructed and poorly constructed test questions.

Tests are composed of short communications called questions or **items.** Each question must be brief and must set a clear problem for the student to think about. Each question must also be complete in itself and independent of other questions. Further, because students will mentally debate the nuances of each word to be sure they are not misinterpreting the intent of the item, it is crucial that questions be stated in clear, precise language. This chapter examines and contrasts different types of selected and constructed response test questions and provides general guidelines for writing or judging the adequacy of each kind of item. Let's begin with an introduction to summative assessment—assessment that takes place after learning has occurred.

SUMMATIVE ASSESSMENT

In Chapters 2 and 4 we talked about diagnostic and formative assessment, respectively. Although critical to teachers' decision making, these forms of assessment should be supplemented by another form of assessment, **summative assessment**, which usually comes at the end of a classroom process, activity, unit, or course. Summative assessment is used mainly to assess the outcomes of instruction and is exemplified by end-of-unit tests, projects, term papers, and final examinations. Table 5.1 contrasts diagnostic, formative, and summative assessments.

Summative assessments help teachers to make decisions that the school bureaucracy requires of them: testing, grading, and grouping of students; recommending whether students should be promoted or placed in special classes; and referring students to special education services if they have special needs. Because they have important consequences for students, summative assessments are generally based on systematically gathered evidence. They almost always focus on students' cognitive performance, usually how well students have learned what has been taught.

It is important to remember that the primary aim of summative assessment is to *provide students with a fair opportunity to demonstrate what they have learned from the instruction they have received*. The primary aim is not to trick students into doing poorly, entertain them, or ensure that most of them get A's. It is not to determine the total knowledge students have accumulated as a result of their learning experiences, both in and out of school. It is simply to let students show what they have learned from the things they have been taught in their classroom.

TABLE 5.1	Comparison Of Diagnostic, Formative, And Summative Assessments		
	Diagnostic	**Formative**	**Summative**
Purpose	To determine the ways in which teachers plan, teach, assess, and evaluate	To monitor and guide instruction while it is still in progress	To judge the success of instruction at its completion
Times of assessment	Beginning of instruction	During instruction	After instruction
Type of assessment technique	Observations, school records, discussions, comments	Observations, questions, seatwork, quizzes, homework	Tests, projects, papers, examinations
Use of assessment information	Hone the content and the method of instruction	Improve and change instruction while it is still going on	Judge the overall success of instruction; grade, place, promote

SELECTED AND CONSTRUCTED RESPONSE TEST ITEMS

Multiple-choice, true-false, and matching questions are examples of selected response items. Constructed response items are those in which the student constructs his or her own answer.

There are two basic types of test questions: **selected response items** and **constructed response items.** As their names suggest, selected response items require the student to select the correct answer from among a number of choices, while constructed response items require the student to supply or construct his or her own answer.

Selected Response Items

Within the general category of selected response items are multiple-choice, true-false, and matching questions.

Multiple-Choice Items

Multiple-choice items consist of a stem, which presents the problem or question, and a set of options from which the student selects an answer.

Multiple-choice items consist of a **stem,** which presents the problem or question to the student, and a set of **options** from which the student selects an answer. The multiple-choice format is widely used in summative tests of all types, primarily to assess learning outcomes at the factual knowledge and comprehension levels. However, with suitable introductory material, this format can also be used to assess higher-level thinking involving application, analysis, and synthesis. The main limitations of the multiple-choice format are that it does not allow students to construct, organize, and present their own answers, and it is susceptible to guessing. However, these concerns about the use of multiple-choice items can be minimized through careful and considered item preparation (Cranton, 2000).

Here are two examples of multiple-choice items.

1. You use me to cover rips and tears. I am made of cloth. What am I?
   A. knot   B. patch   C. perch   D. scratch

2. What is the smallest province in Canada?
   A. New Brunswick
   B. Newfoundland
   C. Nova Scotia
   D. Prince Edward Island

Most often, multiple-choice questions do not effectively test higher-level thinking, but multiple-choice interpretive questions can do so. We will discuss them later in the section "Higher-Level Questions."

True-False Items

The true-false format requires students to classify a statement into one of two categories: true or false; yes or no; correct or incorrect; fact or opinion. True-false items are used mainly to assess factual knowledge and comprehension behaviours, although they also can be used to assess higher-level ones (Frisbie, 1992). The main limitation of true-false questions is their susceptibility to guessing.

The main limitation of true-false questions is their susceptibility to guessing.

The following are typical true-false items.

1. $5 + 4 = 8$ T   F

2. In the equation $E = mc^2$, when m increases E also increases.   T   F

3. Read the statement. Circle T if true and F if false. If the statement is false, rewrite it to make it true by <u>changing only the underlined part of the statement</u>.

   The level of the cognitive taxonomy that describes recall and memory behaviours is called the <u>synthesis</u> level.   T   F

Although primarily used to assess knowledge and comprehension, both multiple-choice and true-false items can be used to assess higher-level thinking.

Matching Items

Matching items consist of a column of **premises,** a column of **responses,** and directions for matching the two. The matching exercise is similar to a set of multiple-choice items, except that in a matching question, the same set of options or responses is used for all the premises. Its chief disadvantage is that it is limited mainly to assessing lower-level behaviours. The following is an example of a matching exercise.

Matching items consist of a column of premises, a column of responses, and directions for matching the two. They assess mainly lower-level thinking.

On the line to the left of each invention in column A, write the *letter* of the person in column B who invented it. Each name in column B may be used only once or not at all.

Column A

_____ (1) basketball
_____ (2) pacemaker
_____ (3) snowmobile
_____ (4) telephone

Column B

A. Alexander Graham Bell
B. Frederick Banting
C. James Naismith
D. Joseph-Armand Bombardier
E. Wilfred Bigelow

Constructed Response Items

Constructed response items consist of short-answer and completion (also called fill-in-the-blank) items, essay questions, or questions requiring the student to create things such as diagrams or concept maps.

Short-Answer and Completion Items

Short-answer items use a direct question to present a problem; completion items use an incomplete sentence. Both tend to assess mainly factual knowledge and comprehension.

Short-answer and completion items are very similar. Each presents the student with a question to answer. The short-answer format presents the problem with a direct question (e.g., What is the name of the first prime minister of Canada?), while the completion format may present the problem as an incomplete sentence (e.g., The name of the first prime minister of Canada is _____) or a picture, map, or diagram that requires labelling. In each case, the student must supply his or her own answer. Typically, the student is asked to reply with a word, phrase, number, or sentence, rather than with a more extended response. Short-answer questions are fairly easy to construct and diminish the likelihood that students will guess answers. However, they tend to assess mainly factual knowledge or comprehension.

The following are examples of completion and short-answer items.

1. Scientists who specialize in the study of plants are called _____.

Next to each province write the name of its capital city.

2. British Columbia _____
3. New Brunswick _____
4. Ontario _____

5. In a single sentence, state one way that inflation lowers consumers' purchasing power.

Essay Items

Essay questions are most useful for assessing higher-level thinking skills but are time-consuming to answer and score and favour the student with writing ability.

Essay questions give students the greatest opportunity to construct their own responses, making them the most useful for assessing higher-level thinking processes like analyzing, synthesizing, and evaluating. The essay question is also the primary way teachers assess students' ability to organize, express, and defend ideas. The main limitations of essays are that they are time-consuming to answer and score, permit testing only of a limited amount of students' learning, and place a premium on writing ability.

Here are some examples of essay questions.

1. What is the value of studying science? Give your answer in complete, correct sentences. Write at least five sentences.

2. "In order for revolutionary governments to build and maintain their power, they must control the educational system." Discuss this statement using your knowledge of the American, French, and Russian revolutions. Do you agree with the statement as it applies to the revolutionary governments in the three countries? Include specific examples to support your conclusion. Your answer will be judged on the basis of the similarities and differences you identify in the three revolutions and the extent to which your conclusion is supported by specific examples. You will have 40 minutes to complete your essay.

Comparing Selected and Constructed Response Items

Constructed response questions are much more useful than selected response questions in assessing students' ability to organize thoughts, present logical arguments, defend positions, and integrate ideas. Selected response questions, on the other hand, are more useful when assessing application and problem-solving skills. Given these differences, it is not surprising that knowing the kind of item that will be on a test can influence the way students prepare for the test. In general, constructed response items encourage global, integrative study, while selected response items encourage a more detailed, specific focus.

Constructed response questions are most useful for assessing students' ability to organize and present their thoughts, defend positions, and integrate ideas.

Selected response items are most useful when application and problem-solving skills are assessed.

TABLE 5.2 Comparison of Selected and Constructed Response Test Items		
	Selected Response Items	**Constructed Response Items**
Types of Items	Multiple-choice, true-false, matching, interpretive exercise	Short-answer, essay, completion
Behaviours Assessed	Factual knowledge and comprehension; thinking and reasoning behaviours like application and analysis when using interpretive exercises	Factual knowledge and comprehension; thinking and reasoning behaviours like organizing ideas, defending positions, and integrating points
Major Advantages	1. Items can be answered quickly so a broad sample of instructional topics can be surveyed on a test. 2. Items are easy and objective to score. 3. Test constructor has complete control over the stem and options so the effect of writing ability is controlled.	1. Preparation of items is relatively easy; only a few questions are needed. 2. Affords students a chance to construct their own answers; only way to test behaviours such as organizing and expressing information. 3. Lessens chance the students can guess the correct answer to items.
Major Disadvantages	1. Time-consuming to construct. 2. Many items must be constructed. 3. Guessing is a problem.	1. Time-consuming to score. 2. Covers small sample of instructional topics. 3. Bluffing is a problem.

While constructed and selected response items consume approximately the same amount of time to construct and score, each format allocates its time differently. Selected response items are time-consuming to construct, but can be scored quickly. Constructed response items are less time-consuming to construct, but are more time-consuming to score. Table 5.2 on page 93 summarizes the differences.

HIGHER-LEVEL QUESTIONS

There is a growing emphasis on teaching and assessing students' higher-level thinking. As the following quotes show, teachers recognize the importance of students' learning how to understand and apply their knowledge. They know that knowledge takes on added meaning when it can be used in real-life situations.

> Facts are important for students to learn in all subjects, but if students do not learn how to understand and use the facts to help them solve new problems, they haven't really learned the most important part of instruction.

> The kids need to go beyond facts and rote learning. You can't survive in society unless you can understand, think, reason, and apply what you know.

> It would be so boring to only teach facts. Some recall or memorization is needed, of course, but day after day of memorization instruction would be demeaning to my students and me. I have to make room in my curriculum for more complex thinking and reasoning skills such as understanding and applying new knowledge.

Many people believe that the only way to test higher-level thinking skills is with essay items. That is not the case! Any test question that demands more from a student than memory is a higher-level item. Thus, any item that requires the student to solve a problem, interpret a chart, explain something in his or her own words, or identify the relationship between two phenomena qualifies as an item of higher-level thinking. Similarly, any assessment that requires students to demonstrate their ability to carry out an activity (e.g., give an oral talk, construct a mobile, or read an unfamiliar foreign language passage aloud) also qualifies as being higher level.

Essay Questions

Essay questions provide an important tool to assess higher-level thinking. Good essay questions require students to organize, understand, apply, integrate, and defend ideas. Questions that can be answered using only factual knowledge are better tested by more structured item types such as multiple-choice, true-false, or completion. The following are examples of essay questions that can elicit higher-level thinking from students. In all cases it is assumed that the students have been taught material similar, though not identical, to that in the items.

1. Explain whether the reasoning in the following statements is correct or incorrect.
    All dogs have tails.
    This animal has a tail.
    Therefore, this animal is a dog.

2. In what ways were the events leading up to the start of World War I the same as the events leading up to the start of World War II? In what ways were they different? Focus your answer on military, social, and economic factors.

3. Describe in your own words how an eclipse of the sun happens.

4. Why are some parts of the world covered by forests, some parts by water, some parts by grasses, and some parts by sand? Tell about some of the things that make a place a forest, an ocean, a grassland, or a desert.

Interpretive Exercises

The interpretive exercise is a common form of multiple-choice item that can assess higher-level thinking. An interpretive exercise gives students some information or data and then asks a series of selection-type questions based on that information. The following is an example of an interpretive exercise:

Interpretive exercises assess higher-level skills because the students must interpret or apply given information.

Read the following passage.
(1) For what men say is that, if I am really just and am not also thought just, profit there is none, but the pain and the loss on the
(3) other hand is unmistakable. But if, though unjust, I acquire the reputation of justice, a heavenly life is promised to me. Since then
(5) appearance tyrannizes over truth and is lord of happiness, to appearance I must devote myself. I will describe around me a
(7) picture and shadow of virtue to be the vestibule and exterior of my house; behind I will trail the subtle and crafty fox.

Which one of the following states the major premise of the passage?
A. For what men say (line 1)
B. if I am really just (line 1)
C. profit there is none, but the pain and the loss (line 2)
D. appearance tyrannizes over truth and is lord of happiness (line 5)
E. picture and shadow of virtue to be the vestibule and exterior of my house (line 7)

Figure 5.1 contains another example, taken from a sample question bank used for large-scale assessment by the Ministry of Education in Alberta. Generally, multiple-choice items that ask for interpretations of graphs, charts, reading passages, pictures, or tables are classified as interpretive exercises. Such exercises can assess higher-level behaviours like recognizing the relevance of information, identifying warranted and unwarranted generalizations, recognizing assumptions, interpreting experimental findings, and explaining pictorial materials.

To answer the questions posed, students have to interpret, comprehend, analyze, apply, or synthesize the information presented. Interpretive exercises assess higher-level skills because they contain all the information needed to answer the questions posed. Thus, if a student answers incorrectly, it is because he or she cannot do the thinking or reasoning required by the question, not because the student failed to memorize background information.

Like the essay question, the interpretive exercise is a useful way to assess higher-level thinking. However, unlike the essay question, interpretive exercises cannot show how students organize their ideas when solving a problem or how well they can produce their own answers to questions.

Other disadvantages of interpretive exercises are the difficulty of constructing them and the heavy reliance they often place on reading ability. Students who read quickly and with good comprehension have an obvious

FIGURE 5.1

Example of an Interpretive Exercise.

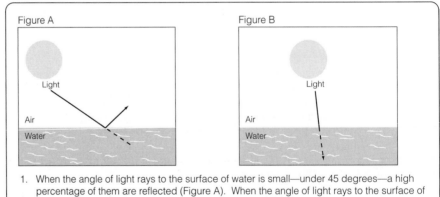

Figure A

Figure B

Light

Light

Air

Water

Air

Water

1. When the angle of light rays to the surface of water is small—under 45 degrees—a high percentage of them are reflected (Figure A). When the angle of light rays to the surface of water is large—near 90 degrees—much of the light passes through the surface and enters the water (Figure B).

    According to the information above, when would the greatest reflection of sunlight from the surface of a lake be observed?

    (1) late in the morning
    (2) when the sky is very cloudy
    (3) early in the afternoon
    (4) noon
    (5) late in the afternoon

SOURCE: "GED Tests: Sample Questions, Test 3: Science," Government of Alberta, 2006, www.education.gov.ab.ca/k_12/testing/Ged/appendix_a_3.asp.

advantage over students who do not. This advantage is particularly evident when the test involves reading and interpreting many passages in a limited amount of time.

Most teachers do not construct their own interpretive exercises, preferring to use exercises supplied by textbook publishers or other sources. Regardless of whether one is constructing or selecting an interpretive exercise, the exercise should meet five general guidelines before it is used to assess student achievement.

1. *Relevance.* The exercise should be related to the instruction provided students.
2. *Similarity.* The material presented in the exercise should be new to the students, but similar to material presented during instruction.
3. *Brevity.* There should be sufficient information for students to answer the questions, but the exercises should not become tests of reading speed and accuracy.
4. *Answers not provided.* The correct answers should not be found directly in the material presented. Interpretation, application, analysis, and comprehension should be needed to determine correct answers.
5. *Multiple questions.* Each interpretive exercise should include more than one question to make most efficient use of time.

Table 5.3 summarizes the pros and cons of the different types of selected and constructed response test items.

GUIDELINES FOR WRITING AND CRITIQUING TEST ITEMS

Whether writing test items or selecting those prepared by others, there are three general guidelines that help insure good tests: (1) cover important objectives; (2) write clearly and simply; and (3) review items before testing. This section discusses and illustrates these guidelines.

Cover Important Objectives

Note that the following discussion pertains to teacher-prepared tests and to textbook tests. Simply because a ready-made test is available with a textbook is no reason for a teacher to assume that the test adequately assesses his or her instruction on the chapter or unit. Each classroom teacher has a responsibility to decide about the suitability of a textbook test for assessing his or her instructional emphases.

Test items should reflect important topics and skills emphasized during instruction, should be stated briefly and clearly, and should be self-contained.

TABLE 5.3 Advantages and Disadvantages of Types of Test Items

Test Type	Advantages	Disadvantages
Multiple-choice items	1. Large number of items can be given in a short period 2. Higher- and lower-level objectives can be assessed 3. Scoring is usually quick and objective 4. Less influenced by guessing	1. Takes substantial time to construct items 2. Not useful when "show your work" is required 3. Often hard to find suitable options 4. Reading ability can influence student performance
True-false items	1. A large number of items can be given in a short time 2. Scoring is usually quick and objective	1. Guessing correct answer is a problem 2. Difficult to find statements that are clearly true or false 3. Items tend to stress recall
Matching items	1. An efficient way to obtain a great deal of information 2. Easy to construct 3. Scoring is usually quick and objective	1. Focus is mainly on lower-level outcomes 2. Homogeneous topics are required
Short-answer items	1. Guessing is reduced; student must construct an answer 2. Easy-to-write items 3. Broad range of knowledge can be assessed	1. Scoring can be time-consuming 2. Not useful for complex or extended outcomes
Essay items	1. Directly assess complex higher-level outcomes 2. Take less time to construct than other item types 3. Assess integrative, holistic outcomes	1. Difficult and time-consuming to score 2. Provide a deep but small sample of students' performance 3. Bluffing and the quality of writing can influence scores
Interpretive exercise items	1. Assess integrative and interpretive outcomes 2. Assess higher-level outcomes 3. Scoring is usually quick and objective	1. Heavily dependent on students' reading ability 2. Difficult to construct items

One important guideline to keep in mind when preparing tests is not to focus exclusively on trivial knowledge and skills. Studies that examined the nature of the test items written by classroom teachers have found that the vast majority assessed memory-level behaviours (Marso & Pigge, 1989,

1991). From elementary school to the university, items that stress recall and memory are used much more extensively than items that assess higher-level thinking and reasoning, mainly because it is much easier to write short-answer or multiple-choice questions. In far too many instances the richness of instruction is undermined by the use of test items that trivialize the breadth and depth of the concepts and skills taught.

Each example that follows states the objective taught, the test item used to assess it, and an alternative item that would have provided a more suitable assessment of the objective. Note that the poor items trivialized higher-level objectives by assessing them with a memory item.

1. **Objective:** Given a description of a literary form, the students can classify the form as fable, mystery, folktale, or fantasy.
   Poor item: What kind of stories did Aesop tell? _____.
   A. fables   B. mysteries   C. folktales   D. fantasies
   Better item: A story tells about the year 2020 and the adventures of a young Martian named Zik, who travelled to other worlds to capture strange creatures for the zoo at Martian City. This story is best classified as a

   _____.
   A. fable   B. mystery   C. folktale   D. fantasy

2. **Objective:** The students describe similarities and differences in chemical compounds and elements.
   Poor item: Chlorine and bromine are both members of a chemical group called the _____.
   Better item: Chlorine and bromine are both halogens. What similarities do they possess that make them halogens? What are two differences in their chemical properties?

There are two main reasons for ensuring that the questions in a test align with the important topics and skills that were emphasized during instruction. First, if there is not a good alignment between instruction and the test questions, performance on the test will be a poor indication of actual learning. Students may have learned what was taught but were stymied by an invalid test. Low grades usually accompany such invalid tests and can diminish students' effort and confidence.

Test items that do not reflect the important topics of instruction are not valid indicators of student achievement.

Second, tests that do not align with instruction have little positive influence on motivating and focusing student study. If students find little relationship between instruction and test content, they will undervalue instruction. You can remember instances when you prepared well for a test based on the teacher's instruction and review only to find that the test contained many questions that focused either on picky, isolated details or on types of problems that were not discussed in class. Recall how you felt when you tried to prepare for the next test given by that teacher.

The problem of mismatch between tests and instruction can be overcome to a large degree by thinking about testing earlier than the day before the test is to be given. With relatively little advance planning, tests that assess the important aspects of instruction can be prepared.

Write Clearly and Simply: Seven Rules

If test questions use ambiguous words or sentence structure, include inappropriate vocabulary, or contain clues to the correct answers, the test will not be a valid indicator of student achievement. The most important skill in writing or selecting good test items is the ability to express oneself clearly and succinctly. Test items should be: (1) briefly stated so students do not spend a disproportionate amount of time reading; (2) clearly expressed so students understand their task; and (3) capable of standing alone since each item provides a separate measurement.

Following are seven rules for writing sound test items. Each is illustrated by some confusing test items prepared by teachers who knew the content they wanted to test but who were unable to clearly state their intent. A better version of the same items is also shown for comparison.

Rule 1: Avoid ambiguous and confusing wording and sentence structure. Students must understand test questions. If the wording or sentence structure is confusing and prevents students from figuring out what they are being asked, students cannot demonstrate their learning. Consider the following test items.

1. All but one of the following is not an element. Which one is not?
   A. carbon   B. plastic   C. salt   D. sugar

2. Newfoundland is not the only province that does not have a border with another province.   T F

In these examples, the wording and sentence construction are awkward and confusing. The student has to sort through multiple negatives to figure out what is being asked. It is better, therefore, to phrase questions briefly, directly, and in the positive voice, as shown in these edited versions.

1. Which one of these is an element?
   A. carbon   B. plastic   C. salt   D. sugar

2. Newfoundland is the only island province in Canada.   T F

Other items, such as examples 3 and 4, are more than just confusing, they are virtually incomprehensible.

3. What is the relative length of the shortest distance between Calgary and Winnipeg and Regina? _____

4. The _____ produced by the _____ is used by the green _____ to change _____ and _____ into _____. This process is known as _____.

What is a reasonable answer to each? Taken individually, the words in example 3 are not overly difficult, but their sequencing makes their intent altogether unclear. Example 4 is so mutilated with blank spaces that a student has to be a mind reader to figure out what is being asked. No student should be confronted by such a question. Students will answer items like examples 3 and 4 incorrectly regardless of how well they have mastered the information and skills taught them. The following changes overcome the problems in these two examples.

Test items should be brief, clearly written, and free of ambiguous words so that comprehension is not an issue.

3. Which is closer to Regina, Calgary or Winnipeg? _____

4. The process in which green plants use the sun's energy to turn water and carbon dioxide into food is called _____.

If a student answers the revised items incorrectly, it is because he or she does not know the desired answer. That is acceptable. Remember, the purpose of a test item is not to guarantee correct answers, but to give students a *fair* chance to show how much they know about the things they were taught. To do this, test items must be readily comprehended.

Another factor that prevents students from being able to focus quickly and clearly on the question being posed is the use of ambiguous words or phrases. Read examples 5, 6, and 7 and try to identify a problem in each that could cause students difficulty in deciding how to answer.

5. Shakespeare was the world's greatest playwright.   T F

6. The most important coastal city in Canada is _____.
   A. Halifax   B. St. John's   C. Vancouver   D. Victoria

7. Write an essay in which you consider the future of atomic energy.

Each example contains an ambiguous term that could be puzzling to students and make their choice of an answer difficult. The true-false example contains the undefined word *greatest.* Did the teacher mean that Shakespeare wrote more plays than any other playwright? that more of his plays are still being performed than those of any other playwright? that his plays are required reading in more Canadian classrooms than those of any other playwright? Until students know what the teacher means by *greatest,* they will have difficulty responding. Example 6 has the same fault. What does the phrase *most important* mean? Each of these cities is important in many ways. Words like *greatest, most important, best,* and similar ambiguous words should be replaced by more specific language, regardless of the type of test item used.

Note the rewritten versions of examples 5 and 6.

5. More of William Shakespeare's plays are required reading in Canadian classrooms than those of any other playwright.   T F

6. The busiest port in Canada is _____.
   A. Halifax   B. St. John's   C. Vancouver   D. Victoria

In example 7 the teacher wants the students to consider the future of atomic energy. Does the teacher mean compare and contrast atomic energy to fossil fuel; discuss the relative merits of fission versus fusion as a means of generating energy; or explain the positive and negative consequences of increased use of atomic energy? It is not clear. The item needs to be more specific for the students to respond in the way the teacher desires as shown in this revised version.

> 7. Describe the advantages and disadvantages of increased use of atomic energy in the automobile manufacturing process.

In most cases, the teachers who wrote the preceding examples knew what they wanted to ask students but were unable to write items that clearly conveyed their intent. Teachers must say precisely what they mean, not assume or hope that their students will interpret their test items in the ways intended.

Rule 2: Use appropriate vocabulary. The difficulty level of test questions can be influenced dramatically by vocabulary. If students cannot understand the vocabulary used in test questions, their test scores will reflect their vocabulary deficiencies rather than how much they have learned from instruction. Based on diagnostic assessments, every teacher should take into account the vocabulary level of his or her students when writing or selecting the items for achievement tests. Note the difference in the following two ways of writing a true-false question to assess students' understanding of capillary action, a principle that explains how liquids rise in narrow passages.

> The postulation of capillary effectuation promotes elucidation of how pliant substances ascend in incommodious veins.   T F
>
> The principle of capillary action helps explain how liquids rise in small passages.   T F

Clearly, vocabulary level can affect the ability of students to understand what is being asked in a test question.

Rule 3: Keep questions short and to the point. Items should quickly focus students on the question being asked. Examine these questions.

Questions should be short, specific, and written at students' vocabulary level.

> 8. Switzerland
>   A. is located in Asia.
>   B. produces large quantities of gold.
>   C. has no direct access to the ocean.
>   D. is a flat, arid plain.
> 9. Billy's mother wanted to bake an apple pie for his aunt and uncle, who were coming for a visit. Billy had not seen them for many months. When Billy's mother saw that she had no apples in the house, she sent Billy to the store to buy some. Her recipe called for 8 apples to make a pie. If apples at the store cost 30 cents for two, how much money will Billy need to buy eight apples?
>   A. $.30   B. $.90   C. $1.20   D. $2.40

In example 8, the stem does not clearly set a problem for the student, that is, after students read the item stem Switzerland, they still have no idea of the question being asked. Only after reading the stem *and* all the options does the point of the item begin to become clear. The item could be more directly stated as follows.

8. Which of the following statements about the geography of Switzerland is true?
   A. It is located in Asia.
   B. It is a flat, arid plain.
   C. It has no direct access to the ocean.
   D. It has a tropical climate.

Example 9 is intended to determine whether the student can correctly calculate the cost of some apples. The information about the aunt and uncle's visit, how long it had been since Billy last saw them, or the lack of apples in the house is not important, can be distracting, and takes time away from relevant items. A better way to state the item is shown here.

9. To make an apple pie Billy's mother needed 8 apples. If apples cost 30 cents for two, how much will 8 apples cost?
   A. $.30   B. $.90   C. $1.20   D. $2.40

In short-answer or completion items, the blanks should come at the end of the sentence so students know what kind of a response is required. Compare these two items and notice how placing the blank at the end helps convey what the item is about.

_____ and _____ are two Canadian First Nations languages.

Two Canadian First Nations languages are _____ and _____.

Matching items can also be written to help students focus more quickly on the questions being asked. Look over example 10 and suggest a change that would focus students more clearly on the questions they have to answer.

10. Draw a line to match the famous scientist in column A with his or her accomplishment in column B.

Column A	Column B
Albert Einstein	derived the equation, $E=mc^2$
Charles Darwin	discovered radium
Marie Curie	invented a form of mathematics called calculus
Sir Isaac Newton	proposed that nebulas were composed of stars
	proposed the theory of natural selection

Most matching items can be improved by placing the column with the lengthier descriptions on the left and the column with the shorter descriptions on the right, as shown next.

10. Draw a line to match the famous scientist in column B with his or her accomplishment in column A.

Column A	Column B
Derived the equation, $E=mc^2$	Albert Einstein
Discovered radium	Charles Darwin
Invented a form of mathematics called calculus	Marie Curie
Proposed that nebulas were composed of stars	Sir Isaac Newton
Proposed the theory of natural selection	

With the exception of essays, most test items should have only one correct answer.

Rule 4: Write items that have one correct answer. With the exception of essay questions, most test items are designed to have students select or construct one best answer. With this goal in mind, read examples 11 and 12. See how many correct answers you can provide for each item.

11. Who was Sir John A. Macdonald? _____

12. Ernest Hemingway wrote _____.

Each of these items has more than one correct answer. Sir John A. Macdonald is most well known for being the first prime minister of Canada. But he was also the second longest serving prime minister, a father of Confederation, a member of the Conservative Party, a lawyer, and a Knight Commander of the Order of St. Michael and St. George. Faced with such an item, students ask themselves which of the many things I know about Sir John A. Macdonald should I answer? Similarly, Ernest Hemingway wrote short stories and letters, in Spain, in pencil, as well as famous novels such as *The Old Man and the Sea*.

Examples 11 and 12 should be restated so that students know precisely what is being asked. Notice how each question asks for something specific—a name—thus indicating to students the nature of the expected answer.

11. What is the name of the first prime minister of Canada? _____

12. The name of the author of *The Old Man and the Sea* is _____.

Items with more than one correct answer occur much more often in short-answer and completion items than in selected response items. Unless short-answer or completion items are stated specifically and narrowly, the teacher can expect many different responses. The dilemma for the teacher then becomes whether to give credit for answers that are technically correct but not the desired one.

Rule 5: Give information about the nature of the desired answer. While the failure to properly focus students is common to all types of test items, it is most often seen in essay items. Despite students' freedom to structure their own responses, essay questions should still require students to demonstrate mastery of key ideas, principles, or concepts that were taught. An essay, like any other type of test item, should be constructed to find out how well students have learned the things they were taught.

Here are two typical essay questions written by classroom teachers.

13. Describe what happened to art during the Renaissance.

14. Why should you study science?

In each of these questions, the students' task is not clearly defined. When students encounter global questions such as these they may have little idea of what the teacher is looking for and may end up with a poor grade because they incorrectly guessed the teacher's intent. This practice is unfair to students and produces test results that do not reflect their achievement.

To determine whether students have learned what was taught, essay questions should be narrowed to focus students on the areas of interest. Students should be informed about the nature and scope of the expected answer. While essay questions should provide the student freedom to select, organize, state, and defend positions, they should not give students total freedom to write whatever they want. Obviously, to develop a well-focused essay question the teacher must give considerable thought to the purpose and scope of the question before actually writing it.

Essay questions should focus students' answers on the major points covered by instruction.

Examples 13 and 14 and have been rewritten to more precisely reflect the teacher's intent. Notice how the vague and ambiguous directions are made clearer to students in the revised questions.

13. Compare art during the Renaissance to art prior to the movement in terms of the portrayal of the human figure, use of colour, and emphasis on religious themes. Your essay will be judged in terms of the distinctions you identify between the two periods and the explanations you provide to account for the differences.

14. Give two reasons for why we should study science. What are some things that studying science teaches us? What are some jobs that use science? Write your answer in at least five complete sentences.

Certainly these are not the only ways that these essay items could have been rewritten, but these revisions point out the need for focus in essay questions. When students approach these revised items, they have a clear sense of what is expected of them; they no longer have to guess what the scope and direction of their answers should be. Note also that it is much more difficult for the student to bluff an answer to the revised items than it is to the initial, broadly stated items. The revised items call for answers specifically related to instruction, and therefore test what was taught and make scoring easier.

To summarize, regardless of the particular type of test item used, students should be given a clear idea of what their task is. In the case of multiple-choice items this may mean elaborating a stem in order to clarify the options. In matching items it may involve putting the longer options in the left column. In short-answer or completion items it may mean placing the blank at the end of the statement or specifying precisely the

For all types of test items, students should have a clear sense of what is expected of them.

nature of the desired answer. In essay questions it may mean elaborating to include information about the scope, direction, and scoring criteria for a desired answer. In all cases, the intent is to allow the student to respond validly and efficiently to the items.

Test item writers should take care not to provide grammatical clues, implausible option clues, sequencing clues, sentence length clues, or specific determiner clues.

Rule 6: Do not provide clues to the correct answer. The item-writing rules discussed thus far have all been aimed at problems that inhibited students from doing their best. However, the opposite problem arises when test items contain clues that help students answer questions correctly even though they have not learned the content being tested. Many types of clues may appear in items: grammatical clues, implausible option clues, sequencing clues, sentence length clues, and specific determiner clues. Try to identify the clue in examples 15 and 16.

15. A figure that has eight sides is called an _____.
    A. pentagon   B. quadrilateral   C. octagon   D. ogive

16. Compared to autos of the 1960s, autos in the 1980s _____.
    A. more horsepower.
    B. to use more fuel.
    C. contain more safety features.
    D. was less often constructed in foreign countries.

These examples contain grammatical clues. In example 15, using the article *a* or *an* at the end of the question or stem indicates to students what letter will begin the next word. The *an* before the blank tells the student that the next word must begin with a vowel, so the options pentagon and quadrilateral cannot be correct. There are two ways to correct this problem: replace the single article with the combined *a(n)* or get rid of the article altogether by writing the question in the plural form.

15. Figures that have eight sides are called _____.
    A. octagons   B. ogives   C. pentagons   D. quadrilaterals

In example 16, only option C grammatically fits the stem. Regardless of students' knowledge, they can select the correct answer because of the grammatical clue. The corrected item might read:

16. Compared to autos of the 1960s autos in the 1980s _____.
    A. are always constructed in foreign countries.
    B. contain more safety features.
    C. have more horsepower.
    D. use more fuel.

Now try to find the clues in examples 17 and 18.

17. Which of the following best describes an electron?
    A. a voting machine
    B. negative particle
    C. neutral particle
    D. positive particle

18. Match the correct phrase in column A with the term in column B. Write the *letter* of the term in column B on the line in front of the correct phrase in column A.

Column A	Column B
_____ 1. type of flower	A. cobra
_____ 2. poisonous snake	B. fission
_____ 3. how amoebae reproduce	C. green
_____ 4. colour of chlorophyll	D. hydrogen
_____ 5. chemical element	E. rose

Example 17 contains a clue that is less obvious than those in examples 15 and 16, but is quite common in multiple-choice items. One of the options is inappropriate or implausible and therefore is immediately dismissed by the students. Choice A, a voting machine, is dismissed as an unlikely answer by all but the most careless readers. As much as possible, options in test questions should be realistic and reasonable. A useful strategy is to have at least three incorrect (but reasonable) options, or **distractors,** in each multiple-choice item.

A distractor is a reasonable but incorrect option in a multiple-choice item.

The more choices students have, the less likely it is that they can guess the correct answer. Understanding this, teachers sometimes write three or four good options for an item and then add a fourth or fifth, such as none of the above or all of the above. It is usually better to avoid such general options.

Example 18 is a very easy question; the topics are so different from one another that many of the options in column B are implausible matches to the statements in column A. The item does not test one homogeneous subject area.

Consider the following matching item, that tests students' knowledge of a single, homogeneous topic. Note the difficulty in answering this item compared to the previous version of example 18.

A matching item should test the students' knowledge of a single homogeneous topic.

18. Match the names of the animals in column A to their correct classification in column B. Write the *letter* of the correct classification on the line in front of each animal name. The choices in column B may be used more than once.

Column A	Column B
_____ 1. alligator	A. amphibian
_____ 2. condor	B. bird
_____ 3. frog	C. fish
_____ 4. porpoise	D. mammal
_____ 5. snake	E. reptile
_____ 6. salamander	

The revised item is a better test of students' knowledge in two ways. First, it does not include the obvious matches and mismatches that occur when many unrelated topics are contained in the same matching item. The revised version focuses on a single topic, classification of animals into groups. Second, unlike example 18, the revised item has an unequal number of entries in columns A and B. Unequal entries in the two columns of a matching item prevent students from getting the last match correct by the process of elimination.

Look for the clues in examples 19 and 20.

19. Some people think the moon is made of green cheese.   T   F

20. One should never phrase a test item in the negative.   T   F

These items contain clues that are called **specific determiners.** In true-false questions, words such as *always, never, all,* and *none* tend to appear in statements that are false, and testwise students tend to answer accordingly. These students often use ordering of options and their varying lengths as clues. Conversely, words like *some, sometimes,* and *may* tend to appear in statements that are true. Thus, in example 19, it is reasonable to assume that *some* people think the moon is made of green cheese, so T should be marked. On the other hand, example 20 must be marked F if there is even a single situation in which a test item can reasonably be stated in the negative (e.g., Which one of these is *not* an example of democracy?).

Rule 7: Don't overcomplicate test items. Occasionally, teachers and textbooks overcomplicate test items. Consider the following item, which was given to Grade 6 students to test their mastery of applying the procedure to calculate simple interest.

> John borrowed $117.55 from Bob at an interest rate of 9.73 percent a year. How much simple interest must John pay Bob at the end of 15 months?

The numbers in this example are difficult and almost ensure that many students in Grade 6 will make computational errors. Unless the teacher was specifically testing computational accuracy, the following example would better assess the students' ability to apply the procedure.

> John borrowed $150.00 from Bob at an interest rate of 9.00 percent a year. How much simple interest must John pay Bob at the end of one year?

The latter item assesses students' mastery of simple interest without complicating the computation so much that errors are likely to occur. Key Assessment Tools 5.1 summarizes advice regarding different types of items.

Review Items before Testing

It is helpful to have a colleague or friend critique test items before the test is administered to students.

The best advice that can be given to improve most classroom tests is to review them before reproducing and administering them to students. Having written or selected the items for a chapter or unit test, it is recommended that a teacher wait one day and then reread them. The teacher should also ask a colleague, spouse, or friend to review the items critically.

Decisions in Planning a Test

Let us refer back to Rita's plan for instruction and assessment of learning outcomes from her Grade 5 unit on weather. She will need to answer four questions in her preparation of an end-of-unit test.

1. What should I test? The first important decision when preparing to assess student achievement is to identify the information, processes, and skills that will be tested. A valid assessment is one that provides students a fair opportunity to show what they have learned from instruction. Therefore, in deciding what to test, it is necessary for Rita to focus attention upon both her objectives and the actual instruction that takes place. Usually the two are very similar, but sometimes it is necessary to add or omit an outcome once teaching begins.

A fair and valid test covers information and skills similar to those covered during instruction.

KEY ASSESSMENT TOOLS 5.1

Writing Test Items

Multiple-choice items
1. Put each test item on a different line.
2. Place the student tasks in the item stem.
3. Put repeated terms in the item stem.
4. Construct at least three alternative choices.
5. Put options in alphabetical order.
6. Avoid grammatical clues to the answer.
7. Be sure that items match students' reading level.
8. Do not include unneeded words.
9. If "no" is used, underline it.
10. Reread the item to identify spelling and other errors.
11. The item stem should clearly state the question to be answered.

True-false items
1. Make items clearly true or false.
2. Be sure that the item is important in the assessment.
3. Avoid specific determiners.
4. Make the true and false items about the same length.
5. Do not use items in a repetitive pattern.
6. Do not use textbook sentences.

(continued)

KEY ASSESSMENT TOOLS 5.1

Writing Test Items (Continued)

Short-answer items

1. Make sure the item relates to the assessment being taught.
2. Provide a clear focus for the intended answer.
3. Make answers possible in short responses; construct item so that student answers are short.
4. Ask students to reply in only one or two responses.
5. Be sure item assesses the intended responses.
6. Put space for the answer at the end of the item.
7. Avoid giving grammatical clues.

Matching answer items

1. Be sure the exercise relates to the assessment.
2. Compare homogeneous topics.
3. Make sure the directions are clear.
4. Put the longer options in the left-hand column.
5. Put options in alphabetical order.
6. Number one set of items; mark the other set with letters.
7. Do not ask for more than 10 responses in the assessment. If more responses are desired, begin a new matching test.
8. Provide one or two additional options in one column to avoid the final option being the correct answer by default.

Essay questions

1. Use several short essays rather than one long one.
2. Be sure that the reading level is appropriate for students.
3. Be sure the essay relates to your objectives.
4. Base the essay on a fresh example, if examples are used.
5. Provide a clear focus of the desired outcome of the essay.
6. Do not use essays that require a great deal of memory.
7. Aid students by focusing them with terms such as "state and defend the topic," "apply the principle to," "develop a valid conclusion," and so on. These kinds of instructions focus students and also help to focus the grading.
8. Provide students with clear directions about the expected length of essay and the amount of time for completion.
9. Provide students with clear scoring criteria, for example, will spelling count?

Based on the expectations or learning outcomes from this Grade 5 unit, Rita knows that she has to determine how well the students are able to discriminate between *weather* and *climate*, predict weather patterns using data from weather reports, describe the water cycle, define terms such as *tem-*

perature, precipitation, humidity, wind chill factor, barometric pressure, and *cloud cover,* and describe ways in which weather conditions affect the activities of humans and animals. But what about other important skills such as designing, constructing, and assessing a variety of weather instruments? These are also covered in the unit, so should they be on Rita's test?

The answer to this question is no! There will always be more expectations or learning outcomes to teach than there is time to teach them. There will always be useful topics and skills that have to be omitted from tests because of a lack of instructional time. Including untaught skills on a test diminishes its validity, making it less than a true and fair assessment of what students have learned from classroom instruction. There also exist other formats such as projects, in-class assignments, portfolios, and performance assessments that can be used to assess those other important skills that are not easily assessed using written tests.

2. What type of assessment should be given? This question is answered by referring back to the expectations or learning outcomes. Each expectation or outcome contains a target process or behaviour that students have been taught. Knowledge outcomes should be tested using *selected response questions*, questions that present the student with a set of choices of which the student selects one or more. Outcomes that refer to comprehending, applying, analyzing, synthesizing, and evaluating may be tested using selected response questions, but are best assessed using *constructed response questions*, questions that require the student to construct an answer or product. Thus the statement of the outcome largely predetermines the format used to assess learning. In any case, written tests primarily assess cognitive skills; affective and psychomotor skills are best assessed using other formats.

The type of assessment procedure chosen depends on the nature of the outcome being assessed.

Many teachers feel that only essay tests are good. Others use multiple-choice items as much as possible, and still others believe that tests should contain a variety of question types. It must be remembered that the main purpose of summative assessment is *to permit students to show how well they have learned the knowledge, behaviours, or processes they were taught.* Thus, no single type of assessment item is applicable all the time. What makes a particular procedure useful is whether it matches the outcomes and instruction provided.

3. How long should the test take? Since time for testing is limited, choices must be made in deciding on the length of a test. Usually, practical matters such as the age of the students or the length of a class period are most influential. Since the stamina and attention span of young students is less than that of older ones, a useful strategy to follow with elementary school students is to test them fairly often using short tests that assess only a few outcomes. Because of their typical attention span, 15- to 30-minute tests, depending on the grade and group, are suggested. Testing in middle, junior, and high school is usually restricted by the length of the class period. Most teachers at these levels plan their tests to last almost one complete class period. For more on length of test time, see Chapter 6.

The age of the students, the subject being tested, and the length of the class period all impact the length of a test.

The number of test questions per outcome depends on the instructional time spent on each outcome and its importance.

In deciding how many questions to ask for each outcome, try to balance two factors: (1) the instructional time spent on each outcome and (2) its importance. Some outcomes are usually more important than others. These outcomes tend to be more general ones that call for the integration of several specialized outcomes. However, if considerable time is spent teaching a specific outcome, it should be tested separately. When teachers focus their tests solely upon the general, integrative outcomes, students may answer questions incorrectly because they cannot successfully integrate the separate skills that they have learned.

4. Should a teacher-made or a textbook test be used? Teachers are inevitably confronted with the question of whether to use the textbook test or construct their own. The very availability of textbook tests is seductive and causes many teachers to think: the test comes with the textbook and seems to measure what is in the chapter that I'm teaching, so why shouldn't I use it?

The main consideration in judging the adequacy of a textbook test is the match between its questions and what students were actually taught in class.

The decision about using a textbook test or constructing one cannot be answered until *after* the teacher has reflected on what was taught and has identified the topics and behaviours to be tested. The usefulness of any test cannot be judged without reference to the planned outcomes and actual instruction.

Textbook tests furnish a ready-made instrument for assessing the outcomes stressed in the textbook and can save teachers much time. Test formats vary across textbook publishers in terms of length, layout, and question type. Look through the teacher's edition of some textbooks to see the range of tests available.

Regardless of whether a teacher is constructing his or her own test or judging the adequacy of a textbook test, he or she must consider the same basic validity issue: Do the items on the test match the instruction provided to the students? The more a teacher alters and reshapes the textbook curriculum, the less valid its accompanying tests become.

It is possible to combine textbook items and teacher-constructed items into an assessment. Often the textbook test has some appropriate assessment items that can be used in conjunction with the items the teacher has constructed. The key issue, however, is the relevance of the assessment items to the instruction provided to the students. Key Assessment Tools 5.2 relates to judging textbook tests.

To summarize, both textbook and teacher-made tests should (1) clearly relate to the outcomes of instruction, (2) include enough questions to assess all or most of the outcomes, and (3) use assessment methods suited to the backgrounds and prior experiences of the students (Joint Advisory Committee, 2002). Tests that meet these criteria will provide a valid indication of student learning. Key Assessment Tools 5.3 provides a summary of common problems teachers encounter in judging tests used for summative purposes.

Assembling Tests

Once items have been written or selected and reviewed, they must be arranged into a test. If a teacher uses a textbook test, the items will already be arranged and ready for copying. Often teachers cut and paste items from various sources into a single test. In assembling a test, similar types of items should be grouped together and kept separate from other item types. For example, all of the short-answer questions should be together and separate from the multiple-choice, matching, completion, and essay questions. Grouping test items by type avoids the necessity of students shifting from one response mode to another as they move from item to item. It also means that a single set of directions can be used for all of the items in that test section, helping students cover more items in a given time. Finally, grouping test items makes scoring easier.

Another important consideration in assembling the test is the order in which the item types are presented. In most tests, selected response items come first and constructed response items come last. Within the constructed response section, short-answer or completion questions should be placed before essay questions. Constructed response items are placed at the end of the test so that students will not devote a disproportionate amount of time to this part of the test.

KEY ASSESSMENT TOOLS 5.2

Key Points to Consider in Judging Textbook Tests

1. The decision to use a textbook test must come *after* a teacher identifies the outcomes that he or she has taught and wants to assess.

2. Textbook tests are designed for the generic classroom, but since few classrooms are generic, most teachers deviate somewhat from the text in order to accommodate their students' needs.

3. The more classroom instruction deviates from the textbook, the less valid the textbook tests are likely to be.

4. The main consideration in judging the adequacy of a textbook test is the match between its test questions and what students were taught in their classes:

    a. Are questions similar to the teacher's objectives and instructional emphases?

    b. Do questions require students to perform the behaviours they were taught?

    c. Do questions cover all or most of the important outcomes taught?

    d. Is the language level and terminology appropriate for the students?

    e. Does the number of items for each outcome provide a sufficient sample of student performance?

> **KEY ASSESSMENT TOOLS 5.3**
>
> ## Common Problems in Developing or Selecting Tests to Assess Student Achievement
>
> 1. Failing to consider outcomes and instructional emphases when planning a test.
> 2. Failing to assess all of the important outcomes and instructional topics.
> 3. Failing to select item types that permit students to demonstrate the desired behaviour.
> 4. Adopting a test without reviewing it for relevance to the instruction provided.
> 5. Including topics or outcomes not taught to students.
> 6. Including too few items to assess the consistency of student performance.
> 7. Using tests to punish students for inattentiveness or acting out.

When arranging items on a test, remember these practices:

1. Designate a space for students to write their names and/or ID numbers (if applicable).
2. Do not split a multiple-choice or matching item across two pages of the test. This can cause unintended errors when students flip from one page to the next to read the second half of a matching question or the last two options of a multiple-choice question.
3. Separate multiple-choice options from the stem by beginning the options on a new line.
4. Number test items, especially if students must record answers on a separate answer sheet or in a special place on the test.
5. Space items for easy reading and provide enough space for students to complete constructed response items. Remember that young students write large and need space to respond. Do not cram items close together.

Each section of a test should have directions that focus students on what to do, how to respond, and where to place their answers. Lack of clear directions is one of the most common faults in teacher-prepared tests and often influences test validity. Here are some sample directions.

➤ Items 1–15 are multiple-choice items. Read each item carefully and write the letter of your answer on the line in front of the question number.
➤ Use words from the boxes to complete the sentences. Use each word only once.
➤ Answer each question by writing the correct answer in the space below the question. No answer should be longer than one sentence.

➤ For items 10 to 15, circle T or F (true or false).

➤ Use the chart to help you answer questions 27–33. Write your answers in the space provided after each question.

Directions such as these at the start of a test section focus students by telling them where and how to respond to the questions. To emphasize a point made earlier, it is especially important that each essay question spell out clearly for students the scope and characteristics of the desired answer. When applicable, it is also helpful to indicate the number of marks that will be given to each test section so they can make decisions about how to allocate their time.

The test should be reproduced so that each student has his or her own copy. Writing the test questions on the blackboard can be time-consuming, create problems for students with poor vision, and encourage students to look around the room during test taking. Orally reading questions can be used to pace students, but this approach places a premium on listening ability and prevents students from working at their own pace. This practice should be avoided unless one is assessing listening skills.

Tests that contribute to valid decisions also need to be reliable, that is, produce consistent scores. Without reliability, a test can hardly provide the kind of information on which a teacher would want to base decisions about students' learning. The main factors in attaining reliable summative tests are (1) the number and representativeness of the items included on the test and (2) the objectivity of scoring. In general, longer tests allow a teacher to look at a greater number of objectives. For example, which test do you think would produce the more stable and consistent information about a student's spelling achievement: a test that consists of a single word selected from a 100-word list or a test that contains a sample of 15 words selected from the same 100-word list? Key Assessment Tools 5.4 summarizes guidelines for assembling tests.

Finally, it is important that the assembled test be reviewed before reproducing and administering it. After constructing a test, it is recommended that a teacher wait one day and reread the test. If possible, the teacher should also ask a colleague to review the test format and individual test items critically.

TECHNOLOGY AND ASSESSMENT

http://escholarship.bc.edu

The *Journal of Technology, Learning and Assessment* (JTLA) is a peer-reviewed, scholarly online journal that produces interdisciplinary articles combining technology, learning theory, and assessment.

Find a link to this site and others on our OLC at

www.mcgrawhill.ca/college/airasian.

ACCOMMODATIONS: SUBSTITUTIONS FOR WRITTEN TESTS

There are a number of alternatives to written tests for students with exceptionalities. For example, the simplest way to accommodate a student who is physically unable to respond in writing to a test of subject knowledge and ideas is to present the test items orally. In some cases it may be appropri-

> ## KEY ASSESSMENT TOOLS 5.4
>
> ### Guidelines for Assembling a Test
>
> This list combines some suggestions to consider when assembling a test:
>
> ➤ Organize the test by item type: selected response before constructed response, essay last.
>
> ➤ Indicate the purpose of the test on the top of the first page of the test.
>
> ➤ Allow sufficient space for written responses, especially for young students.
>
> ➤ Do not split multiple-choice or matching items across two pages.
>
> ➤ Separate stem from options in multiple-choice questions.
>
> ➤ Number test items.
>
> ➤ Provide clear directions for each section of the test; for older students, indicate the value of each section or question.
>
> ➤ Provide enough questions to ensure reliability.
>
> ➤ Proofread the test before copying.

ate for a student with a physical disability to use a computer in place of paper and pencil. In other cases, special equipment may be needed to make the computer itself accessible to such a student. For students with extreme physical limitations there may be workable accommodations, such as speech-to-text software for students unable to type. There may be a special education teacher or classroom in your school that can help with this type of problem, which is likely to require some forethought. Figure 5.2 is a suggestive rather than definitive list of products and Web site resources that can be useful for accommodating students with exceptionalities when assessing for summative purposes.

FIGURE 5.2   *Resources for Universal Design.*

Software

***Built-in Accessibility
of Operating Systems***

Apple Special Needs
www.apple.com
(search for special needs)

Microsoft Enable
www.microsoft.com/enable

***Text-to-Speech Software
Programs***

CAST eReader www.cast.org

Kurzwell 3000
www.kurzweiledu.com

ReadPlease 2003
www.readplease.com

TextHELP! www.texthelp.com

Write: OutLoud
www.donjohnston.com

WYNN
www.freedomscientific.com

***Speech-to-Text Software
Programs***

Dragon Naturally Speaking
www.scansoft.com

IBM ViaVoice
www.nuance.com/viavoice/
pro

Accessible Multimedia

HiSoftware
www.hisoftware.com

Hardware

Portable Word Processors

AlphaSmart
www.alphasmart.com

CalcuScribe
www.calcuscribe.com

DreamWriter
www.brainium.com

LaserPC6
www.perfectsolutions.com

QuickPad www.quickpad.com

***Handwriting Recognition
Technologies***

InkLink
www.siibusinessproducts.com

InkWell
www.apple.com/macrosx/
features/inkwell

Logitech io Personal Digital Pen
www.logitech.com

PenReader
www.smarttech.com

Electronic Whiteboards

Mimio
www.mimio.com

SMARTBoard
www.smarttech.com

Online Resources

Digital Text

American Library Association
Great Sites for Children
www.ala.org/parentspage/
greatsites/lit.html

Berkeley Digital Library SunSite
www.sunsite.berkeley.edu

The Children's Literature Web
Guide
www.ucalgary.ca/~dkbrown

Internet Public Library
www.ipl.org

Project Gutenberg
www.gutenberg.org

University of Virginia Library
Electronic Text Center
www.etext.lib.virginia.edu/
ebooks

Organizations

Technology in Education

Association for the Advancement
of Computing in Education
(AACE)
www.aace.org

Association for Educational
Communications and
Technology (AECT)
www.aect.org

International Society for
Technology in Education (STE)
www.iste.org

U.S. Department of Education
Office of Educational Technology
www.ed.gov/Technology

Accessibility

CPB/WGBH National Center
for Accessible Media
www.ncam.wgbh.org

SOURCE: Curry, C. (2003). Universal design accessibility for all learners. *Educational Leadership,* (61) 2, 55–60.

CHAPTER REVIEW

CHAPTER REVIEW

Visit Chapter 5 of the
Online Learning
Centre at
**www.mcgrawhill.ca/
college/airasian**
to take chapter
quizzes, link to related
Web sites, and read
PowerWeb articles and
news feed updates.

What are summative assessments?

➤ Summative assessments are assessments that take place after learning has occurred in order to judge the success of the instruction. They usually take the form of tests, projects, papers, or examinations.

➤ Summative assessments are useful for student promotion and placement considerations.

➤ Written tests almost always focus on students' cognitive performance.

What are the two basic types of written test items?

➤ The two basic types of test items are selected response and constructed response.

➤ Selected response items are those in which the student selects the correct answer from among a number of choices. Examples of selected response items include multiple-choice items, true-false items, matching items, and interpretive exercises.

➤ Constructed response items are those that require the student to construct his or her own answer. Examples of constructed response items include short-answer items, completion items, and essay items.

What are the parts of any multiple-choice item?

➤ Multiple-choice items consist of a *stem*, which presents the problem or question, and a set of *options* from which the student selects an answer.

➤ Among the set of options, there is one correct option and, usually, at least three incorrect (but reasonable) options, or *distractors*.

What are some rules for writing sound test items?

➤ Avoid ambiguous and confusing wording and sentence structure.

➤ Use appropriate vocabulary.

➤ Keep questions short and to the point.

➤ Write items that have one correct answer.

➤ Give information about the nature of the desired answer.

➤ Do not provide clues to the correct answer.

➤ Do not overcomplicate test items.

What are specific determiners?

➤ Specific determiners are clues in true-false questions that assist the student in answering the question correctly.

➤ Examples of specific determiners are words such as *always*, *never*, *all*, and *none*, which tend to appear in statements that are false, and words like *some*, *sometimes*, and *may*, which tend to appear in statements that are true.

➤ Specific determiners are to be avoided in the construction of test items.

QUESTIONS FOR DISCUSSION

1. What are some expectations or learning outcomes that are best assessed by selected response items? What are some expectations or learning outcomes that are best assessed by constructed response items?

2. How are diagnostic assessment and instruction related to written tests of student learning?

3. What are the pros and cons of giving students choices in answering essay items?

4. What harm could result if a teacher's tests produced invalid information about student learning?

5. Are higher-level expectations or learning outcomes harder to teach and assess than lower-level ones? Why or why not?

6. Why is the development of higher-level thinking in students important to society?

7. What are the specific challenges that children with exceptionalities face when working with written tests?

ACTIVITIES

Each of the following five test items has at least one fault. Read each item, identify the fault(s) in it, and rewrite the item to correct the fault(s).

1. Alexander Graham Bell, who was born in Scotland in 1847 and moved to Ontario, is best known for his invention of the telephone, which he called his "electrical speech machine."   T   F

2. Minor differences among organisms of the same species are known as
   A. heredity
   B. variations
   C. adaptation
   D. natural selection

3. The recall of factual information can be best assessed with a _____ item.
   A. essay
   B. objective
   C. matching
   D. short-answer

4. Although the experimental research completed, particularly that by Hansmocker, must be considered too equivocal and the assumptions viewed as too restrictive, most testing experts would recommend that the easiest method of significantly improving written achievement test reliability would be to
   A. increase the size of the group
   B. increase the weighting of items
   C. increase the number of items
   D. increase the amount of testing time

5. An electric transformer can be used
   A. alternating current is changed to direct current
   B. for storing up electricity
   C. it converts electrical energy into direct current
   D. to increase the voltage of alternating current (correct answer)

CHAPTER 6

ADMINISTRATION OF SELECTED AND CONSTRUCTED RESPONSE TESTS

After reading this chapter, you will be able to:

➤ State activities that help prepare students for tests

➤ Outline basic principles for test administration

➤ Identify strategies to reduce cheating on tests

➤ Distinguish between objective and subjective scoring and holistic and analytic scoring

➤ Understand how to analyze the evidence of validity for test items

➤ Identify strategies for testing students with exceptionalities

urjit Mohammed has been supply teaching for a year and has now received his first long-term teaching assignment. Just two days into his term, he had to administer a history test that the Grade 7 teacher constructed prior to her leave. The test was comprised of both selected and constructed response items. Since the previous teacher did not supply Surjit with a scoring key for marking, he spent an evening reading and researching the information that was covered on the history test. He devised an answer key for the selected response items and an analytic rubric for each of the constructed response short essay questions. Surjit was then faced with the challenge of allocating marks for each set of test items and explaining his scoring protocol to students. In the end, he could not believe how much thought had gone into the administration of a history test.

Chapter 5 discussed the decisions that teachers must make in planning and constructing tests. The process of selecting test items that give students a fair chance to demonstrate their learning is an important responsibility. There are five other considerations that influence the adequacy of selected and constructed response tests: (1) preparing students for tests, (2) administering the test, (3) understanding and dealing with cheating, (4) scoring the test, and (5) giving feedback to students about the results. Chapter 6 addresses these topics along with test administration considerations for students with exceptionalities.

PREPARING STUDENTS FOR SELECTED AND CONSTRUCTED RESPONSE TESTS

This chapter begins with a discussion of how to prepare students for testing. Many of these practices may appear to be sensible ones that all teachers would normally do. However, such is not the case. It is remarkable how often these commonsense practices are ignored or overlooked. Failure to carry out these activities can jeopardize the validity of tests.

Issues of Test Preparation

Fair and valid assessment involves preparing appropriate objectives, providing good instruction on these objectives, and determining how these objectives are best assessed.

We use tests and other assessments to help make decisions about students' learning in some content area. A student's performance on a test or assessment is meant to represent the student's mastery of a broader body of knowledge and skills than just the specific examples included on the test or assessment. Thus, tests and other assessments gather a sample of a student's behaviour and use that sample to generalize how the student is likely to perform if confronted with similar tasks or items. For example, the performance of a student who scores 90 percent on a test of poetry analysis, chemical equation balancing, or capitalization rules is interpreted as indicating that the student has mastered about 90 percent of the general content domain on which he was taught and tested. The specific tasks or test items are selected to represent the larger group of similar tasks and items.

Objectives, instruction, and assessment *should* all be related to each other. After all, the purpose of a test is to determine how well students have learned what they were taught. The important question, however, is: When does the relationship among objectives, instruction, and assessment become so close that it is inappropriate or unethical?

There is an important ethical difference between teaching to the test and teaching the test itself. Teaching to the test involves teaching students the general skills, knowledge, and processes that they need to answer the questions on a test. This is an appropriate and valid practice. It is what good teaching and testing are all about. But teaching the test itself—that is, teaching students the answers to specific questions that will appear on the test—is neither appropriate nor ethical. It produces a distorted, invalid picture of student achievement. Such a test will give information about how well students can remember the specific items they were taught, but it will not tell how well they can do on questions that are similar, but not identical, to the ones they have been taught. Teachers have an educational and ethical responsibility not to corrupt the validity of students' test performance by literally teaching them the exact items that will be on the test.

There is an important difference between teaching to the test and teaching the test itself.

Another problematic practice difficult to classify is teachers' limiting instruction to overly narrow objectives that sometimes accompany a text. When working with a predetermined curriculum, it is appropriate for teachers to confine their instruction to the objectives that will be tested, so long as they do not prepare the students for the specific test items that will be used to measure these objectives. However, it is improper for teachers to consciously exclude important objectives from their instruction solely because those objectives are not on the test provided by a text or other outside source. Instead of linking assessment to the curriculum objectives, such teachers have let the test objectives define their curriculum.

The following sections describe other actions that teachers should carry out to prepare their students for tests. As you read these sections, bear in mind the "Do No Harm" testing practices in Key Assessment Tools 6.1. Also bear in mind that concern about test preparation is not confined to tests, but also includes other summative assessment tasks.

Review Before Testing

While teaching a unit or chapter, many objectives are introduced, some early and others at the end of instruction. Because the topics students most remember are the ones taught at the beginning and the end of a unit, it is good practice to provide students a review prior to testing. The review can take many forms: a question and answer session, a written or oral sum-

KEY ASSESSMENT TOOLS 6.1

"Do No Harm" Testing Practices

1. When a student does poorly on a test, determine which link in the learning chain is uncoupled. Always have constructive, nonpunitive contingency plans for students who perform poorly on a test. Testing should not be an end in itself, but rather a call to action.

2. Not all students can demonstrate their strengths in the same manner. Allow different students to demonstrate their learning differently, using the means of their choice (portfolios, expert papers, oral presentations, and projects, as well as multiple-choice tests).

3. Some students who excel on tests might develop a false sense of security and confidence, failing to realize that there are many other abilities that no test can elicit. Take care to nurture vital capacities that are not testable.

4. Avoid the hazard of teaching to the tests because your work or school is being judged solely on the basis of examination scores. Teachers should never have their students rehearse or explicitly prepare for tests. Good results on such tests should be the product of the regular, undisturbed curriculum.

Source: Levine (2003).

mary of main ideas, or administration of a review test. The review exercises should be similar, but not identical, to the exercises that will make up the test. In essence, the review should provide one last chance to review newly acquired knowledge and practise important skills, and to afford an opportunity to ask questions about things that are unclear. Often, the review exercise itself provokes questions that help students grasp partially understood ideas.

Test reviews often provoke questions that help students grasp partially understood ideas.

The review should cover the main ideas and skills that were taught. Many teachers fail to conduct a review because they feel the review might "tip off" students to the kinds of things that will be on the test. This is faulty reasoning. A review is the final instructional act in the chapter or unit. It provides students an opportunity to practise skills and clarify misunderstandings about the content. If the review focuses mainly on peripheral topics and behaviours in an attempt to "protect" the areas to be tested, students will not be afforded a final practice on the important outcomes. They will not have their questions answered, and, after experiencing a few irrelevant review sessions, will cease taking them seriously.

The purpose of a review, especially a review for a test or assessment, is to prepare students for the test. A test should not trick students, make them answer topics they haven't been taught, or create a high-anxiety test situation. It should give students a fair chance to show what they have learned. A pertinent review prior to the test will help them do this.

Ensure Familiarity with Question Formats

If a classroom test contains questions that use an unfamiliar format, students should be given practice with or examples of that format prior to testing. The need for such practice is especially important in the elementary and middle grades where students first encounter matching, multiple-choice, true-false, short-answer, and essay questions. Students must learn what is expected of them for each type of question, and how to record their answer. One opportune time to familiarize students with question formats is during the review exercises prior to the chapter or unit test. Pretest practice with new types of question and response formats can reduce anxiety and permit a more valid assessment of student learning. Provide students with suggestions such as those in Table 6.1 that help them prepare for specific types of response formats.

If students are not familiar with the types of questions used on a test, the test does not produce a valid assessment of what they have learned.

In addition to familiarizing students with new types of questions and response formats, there is a general set of test-taking guidelines that can help students do their best on tests. These guidelines will not enable students to overcome the handicaps of poor teaching and lack of study, but they can help focus students during testing. Table 6.2 lists some advice that you may want to give students before a test (Ebel & Frisbie, 1991).

Scheduling the Test

As you consider when to schedule the test, bear in mind both the estimated length of time to complete the test, as well as when the test can be accommodated in the students' timetable. The Canadian Personnel Psychology Centre (2005) has some guidelines with respect to test completion considerations. First, the time limit should be set to allow the majority of students to finish within the allotted time. Estimating this time limit can be tricky, especially for constructed response items—use your best judgment. For selected response items, you should allow about 1 minute per multiple-choice question and 30 seconds per true/false question or matching items.

As the teacher, you may opt to test your students immediately after completing instruction on a chapter or unit in order to provide them with the opportunity to review, study, and reflect on the instruction before being tested. However, there are other considerations about the times when students are most likely to show their best performance. For example, if a teacher were to test students the day of the school's championship basketball game, the period after an assembly or lunch, or on the first day after a long school vacation, it is likely that students would give a substandard test performance. Likewise, a teacher should not schedule a test on a day that he or she will be away just so the supply teacher will have something to keep the students busy. The supply teacher may not be able to answer students' questions about either the test or the meaning of particular questions.

TABLE 6.1 Suggestions for Students for Writing Multiple-Choice Exams

Establish the appropriate attitude.

➤ There are many ways to prepare, even if you cannot study specific content.

Build vocabulary.

➤ Keep a personal dictionary with a list of unfamiliar words, with definitions, synonyms and contextual use.

➤ Identify and look up unfamiliar vocabulary in all the text you read.

Understand how questions are constructed.

➤ Use practice tests available to practise reading a selection and completing its questions, then checking your answers. Try to determine why a certain answer is correct, and why the other choices are incorrect.

Understand how the exam is constructed.

➤ You may want to read all the questions before reading the passage. Similarly, you may want to read all the questions before you begin to answer any.

Write on the test.

➤ Make notes in the margins of ideas or reminders.

➤ Use visual clues such as underlining to focus your attention on what is being asked.

➤ Circle key words in the stem of the question:
  ➤ negative words—"none," "not," "never," "neither," "only"
  ➤ superlatives— "every," "all," "none," "always"
  ➤ qualifiers— "usually," "often," "generally," "may," "best," "most"
➤ Cross out choices which are not possible.

Read carefully.

➤ Read everything. All material included with the reading selection is important.

➤ When reading a drama selection, create internal voices or visual images to associate with each character.

Checking answers.

➤ Write in the answer booklet:
  ➤ circle possible answers
  ➤ put question marks beside difficult questions
  ➤ cross out or eliminate choices
➤ Changing answers on a multiple-choice exam is neither good nor bad; if you have a good reason for changing your answer, change your answer.

SOURCE: Sandra Ens, Cochrane High School, Cochrane, Alberta.

TABLE 6.2 Common Test-Taking Strategy Advice for Students

➤ Read test directions carefully.

➤ Find out how questions will be scored. Will all questions count equally? Will points be taken off for spelling, grammar, neatness?

➤ Pace yourself to ensure that you can complete the test.

➤ Plan and organize any essay questions before writing.

➤ Attempt to answer all questions. If guessing is not penalized, guess when you don't know the answer.

➤ When using a separate answer sheet, check often to make certain that you are marking your responses in the correct space.

➤ Be well rested at the time of testing by avoiding late-night cram sessions.

In secondary level schools there is usually little flexibility in scheduling tests, where limited periods and departmentalized instruction mean that students must be in certain places at certain times. The math teacher who has a class immediately after lunch has no choice but to test students then. While no teacher has complete control over scheduling tests, it is useful to bear in mind that there are some times when students are able to perform better on tests than others.

Giving Students Information about the Test

It is a good idea to let students know when a test will be given, what areas will be covered, what types of questions it will contain, how much it counts, and how long it will take. These factors undoubtedly influence your own test preparation. By providing this information, the teacher can help reduce some of the anxiety that inevitably accompanies the announcement of a test. When information is provided, the test becomes an incentive to make students study.

The hardest test for students to prepare for is the first one they take in a class. Even if a teacher provides detailed information about topics to be covered, types of items, number of questions, and the like, students always have some uncertainty about the test. It is not until they take a teacher's first test that they get a sense of how that teacher tests and whether the review given by the teacher can be trusted as a basis for test preparation. Once students know the teacher's style, they have a sense of what to expect on subsequent tests and whether the teacher's pretest information is useful.

Of course, unless a teacher has thought about the nature of the test to be given, it is impossible to provide all the pretest information students need to prepare for the test. The specifics of test content, types of questions, and

Hastily planned tests too often focus on memory items and fail to cover a representative sample of the instruction provided.

test length need to be considered well before the test is given. Hastily planned tests too often focus mainly on memorization skills and fail to cover a representative sample of the instruction provided to students. Thus, to inform students about test characteristics, a teacher cannot put off planning the test until the last minute.

ADMINISTERING TESTS

The aim of test administration is to establish both a physical and psychological setting that permits students to show their best performance. The setting should also make it easy for students to keep track of the time.

Physical Setting

One way to minimize interruptions is to post a sign on the door indicating testing is occurring.

Students should have a quiet, comfortable environment in which to take the test. Interruptions should be minimized; some teachers post a sign on the door indicating that testing is in progress. During testing there is little one can do about interruptions like fire drills or announcements from the classroom intercom. When such interruptions occur, the teacher must make a judgment about whether it is fair for students to continue with testing. Obviously a 1-minute interruption from the intercom is less disruptive than a 20-minute fire drill, during which students may talk to one another about the test. If an interruption is judged sufficiently disruptive to diminish students' ability to provide a fair and representative indication of their achievement, testing should be terminated and repeated at another time.

Often interruptions occur when students ask questions during testing. A good way to minimize many of these questions is to proofread items and directions prior to administering the test. Occasionally, typographical errors or unclear items are not detected until testing has begun. Usually, a student raises his or her hand or approaches the teacher to ask a question or point out a problem. When such situations arise, an announcement should be made to the whole class informing them of the problem (e.g., "Please correct item 17 in the following way," or "Option B in item 29 should be changed to . . ."). In the end, the decision of whether and how to answer student questions rests with the individual teacher. Answering questions during testing is appropriate as long as the teacher is consistent in responding to all students who ask questions.

Test anxiety is diminished by giving students advance notice of the test, an opportunity to prepare for it, and a pre-test review.

Psychological Setting

Establishing a productive psychological setting that reduces student anxiety and sets a proper atmosphere for testing is as important as providing a comfortable physical environment. Giving students good instruction, advance notice of the test, a day or two to prepare for it, prior knowledge of the kind of test items, and a good chapter or unit review will help diminish students' test anxiety. Even so, it is probably impossible to completely allay all test anxiety.

No teacher should precede test administration with a comment like, "This is the most important test you will take this term. Your grade will be determined primarily by how you do on this test." A speech like this will raise students' anxiety levels appreciably and hamper their ability to show what they have learned. Conversely, test administration should not be prefaced with remarks such as, "Everybody knows that tests don't mean much; I just give tests because I have to" or "Don't worry about it—it counts very little in your final grade." Describing and treating a test as if it were a trivial interruption in the school day will diminish its ability to motivate student study and will interfere with students' test performances.

The line between overemphasizing and underemphasizing the importance of a test is hard to draw. Students should take tests seriously and they should be encouraged to do their best. The appropriate middle ground between over- and underemphasizing the importance of tests will vary with the age and characteristics of students. The more students know about the test, the more likely their anxiety will be lowered. Of course, fair, valid test items and no "surprises" such as unannounced tests, unfamiliar item types, and untaught topics will help allay test anxiety. Each teacher must find the middle ground for his or her class, knowing that whatever is done, there will be some students who will be very anxious about their performance and some who will not care.

Keeping Track of Time

During testing it often helps students if the teacher keeps track of the remaining time with announcements such as, "There are 20 minutes left until the test is over." Such reminders can initially be made at 15-minute intervals, then changed to 5-minute intervals near the end of the test. Such reminders are most useful at the secondary school level during final exams, which usually take longer than a single class period to administer. In self-contained elementary school classrooms, where testing and instruction are ruled less by the bell schedule, the teacher has discretion regarding when and how to start and end testing.

ISSUES OF CHEATING

Teachers should be alert to the possibility of cheating on tests, projects, quizzes, and assignments. Unfortunately, cheating is a common occurrence, both in school and in life. Students cheat for many reasons: external pressure from teachers or parents; failure to prepare and study for tests;

Teachers can discourage cheating with seating arrangements, careful proctoring, and swift punishment of those who do cheat.

internal pressure from being in an intensively competitive school that gives a limited number of high grades; danger of losing a scholarship; and, unfortunately, because "everybody else does it." Some even blame their cheating on the practices of others. For example, some try to justify cheating with excuses like, "No one near me was attempting to cover up their exam paper," "The material is too difficult," "There's just too much material to learn," or "The teacher gives tests that are unfair."

However, no matter how and why it is done, cheating is an unacceptable, dishonest, and immoral classroom behaviour. The argument that says, "So what, everybody does it. It's no big deal," is wrong. It *is* a big deal. Cheating is analogous to lying. When students cheat and turn in work or a test under the pretense that they did the work themselves, that should be recognized and called lying (Summergrad, 1999).

Types of Cheating on Tests

How do students cheat on tests? Cizek (1999) has written a useful and comprehensive book that explores cheating in depth and with understanding. He identifies and gives examples of a very large number of the ways that students cheat. The following examples represent a small sample of common ways students cheat:

1. Looking at another student's test paper during a test.
2. Dropping one's paper so that other students can cheat off it.
3. Dropping one's paper and having another student pick it up, cheat from it, and dropping it again so the original dropper can reclaim his or her paper.
4. Passing an eraser between two students who write test information on the eraser.
5. Developing codes such as tapping the floor three times to indicate that a multiple-choice item should be answered "C."
6. Looking at students' papers while walking up to the teacher to ask a question about the test.
7. Using crib notes or small pieces of paper to cheat. Crib notes can be hidden in many ingenious places.
8. Wearing a T-shirt with useful test information written on it.

Deterring Cheating

Teachers should monitor test taking in order to deter cheating and to enhance test validity. There are a number of methods that can be used to deter cheating, some relatively easy to apply and others more complicated. Three general approaches that help eliminate or lessen cheating

CHAPTER CASE STUDY

Visit the text OLC to read the case of Karen Lee, a first-year French teacher. Karen takes over a secondary school French class midyear and faces an unruly group of students.

www.mcgrawhill.ca/ college/airasian

are (1) providing students good instruction and information about the test, (2) knowing the common methods of student cheating, and (3) observing students during testing. Prior to testing, students' books and other materials should be out of sight under their desks or elsewhere. Students' seats should be spread out in the classroom as much as possible. Consider a ban on wearing baseball caps during testing because when the visors are tilted below the eyes, the teacher cannot see where the students' eyes are looking. During testing, the teacher should quietly move about the classroom and observe students as they take the test. While observation rarely "catches" a student cheating, the presence of the teacher moving about the classroom is a deterrent to cheating.

Many schools and districts develop honour codes or cheating rules that all students are to respect. Such codes or rules spell out in detail what is and is not cheating. Table 6.3 excerpts a cheating policy from a secondary school in British Columbia.

It is the teacher's responsibility to discourage cheating with seating arrangements, careful proctoring, and other activities. If some students do cheat, those who do not can be unfairly penalized for their appropriate and ethical behaviour, by receiving lower grades and the honours that come from grades. Teachers should discourage cheating and penalize students caught doing it, as it is an immoral activity and it provides an invalid picture of a student's achievement. It is, however, important to have strong evidence to support charges of cheating, because students have due process rights if accused.

SCORING SELECTED AND CONSTRUCTED RESPONSE TESTS

The product of test administration is a stack of tests that contain information about each student's achievement. However, to use this information, the teacher must summarize and score it. Scores provide a summary of each student's performance on the test. The process of scoring a test involves **evaluation**—that is, assigning a number to represent a student's performance.

The complexity of scoring tests varies with their type. Selected response items are easiest to score, short-answer and completion items are next easiest, and essays are the most difficult. The reason for this is obvious if one thinks about what a teacher has to do to score each item type. How much time and judgment is involved in scoring each? What precisely does the teacher have to look at to determine whether an item is correct or incorrect? Which type of item requires the most consideration to score? The answers to these questions illustrate the range of ease and difficulty encountered when scoring various item types.

TABLE 6.3 Excerpts from the Cheating Policy of Frances Kelsey Secondary School

Definition of Cheating

For the purposes of this policy, cheating may be described as "academic dishonesty." Academic dishonesty means presenting, as your own work, material produced by or in collaboration with others, or permitting or assisting others to present your work as their own.

Dishonesty has occurred:

➤ when a student turns in the work of another student and misrepresents this work as his or her own work. (e.g., handwritten material, computer reproduced work, copied test answers, duplicated audio or visual tapes, compact discs or digital video discs).

➤ when a student knowingly permits another student to duplicate work and to deliberately misrepresent that work as his/her own.

➤ when a student writes a test for another student.

➤ when a student steals or obtains examinations, answer keys, or other testing information from the teachers' files, computer directories, or computer disk or other sources.

➤ when written or printed material is used in a test situation without the subject teacher's permission.

Determination of Cheating

Any teacher who has *reason to suspect* that a student has cheated will follow the steps outlined below:

➤ Meet with the student(s) involved, provide evidence of cheating, discuss the matter, and determine whether cheating has actually occurred.

➤ If there is sufficient evidence of cheating or an admission of guilt by the student, inform the department head.

➤ Consult the recommended penalties listed below for an appropriate response.

➤ Inform the student's adviser as soon as possible.

➤ Phone the parents or guardians and inform them of the cheating offence and the penalty.

Recommended Penalties for Cheating (one example only)

If a student uses non-approved materials written materials or electronic devices in a testing situation:

For the first offence, the student may receive zero on test or rewrite test. For the second offence, the student receives zero on the test and no rewrite is permitted.

Appeal Procedure

The student and/or parent of the student accused of cheating may appeal to the principal of the school within 14 days of notification of the cheating infraction. The principal and/or designates will review the evidence and make a final determination.

SOURCE: Excerpted from "Frances Kelsey Secondary School Cheating Policy," Frances Kelsey Secondary School, www.fkss.ca/community/CheatPolicy.html.

Scoring Selected Response Items

Students respond to selected response items by writing, circling, or marking the letter of their response. Scoring selected response items is essentially a clerical task in which the teacher compares an answer **key** containing the correct answers to the answers the student has given. The number of matches indicates the student's score on the test. Before using an answer key, it is a good idea to check to make sure that the key is correct.

Scoring selected response test items is relatively **objective**—that is, independent scorers will usually arrive at the same or very similar scores for a given student's test. Conversely, **subjective** scoring means that independent scorers would not arrive at the same or similar scores for a given student's test. In a subjective test, a student's performance may depend on *who* scores the test in addition to the quality of the student's answers. Selected response items produce objective scores because there usually is one clearly correct answer to each item, and that answer is identified by a single letter. However, as students' responses become more lengthy and complex—as they do with constructed response items—the judgment of what is a correct or incorrect answer often blurs and scoring becomes more subjective. It has long been known that even when the same person scores the same essay test twice, there is no guarantee that the scores will be the same or similar (Starch & Elliott, 1912, 1913). This is a problem because, if we are to have confidence in a test score, it is important that the scores be objective. Fortunately, there are some ways to make the scoring of constructed response items less subjective, as we will now examine.

Selected response items can be scored objectively because they are usually brief and have only one correct answer.

Subjective test scores are those for which independent scorers have difficulty arriving at the same or similar scores.

To instill confidence in a test score, it is important that the score is as objective as possible.

Scoring Short-Answer and Completion Items

As long as short-answer and completion items are clearly written, focus students on their task, and call for a succinct response, scoring can be objective. However, as items require lengthier responses from students, subjectivity of scoring will increase as interpretations of what students know or meant to say will have to be made.

No matter how well a teacher has prepared and reviewed test items, he or she never knows how an item will work until *after* it is administered to students. Inevitably, there are times when student responses to an item reveal that most students misinterpreted it, and that the students' answers are correct given their interpretation, but incorrect given the teacher's intention. How should such responses be scored?

In reviewing unexpected responses and untaught items, the teacher must decide if wrong answers are the result of faulty items or a lack of student learning. Test scores should not automatically be raised simply because many students got an item wrong, but the teacher must make a judgment about the likely source of the problem and how it is best handled. At the very least, the problem items should be examined and analyzed.

In scoring unexpected responses, teachers must decide if wrong answers are the result of faulty test items or a lack of student learning.

*Test scores that reflect
ambiguous or untaught
items are less valid
indicators of student
achievement.*

In the end, scoring decisions rest with the teacher. Teachers must decide who is at fault when students misinterpret an item and whether students should lose credit for wrong answers on items that were not discussed in class. Two principles should be considered in making such decisions. First, since the test scores should reflect students' achievement on the chapter or unit, the scores should deal only with topics that were taught and items that are clearly written. If points are deducted for items not taught or for misinterpreting ambiguous questions, scores will not reflect students' true achievement. Second, whatever decision is made regarding the scoring of poor or untaught items, it should be applied uniformly to all students.

Three guidelines can help teachers overcome problems of scoring short-answer and completion items.

1. Prepare an answer key before scoring. Know what you are looking for in student responses *before* scoring.

2. Determine how factors such as spelling, grammar, and punctuation, which are usually ancillary to the main focus of the response, will be handled in scoring. Should points be taken off for such factors? Decide before scoring and inform students before testing.

3. If student responses are technically correct but not initially considered in the scoring guideline, give credit to each unexpected but correct responses.

Scoring Essay Items

Essay questions represent the ultimate in scoring complexity because they permit each student to construct a unique and lengthy response to the question posed. This means that there is no single definitive answer key that can be applied uniformly to all responses. Interpretation of the responses is necessary. Moreover, the answer to an essay question is presented in a form that contains many distracting factors that contribute to subjective scoring.

Think of an essay answer that you have written. Remember how it looked spread out over the page. Visualize your handwriting and the overall appearance of the written answer. Remember that the essay question was intended to determine how well you understood and could communicate the ideas and information you had been taught. However, the teacher who scored your essay was probably influenced by one or more of the following factors:

➤ Handwriting legibility
➤ Writing style, including sentence structure and flow

➤ Spelling and grammar

➤ Neatness

➤ Fatigue of the scorer

➤ Identity of the student

➤ Location of the test paper in the pile of test papers

Each of these factors can influence a teacher's reaction to an essay answer, although none of them has anything to do with the actual content of the student's response (Gentile, 2000). For example, a student whose handwriting is so poor that it forces the teacher to decipher what each scribbled word means will frustrate the teacher and divert attention away from the content of the answer. The essay likely will get a lower score than that of another student who provides the same answer in more legible handwriting. A student who uses interesting words in a variety of sentence structures to produce an answer that flows smoothly from point to point likely will get a better score than a student who states the same points in a string of simple declarative sentences. Poor grammar and misspelled words create a negative impression in a teacher's mind; neatness does count with teachers too.

Many types of scorer subjectivity can influence how an essay item is scored.

Scoring essays is a time-consuming and difficult task, so student scores may be influenced by how alert the teacher is when the essays are read. The first few essays that are read seem new and fresh, and students who wrote them tend to get good scores. However, after the teacher has read the same response 15 or more times, familiarity and fatigue set in, and responses similar to the initial ones often get lower scores. Thus, students who provide essentially the same answer to an essay question may get different scores depending upon when the scorer read their answer.

Knowledge of who wrote the essay can also influence the scoring process. In almost all essay questions there is at least one point when the teacher must interpret what a student was trying to say. Knowledge of who wrote the answer can influence the teacher's interpretation. For example, two students, Erica and Keyshawn, have each written an essay that has some ambiguous statements. The teacher knows that Erica is an interested, able student who always does well on tests and in class discussions. The teacher thinks, "Although Erica didn't make this point clearly and it's not evident that she understands it, she probably knew the answer even though it didn't come out right. I'll give her the credit." The teacher also knows that Keyshawn generally does poorly in school and remembers his indifference to the topic during a recent class discussion. The teacher thinks, "Since Keyshawn doesn't care about this subject, rarely says anything in class except to disagree with me, and didn't make this point clearly, he probably had no idea of what this question was asking of him. He will get no credit." One way to avoid such biased scoring is to identify papers by number or have students put their names on the last page of a test.

Holistic Versus Analytic Scoring

Holistic scoring provides a single, overall impression of the complete essay. Analytic scoring provides a separate score for each component of the essay.

Teachers typically use two approaches to scoring essay questions: holistic scoring and analytic scoring. **Holistic scoring** reflects a teacher's *overall impression* of the whole essay by providing a *single score or grade.* **Analytic scoring,** on the other hand, views the essay as being made up of many components and provides *separate scores* for each component. Thus, an essay that is scored analytically might result in separate scores for accuracy, organization, supporting arguments, grammar, and spelling. Analytic scoring provides detailed feedback that students can use to improve different aspects of their essays. According to Robert Runté at the University of Lethbridge in Alberta (2002), analytic scoring is good for scoring a large number of short, specific essay items, whereas, holistic scoring is appropriate for longer, general essay items. A tip for analytic scoring is not to allocate a large number of marks per item (e.g., 100 points) as this degree of distinction is difficult to justify. As well, for holistic scoring, ensure that the rubric is clear and focused on common characteristics, dimensions, and expectations that are reflected in the essay question. In both holistic and analytic scoring, teachers should give helpful and encouraging suggestions on students' essay item responses. In Chapter 7 we will discuss the use of holistic and analytic scoring rubrics.

Steps to Ensure Objectivity

Regardless of whether a teacher uses holistic or analytic scoring, certain steps should be followed to ensure that students' essays are scored objectively. Although the following suggestions are time-consuming, they are necessary if scores are to be valid for decision making:

A well-focused essay item includes scoring criteria and specific information about the students' task.

1. *Ensure that the response scoring criteria matches the essay question.* In Chapter 5, it was recommended that essay questions should be narrowly focused and include information about the scope of the students' responses. In this way, the criteria that focus students' responses are also the basic criteria that can be used in scoring the students' answers. Students should be provided with this information about the scoring criteria in the essay question directions. If the essay question communicates a precise set of teacher expectations, scoring subjectivity is likely to be diminished.

2. *Decide and tell students how handwriting, punctuation, spelling, and organization will be scored.* Students should know in advance what factors will count in scoring the essay.

3. *If possible, score students anonymously.* This will help keep the scoring objective by eliminating knowledge and accompanying perceptions of students' effort, ability, interest, and past performance. Each student should be scored on the basis of present performance, not in terms of teacher perceptions.

4. *In tests with multiple essay items, score all students' answers to the first question before moving to the second question.* It is difficult to score two or three different essay questions in succession, as you must shift content orientation and criteria for each question. Scoring all the answers to a single essay question at one time also ensures against the "carryover" effect, which is the tendency to let your reaction to a student's initial essay influence your perception of succeeding essays written by that same student. Further to this, the Queen's University Instructional Development Centre (2005, www.queensu.ca/idc/idcresources/handouts/Guide_Scoring_Essay.htm) suggests that a strategy to offset subjectivity is to shuffle all of the students' papers after scoring a question.

5. *Read essay answers a second time after initial scoring.* The best way to check for objectivity in essay scoring is to have a second individual read and score students' papers using the same criteria that you used to score them. Since this is usually impractical, an acceptable procedure is for you to reread and, if necessary, rescore a selection of the essays before finalizing the scores. Two scorings by the same person, even if done quickly and on only a selection of essays, lead to more objective decision making.

Before scores of essay items are finalized, the teacher should check for objectivity by rereading and, if necessary, rescoring a selection of essays.

Essay questions permit the assessment of many thought processes that can be assessed in no other way. When such thought processes are part of the instructional objectives and are actively taught to students, they should be assessed fairly to obtain a representative picture of student learning. Nevertheless, when using essay questions, a teacher must realize the difficulty inherent in scoring them and the implications of scoring them improperly. Time should be set aside to score essay responses objectively so that results can be used with confidence.

ANALYZING ITEM VALIDITY

Even though one has prepared students for testing and written or selected appropriate test items, poor test assembly, administration, and scoring can still impair test validity. (See Appendix C on page 305 for a discussion of normal distribution and standard deviation of scores.)

The steps described in the preceding section are intended to produce valid test scores. Although these steps will eliminate most of the common pitfalls found in classroom tests, a teacher never really knows how well test items will work until after they have been administered to students. Thus, a review of student performance after testing in order to identify faulty items is an important final step to ensure the validity of the test results. There are two reasons for performing such after-test analyses: (1) to identify and make scoring adjustments for any items that students' answers show were misunderstood or ambiguous and (2) to identify ways to improve items for use on future tests.

After-Test Analyses

The following two examples illustrate the importance of after-test analyses.

Example 1. A Grade 9 geography teacher who taught a unit on the Low Countries (e.g., East Frisia, Limburg, Belgium, Luxembourg, and Holland) asked the following short answer question and allocated four marks to the response:

"What are the Low Countries?"

Even though the item did not explicitly ask for the names, she expected that her students would respond with the names of some of the regions and/or nations collectively known as the "Low Countries." While many students did supply the names, many others responded that the Low Countries were "a group of countries in Europe that are largely below sea level." How should the teacher score the responses of this latter group of students?

Example 2. As part of an end-of-unit test to measure student achievement of concepts from a Grade 5 unit on physical fitness, a teacher wrote the following multiple-choice question:

"The main value of a daily exercise program is to:
   A. eat less
   B. develop musculature
   C. raise intelligence
   D. keep physically fit"

Choice B was the intended correct answer, but many students selected D as their answer. What should the teacher do about the students who selected option D?

Notice that these problems did not become apparent until *after* the teacher looked over the student responses and found unexpected or odd response patterns. These exceptionalities may include: almost every student missing a particular item; some students giving strange or unexpected answers to an item; all of the bright students doing poorly on an item; no consistency in the wrong answers to an item. As these scoring patterns emerge, teachers should inspect student responses to determine whether the problem was related to test construction or student learning. It is important to emphasize that test scores should not automatically be raised simply because many students got an item wrong. In each case, the teacher must make a judgment regarding the source of the problem and how it will be rectified, if at all. Recognize, however, that if problem items are not examined and analyzed, no reasonable decision can be made.

Problems in constructed response items (like Example 1) usually become evident when reading students' answers. The written responses give a good indication of how students understood and interpreted a test item. For example, in the preceding geography item on the Low Countries, students' answers made it clear that the item did not focus students on the names of the Low Countries and, consequently, produced other responses that were correct but not what the teacher wanted.

After-Test Analyses of Multiple-Choice Items

Problems in selected response items, especially multiple-choice ones, are harder to detect because students select rather than construct their own response, which provides little insight into their thinking. To identify problems with multiple-choice items, teachers must view response patterns on the various options provided. While it is desirable to review all items in a multiple-choice test, limitations in time make it more realistic to review those items that half or more of the students answered incorrectly. This is where most, if not all, of the faulty items are likely to be found.

There are many ways that response patterns for multiple-choice items can be examined. A number of statistical indices can be calculated to describe each test item (Kubiszyn & Borich, 1999). For example, the **difficulty index** of an item describes the proportion of students who answered it correctly. Thus, an item of .70 difficulty (70 percent of the class answered correctly) is easier than one of .40 difficulty (40 percent of the class answered correctly). Items can be ranked in terms of their difficulty to identify students' strengths and weaknesses. As illustration, Patricia Seaman (2003) at The University of New Brunswick considers an item moderately difficult if 70–85 percent of students answer it correctly. Only a few questions should have a difficulty index of 90 percent. For any question, if less than 50 percent of students respond correctly, the question should be examined and revised. The **discrimination index** describes how an individual item fares with students who scored high and low on the overall test. An item with positive discrimination is one that is more frequently answered correctly by students who score high on the test as a whole than by students who score low. (See Appendix C on page 305 for elaboration of these two indices.)

Because most classroom teachers lack the time and resources to perform the numerical analyses required to calculate difficulty and discrimination indices, they must rely upon simple methods to understand and improve those items that a large proportion of the class answered incorrectly. The following are examples of item response patterns teachers can use to answer the question "What's the problem with this item?" Each of these patterns indicates a different possible reason why large numbers of students might answer incorrectly. In each of the three cases, an asterisk indicates the keyed answer.

This first response pattern is typical of multiple-choice items that have two correct or defensible answers, similar to Example 2 shown previously. For this example, two choices, A and C, were rarely selected. The majority of students split themselves between options B and D. Only the students who marked B, the keyed response, received credit on the item when it was initially scored.

Options	A	*B	C	D
Number of students choosing option	2	8	2	8

When the teacher saw that a number of students missed this item, he looked at option D, decided that it was also a correct choice, and decided to give full credit to those who selected D.

The next pattern is one where most students select an option other than the keyed one. In the example below, most students chose C rather than D, the keyed option. Sometimes this pattern is simply the result of miskeying on the part of the teacher. In this case the teacher wrote D next to this item when she meant to write C. If the item was not miskeyed, closer inspection of option C should provide a clue about why it was chosen so often. If not, students should be consulted to explain their answers.

Options	A	B	C	*D
Number of students choosing option	2	1	15	2

Finally, consider the following pattern in which all options are selected by about the same number of students. Such a pattern may be an indication that students are guessing the correct answer. They probably have no idea which option is correct. Faulty item wording or untaught material are likely explanations for such a response pattern.

Options	*A	B	C	D
Number of students choosing option	5	6	4	5

After-test analyses using the above strategies can help teachers better understand how well their items are working and why students responded as they did. Asking students why they answered an item in a particular way can also produce useful information. While the decision about how to score an item ultimately rests with the classroom teacher, information of the kind described in this section is helpful in making that decision. An after-test analysis will enhance the validity of the test scores and the decisions made from them.

DISCUSSING TEST RESULTS WITH STUDENTS

Students want information about their test performance. Teachers can provide this information through comments written on papers or tests that indicate to students what they did well and how they might improve. It also is helpful to go over the results of a test with students. This is especially useful when the students have their marked tests in front of them during the review. The teacher should pay special attention to items that a large proportion of the class got wrong in order to clear up misconceptions and to indicate the nature of the desired answer. For older students it also is helpful to explain how the tests were scored and graded. Finally, opportunity should be provided for shy students to discuss the test in private with the teacher.

Going over test results when students have the graded test in front of them is useful.

The Manitoba Teachers' Society has made a series of recommendations in the form of a model for the assessment of student achievement. In this model, the Society addresses points with respect to teachers' obligation to be responsive to students' test performance:

➤ Justify how assessment methods and strategies are connected to the curriculum and the instruction that students have received

➤ Provide timely feedback to students

➤ Discuss a student's learning activity and achievement with his/her parents/guardians

SOURCE: Excerpted from Manitoba Teachers' Society, www.mbteach.org/studassess.htm.

TESTING STUDENTS WITH EXCEPTIONALITIES

In Chapter 5 we noted some alternatives to pencil-and-paper testing for students with exceptionalities. In this chapter the focus is on other ways of accommodating students with exceptionalities during selected and constructed response tests. There is some overlap between student accommodations for instruction and those for assessment, in large part because many exceptionalities call for the same or similar accommodations for both instruction and testing. In all cases, the purpose of accommodations is to minimize the effect of student attributes that are not related to the primary focus of the test. The goal is to provide an accommodation that will provide the student a fair chance to show what he or she knows, unencumbered by the exceptionality.

Accommodations can be made by modifying the format of presentation or response or the setting or timing of a test.

Student accommodations in testing can be divided into four general categories: modifying the presentation format of the test, modifying the response format of the test, modifying test timing, and modifying test setting. Following are common examples of accommodations in these four areas. The specific accommodations required for a given student will be guided by his or her Individual Education Plan (IEP).

Modifying the Presentation Format

➤ Read directions for each test section; read slowly.

➤ Provide verbal or oral directions as needed.

➤ Present directions as a sequence of steps for the student to follow.

➤ Have student repeat directions to ensure understanding.

➤ Read test questions aloud.

➤ Spread items over the page; put each sentence on a single line.

➤ Present test in Braille, large print, sign language, native language, or bilingually.

➤ Revise or simplify reading level.

Modifying the Response Format

➤ Allow dictionaries, texts, or calculators.

➤ Allow responses in Braille, large print, sign language, native language, or tape recording.

➤ Provide verbal prompts to items.

➤ Provide a scribe to write student answers.

➤ Provide examples of expected test responses as a model.

➤ Give student an outline for essay items.

➤ Include definitions or formulas for the student; allow the use of notes for reference.

➤ Double-check student's understanding of the items and desired responses.

➤ Make the test similar to what was taught during instruction.

Modifying Test Timing

➤ Provide extra time.

➤ Avoid timed tests.

➤ Test over a period of discrete testing sessions.

➤ Give extra breaks during testing.

Modifying Test Setting

➤ Test in a separate and quiet location.

➤ Seat student away from distractions.

➤ Test one-on-one.

There are, of course, many other accommodations that can be applied to provide valid assessment of students with exceptionalities, but this list provides a useful beginning for our exploration into this area. One additional issue requires attention. The above accommodations are generally those that all students in a classroom will notice during a test. Teachers should try not to bring undue attention to students with exceptionalities during testing. For example, teachers could confer privately with students with exceptionalities when setting up needed accommodations. They can make the modified test similar in appearance to the regular test. They can try to be unobtrusive when helping students with exceptionalities during testing and try to monitor all students in the same way. The aim of such practices is to be sensitive to embarrassment to students with exceptionalities during testing and avoid it as much as possible.

In sum, the Ontario Secondary School Teachers' Federation has made recommendations with respect to student testing. Here are excerpts from the "Ten Ways Teachers Test Effectively—Success for All Students." (Note Recommendation 6.)

Teachers know these are the effective ways to evaluate their students:

1. Tests are only one tool teachers use to evaluate students' work in a course. Teachers design tests to fairly assess student progress.

2. Use of different methods of evaluation provides students with several opportunities and a variety of ways to demonstrate their learning. Assessment instructions are based on students' daily classroom experience.

3. Students who are absent from tests or other evaluated activities have opportunities to write the test or complete an alternate activity upon their return to class.

4. Students get their tests and assignments back. They can review their marked exams. This helps to identify student strengths and weaknesses on which to plan next steps.

5. Teachers provide their students with marking schemes for tests and assignments. Students know how they will be evaluated.

6. *Teachers make accommodations for the identified physical and learning needs of students. Teachers' assessment practices for these students reflect the students' needs and learning styles.*

SOURCE: "Ten Ways Teachers Test Effectively—Success for All Students," Ontario Secondary School Teachers' Federation, www.osstf.on.ca/www/issues/studenttesting/10wayseffective.html.

TECHNOLOGY AND ASSESSMENT

Accommodating Students with Exceptionalities During Testing

For more information about accommodating students with exceptionalities during testing, visit Chapter 6 of the text Web site to link to the following resources.

http://canadian.cec.sped.org

Canadian Council for Exceptional Children (CCEC)

The CCEC belief has always been that students with special needs have the right to the highest quality education. The CCEC is committed to those who work with special students— educators, support personnel, and parents.

www.ldac-taac.ca/index-e.asp

Learning Disabilities Association of Canada (LDAC)

The LDAC provides understanding and support to people with learning disabilities, their parents, and teachers and other professionals. Working with a network of provincial/territorial and local partners, they provide information on learning disabilities, practical solutions, and tools for assisting students with learning disabilities.

Find links to these sites and others on our OLC at

www.mcgrawhill.ca/college/airasian.

CHAPTER REVIEW

CHAPTER REVIEW

Visit Chapter 6 of the Online Learning Centre at **www.mcgrawhill.ca/ college/airasian** to take chapter quizzes, link to related Web sites, and read PowerWeb articles and news feed updates, and access study tools, including the case study referenced in this chapter.

What considerations should teachers take into account in order to prepare students for tests?

➤ Do not teach students the exact items that will be on the test.

➤ Give students practice with question formats prior to testing.

➤ Bear in mind that there are times when students are able to perform better on tests than others.

➤ Give students information about the nature of the test.

What are three considerations for test administration?

➤ Physical setting—Students should have a quiet testing environment with minimal interruptions.

➤ Psychological setting—Reduce student anxiety by providing advance notice of a test, preparation, and review.

➤ Keeping track of time—Remind students of the test time remaining with announcements.

How do you as a teacher discourage cheating?

➤ Consider seating arrangements.

➤ Know common methods of student cheating.

➤ Carefully proctor during testing.

➤ Reprimand students who do cheat.

What is a guideline for scoring selected response items?

➤ Prepare an answer key and ensure that it is correct.

What are some guidelines for scoring short-answer and completion items?

➤ Prepare an answer key.

➤ Determine how factors such as spelling, grammar, and punctuation will be handled in scoring.

➤ Be prepared to consider unexpected responses and decide if these responses are the result of faulty test items or a lack of student learning.

What are some guidelines for scoring essay items?

➤ Define what constitutes a good answer and decide on the scoring method (analytic or holistic).

➤ Be alert to factors that might affect the objectivity of essay scoring such as students' writing style, grammar and spelling, neatness, scorer fatigue, prior performance, students' identity, and carryover effects.

➤ Ensure that the response scoring criteria matches the essay question.

➤ Tell students how handwriting, punctuation, spelling and organization will be scored.

➤ If possible, score students' tests anonymously.

➤ Score all responses to the first essay question before moving on to score succeeding questions.

➤ Read essay questions a second time after initial scoring.

Why should teachers perform after-test analyses?

➤ To identify and make scoring adjustments for any items that students' answers show were misunderstood or ambiguous.

➤ To identify ways to improve items for use on future tests.

What is the difficulty index and the discrimination index?

➤ The difficulty index of an item describes the proportion of students who answered the item correctly.

➤ The discrimination index describes how an individual item fares with students who scored high and low on the overall test.

What are the accommodations in testing that can be made for students with exceptionalities?

➤ Presentation format (read directions and test questions, simplify reading level).

➤ Response format (tape record responses, provide a scribe, provide models, outlines, or formuli).

➤ Test timing (provide extra time, give breaks, test over a period of days).

➤ Test setting (one-on-one, away from distractions).

QUESTIONS FOR DISCUSSION

1. What are some ways that scoring essay questions can be made more objective? What are some consequences of subjective essay scoring?

2. How can a teacher reduce students' test anxiety while maintaining their motivation to do well on a test?

3. How should a teacher respond to cheating? Should all forms of cheating be treated in the same way? What cautions should a teacher keep in mind before accusing a student of cheating?

4. Assume that you are teaching Grade 8 and you have a student who perpetually is absent due to illness on the day of a test. What would be your course of action to address this problem? Who will you seek assistance from to get information about the student? How will you approach the student about the problem?

5. Consider the recommended accommodations in testing that can be made for students with exceptionalities. Assume that you are teaching

Grade 10 Canadian history and you have a student with a reading disability. This student is reading and comprehending at a Grade 5 reading level. Specifically describe how you will exact some of these accommodations.

ACTIVITIES

1. Using information from Chapter 5, rewrite the following essay question to make it more focused for students. Then state a set of criteria you would use to judge the quality of your students' answers.

   "Compare the Conservative and the Liberal parties."

2. Talk to two teachers about how they deal with and prevent cheating on tests. Ask them specific questions about their proactive strategies.

3. In a small group, talk with your colleagues about types of cheating they have noticed and what can be done to reduce it. Generate a list of these brainstormed ideas and retain it with your notes on this chapter.

4. Assume that you are a Grade 12 science teacher. You have four classes that you teach (Class V—29 students, Class W—25 students, Class X—29 students, and Class Y—32 students). The total number of students across these four classes equals 115. You give your students a short multiple-choice 10-question quiz. The following table indicates the number of incorrect responses for each of the 10 questions for each of your four classes.

Difficulty Index Analysis—Quiz #1—October 3, 2006

Multiple-Choice Question	Class V (N = 29)	Class W (N = 25)	Class X (N = 29)	Class Y (N = 32)	Totals (N = 115)
1	1	1	1	3	6
2	0	0	0	1	1
3	5	1	2	2	10
4	4	2	5	4	15
5	7	6	4	8	25
6	0	0	0	0	0
7	0	1	1	2	4
8	0	0	0	0	0
9	0	3	0	2	5
10	4	3	3	4	14
	mean = ?%	mean = ?%	mean = ?%	mean = ?%	mean = ?%

   a. Calculate the means for each class and the overall mean across all classes. What conclusions do you draw from these means?

   b. Calculate the Difficulty Index for each test item. What conclusions do you draw about the degree of difficulty for each of these 10 questions?

CHAPTER 7

PERFORMANCE ASSESSMENTS

CHAPTER OBJECTIVES

After reading this chapter, you will be able to:

- Define anecdotal record, checklist, rating scale, rubric, performance criteria, portfolio, and other basic terms

- Contrast performance processes and performance products

- Contrast performance assessment with other assessment types

- Write well-stated performance criteria for a given process or performance

- Apply different scoring approaches for performance assessments

- Construct a scoring rubric

- Discuss portfolios and their use in assessment

- Identify strategies to improve the validity and reliability of classroom performance assessments

M s. Landers taught her Grade 9 science class a unit on microscopes. She taught her students how to set up, focus, and use a microscope. Each student used a microscope to identify and draw pictures of three or four objects on glass slides. At the end of the unit, she assessed the students' achievement by giving a paper-and-pencil test that asked them to label parts of a diagrammed microscope and answer multiple-choice questions about the history of the microscope.

This example illustrates an important limitation of many paper-and-pencil tests: they allow teachers to assess some, but not all, important learning outcomes. Ms. Landers relied solely on tests that measured *knowledge of performance* (remember factual knowledge), but not the ability to actually *perform the skill* (apply procedural knowledge).

This chapter describes **performance assessment**, which is any form of assessment in which students carry out an activity or produce a product in order to demonstrate learning. This chapter tells how to develop such assessments and discusses their pros and cons, including questions of validity and reliability.

THE GENERAL ROLE OF PERFORMANCE ASSESSMENTS

Performance assessments allow students to demonstrate what they know and can do in a real situation. Performance assessments are also called alternative and authentic assessments.

There are many classroom situations for which valid assessment requires that teachers gather formal information about students' performances or products. Teachers collect student products such as written stories, paintings, lab reports, and science fair projects, as well as performances such as giving a speech, holding a pencil, typing, and cooperating in groups. Generally, products produce tangible outcomes—things you can hold in your hand—while performances are things you observe or listen to.

Performance assessments may also be called alternative or authentic assessments. They permit students to show what they can do in real situations (Wiggins, 1992). The difference between describing how a skill should be performed and actually knowing how to perform it is an important distinction in classroom assessment.

Some types of paper-and-pencil test items can be used to provide information about the thinking processes that underlie students' performance. For example, a math problem in which students have to show their work provides insight into the mental processes used to solve the problem. An essay question can show students' organizational skills, thought processes, and application of capitalization and punctuation rules. These two forms of paper-and-pencil test items can assess what students can do as opposed to the majority of paper-and-pencil test questions that reveal what students know. With most selected and constructed response questions, the teacher observes the *result* of the student's intellectual process, but not the thinking process that produced the result. If the student gets a multiple-choice, true-false, matching, or completion item correct, the teacher *assumes* that the student must have followed the correct process, but there is little direct evidence to support this assumption, since the only evidence of the student's thought process is a circled letter or a single written word. On the other hand, essays and other constructed response items provide a product that shows how students think about and construct their responses. They permit the teacher to see the logic of arguments, the manner in which the response is organized, and the basis of conclusions drawn by the student (Bartz, Anderson-Robinson, & Hillman, 1994). Thus, paper-and-pencil assessments like stories, reports, or "show-your-work" problems are important forms of performance assessments. Table 7.1 shows some of the differences between selected response test items, essays, oral questions, and performance assessments.

Chapters 2 and 4 discussed how teachers observe their students' performance in order to learn about them and also to obtain information about the moment-to-moment success of their instruction. Such observations are primarily informal and spontaneous. In this chapter, we are concerned with assessing more formal, structured performances and products, those that the teacher plans in advance, helps each student to perform, and formally assesses. These assessments can take place during normal classroom instruction (e.g., oral reading activities, setting up laboratory equipment) or in some special situation set up to elicit a performance (e.g., giving a speech in an auditorium). In either case, the activity is formally structured—the teacher arranges the conditions in which the performance or product is demonstrated and judged. Such assessments permit each student to show his or her mastery of the same process or task, something that is impossible with informal observation of spontaneous classroom performance and events.

PERFORMANCE ASSESSMENT IN SCHOOLS

The amount of attention that has recently been focused on performance assessment in classrooms might lead one to believe that it is new and untried. But, in actuality, performance assessment has been used in classrooms for a very long time. Its growth in popularity may be attributed to a number of factors (Ryan & Miyasaka, 1995; Quality Counts, 1999). First, performance assessment has been proposed or mandated in schools and districts across Canada. Second, increased classroom emphasis on problem solving, higher-level thinking, and real-world reasoning skills has created a reliance on performance and product assessments to demonstrate student learning. Third, performance assessments can provide some students who do poorly on selected response tests with an opportunity to show their achievement in alternative ways. Visit the text OLC (www.mcgrawhill.ca/college/airasian) for an example of a performance assessment task designed by a beginning teacher.

Performance assessments reflect the recent emphasis on real-world problem solving.

TABLE 7.1 Comparison of Various Types of Assessments

	Selected Response Test	Essay	Oral Question	Performance Assessment
Purpose	Sample knowledge with maximum efficiency and reliability	Assess thinking skills and/or mastery of how a body of knowledge is structured	Assess knowledge during instruction	Assess ability to translate knowledge and understanding into action
Student's Response	Read, evaluate, select	Organize, compose	Oral answer	Plan, construct, and deliver an original response
Major Advantage	Efficiency—can administer many items per unit of testing time	Can measure complex cognitive outcomes	Joins assessment and instruction	Provides rich evidence of performance skills
Influence on Learning	Overemphasis on recall encourages memorization; can encourage thinking skills if properly constructed	Encourages thinking and development of writing skills	Stimulates participation in instruction, provides teacher immediate feedback on effectiveness of teaching	Emphasizes use of available skill and knowledge in relevant problem contexts

SOURCE: Adapted from R. J. Stiggins, "Design and Development of Performance Assessments," *Educational Measurement: Issues and Practice,* 1987, 6(3), p. 35. Copyright 1987 by the National Council on Measurement in Education. Adapted by permission of the publisher.

Performance-Oriented Subjects

Assessing students' understanding of concepts through hands-on demonstrations is becoming more common.

There is a growing emphasis on using performance assessment to determine students' understanding of the concepts they are taught and measure their ability to apply procedural knowledge. The argument is that if students really grasp a concept or process, they can explain and use it to solve real-life problems. For example, after teaching students about money and making change, the teacher may assess learning by having students count out the money needed to purchase objects from the classroom "store" or act as storekeeper and make change for other students' purchases. Or, rather than giving a multiple-choice test on the chemical reactions that help identify unknown substances, the teacher could give students an unknown substance and have them go through the process of identifying it. These kinds of hands-on demonstrations of concept mastery are growing in popularity.

Teachers also constantly assess students' feelings, values, attitudes, and emotions. When a teacher checks the "satisfactory" rating under the category "works hard" or "obeys school rules" on a student's report card, the teacher bases this judgment on observations of the student's performance. Teachers rely upon observations of student performance to collect evidence about important behaviours such as getting along with peers, working independently, following rules, and self-control.

DEVELOPING PERFORMANCE ASSESSMENTS

A diving competition is an instructive example of a skill that is assessed by a performance assessment. Submitting a written essay describing how to perform various dives or answering a multiple-choice test about diving rules are hardly appropriate ways to demonstrate one's diving *performance.* Rather, a valid assessment of diving performance requires seeing the diver actually perform. To make the assessment reliable, the diver must perform a series of dives, not just one.

Diving judges rate dives using a scale that has 21 possible numerical scores that can be awarded (e.g., 0.0, 0.5, 1.0 . . . 5.5, 6.0, 6.5, . . . 9.0, 9.5, 10.0). They observe a very complicated performance made up of many body movements that together take about 2 seconds to complete. The judges do not have the benefit of slow motion or instant replay to review the performance and they cannot discuss the dive with one another. If their attention strays for even a second, they miss a large portion of the performance. Yet, when the scores are flashed on the scoreboard the judges inevitably are in very close agreement. Rarely do all judges give a dive the exact same score, but rarely is there more than a 1-point difference between any two judges' scores. This is amazing agreement among observers for such a short, complicated performance.

With this example in mind, let's consider the four essential features of all formal performance assessments, whether it be a diving competition, an oral speech, a book report, a typing exercise, a science fair project, or something else. This overview will then be followed by a more extensive discussion of each feature. Briefly, every performance assessment should:

1. Have a clear purpose that identifies the decision to be made from the performance assessment.
2. Identify observable aspects of the student's performance or product that can be judged.
3. Provide an appropriate setting for eliciting and judging the performance or product.
4. Provide a judgment or score to describe performance.

Define the Purpose of Assessment

In a diving competition, the purpose of the assessment is to rank each diver's performance in order to identify the best divers. Each dive receives a score and the highest total score wins the competition. Suppose, however, that dives were being performed during practice, prior to a competition. The diver's coach would observe the practice dives, but the coach's main concern would be not with the overall dive, but with examining the many specific features of each dive that the judges will score during a competition. Consequently, the coach would "score" the practice dive formatively, identifying the diver's strengths and weaknesses for all aspects of each dive. The specific areas in which the diver was weak would likely be emphasized in practice.

Performances and products are normally broken down into specific, observable criteria, each of which can be judged independently.

Performance assessments are particularly suited to such diagnosis because they can provide information about how a student performs each of the specific criteria that make up a more general performance or product. This criterion-by-criterion assessment makes it easy to identify the strong and weak points of a student's performance. When the performance criteria are stated in terms of observable student behaviours or product characteristics, as they should be, remediation is made easy. Each suggestion for improvement can be described in specific terms—for example, "report to group project area on time," "wait your turn to speak," "do your share of the group work."

Performance assessments are particularly suited to diagnosis because they provide information about how students perform each specific criterion in a general performance.

Teachers use performance assessment for many purposes: grading students' work, constructing portfolios of student work, diagnosing student learning, helping students recognize the important steps in a performance or product, providing concrete examples of student work for parent conferences. Whatever the purpose of performance assessment, it should be specified at the beginning of the assessment process so that proper performance criteria and scoring procedures can be established.

Teachers need to think ahead about whether a performance assessment's purposes will be formative or summative because their judgment task is very different depending on which is the case. When the goal of assessment is formative, the focus is on giving feedback to students about their strengths and weaknesses for reinvestment. When the goal is summative, the focus is on rating the ultimate level of achievement for administrative purposes.

Identify Performance Criteria

Performance criteria are the specific behaviours a student should display in properly carrying out a performance or creating a product. They are at the heart of successful performance assessment, yet they are the area in which most judgment problems occur.

When teachers first think about assessing performance, they tend to think in terms of general performances such as oral reading, giving a speech, following safety rules in the laboratory, printing or handwriting, writing a book report, organizing ideas, or getting along with peers. In reality, such performances cannot be assessed until they are broken down into the more specific aspects or characteristics that comprise them. These narrow aspects and characteristics are the performance criteria that teachers will observe and judge.

Key Assessment Tools 7.1 shows three sets of criteria for assessing students' performance when (1) working in groups, (2) playing the piano, and (3) writing a book report. Criteria such as these focus teachers' instruction and assessments in the same way that diving criteria enable judges to evaluate diving performance. Notice how the performance criteria clearly identify the important aspects of the performance or product being assessed. Well-stated performance criteria are at the heart of successful efforts to instruct and assess performances and products.

To define performance criteria, a teacher must first decide if a process or a product will be observed. Will processes such as typing or oral reading be assessed, or will products such as a typed letter or book report be assessed? In the former case, criteria are needed to judge the student's actual performance of targeted criteria; in the latter, criteria are needed to judge the end product of those behaviours. In some cases, both process and

Performance criteria can focus on processes, products, or both.

KEY ASSESSMENT TOOLS 7.1

Examples of Performance Criteria

Working in Groups	Playing the Piano	Writing a Book Report
Reports to group project area on time	Sits upright with feet on floor (or pedal, when necessary)	States the author and title
Starts work on own	Arches fingers on keys	Identifies the type of book (fiction, adventure, historical, etc.)
Shares information	Plays without pauses or interruptions	Describes what the book was about in four or more sentences
Contributes ideas	Maintains even tempo	
Listens to others	Plays correct notes	States an opinion of the book
Waits turn to speak	Holds all note values for indicated duration	Gives three reasons to support the opinion
Follows instructions		
Courteous to other group members	Follows score dynamics (forte, crescendo, decrescendo)	Uses correct spelling, punctuation, and capitalization
Helps to solve group problems	Melody can be heard above other harmonization	
Considers viewpoints of others		
Carries out share of group-determined activities	Phrases according to score (staccato and legato)	
Completes assigned tasks on time	Follows score pedal markings	

product can be assessed. For example, a Grade 1 teacher assessed both process and product when she (1) observed a student writing to determine how the student held the pencil, positioned the paper, and manipulated the pencil and (2) judged the finished, handwritten product to assess how well the student formed his letters. Notice that the teacher observed different things according to whether she was interested in the student's handwriting *process* or handwriting *product*. It is for this reason that teachers must know what they want to observe before performance criteria can be identified.

The key to identifying performance criteria is to break down an overall performance or product into its component parts. It is these parts that will be observed and judged. Consider, for example, a product assessment of Grade 8 students' written paragraphs. The purpose of the assessment is to judge students' ability to write a paragraph on a topic of their choice. In preparing to judge the completed paragraph, a teacher initially listed the following performance criteria:

➤ First sentence
➤ Appropriate topic sentence
➤ Good supporting ideas
➤ Good vocabulary
➤ Complete sentences
➤ Capitalization
➤ Spelling
➤ Conclusion
➤ Handwriting

These performance criteria do identify important areas of a written paragraph, but the areas are vague and poorly stated. What, for example, is meant by "first sentence"? What is an "appropriate" topic sentence or "good" vocabulary? What should be examined in judging capitalization, spelling, and handwriting? If a teacher cannot answer these questions, how can he or she provide suitable examples or instruction for students? Performance criteria need to be specific enough to focus the teacher on well-defined characteristics of the performance or product. They must also be specific enough to permit the teacher to convey to students, in terms they can understand, the specific features that define the desired performance or product. Once defined, the criteria permit consistent teacher assessments of performance and consistent communication with students about their learning.

Following is a revised version of the performance criteria for a well-organized paragraph. Note the difference in clarity and how the revised version focuses the teacher and students on very specific features of the paragraph—ones that are important and will be assessed. Before assigning the task, the teacher wisely decided to share and discuss the performance criteria with the students.

➤ Indents first sentence.

➤ Topic sentence sets main idea of paragraph.

➤ Following sentences support main idea.

➤ Sentences arranged in logical order.

➤ Uses age-appropriate vocabulary.

➤ Writes in complete sentences.

➤ Capitalizes proper nouns and first words in sentences.

➤ Makes no more than three spelling errors.

➤ Conclusion follows logically from prior sentences.

➤ Handwriting is legible.

Cautions in Developing Performance Criteria

Three points of caution are appropriate here. First, it is important to understand that the previous example of performance criteria is not the only one that describes the characteristics of a well-written paragraph. Different teachers might identify varying criteria that they feel are more important or more suitable for their students than some of the ones in our example. Thus, emphasis should not be upon identifying the best or only set of criteria for a performance or product, but rather upon stating criteria that are meaningful, important, and can be understood by the students.

Second, it is possible to break down most school performances and products into many very narrow criteria. However, a lengthy list of performance criteria becomes ineffective because teachers rarely have the time to observe and assess a large number of very specific performance criteria for each student. Too many criteria make the observation process intrusive, with the teacher hovering over the student, rapidly checking off behaviours, and often interfering with a student's performance.

Very long lists of performance criteria (over 15) become unmanageable and intrusive.

For classroom performance assessment to be manageable and meaningful, a balance must be established between specificity and practicality. The key to attaining this balance is to identify the *essential* criteria associated with a performance or product; 6 to 12 performance criteria are a manageable number for most classroom teachers to emphasize.

Third, the process of identifying performance criteria is an ongoing one that is rarely completed after the first attempt. Initial performance criteria will need to be revised and clarified, based on experience from their use, to provide the focus needed for valid and reliable assessment. To aid this process, teachers should think about the performance or product they wish to observe and reflect on its key aspects. They can also examine a few actual products or performances as bases for revising their initial list of criteria.

The following list shows the initial set of performance criteria a teacher wrote to assess students' oral reports.

➤ Speaks clearly and slowly.

➤ Pronounces correctly.

➤ Makes eye contact.

➤ Exhibits good posture when presenting.

➤ Exhibits good effort.

➤ Presents with feeling.

➤ Understands the topic.

➤ Exhibits enthusiastic attitude.

➤ Organizes.

Like other writing assignments, good performance criteria need to be revised and clarified over time.

Note the lack of specificity in many of the criteria: "slowly," "correctly," "good," "understands," and "enthusiastic attitude." These criteria hide more than they reveal. After reflecting on and observing a few oral presentations, the teacher revised and sharpened the performance criteria as shown in the following list. Note that the teacher first divided the general performance into three areas (physical expression, vocal expression, and verbal expression) and then identified a few important performance criteria within each of these areas. It is not essential to divide the performance criteria into separate sections, but sometimes it is useful in focusing the teacher and students.

1. Physical expression

   ➤ Stands straight and faces audience.

   ➤ Changes facial expression with changes in tone of the report.

   ➤ Maintains eye contact with audience.

2. Vocal expression

   ➤ Speaks in a steady, clear voice.

   ➤ Varies tone to emphasize points.

   ➤ Speaks loudly enough to be heard by audience.

   ➤ Paces words in an even flow.

   ➤ Enunciates each word.

3. Verbal expression

   ➤ Chooses precise words to convey meaning.

   ➤ Avoids unnecessary repetition.

   ➤ States sentences with complete thoughts or ideas.

   ➤ Organizes information logically.

   ➤ Summarizes main points at conclusion.

Developing Observable Performance Criteria

The value of performance assessments depends on identifying performance criteria that can be observed and judged.

The value and richness of performance and product assessments depend heavily on identifying performance criteria that can be observed and judged. It is important that the criteria be clear in the teacher's mind and that the students be taught the criteria. The following guidelines should prove useful for this purpose.

1. *Select the performance or product to be assessed and either perform it yourself or imagine yourself performing it.* Think to yourself, "What would I have to do in order to complete this task? What steps would I have to follow?" It isn't a bad idea to actually carry out the performance yourself, recording and studying your performance or product.

2. *List the important aspects of the performance or product.* What specific behaviours or attributes are most important to the successful completion of the task? What behaviours have been emphasized in instruction? Include important aspects and exclude the irrelevant ones.

3. *Try to limit the number of performance criteria, so they all can be observed during a student's performance.* This is less important when one is assessing a product, but even then it is better to assess a limited number of key criteria than a large number that vary widely. Remember, you will have to observe and judge performance on each of the criteria identified.

4. *If possible, have groups of teachers think through the important criteria included in a task.* Because all Grade 1 teachers assess oral reading in their classrooms and because the criteria for successful oral reading do not differ much from one Grade 1 classroom to another, a group effort to define performance criteria will likely save time and produce a more complete set of criteria than that produced by any single teacher. Similar group efforts are useful for other common performances or products such as book reports and science fair projects.

5. *Express the performance criteria in terms of observable student behaviours or product characteristics.* Be specific when stating the performance criteria. For example, do not write "The child works." Instead, write "The child remains focused on the task for at least 4 minutes." Instead of "organization," write " Information is presented in a logical sequence."

6. *Do not use ambiguous words that cloud the meaning of the performance criteria.* The worst offenders in this regard are adverbs that end in *ly*. Other words to avoid are "good" and "appropriate." Thus, criteria such as "appropriate organization," "speaks correct*ly*," "writes neat*ly*," and "performs graceful*ly*" are ambiguous and leave interpretation of performance up to the observer. The observer's interpretation may vary from time to time and from student to student, diminishing the fairness and usefulness of the assessment.

7. *Arrange the performance criteria in the order in which they are likely to be observed.* This will save time when observing and will maintain primary focus on the performance.

8. *Check for existing performance criteria before defining your own.* The performance criteria associated with giving an oral speech, reading aloud, using a microscope, writing a persuasive paragraph, cutting with scissors, and the like have been listed by many people. No

When teachers within a school develop similar performance criteria across grade levels, it is reinforcing to students.

one who reads this book will be the first to try to assess these and most other common school performances. The moral here is that one need not reinvent the wheel every time a wheel is needed.

Regardless of the particular performance or product assessed, clearly stated performance criteria are critical to the success of both instruction and assessment. The criteria define the important aspects of a performance or product, guide what students should be taught, and produce a focus for both the teacher and student when assessing performance. Clear performance criteria are needed, and the tasks used to teach and assess the desired performance should be aligned to the criteria (McTighe, 1996).

Provide a Setting to Elicit and Observe the Performance

Teachers may observe and assess naturally occurring classroom behaviours or set up situations in which they assess carefully structured performances.

Once the performance criteria are defined, a setting in which to observe the performance or product must be selected or established. Depending on the nature of the performance or product, the teacher may observe behaviours as they naturally occur in the classroom or set up a specific situation in which the students must perform. There are two considerations in deciding whether to observe naturally occurring behaviours or to set up a more controlled exercise: (1) the frequency with which the performance naturally occurs in the classroom and (2) the seriousness of the decision to be made.

Formally structured performance assessments are needed when teachers are dealing with low-frequency behaviours and making important decisions.

If the performance occurs infrequently during normal classroom activity, it may be more efficient to structure a situation in which students must perform the desired behaviours. For example, in the normal flow of classroom activities, students rarely have the opportunity to give a planned 5-minute speech, so the teacher should set up an exercise in which each student must develop and give a 5-minute speech. Oral reading, on the other hand, occurs frequently enough in many elementary classrooms that performance can be observed as part of the normal flow of reading instruction.

The importance of the decision to be made from a performance assessment also influences the context in which observation takes place. In general the more important the decision, the more structured the assessment environment should be. A course grade, for example, represents an important decision about a student. If performance assessments contribute to grading, evidence should be gathered under structured, formal circumstances so that every student has a fair and equal chance to exhibit his or her achievement. The validity of the assessment is likely to be improved when the setting is similar and familiar to all students.

Regardless of the nature of the assessment, evidence obtained from a single assessment describes only one example of a student's performance. For a variety of reasons such as illness, home problems, or other distractions, student performance at a single time may not provide a reliable indication of the student's true achievement. To be certain that one has an accurate indication of what a student can and cannot do, multiple observations and products are useful. If the different observations produce similar performance, a teacher can have confidence in the evidence and use it in decision making. If different observations contradict one another, more information should be obtained.

Multiple observations of student performances provide more reliable and accurate information.

Develop a Score to Describe the Performance

The final step in performance assessment is to score students' performance. As in previous steps, the nature of the decision to be made influences the judgmental system used. Scoring a performance assessment can be holistic or analytic, just like scoring an essay question. In situations such as group placement, selection, or grading, holistic scoring is most useful. To make such decisions, a teacher seeks to describe an individual's performance using a single, overall score. On the other hand, if the assessment purpose is to diagnose student difficulties or certify student mastery of each individual performance criterion, then analytic scoring, with a separate score or rating on each performance criterion, is appropriate. In either case, the performance criteria dictate the scoring or rating approach that is adopted.

Holistic scoring (a single overall score) is good for such things as group placement or grading; analytic scoring (scoring individual criteria) is useful in diagnosing student difficulties.

In most classrooms, the teacher is both the observer and the scorer. In situations where an important decision is to be made, additional observers/scorers may be added. Thus, it is common for performance assessments in athletic, music, debate, and art competitions to have more than a single judge in order to make scoring more fair.

A number of options exist for collecting, recording, and summarizing observations of student performance: anecdotal records, checklists, rating scales, and rubrics, and portfolios. The following sections explore these options in detail.

ANECDOTAL RECORDS, CHECKLISTS, AND RATING SCALES

Anecdotal Records

Written accounts of significant, individual student events and behaviours the teacher has observed are called **anecdotal records**. Only those observations that have special significance and that cannot be obtained from other classroom assessment methods should be included in an anecdotal record. Figure 7.1 shows an example of an anecdotal record of student Lynn Gregory. Notice that it provides information about the learner, the date of observation, the name of the teacher observing, and a factual description of the event.

FIGURE 7.1
Anecdotal Record for Lynn Gregory.

STUDENT   *Lynn Gregory*   DATE   *9/22/2006*

OBSERVER   *J. Ricketts*

All term Lynn has been quiet and passive, rarely interacting w/classmates in class or on the playground. Today Lynn suddenly "opened up" and wanted continual interaction w/classmates. She could not settle down, kept circulating around the room until she became bothersome to me and her classmates. I tried to settle her down, but was unsuccessful.

Most teachers have difficulty identifying particular events or behaviours that merit inclusion in an anecdotal record. What is significant and important in the life of a student is not always apparent at the time an event or behaviour occurs. From the hundreds of observations made each day, how is a teacher to select the one that might be important enough to write down? It may take many observations over many days to recognize which events really are significant. Moreover, anecdotal records are time-consuming to prepare and need to be written up soon after the event or behaviour is observed, while it is fresh in the teacher's mind. This is not always possible. For these reasons, anecdotal records are not used extensively by teachers. This does not mean that teachers do not observe and judge classroom events—we know they do. It simply means that they seldom write down descriptions of these events.

Anecdotal records are written accounts of significant events and behaviours the teacher has observed in a student.

Checklists

A checklist, which is a written list of performance criteria, can be used repeatedly over time to diagnose strengths, weaknesses, and changes in performances.

A **checklist** is a written list of performance criteria. As a student's performance is observed or product judged, the scorer determines whether the performance or the product meets each performance criterion. If it does, a checkmark is placed next to that criterion, indicating that it was observed; if it does not, the checkmark is omitted. Figure 7.2 shows a completed checklist for Rick Gray's oral presentation. The performance criteria for this checklist were presented earlier in this chapter.

Checklists are diagnostic, reusable, and capable of charting student progress. They provide a detailed record of students' performances, one that can and should be shown to students to help them see where improvement is needed. Rick Gray's teacher could sit down with him after his presentation and point out both the criteria on which he performed well and the areas that need improvement. Because it focuses on specific performances, a checklist provides diagnostic information. The same checklist can be reused, with different students or with the same student over time. Using the same checklist more than once is an easy way to obtain information about a student's improvement over time.

FIGURE 7.2   *Checklist Results for an Oral Presentation*

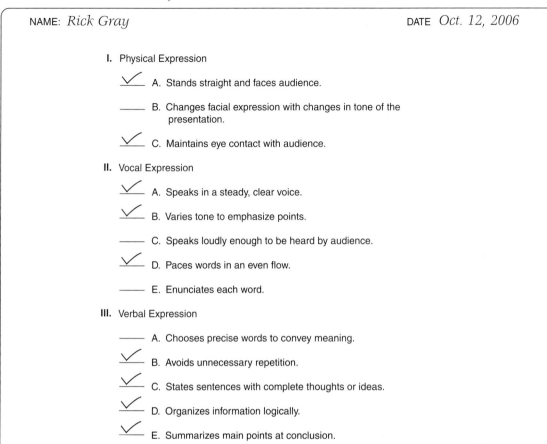

NAME: *Rick Gray*   DATE *Oct. 12, 2006*

I. Physical Expression

    ✓ A. Stands straight and faces audience.

    _____ B. Changes facial expression with changes in tone of the presentation.

    ✓ C. Maintains eye contact with audience.

II. Vocal Expression

    ✓ A. Speaks in a steady, clear voice.

    ✓ B. Varies tone to emphasize points.

    _____ C. Speaks loudly enough to be heard by audience.

    ✓ D. Paces words in an even flow.

    _____ E. Enunciates each word.

III. Verbal Expression

    _____ A. Chooses precise words to convey meaning.

    ✓ B. Avoids unnecessary repetition.

    ✓ C. States sentences with complete thoughts or ideas.

    ✓ D. Organizes information logically.

    ✓ E. Summarizes main points at conclusion.

There are, however, disadvantages associated with checklists. One important disadvantage is that checklists give a teacher only two choices for each criterion: performed or not performed. A checklist provides no middle ground for scoring. Suppose that Rick Gray stood straight and faced the audience most of the time during his oral presentation, or paced his words evenly except in one brief part of the speech when he spoke too quickly and ran his words together. How should his teacher score him on these performance criteria? Should Rick receive a check because he did them most of the time, or should he not receive a check because his performance was flawed? Sometimes this is not an easy choice. A checklist forces the teacher to make an absolute decision for each performance criterion, even though a student's performance is somewhere between these extremes.

A second disadvantage of checklists is the difficulty of summarizing a student's performance into a single score. We saw how useful checklists can be for diagnosing students' strengths and weaknesses. But what if a

Checklists cannot record gradations in performances.

teacher wants to summarize performance across a number of criteria to arrive at a single score for grading purposes?

One way to summarize Rick's performance into a single score is to translate the number of performance criteria he successfully demonstrated into a percentage. For example, there were 13 performance criteria on the oral presentation checklist and Rick demonstrated 9 of them during his presentation. Assuming each criterion is equally important, Rick's performance translates into a score of 69 percent ($9/13 \times 100 = 69\%$). Thus, Rick demonstrated 69 percent of the desired performance criteria. (In Chapter 8 we will discuss the way scores like Rick's 69 percent are turned into grades.)

A second, and better, way to summarize performance would be for the teacher to set up standards for rating students' performance. Suppose Rick's teacher set up the following set of standards:

Excellent	12 or 13	performance criteria shown
Good	9 to 11	performance criteria shown
Fair	5 to 8	performance criteria shown
Poor	5 or less	performance criteria shown

Summarizing performances from a checklist can be done by setting up rating standards or by calculating the percentage of criteria accomplished.

These standards allow the teacher to summarize performance on a scale that goes from excellent to poor. The scale could also go from a grade of A to one of D, depending on the type of scoring the teacher uses. The same standard would be used to summarize each student's performance. Rick performed 9 of the 13 criteria, and the teacher's standard indicates that his performance should be classified as "good" or "B." Of course, there are many such standards that can be set up and the one shown is only an example. In establishing standards, it is advisable to keep the summarizing rules as simple as possible.

Rating Scales

Although they are similar to checklists, **rating scales** allow the observer to judge performance along a continuum rather than as a dichotomy. Both checklists and rating scales are based upon a set of performance criteria, and it is common for the same set of performance criteria to be used in both a rating scale and a checklist. However, a checklist gives the observer two categories for judging, while a rating scale gives more than two.

The three most common types of rating scales are numerical, graphic, and descriptive (also called scoring rubrics).

Three of the most common types of rating scales are the numerical, graphic, and descriptive scales. Figure 7.3 shows an example of each of these scales as applied to two specific performance criteria for giving an oral presentation. In numerical scales, a number stands for a point on the rating scale. Thus, in the example, "1" corresponds to the student *always* performing the behaviour, "2" to the student *usually* performing the behaviour, and so on. Graphic scales require the rater to mark a position on a line divided into sections based upon a scale. The rater marks an "X" at that point on the line that best describes the student's performance. Descriptive rating scales, also called **scoring rubrics** (see pages 166–173 also), require the rater to choose among different descriptions of actual performance (Wiggins & McTighe, 1998; Goodrich, 1997). In descriptive rating scales, different descriptions are used to represent different levels of student performance. To score, the teacher picks the description that comes closest to the student's actual performance. A judgment of the teacher determines the grade.

Regardless of the type of rating scale one chooses, two general rules will improve their use. The first rule is to limit the number of rating categories. There is a tendency to think that the greater the number of rating categories to choose from, the better the rating scale. In practice, this is not the case. Few observers can make reliable discriminations in performance across more than five rating categories. Adding a larger number of categories on a rating scale is likely to make the ratings less, not more, reliable. Stick to three to five well-defined and distinct rating scale points, as shown in Figure 7.3.

The second rule is to use the same rating scale for each performance criterion. This is not usually possible in descriptive rating scales where the descriptions vary with each performance criterion. For numerical and graphic scales, however, it is best to select a single rating scale and use it for all performance criteria. Using many different rating categories requires the observer to change focus frequently and will decrease rating accuracy by distracting the rater's attention from the performance.

Figure 7.4 shows a complete set of numerical rating scales for Sarah Jackson for an oral presentation. Note that its performance criteria are identical to those on the checklist shown in Figure 7.2. The only difference between the checklist and the numerical rating scales is the way performance is scored.

While rating scales provide more categories for assessing a student's performance, and thereby provide detailed diagnostic information, the multiple rating categories complicate the process of summarizing performance across criteria to arrive at a student's overall score. With a checklist, summarization is reduced to giving credit for checked criteria and no credit for unchecked criteria. This cannot be done with a rating scale because performance is judged in terms of *degree,* not presence or absence. A teacher must treat ratings of "always," "usually," "seldom, and "never" differently from each other, or there is no point to having the different rating categories.

Numerical summarization is the most straightforward and commonly used approach to summarizing performance on rating scales. It assigns a point value to each category in the scale and sums the points across the performance criteria. For example, consider Sarah Jackson's ratings in Figure 7.4. To obtain a summary score for Sarah's performance, one can assign 4 points to a rating of "always," 3 points to a rating of "usually," 2 points to a rating of "seldom," and 1 point to a rating of "never." The numbers 4, 3, 2, and 1 match the four possible ratings for each performance cri-

Descriptive rating scales, or scoring rubrics, require the rater to choose among different descriptions of actual performance.

Having too many scales tends to distract the rater from the performance, making the ratings unreliable.

Whereas checklists measure only the presence or absence of some performance, a rating scale measures the degree to which the performance matches the criteria.

FIGURE 7.3   *Three Types of Rating Scale for an Oral Presentation.*

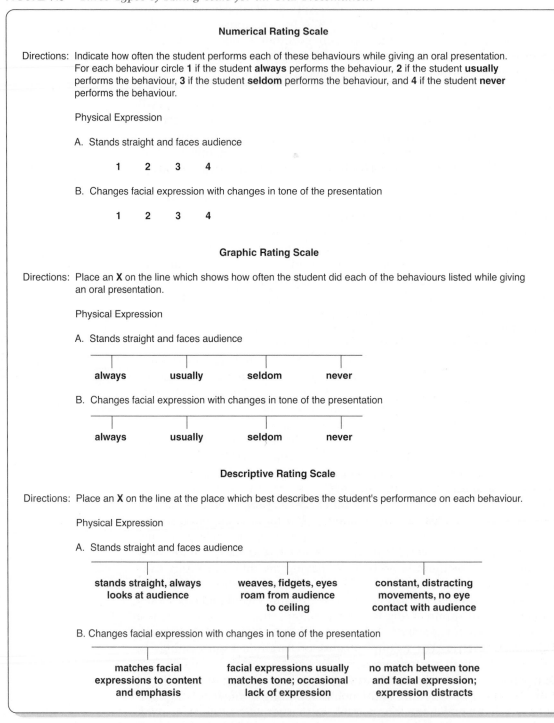

Numerical Rating Scale

Directions: Indicate how often the student performs each of these behaviours while giving an oral presentation. For each behaviour circle **1** if the student **always** performs the behaviour, **2** if the student **usually** performs the behaviour, **3** if the student **seldom** performs the behaviour, and **4** if the student **never** performs the behaviour.

Physical Expression

A. Stands straight and faces audience

           1   2   3   4

B. Changes facial expression with changes in tone of the presentation

           1   2   3   4

Graphic Rating Scale

Directions: Place an **X** on the line which shows how often the student did each of the behaviours listed while giving an oral presentation.

Physical Expression

A. Stands straight and faces audience

      always   usually   seldom   never

B. Changes facial expression with changes in tone of the presentation

      always   usually   seldom   never

Descriptive Rating Scale

Directions: Place an **X** on the line at the place which best describes the student's performance on each behaviour.

Physical Expression

A. Stands straight and faces audience

      stands straight, always   weaves, fidgets, eyes   constant, distracting
        looks at audience   roam from audience   movements, no eye
                                            to ceiling   contact with audience

B. Changes facial expression with changes in tone of the presentation

        matches facial   facial expressions usually   no match between tone
      expressions to content   matches tone; occasional   and facial expression;
         and emphasis   lack of expression   expression distracts

FIGURE 7.4   *Types of Rating Scales.*

NAME: *Sarah Jackson*   DATE: *Nov. 8, 2006*

Directions: Indicate how often the student performs each of these behaviours while giving an oral presentation. For each behaviour **circle 4** if the student **always** performs the behaviour, **3** if the student **usually** performs the behaviour, **2** if the student **seldom** performs the behaviour, and **1** if the student **never** performs the behaviour.

I. Physical Expression

(4) 3 2 1   A. Stands straight and faces audience

4 3 (2) 1   B. Changes facial expression with changes in tone of the presentation

4 (3) 2 1   C. Maintains eye contact with audience

II. Vocal Expression

(4) 3 2 1   A. Speaks in a steady, clear voice

4 (3) 2 1   B. Varies tone to emphasize points

4 3 (2) 1   C. Speaks loudly enough to be heard by audience

4 (3) 2 1   D. Paces words in an even flow

4 3 (2) 1   E. Enunciates each word

III. Verbal Expression

4 3 (2) 1   A. Chooses precise words to convey meaning

4 (3) 2 1   B. Avoids unnecessary repetition

(4) 3 2 1   C. States sentences with complete thoughts or ideas

(4) 3 2 1   D. Organizes information logically

4 (3) 2 1   E. Summarizes main points at conclusion

terion, with 4 representing the most desirable response and 1 the least desirable. Thus, high scores indicate good performance. Note that before summarizing Sarah's performance into a single score, it is important for the teacher to identify areas of weakness so that Sarah can be guided to improve her oral presentations.

Sarah's total score, 39, can be determined by adding the circled numbers. The highest possible score on the rating scale is 52; if a student was rated "always" on each performance criterion, the student's total score would be 52 (4 points × 13 performance criteria). Thus, Sarah scored 39 out of a possible 52 points. In this manner, a total score can be determined for each student rated. This score can be turned into a percentage by dividing it by 52, the total number of points available (39/52 × 100 = 75%).

RUBRICS

Besides numerical summaries, scoring rubrics or descriptive summarizations provide another way to summarize performance. A rubric is a set of clear expectations or criteria used to help teachers and students focus on what is valued in a subject, topic, or activity. A rubric describes the level at which a student may be performing a process or completing a product. It focuses on academic work and is based on and linked to the teacher's curriculum. A rubric describes what is to be learned rather than on how to teach. It lays out criteria for different levels of performance, which are usually descriptive, rarely numerical.

Rubrics are useful to both teachers and students. Rubrics are helpful for teachers in the following ways:

➤ specifying criteria to focus instruction on what is important;

➤ specifying criteria to focus student assessments;

➤ increasing the consistency of assessments;

➤ limiting arguments over grading because of the clear criteria and scoring levels that reduce subjectivity; and

➤ providing descriptions of student performance that are informative to both parents and students.

In addition to providing teachers with an assessment measure, rubrics are also useful tools for students as they can help students by:

➤ clarifying the teacher's expectations about performance;

➤ pointing out what is important in a process or product;

➤ helping them to monitor and critique their own work;

➤ providing informative descriptions of performance; and

➤ providing clearer performance information than traditional letter grades provide.

Two Methods of Scoring

There are two basic methods of scoring rubrics, holistic and analytic, similar to essay scoring methods. Holistic scoring is used to assess the overall performance of a student across all the performance criteria. The teacher selects the description that most closely matches the student's overall performance on the process or product. Analytic scoring is used to assess individually each performance criterion stated in the rubric. Each criterion is rated separately using different levels of performance. Figure 7.5 illustrates a holistic scoring rubric for writing assessment. There are five scoring levels, each including multiple criteria. The assessor selects the scoring level

FIGURE 7.5 *An Example of a Holistic Scoring Rubric.*

5/5 Ideas are insightful and well considered. This writing has a strong central focus and is well organized. The organizational pattern is interesting, perhaps original, and provides the piece with an
introduction that hooks the reader and carries the piece through to a satisfying conclusion. The
writer has chosen appropriate details and established a definite point of view. Sentences are clear
and varied. Word choices are vivid. The writer's voice and tone consistently sustain the reader's
interest. If there are errors in mechanics, they are the result of the student taking a risk with more
complex or original aspects of writing.

4/5 Ideas are thoughtful and clear. This writing has a clear and recognizable focus. A standard organizational pattern is used, with clear introduction, transitions, and conclusion. A point of view is
established and a sense of audience is clear. The writer has used appropriate details, clear and correct sentence structures, and specific word choices. The writer's voice and tone maintain the
reader's interest. The few errors in mechanics do not impede communication or annoy the reader
unduly.

3/5 Ideas are straightforward and clear. This piece of writing has a recognizable focus, though there
may be superfluous information provided. The organizational pattern used is clear and includes a
basic introduction and conclusion though it may be formulaic or repetitive. The point of view is
clear and consistent. The word choices and sentence structures are clear but not imaginative. The
writer's voice and tone establish, but may not maintain, the reader's interest. The mechanics show
less effort and attention to proofreading than needed.

2/5 Ideas are limited and overgeneralized but discernible. This piece of writing has an inconsistent or
meandering focus. It is underdeveloped and lacks clear organization. Incorrect or missing transitions make it difficult to follow. There may be an introduction without a conclusion, or the
reverse, a conclusion with no introduction. The point of view is unclear and there are frequent
shifts in tense and person. The writer exhibits superficial and/or minimal awareness of the reader.
Mechanical errors interfere with the reader's understanding and pleasure.

1/5 Ideas are elementary and may not be clear. This piece of writing lacks focus and coherence. The
organizational pattern and development of the topic are confusing. Point of view may shift in a
confusing way. Mechanical errors are abundant and interfere with understanding. The piece must
be read several times to make sense of it. Awareness of the reader is not apparent.

that best describes the student's overall writing proficiency. Figure 7.6 provides an example of an analytic scoring rubric for speaking tasks. Each of
the six categories that are considered when assessing oral speaking proficiency is assessed separately. Each category is scored from 1 (low) to 4
(high).

FIGURE 7.6 *An Example of an Analytic Scoring Rubric.*

Task Completion
1. Minimal completion of the task and/or responses frequently inappropriate
2. Practical completion of the task, responses mostly appropriate yet undeveloped
3. Completion of the task, responses appropriate and adequately developed
4. Superior completion of the task, responses appropriate and with elaboration

Comprehensibility
1. Responses barely comprehensible
2. Responses mostly comprehensible, requiring interpretation on the part of the listener
3. Responses comprehensible, requiring minimal interpretation on the part of the listener
4. Responses readily comprehensible, requiring no interpretation on the part of the listener

Fluency
1. Speech halting and uneven with long pauses and/or incomplete thoughts
2. Speech choppy and/or slow with frequent pauses, few or no incomplete thoughts
3. Some hesitation but manages to continue and complete thoughts
4. Speech continuous with few pauses or stumbling

Pronunciation
1. Frequently interferes with communication
2. Occasionally interferes with communication
3. Does not interfere with communication
4. Enhances communication

Vocabulary
1. Inadequate and/or inaccurate use of vocabulary
2. Somewhat inadequate and/or inaccurate use of vocabulary
3. Adequate and accurate use of vocabulary
4. Rich use of vocabulary

Grammar
1. Inadequate and/or inaccurate use of basic language structures
2. Emerging use of basic language structures
3. Emerging control of basic language structure
4. Control of basic language structures

Source: Adapted from www.fcps.edu/DIS/OHSICS/forlng?PALS/rubrics/1spk_an.htm.

Devising Rubrics

Consider the following set of performance criteria that were developed for a Grade 5 book report.

1. Tell why you chose the book.
2. Describe the main characters of the book.

3. Explain the plot of the book in three to five sentences.
4. Describe the main place or setting of the book.
5. Explain in three sentences how the main characters have changed through the book.
6. Write in complete sentences.
7. Check spelling, grammar, punctuation, and capitalization.
8. Describe whether or not you enjoyed the book and why.

Of course, these criteria could be added to or subtracted from, based on the students in a class and what characteristics of a book report the teacher wishes to emphasize. Different teachers might select different perform-ance criteria.

Scoring rubrics for processes and products are developed by stating lev-els of the performance criteria that indicate different qualities of student performance. For example, the holistic rubric constructed for the Grade 5 book report contained three levels of performance labelled "excellent," "good," and "poor." Read each description and note how the teacher describes different levels of performance for the criteria.

Excellent: Student gives two reasons why the book was chosen; all main char-acters described in great detail; describes the plot in a logical, step-by-step sequence; gives detailed description of the place in which the book takes place; describes how each main character changed during the book in five sentences; all sentences are complete; no more than a total of five spelling, grammar, punc-tuation, or capitalization errors; states opinion of the book based on book con-tent.

Good: Student gives one reason why the book was chosen; all main characters described too briefly; plot described but one main aspect omitted; provides gen-eral description of the book setting; briefly describes how most of the main char-acters changed during the book; a few nonsentences; more than five spelling, grammar, punctuation, or capitalization errors; states opinion of the book but no reference to the book content.

Poor: Student fails to state why book was chosen; not all main characters are described; superficial plot description with key aspects omitted; little informa-tion about where the book takes place; incorrectly describes changes in the main characters during the book; a few nonsentences; many spelling, grammar, punc-tuation, or capitalization errors; no opinion of the book provided.

To score the book report, the teacher would read a student's book report, compare it to the three levels, and determine which of the three levels best describes the quality of the student's book report. Is it most like the "excel-lent" description, the "good" description, or the "poor" description? The selected description determines the grade for the student's book report. Different rubrics can have different numbers of scoring levels and differ-ent descriptions for the levels. Key Assessment Tools 7.2 gives the steps in preparing and using rubrics.

KEY ASSESSMENT TOOLS 7.2

General Steps in Preparing and Using Rubrics

1. Select a process or product to be taught.
2. State performance criteria for the process or product.
3. Decide on the number of scoring levels for the rubric, usually three to five.
4. State description of performance criteria at the highest level of student performance (see "excellent" description of the book report rubric).
5. State descriptions of performance criteria at the remaining scoring levels (e.g., the "good" and "poor" levels of the book report rubric).
6. Compare each student's performance to each scoring level.
7. Select the scoring level closest to a student's actual performance or product.
8. Grade the student's work.

Consider the rubric in Table 7.2 that is used to assess students' response journal questions. The rubric has four scoring levels ranging from "excellent" to "poor" performance. After reading the "excellent" scoring level, can you identify the teacher's intended performance criteria? If the criteria are clear you should be able to identify them from the "excellent" level.

We can apply the steps in Key Assessment Tools 7.2 to the response journal rubric in Table 7.2:

Step 1: Select a performance process or product: response journal questions.

Step 2: Identify performance criteria based on best student performance:
- ➤ Answers complete and accurate
- ➤ Answers supported with information from readings
- ➤ Answers include direct quotations
- ➤ Answers show varied and detailed sentences
- ➤ Appropriate spelling, capitals, and punctuation

Step 3: Decide on the number of scoring levels: four.

Step 4: State the description of the performance criteria at the highest level: see the "excellent" category in Table 7.2.

Step 5: State descriptions of criteria at the remaining scoring levels: compare the quality of the "excellent" scoring level to the "good," "needs improvement," and "poor" levels.

Step 6: Compare each student's performance to the four scoring levels.

Step 7: Select the scoring level that best describes the level of the student's performance on the response journal.

Step 8: Assign a grade to student's work.

One important aspect of developing and using rubrics is the construction of scoring levels. The bases for developing good scoring levels are the performance criteria and a set of terms that differentiate levels of student performance. For example, go to Table 7.2 and read the four scoring levels. Notice that in each scoring level except the "poor" one, we can see the same aspects of the performance criteria: answers complete and accurate, supported from readings, sentence structure, and mechanics. Even the "poor" level includes three of the four criteria. Note what makes the scoring levels different. It is not the criteria per se. It is the level of performance used to describe each criterion. For example, in the "excellent" level, answers are *very* complete and accurate; in the "good" level, answers are *usually* complete and accurate; in the "needs improvement" level, answers are *partially* accurate; and in the "poor" level, answers are *inaccurate or not attempted*. Try the same analysis with the remaining criteria in the table.

Many common descriptors are used to describe scoring levels in rubrics. For instance, excellent, good, needs improvement, poor were used in the preceding examples. Other descriptors are always, mostly, sometimes, seldom, never; exemplary, competent, inconsistent, lacking; advanced, proficient, basic, in progress; and all, some, few, incomplete. In any case, as recommended by Tierney and Simon (2000), performance assessment criteria "descriptors for each level deal with the same performance criteria and attributes in order for the progressive scale to be continuous and consistent from one level to the other" (para. 9).

There are also generic rubrics that can be used to assess a variety of processes and products. Usually, generic rubrics state only the description of the highest level of the scoring rubric. The user must provide his or her own scoring levels to differentiate student performance. One example of a

---

TABLE 7.2 Scoring Rubric for Grade 5 Response Journal Questions

3—Excellent. Answers are very complete and accurate. Most answers are supported with specific information from the reading, including direct quotations. Sentence structure is varied and detailed. Mechanics are generally accurate, including spelling, use of capitals, and appropriate punctuation.

2—Good. Answers are usually complete and accurate. These answers are supported with specific information from the reading. Sentence structure is varied. Mechanics are generally accurate, including spelling, use of capitals, and appropriate punctuations.

1—Needs improvement. Answers are partially to fully accurate. These answers may need to be supported with more specific information from the reading. Sentence structure is varied, with some use of sentence fragments. Mechanics may need improvement, including spelling, use of capitals, and appropriate punctuation.

0—Poor. Answers are inaccurate or not attempted at all. Sentence structure frequently incomplete. Mechanics need significant improvement.

SOURCE: Used with permission of Gwen Airasian.

description from a generic rubric is "goes beyond expectation, includes extra information, makes no mistakes, demonstrates exceptional grasp of the topic, understands abstract concepts, and finds links among parts." This generic rubric could be applied to many types of performance assessments.

What descriptions for an average and a poor scoring level might follow from the exemplary generic description? For example, if a particular exemplary description is "goes beyond expectation," what phrasing could be used to describe an average or poor level for "goes beyond expectation?" Two possible "average" examples might be "performs adequately" or "exhibits average expectation." A description of a third, poor level of performance might be stated as "performs inadequately" or "exhibits below average expectation." Now, given the generic exemplary description "makes no mistakes," what average and poor level examples can you identify for the generic example? Scoring rubrics may have only two levels or may use up to six, but rarely does the number of scoring levels exceed four or five.

Involving Students in the Use of Rubrics

When using rubrics a teacher should inform the students about the criteria that will be used to judge their performance or product *before* assessment takes place. Obviously, the teacher should have identified the criteria before the beginning of instruction and assessment. The criteria—and, ideally, specific examples of good and poor performance—should be described and illustrated for the students. Students should know what makes a good lab report, oral speech, persuasive essay, "show-your-work" math problem, dissection of a frog, analysis of a poem, bar graph, journal response, or any of a thousand other classroom processes and products.

Knowing the criteria of quality performance before assessment leads to a number of benefits for both students and teacher. First, knowledge of performance criteria provides information to students about what is expected of their work—what characteristics make the work good work. Second, knowledge of the criteria lends focus and structure to students' performances and product. They know what is expected of them and thus can concentrate on learning and demonstrating the desired knowledge and behaviours. This, in turn, saves the teacher time in scoring students' products or processes because the criteria narrow the breadth of student responses.

Many teachers let students help identify the important performance criteria for a classroom process or product. Involving students in identifying performance criteria gives them a sense of ownership of the rubric as well as an early preview of the important characteristics of the process or product they will be working on. Some teachers provide students with good and poor examples of the process or product they are teaching and ask students to identify what makes a good example. In the process of determining what makes good examples, the students are also identifying relevant criteria for the process or product.

It is very important to understand that there is a learning curve for mastering the construction and use of rubrics. It takes time to learn to use rubrics well. Trial and error as well as practice for both students and teachers are needed to help each gain the most out of rubrics. Start with simple and limited performance criteria and scoring levels—perhaps three or four criteria and two or three scoring levels. Explain the rubric process to the students: what rubrics are, why we use them, how they can help improve learning and clarify grading. Practise with the students. One approach is to have students use a rubric to revise their work before passing it in. A teacher should expect to revise a rubric a few times before he or she and the students feel comfortable with it.

PORTFOLIOS

An important addition to the growing use of classroom performance assessments is portfolio assessment. This assessment method is gaining use in schools and classrooms (Ryan & Miyasaka, 1995). A **portfolio** is a collection of selected student work. The term *portfolio* derives from the collections that models, photographers, and artists assemble to demonstrate their work. In the classroom, portfolios have the same basic purpose: to collect student performances to show their work and accomplishments over time. Portfolios do not contain haphazard, unrelated collections of a student's work. They contain consciously selected examples of work that is intended to show student growth and development toward important curriculum goals. According to Forgette-Giroux and Simon (2000), portfolio assessment should serve as an opportunity to empower students to judge their progress on clearly articulated competencies. Portfolios, therefore, should support instruction and be related to learning expectations and outcomes.

A portfolio can be made up of many different student performances or it can be made up of a single performance. For example, a multifocused writing portfolio might contain writing samples, lists of books read, journal entries about books read, and descriptions of favourite poems. Conversely, a single-focus portfolio might contain multiple pieces of the same process or product, such as a portfolio containing only book reports, only written poems, or only chemistry lab reports. Key Assessment Tools 7.3 samples the range of materials that can go into a portfolio.

In one Grade 1 class, students developed a reading portfolio. Every third week the students read a paragraph or two into their audiotape "portfolio." The teacher monitored student improvement over time and students could play back their pieces to measure their reading improvement. Also, periodically the students' reading portfolios were sent home for the parents to listen to their child's reading improvement, an opportunity parents appreciated.

KEY ASSESSMENT TOOLS 7.3

What Can Go Into a Portfolio

Media: videos, audiotapes, pictures, artwork, computer programs

Reflections: plans, statements of goals, self-reflections, journal entries

Individual work: tests, journals, logs, lab reports, homework, essays, poems, maps, inventions, posters, math work

Group work: cooperative learning sessions, group performances, peer reviews

Work in progress: rough and final drafts, show-your-work problems, science fair projects

Portfolios can contribute to instruction and learning in many ways:

➤ Showing students' typical work.
➤ Monitoring student progress and improvement over time.
➤ Helping students self-evaluate their work.
➤ Providing ongoing assessment of student learning.
➤ Providing diagnostic information about student performance.
➤ Helping teachers judge the appropriateness of the curriculum.
➤ Facilitating teacher meetings and conferences with students, parents, and both students and parents.
➤ Grading students' work.
➤ Reinforcing the importance of processes and products in learning.
➤ Showing students the connections among their processes and products.
➤ Providing concrete examples of student work.
➤ Encouraging students to think about what is good performance in varied subject areas.
➤ Focusing on both the process and final product of learning.
➤ Informing subsequent teachers about students' prior work.

Whatever a portfolio's use and contents, it is important that it have a defined, specific purpose that will focus the nature of the information that will be collected in the portfolio. Too often, teachers defer the question of the portfolio's purpose until *after* students have collected large amounts of their work in their portfolios. At that time the teacher is likely to be confronted with the question of what to do with a vast, undifferentiated collection of student information.

Perhaps the greatest contribution that portfolios provide for learning is that they give students a chance to revisit and reflect on the products and processes they have produced. For many students, life in school is an ongoing sequence of papers, performances, assignments, and productions. Each day a new batch of paperwork is produced and the previous day's productions are tossed away or lost, both mentally and physically. Collecting pieces of students' work in a portfolio retains them for subsequent student review, reflection, demonstration, and grading. With suitable guidance, students can be encouraged to think about and compare their work over time, providing them an opportunity rarely available in the absence of portfolios. For example, students might be asked to reflect on the following questions. Which of these portfolio items shows the most improvement and why? Which did you enjoy most and why? From which did you learn the most and why? In what areas have you made the most progress over the year and what was the nature of that progress? Portfolios allow students to see their progress and judge their work from the perspectives of time and personal development.

As noted, there is a great deal more to successful portfolio assessment than simply collecting bunches of students' work. Portfolio assessment is a type of performance assessment and thus depends on the same four elements that all types of performance assessment require: (1) a clear purpose, (2) appropriate performance criteria, (3) a suitable setting, and (4) scoring performance. There are a number of questions that must be answered in developing and assessing portfolios. The following are examples of some of these questions:

1. What is the purpose of the portfolio?
2. What will go into and be removed from the portfolio during its use?
3. Who will select the entries that go into the portfolio: teacher, students, or both?
4. How will the portfolio be organized and maintained?
5. How will the portfolio be assessed?

Purpose of Portfolios

The items that go into a portfolio, the criteria used to judge the items, and the frequency with which items are added to or deleted from the portfolio all depend on the portfolio's purpose. If the purpose is to illustrate a student's typical work in various school subjects for a parent's night at the school, the portfolio contents would likely be more wide ranging than if its purpose is to assess the student's improvement in math problem solving over a single marking period. In the latter case, math problems would have to be obtained periodically throughout the marking period and collected in the portfolio.

It is important to determine the purpose and guidelines for a portfolio's content before compiling it. Is it to grade, group, instruct, or diagnose students?

If a portfolio is intended to show a student's best work in a subject area, the contents of the portfolio would change as more samples of the student's performance became available and as less good ones were removed. If the purpose is to show improvement over time, earlier performances would have to be retained and new pieces added.

Given the many and varied uses of portfolios, purpose is a crucial issue to consider and define in carrying out portfolio assessment. It is important to determine the purpose and general guidelines for the pieces that will go into the portfolio *before* starting the portfolio assessment. It is also critical that all pieces going into a portfolio be dated, especially in portfolios that aim to assess student growth or development. Without recorded dates for each portfolio entry, it may be impossible to assess growth and improvement.

Allowing students to help determine what goes into their portfolios gives them a sense of ownership.

To promote students' ownership of their portfolios, it is useful to allow students to choose at least some of the pieces that will go into their portfolios. Some teachers develop portfolios that contain two types of pieces, those required by the teacher and those selected by the student. It is also important that all student portfolio selections are accompanied by a brief written explanation of why the student feels that a particular piece belongs in her or his portfolio. This will encourage the student to reflect on the characteristics of the piece and why it belongs in the portfolio.

Performance Criteria

Performance criteria are needed to evaluate each of the individual pieces within a portfolio and the whole portfolio itself.

Performance criteria are needed to assess the individual pieces that make up a portfolio and the whole portfolio itself. Without such criteria, assessment cannot be consistent within and across portfolios. The nature and process of identifying performance criteria for portfolios is the same as that for checklists, rating scales, and rubrics. Depending on the type of performance contained in a portfolio, many of the performance criteria discussed earlier in this chapter can be used to assess individual portfolio pieces.

If student portfolios are required for all teachers in a grade or if portfolios are to be passed on to the student's next teacher, it is advisable for all affected teachers to cooperate in formulating a common set of performance criteria. Cooperative teacher practice is useful because it involves groups of teachers in the process of identifying important performance criteria. It also helps produce common instructional emphases within and between grades and fosters discussion and sharing of materials among teachers (Herbert, 1992).

It is valuable to allow students to help identify performance criteria used for assessing the contents of a portfolio because this can give students a sense of ownership over their performance and help them think through the nature of the portfolio pieces they will produce. Beginning a lesson with joint teacher and student discussion of what makes a good book report, oral reading, science lab, or sonnet is a useful way to initiate instruction and get the students thinking about the characteristics of the process or product they will have to develop.

There is another very important reason why performance criteria are needed for portfolio assessment. The processes or products that will make up a portfolio should, like all forms of assessment, be related to the instruction provided to students. Performance criteria are like the teacher's objectives, identifying the important learning outcomes or expectations that students need to learn. Without explicit criteria, instruction may not provide all the experiences necessary to carry out the desired learning, thereby reducing the validity of the portfolio.

The performance criteria used in evaluating portfolios should align with a teacher's instructional objectives.

Setting

In addition to a clear purpose and well-developed performance criteria, portfolio assessments must take into account the setting in which students' performances will be gathered. While many portfolio pieces can be gathered by the teacher in the classroom, other pieces cannot. When portfolios include oral speaking, science experiments, artistic productions, and psychomotor activities, special equipment or arrangements may be needed to properly collect the desired student performance. Many teachers underestimate the time it takes to collect the processes and products that make up portfolios and the management and record keeping needed to maintain them. Checking, managing, maintaining, and assessing student portfolios is time-consuming, but important.

An important dimension of using portfolios is the logistics of collecting and maintaining student portfolios. Portfolios require space. They have to be stored in a safe but accessible place. A system has to be established for students to add or subtract pieces of their portfolios. Can students go to their portfolio at any time or will the teacher set aside special times when all students deal with their portfolios? If the portfolio is intended to show growth, how will the order of the entries be kept in sequence? Maintaining portfolios requires time and organization. Materials such as envelopes, crates, tape recorders, and the like will be needed for assembling and storing student portfolios.

Scoring

Scoring portfolios can be a time-consuming task. Not only does each individual portfolio piece have to be assessed, but the summarized pieces must also be assessed to provide an overall portfolio performance. Depending on the complexity and variety of the contents of the portfolio, assessing may require considerable time and attention to detail, further increasing assessment time.

Scoring portfolios is a time-consuming process that involves judging each individual piece and the portfolio as a whole.

Summative Scoring

Consider the difference in managing and scoring portfolios that contain varied processes or products compared to portfolios that contain examples of a single process or product. The multifocused portfolio provides a wide range of student performance, but at a substantial logistical and scoring cost to the teacher. The single-focus portfolio does not provide the breadth of varied student performances of the multifocused portfolio, but can be managed and scored considerably more quickly.

Figure 7.7 provides an example of a teacher's anecdotal notes of one student's writing portfolio. When the purpose of a portfolio is to provide descriptive information about student performance for a parent-teacher night or to pass student information on to the next year's teacher, no scoring or summarization of the portfolio contents will be necessary. The contents themselves provide the desired information. However, when the purpose of a portfolio is to diagnose, track improvement, assess the success of instruction, encourage students to reflect on their work, or grade students' work, some form of summarization or scoring of the portfolio pieces is required.

Performance criteria used to assess an entire portfolio are different from those used to assess individual portfolio items.

The purpose of assessing an entire portfolio, as opposed to the individual pieces, is usually summative—to assign a grade. Such holistic portfolio assessment requires the development of a set of summarizing criteria. For example, improvement in writing might be judged by comparing a student's early pieces to later pieces in terms of these performance criteria: (1) number of spelling, capitalization, and punctuation errors, (2) variety of sentence structures used, (3) use of supporting detail, (4) appropriateness of detail to purpose, (5) ability to emphasize and summarize main ideas, (6) link and flow between paragraphs, and (7) personal involvement in written pieces. An alternative approach might be for the teacher to rate earlier written pieces using a general scoring rubric and compare the level of early performances to later performances using the same rubric.

Different portfolios with different purposes require different summarizing criteria. For example, how would you summarize a portfolio containing a number of tape recordings of a student's French pronunciation or a portfolio made up of poems a student wrote as part of a poetry unit? What criteria would you use to judge *overall* progress or performance?

Scoring the Pieces

Individual portfolio pieces are normally judged using performance criteria that have been assembled into some form of checklist, rating scale, or rubric.

Individual portfolio pieces are typically appraised using methods we have discussed: checklists, rating scales, and rubrics. Table 7.3 gives examples of tools to assess a Grade 7 science portfolio. Thus, each story, tape recording, lab report, handwriting sample, persuasive essay, or cooperative group product can be judged by organizing the performance criteria into a checklist, rating scale, or rubric.

Of course, the teacher does not always have to be the one who assesses the pieces. It is desirable and instructive to allow students to self-assess some of their portfolio pieces in order to give them practice in critiquing their own work in terms of the performance criteria.

FIGURE 7.7 *Anecdotal Notes of a Student's Writing Portfolio.*

Date	Genre	Topic	Reason	Length	Drafts
9/??	Self-Reflection	Thinking About Your Writing	Requested	1 page	1 draft
10/17	Narrative/Dramatic	Personal Monologue	Important	1 page	2 drafts
1/16	Response to Literature	On *The Lord of the Flies*	Unsatisfying	1 page	4 drafts
2/??	Self-Reflection	Response to Parent Comments	Requested	1 page	1 draft
2/28	Narrative/Dramatic	"The Tell-Tale Heart"	Free Pick	3 pages	2 drafts
5/22	Response to Literature	On *Animal Farm*	Satisfying	5 pages	2 drafts
6/??	Self-Reflection	Final Reflection	Requested	2 pages	1 draft

As a writer, Barry shows substantial growth from the beginning of the year in his first personal monologue to his last piece, a response to Animal Farm. Initially, Barry seems to have little control over the flow and transition of his ideas. His points are not tied together, he jumps around in his thinking, and he lacks specificity in his ideas. By January, when Barry writes his response to The Lord of the Flies, he begins a coherent argument about the differences between Ralph's group and Jack's tribe, although he ends with the unsupported assertions that he would have preferred to be "marooned on a desert island" with Ralph. Barry includes three reasons for his comparison, hinges his reasons with transition words, but more impressively, connects his introductory paragraph with a transition sentence to the body of his essay. In the revisions of this essay, Barry makes primarily word and sentence level changes, adds paragraph formatting, and generally improves the local coherence of the piece.

By the end of February when he writes his narrative response to Poe's "The Tell-Tale Heart," Barry displays a concern for making his writing interesting. "I like the idea that there are so many twists in the story that I really think makes it interesting." He makes surface-level spelling changes, deletes a sentence, and replaces details, although not always successfully (e.g., "fine satin sheets and brass bed," is replaced with the summary description "extravagant furniture"). Overall, it is an effective piece of writing showing Barry's understanding of narrative form and his ability to manipulate twists of plot in order to create an engaging story.

Barry's last selection in his portfolio is an exceptional five-page, typed essay on Orwell's Animal Farm. The writing is highly organized around the theme of scapegoating. Using supporting details from the novel and contemporary examples from politics and sports, Barry creates a compelling and believable argument. The effective intertextuality and the multiple perspectives Barry brings to this essay result largely from an exceptional revision process. Not only does he attempt to correct his standard conventions and improve his word choices, he also revises successfully to the point of moving around whole clumps of text and adding sections that significantly reshape the piece. This pattern of revision shows the control Barry has gained over his writing.

In Barry's final reflection he describes his development, showing an awareness of such issues as organizing and connecting ideas, choosing appropriate words and details, and making his writing accessible to his readers. "I had many gaps in my writing. One problem was that I would skip from one idea to the next and it would not be clear what was going on in the piece. . . . Now, I have put in more details so you don't have to think as much as you would. I also perfect my transitions and my paragraph form. . . . My reading . . . has improved my vocabulary and it helped me organize my writing so it sounds its best and makes the most sense possible. . . . There are many mistakes I have made throughout the year, but I have at least learned from all of them." I agree with him.

Source: P. A. Moss, et al., "Portfolios, accountability, and an interpretive approach to validity," *Educational Measurement: Issues and Practice*, 1992, *11*(3), p. 18. Copyright 1992 by the National Council on Measurement in Education. Used by permission of AERA.

TABLE 7.3 Assessing Individual Portfolio Pieces			
Checklist			
Selects correct solution method	Yes	No	
Draws and labels diagrams	Yes	No	
Shows work leading to solution	Yes	No	
Gets correct answer	Yes	No	
Rating Scale			
Selects correct solution method	Quickly	Slowly	Not at all
Draws and labels diagrams	Completely	Partially	Not at all
Shows work leading to solution	Completely	Partially	Not at all
Gets correct answer	Quickly	Slowly	Not at all
Rubric			
Selects correct solution method; draws complete, labelled diagrams; shows all work; gets correct answer			
Selects correct solution method; draws complete but poorly labelled diagrams; shows partial work; gets partially correct answer			
Selects incorrect solution method; neither draws nor labels diagrams; shows very little work; gets incorrect answer			

Allowing students to self-assess their portfolio encourages student reflection and learning.

Consider how much more student involvement in the writing process portfolios provide, compared to when an assignment is given, passed in to the teacher, graded, returned to the student, and soon forgotten. Note also how this kind of assessment encourages student reflection and learning.

From the teacher's point of view, clearly there are both advantages and disadvantages to performances, product, and portfolio assessments. Table 7.4 summarizes the major trade-offs.

VALIDITY AND RELIABILITY OF PERFORMANCE ASSESSMENTS

Since formal performance assessments are used to make decisions about students' work, it is important for them to be valid and reliable. This section describes steps that can be taken to obtain high-quality performance assessments.

Scoring performance assessments is a difficult and often time-consuming activity. The process is often complex and lengthy. Unlike when scoring selected response items, teachers' interpretation and judgment are neces-

---

TABLE 7.4 Advantages and Disadvantages of Performance, Product, and Portfolio Assessments

Advantages

➤ Chart student performance over time.

➤ Conduct student self-assessment of products and performances.

➤ Conduct peer review of products and performances.

➤ Provide diagnostic information about performances and products.

➤ Integrate assessment and instruction.

➤ Promote learning through assessment activities.

➤ Give students ownership over their learning and productions.

➤ Clarify lesson, assignment, and test expectations.

➤ Report performance to parents in clear, descriptive terms.

➤ Permit student reflection and analysis of work.

➤ Provide concrete examples for parent conferences.

➤ Assemble cumulative evidence of performance.

➤ Reinforce importance of student performance.

Disadvantages

Most disadvantages associated with performance, product, and especially portfolio assessments involve the time they require:

➤ To prepare materials, performance criteria, and scoring formats.

➤ To manage, organize, and keep records.

➤ For teachers and students to become comfortable with the use of performance assessments and the change in teaching and learning roles they involve.

➤ To score and provide feedback to students.

---

sary for scoring performances and products. Each student produces or constructs a performance or product that is different from that of other students. This makes scoring difficult; the more criteria to address and the more variation in the products or performances students produce, the more time-consuming, fatiguing, and potentially invalid.

Scoring performance assessments is a difficult, time-consuming activity.

Further, like essays, performance assessments are subject to many ancillary factors that may not be relevant to scoring but may influence the teacher's judgment of the performance assessments. For example, teachers' scoring of products such as essays or reports are often influenced by the quality of a student's handwriting, neatness, and knowledge of the student being scored. These and similar factors are not key aspects of the product, but they often weigh heavily in scoring. Teachers can rarely be completely unbiased observers of what their students do, because they know their students too well and have a set of built-in predispositions regarding each one. In each case, there are many irrelevant and distract-

Distractions and personal feelings can introduce error into either the observation or judging process, thereby reducing the validity and reliability of the assessment.

ing factors that can influence the teacher's judgments and the validity and reliability of performance assessments.

The key to improving rating or scoring skills is to try to eliminate the distracting factors so that the assessment more closely reflects the student's actual performance. In performance assessments, the main source of error is the observer, who judges both what is happening during a performance and the quality of the performance. Beyond the issue of distractions, teachers can prepare their students well and ensure validity and reliability in various other ways.

Preparing Students

There are many ways teachers prepare their students for performance assessment. First and foremost, they provide good instruction. Students learn to set up and focus microscopes, build bookcases, write book reports, give oral speeches, measure with a ruler, perform musical selections, and speak French the same way they learn to solve simultaneous equations, find countries on a map, write a topic sentence, or balance a chemical equation. They are given instruction and practice. Achievement depends upon their being taught the things on which they are being assessed. One of the advantages of performance assessments is their explicit criteria, which focus instruction and assessment.

Unless students are informed about the performance criteria upon which they will be judged, they may not perform up to their abilities.

In preparing students for performance assessment, the teacher should inform and explain the criteria on which they will be judged (Mehrens, Popham, & Ryan, 1998). In many classrooms, teachers and students jointly discuss and define criteria for a desired performance or product. This helps them to understand what is expected of them by identifying the important dimensions of the performance or product. Another, less interactive way to do this is for the teacher to give students a copy of the checklist or rating form that will be used during their assessment. If performance criteria are not made clear to students, they may perform poorly, not because they are incapable, but because they were not aware of the teacher's expectations and the criteria for a good performance. In such cases, the performance ratings do not reflect the students' true achievement, and the grades they receive could lead to invalid decisions about their learning.

Validity

When irrelevant, subjective factors differentiate the scores of one group of students from another, the scores are said to be biased.

Validity is concerned with whether the information obtained from an assessment permits the teacher to make a correct decision about a student's learning. As discussed previously, either failure to instruct students on desired performances or the inability to control personal expectations can produce invalid information. Another factor that can reduce the validity of formal performance assessment is **bias**. When some factors such as ethnicity, native language, prior experience, gender, or exceptionality differentiates the scores of one group from those of another, we say the scores are biased. That is, judgments regarding the performance of one group of students are influenced by the inclusion of irrelevant, subjective criteria.

Suppose that oral reading performance was being assessed in a Grade 2 classroom. Suppose also that in the classroom there was a group of students whose first language is Arabic. The oral reading assessment involved reading aloud from a storybook written in English. When the teacher reviewed her notes on the students' performances, she noticed that the Arabic-speaking students as a group did very poorly. Would the teacher be correct in saying that the Arabic-speaking students have poor oral reading skills? Would this be a valid conclusion to draw from the assessment evidence? A more reasonable interpretation would be that the oral reading assessment was measuring the Arabic-speaking students' familiarity with the English language rather than their oral reading performance. In essence, the assessment provided different information about the two groups (oral reading proficiency versus knowledge of English language). It would be a misinterpretation of the evidence to conclude that the Arabic-speaking students had poor oral reading skills without taking into account the fact that they were required to read and pronounce unfamiliar English words. The results of the assessment were not valid for the teacher's desired decision about oral reading for the Arabic-speaking students.

Teachers should select performance criteria and settings that do not give an unfair advantage to any group of students.

When an assessment instrument provides information that is irrelevant to the decisions it was intended to help make, it is invalid. Thus, in all forms of assessment, but especially performance assessment, a teacher must select and use procedures, performance criteria, and settings that do not give an unfair advantage to some students because of cultural background, language, exceptionality, or gender. Other sources of error that commonly affect the validity of performance assessments are teachers' reliance on mental rather than written record keeping and their being influenced by prior perceptions of a student. The longer the interval between an observation and the written scoring, the more likely the teacher is to forget important features of students' performance.

Teachers should write down performance assessments at the time they are observed in order to avoid memory error.

Often, teachers' prior knowledge of their students influences the objectivity of their performance ratings. Personality, effort, work habits, cooperativeness, and the like are all part of a teacher's perception of the students in his or her class. Often, these prior perceptions influence the rating a student is given: the likable, cooperative student with the pleasant personality may receive a higher rating than the standoffish, belligerent student, even though they performed similarly. Assessing students on the basis of their personal characteristics rather than their performance lowers the validity of the assessment. Each of these concerns threatens the validity of teacher interpretations and scores. These concerns are particularly difficult to overcome because of the complexity of performance assessment.

Assessing students on the basis of their personal characteristics rather than on their performance lowers the validity of the assessment.

Reliability

Observing a performance more than once increases the reliability of the assessment but is time-consuming.

Reliability is concerned with the stability and consistency of assessments. Hence, the logical way to obtain information about the reliability of student performance is to observe and score two or more performances or products of the same kind. Doing this, however, is not reasonable in most school settings; once a formal assessment is made, instruction turns to a new topic. Few teachers can afford the class time necessary to obtain multiple assessments on a given topic. This reality raises an important problem with the reliability of performance assessments: they may lack generalization. Performances, products, and portfolios are more complex and fewer in number than selected response assessments. Because of such discrepancies in the quantity of information obtained from particular assessments, the teacher who employs performance assessments sees fewer examples of student mastery than when more narrow assessment approaches are used. The teacher's question then becomes how reliable is the limited information I have obtained from students? Does a single essay, a few show-your-work problems or a portfolio provide enough evidence that students will perform similarly on other essays, show-your-work problems, or portfolios?

An important concern in interpreting performance assessments is the often low generalizability of students' performances, products, or portfolios.

Teachers are put on the horns of a dilemma. Because they want their students to learn more than facts and narrow topics, they employ performance assessments to ensure deeper, richer learning. However, by employing an in-depth and time-consuming approach, they often diminish the reliability of the assessment. This is a dilemma faced in classroom teachers' own assessments and in more general, large-scale student assessments. There are few easy ways to overcome the dilemma. However, it is better to use evidence from imperfect performance assessments than to make uninformed decisions about important student achievement.

Unclear or vague performance criteria increase teacher interpretation, which introduces inconsistency into the assessment.

Reliability is also affected when performance criteria or rating categories are vague and unclear. This forces the teacher to interpret them, and because interpretations often vary with time and situation, this introduces inconsistency into the assessment. One way to eliminate much of this inconsistency is to be explicit about the purpose of a performance assessment and to state the performance criteria and rubrics in terms of observable student behaviours. The objectivity of an observation can be enhanced by having several individuals independently observe and rate a student's performance. In situations where a group of teachers cooperate in developing criteria for a student performance, product, or portfolio, it is not difficult to have more than one teacher observe or examine a few students' products or performances to see whether scores are similar across teachers.

Having more than one person observe and rate a performance increases the objectivity of the assessment.

Performance criteria should be realistic in terms of the students' developmental level.

At the classroom level, there are some guidelines for teachers to improve the validity and reliability of performance, product, and portfolio assessments. First, students should know the purpose of the assessment from the beginning, then you should teach and give students practice in the performance criteria. Teachers should state the performance criteria in terms of observable behaviours and avoid using adverbs such as "appropriately," "correctly," or "well" because their interpretation may shift from student to student. Instead try to use overt, well-described behaviours that can be seen by an observer and therefore are less subjective to interpretation. The performance criteria that you select should be at an appropriate level of difficulty for the students and limited to a manageable number. A large number of criteria makes observation difficult and causes errors that reduce the validity of the assessment information. Teachers should maintain a written record of student performance. To make this task manageable you should use checklists, rating scales, and rubrics, although descriptive anecdotal notes are often desirable and informative. Tape recordings or videotapes may be used to provide a record of performance, so long as their use does not upset or distract the students. Finally, be sure that the performance assessment is fair to all students.

CHAPTER REVIEW

CHAPTER REVIEW

Visit Chapter 7 of the Online Learning Centre at **www.mcgrawhill.ca/ college/airasian** to take chapter quizzes, link to related Web sites, and read PowerWeb articles and news feed updates.

What is performance assessment?

➤ Performance assessment is any form of assessment in which students carry out an activity or produce a product in order to demonstrate learning.

What are other names for performance assessments?

➤ Performance assessments may also be called alternative and authentic assessments.

What are some areas of learning for which performance assessments may be used?

➤ Performance assessments are useful for determining student learning in performance-oriented areas such as communication skills, psychomotor skills, athletic activities, concept acquisition, and affective characteristics.

What are some uses for performance assessments?

➤ Chart student performance over time;

➤ Assess the quality of a product of student work;

➤ Provide diagnostic information about student learning;

➤ Give students ownership of their learning;

➤ Integrate instructional and assessment processes;

➤ Foster students' self-assessment of their work; and

➤ Assemble into portfolios both cumulative evidence of performance and concrete examples of students' work for parent conferences.

What are the components required for successful performance assessment?

➤ Successful performance assessment requires a well-defined purpose for assessment; clear, observable performance criteria; an appropriate setting in which to elicit performance; and a scoring or rating method.

What are performance criteria?

➤ Performance criteria are the specific behaviours a student should display when carrying out a performance or the characteristics a student should possess. The key to identifying performance criteria is to break down an overall performance or product into its component parts. It is these parts that will be assessed.

What are some guidelines for developing performance criteria?

➤ Select the performance or product to be assessed and either perform it yourself or imagine yourself performing it;

➤ List the important aspects of the performance or product;

➤ Try to limit the number of performance criteria, so they can all be observed during a student's performance;

➤ If possible, have groups of teachers think through the important criteria included in a task;

➤ Express the performance criteria in terms of observable student behaviours or product characteristics;

➤ Do not use ambiguous words (e.g., adequately, correctly, appropriate) that cloud the meaning of the performance criteria;

➤ Arrange the performance criteria in the order in which they are likely to be observed; and

➤ Check for existing performance criteria before defining your own.

What is the difference between holistic scoring and analytic scoring?

➤ Holistic scoring provides a single overall score for a performance process or product. With analytic scoring, a separate score is given for each performance criterion.

In what ways may student performance be collected, recorded, and/or summarized?

➤ Options for collecting, recording, and summarizing student performance include the use of anecdotal records, checklists, rating scales, rubrics, and portfolios.

What are anecdotal records?

➤ Anecdotal records are written accounts of significant, individual student events and behaviours the teacher has observed.

What is a checklist?

➤ A checklist is a written list of performance criteria that only indicates whether or not a student has met each criterion. A checklist gives a teacher only a dichotomy of choices: performed or not performed.

What are rating scales?

➤ Rating scales are lists that allow the observer to judge performance along a continuum (e.g., always, sometimes, never) rather than as a dichotomy.

➤ Performance can be summarized across performance criteria either numerically or descriptively. Descriptive summarization provides text-based, diagnostic information about a student's strengths and weaknesses. Numerical summarization assigns a point value to each category in the scale and sums the points across the performance criteria.

What are rubrics?

➤ Rubrics are a type of rating scale; more specifically, rubrics are descriptive rating scales, which require the rater to choose from among different descriptions of actual performance.

What are portfolios?

➤ Portfolios are collections of students' work in an area that show change and progress over time. Portfolios may contain student products or performances.

What are the educational uses of portfolios?

➤ Focusing instruction on important performance activities;
➤ Reinforcing the point that performances are important school outcomes;
➤ Providing parents, students, and teachers with a perspective on student improvement.
➤ Diagnosing weaknesses;
➤ Allowing students to revisit, reflect on, and assess their work over time;
➤ Grading students; and
➤ Integrating instruction with assessment.

How can the validity of performance assessment be improved?

➤ Stating performance criteria in observable terms;
➤ Setting performance criteria at an appropriate difficulty levels for students;
➤ Limiting the number of performance criteria;
➤ Maintaining a written record of student performance; and
➤ Checking to determine whether extraneous factors influenced a student's performance.

How can the reliability of performance assessment be improved?

➤ The reliability of performance assessments can be improved through multiple observations of performance or by checking for agreement among observers viewing the same performance, product, or portfolio and using the same assessment criteria.

QUESTIONS FOR DISCUSSION

1. What types of objectives are most suitably assessed using performance assessment?

2. How do formal and informal performance assessments differ in terms of student characteristics, validity and reliability of information, and usefulness for teacher decision making?

3. What are the advantages and disadvantages of performance assessments for teachers? For students?

4. How should a teacher determine the validity of a performance assessment?

5. How might instruction differ when a teacher desires to assess students' performances and products rather than their responses to selection-type tests?

6. What are some examples of how performance assessment can be closely linked to instruction? For example, how can performance assessment be used to involve students in the instructional process?

7. How does performance assessment relate to formative and summative assessment?

ACTIVITIES

1. Select a subject area you might like to teach and identify one objective in that subject matter that cannot be assessed by selected or constructed response questions. Construct a performance or product assessment instrument for this objective. Provide the following information:

    (a) the objective and a brief description of the behaviour or product you will assess and the grade level at which it will be taught.

    (b) a set of at least 10 observable performance criteria for judging the performance or product.

    (c) a method to score student performance.

    (d) a method to summarize performance into a single score.

    The assessment procedure used may be in the form of a checklist or a rating scale. A two- to three-page document should adequately provide the needed information. Be sure to focus on the clarity and specificity of the performance criteria and on the clarity and practicality of the scoring procedure.

2. Rewrite in clearer form the following performance criteria for assessing a student's poem. Remember that you are trying to write performance criteria that most people will understand and interpret the same way.

➤ Poem is original
➤ Meaningfulness
➤ Contains rhymes
➤ Proper length
➤ Well-focused
➤ Good title
➤ Appropriate vocabulary level

GRADING

After reading this chapter, you will be able to:

➤ Identify the purposes and difficulties of grading

➤ Understand grading as a judgment process

➤ Contrast the four types of grading (norm-reference, criterion-referenced, comparison to student's own ability, comparison to student's prior performance)

➤ Outline considerations around what to grade

➤ State methods for summarizing varied types of assessment information

➤ Distinguish between the two approaches to assigning grades (criterion-referenced vs. norm-referenced)

➤ Describe approaches for grading students with exceptionalities

➤ Propose strategies for conducting effective parent-teacher conferences

A s a beginning teacher, Lillian Hong is faced with the task of compiling her first set of report card grades. Throughout the term, Lillian has been gathering various assessment data from her Grade 3 students across all of the curricular areas. In some subjects such as mathematics, Lillian has several quiz and test grades recorded in her grade book. In other subjects, such as social studies, Lillian has just a few letter grades noted as students completed projects over the course of the term. Lillian is overwhelmed by all of these data that represent different scales; she is discouraged by the thought of combining this information into report card grades. Moreover, Lillian is also anxious about the prospect of meeting with her students' parents at the conferences scheduled for the days after report card dissemination for the purpose of discussing her students' grades.

Chapters 2 through 7 offer teachers a variety of techniques to assess or gather information about their students' learning. This is only the beginning of the assessment and evaluation process, teachers must use this information to make decisions or judgments about students or instruction. Recall from Chapter 1 that **measurement** is the process of quantifying or assigning a number to performance. The most common example of measurement in the classroom is when a teacher **scores** a quiz or test. **Scoring** produces a numerical description of performance that is used to represent a student's performance. Finally, there is **evaluation** which is the process of making judgments about what is good or desirable as in, for example, judging the quality of students' essays or the desirability of a particular instructional activity. Evaluation occurs after assessment data have been collected, synthesized, and interpreted because this is when the teacher is in a position to make informed judgments.

Grading is the process of judging the quality of a student's performance by comparing it to some standard of performance.

The process of judging the quality of a student's performance by comparing it to some standard of performance is called **grading**. The process of grading involves translating assessment information into letters, numbers, or marks to indicate the quality of a student's learning and performance—grading is a part of the evaluation process. Teachers assign grades to single assessments; for example, a student may get a 78 on a science test or a Level 3+ on an oral presentation. Report card grades, on the other hand, represent a student's performance across a variety of assessments that were completed during a term or grading period. Assigning grades is an exceptionally important professional responsibility, one that a teacher carries out several times during the school year and one that has important consequences for students. The Alberta Assessment Consortium (2002) cautions that, "this symbolic representation called a grade should be as objective as possible and not open to interpretation."

PURPOSES AND DIFFICULTIES OF GRADING

The purpose of this chapter is to raise the questions teachers face when grading and to help answer these questions. While the main focus is on the process of assigning report card grades in academic subjects, the principles discussed are also appropriate for grading single tests or assessments. A logical place to begin discussion is with the question, "Why grade?"

Why Grade?

The question, "Why grade?" is a seemingly simple one. A simple response to that question is that the purpose of grading is to communicate symbols that summarize performance over time (O'Connor, 2002). It is a reality that all school systems require that classroom teachers make periodic judgments about their students' performance. Therefore, the most compelling reason that classroom teachers have to grade their students is that they are required to grade as part of their professional responsibilities. However, the ultimate purpose of grading should be to communicate meaningful information about a student's learning and achievement to students, parents, and others. This speaks to what Earl and Katz (2000) call, "a paradox": teachers have to communicate something about the learner to the learner and to others. In this sense, grades are a way that students come to regard themselves as competent or incompetent (Earl & Katz, 2000). With this general purpose are four more specific purposes for grading: administrative, informational, motivational, and guidance (Salend & Duhaney, 2002).

Administratively, grades help determine such things as a student's instructional placement, credits for graduation, and suitability for promotion to the next level. They may also be used to judge different teaching approaches and the quality of both teachers and administrators.

Administrative reasons for grading include determining a student's instructional placement, credits for graduation, and readiness for promotion.

Informationally, grades are used to inform parents, students, and others about a student's academic performance and effort. Grades represent the teacher's summary judgment about how well students have mastered the content and processes taught in a subject area during a particular term or grading period. Because report card grades are given only a few times a year, the judgments that they contain are a summary. Grades provide information with respect to how students have met the learning objectives. Grades are important, but bear in mind that grades are only one means of communicating with students and parents. Other methods such as parent conferences can provide more detailed information about school progress, and will be described later in this chapter.

Grades are used to motivate students to study and to guide them toward appropriate courses and programs.

Grades are also used to motivate students to study. A high grade is a reward for learning. This motivational aspect of grading is, however, a two-edged sword. Student motivation may be enhanced when grades are high, but may be diminished when grades are lower than expected or when students continue to get low grades. Moreover, it is not desirable to have students study solely to get a good grade, so teachers should try to balance grading rewards with other kinds of rewards.

Lastly, grades are used for guidance. They help students, parents, teachers, and counsellors to choose appropriate courses and course levels for students. They help identify students who may be in need of special services and they provide information to post secondary institutions about the student's academic performance in high school.

Grades are used in schools for many reasons, and while there are periodic calls to abolish grades, it is difficult to envision schools in which judgments about students' performance would not be made by teachers and communicated to various interested parties. The basis on which teacher judgments are made may change or the format in which the grades are reported may be altered, but the basic process of teachers judging and communicating information about student performance—that is, "grading"—will still go on.

Because grades can affect students' chances in life, teachers are ethically bound to be as fair and objective as possible when grading students.

Grades in whatever form are potent symbols in our society, symbols that are taken very seriously by teachers, students, parents, and the public at large. Regardless of your personal biases about the value and usefulness of grades and grading, it is necessary to take the grading process seriously. That means teachers should devise a grading system for students that (1) is fair to students and (2) delivers the message about student performance that is valid and reliable. Teachers have a responsibility to be objective in assigning grades and should never use grades to punish or reward students.

The Difficulty of Grading

The difficulty of grading lies in the reality that a grade is a single symbol that must represent several pieces of assessment data. Blending such a variety of assessment data may make it difficult to discern what a grade means (O'Connor, 2002). Grading can be a very difficult task for teachers for four reasons: (1) few teachers have had formal instruction in how to grade their students (Brookhart, 1999); (2) school boards and administrators provide little guidance to teachers regarding specific grading policies and expectations (Hubelbank, 1994); (3) teachers know that grades are taken seriously by parents and may be scrutinized and often challenged; and (4) the knowledge of each student's needs and characteristics that teachers have is difficult to ignore when the teacher is called upon to be a dispassionate, objective dispenser of grades.

Teachers inevitably face the dilemma of what constitutes fairness in grading. Must a teacher always be steadfast to the institution that expects dispassionate grading, or can fairness include consideration of a student's unique needs, circumstances, and challenges? Which is the greater misuse of knowledge, to ignore or to take into account individual student circumstances when grading? Is it any wonder that teachers hold some ambivalence about grading when the reality is that grading has real consequences for students and can influence students' educational or even future occupational status?

Some teachers agonize over the grades that they give students. The first report card of the academic year often sets up future expectations for the student and his or her parents. At times teachers may express concern about the effect that grades have on their students as some students define their self-image by their grades. It is especially difficult to ensure that subject matter report card grades clearly reflect academic performance. Students' work and study habits are usually reported on the report card as comments or reserved as a separate reporting component. The Alberta Assessment Consortium (2002) concurs that a teacher's evaluation of students' effort, attitude, behaviour, participation, and attendance should be reported separately from students' academic performance.

Grading is a difficult, time-consuming process that demands considerable mental and emotional energy from teachers because grades have important consequences for students and others. Grading is further complicated by the lack of uniformly accepted strategies for assigning grades. Grading systems are not comparable from school to school nor from teacher to teacher, so each teacher must find his or her own answer to the many questions associated with the grading process.

There are no uniformly accepted strategies for assigning grades.

Why is there so much controversy and debate about grading? O'Connor (2002) offers seven plausible reasons or perspectives that he has distilled from the writings of several other assessment specialists. First, *learning actually does take place in the absence of grading*. In other words, students can be intrinsically motivated to complete activities and learn. Yet, the second reason almost contradicts the first: *grading is inescapable*. In our current era of accountability, grades are used as vehicles of measurement and are therefore difficult to abolish. The third and fourth perspectives are related in that *faulty grading is damaging to both students and teachers* and *grading is subjective and emotional*. Faulty grading practices damage students' achievement and confidence as well as the interpersonal relationship that they have with their teachers. These teachers have made subjective decisions about the kinds of assessments to use, the scoring of the data and the ultimate use of the data in grading. It should be noted that *there is no single best practice for grading* and this contributes to the notion that *grading is complicated*. Finally, it is surprising that *there is a limited research base for grading* and consequently, the current process of grading has not changed much over the last century. These seven perspectives address the question concerning the debate about grading.

Grading in Cooperative Learning

Classrooms at all levels of education are increasingly emphasizing group-based or cooperative learning strategies. In cooperative learning, small groups of two to six students are presented with a task or problem situation that they must solve together. While the problem given in a cooperative group can be posed in virtually any subject area, the main purpose of cooperative learning is to have students learn to work together to arrive at a single, group-generated solution.

In grading cooperative learning, teachers are usually concerned with assessing three important outcomes: (1) the interactive, cooperative processes that go on within the group, (2) the quality of the group's solution, and (3) each member's contribution to and understanding of that solution. While the assessment of the group processes is important, assessment of subject matter learning is equally important. However, conducting assessment of each individual group member is difficult because the group turns in a single, cooperatively reached product. At issue is how a teacher should assign individual student grades on the basis of a single group production.

The most common grading practice in cooperative learning is to assign a single grade to a group's solution and to give that grade to each group member. The difficulty with such a strategy is that it assumes equal contributions and understanding on the part of each group member. Both the student who contributed and learned a great deal and the student who contributed and learned very little receive the same grade. On the other hand, to push too hard for individual student solutions and contributions can destroy many of the benefits of cooperative problem solving. Thus, for many teachers, grading in cooperative learning situations creates problems not encountered in grading individual student performance.

There is no single acceptable solution to these problems. Many teachers see no difficulty in assuming equal contributions and learning from each group member and give identical grades to all of them. Other teachers mingle assessment of the group process with assessment of the group product, relying on their observations and interactions with students to provide them with an indication of the contribution and comprehension of each group member. Teachers then adjust individual grades according to their observations of student participation, contribution, and understanding. Still other teachers let the students self-assess their own contribution and understanding by grading themselves. This approach is less than ideal because students' self-assessments will often be based as much on their self-perceptions and self-confidence as on their actual contribution and learning.

Teachers can use follow-up activities with individual students to determine how well they understand the processes used in a group-based solution.

Another strategy that has some advantages over the preceding ones combines group and individual grades. All members of the group get the same grade for their single, group-based solution or product. Subsequently, the teacher requires each student to individually answer or perform follow-up or application activities related to the group problem or task. The purpose of these follow-up activities is to determine how well each student understands and can apply the group solution in solving similar types of problems. This approach blends both participation and contribution with subject matter learning in a way that helps the teacher know what each student has learned.

GRADING AS JUDGMENT

The grading process is dependent upon teacher judgments. Ultimately, all grades are based on judgment. Although there may be guidelines to help develop a classroom grading system, all such systems rely on teacher judgment because the teacher knows the students and their accomplishments better than anyone else. Consequently, in assigning grades, teachers are granted considerable discretion and autonomy; no one else can or should make grading judgments for a teacher's students.

The most important aspect of the grading process is its dependence on teacher judgments.

Teacher judgments require two things: (1) data about the student being judged (e.g., test scores, book reports, performance assessments) and (2) a basis of comparison that can be used to translate that data into grading judgments (e.g., what level of performance is worth an A, B, C, D, or F). Data provides the basis for judgment, but note that judgment is different from mere guessing. To *judge* implies that the teacher has some evidence to consider in making the judgment. Thus, a teacher gathers evidence of various kinds to help make judgments and decisions about student learning.

A judgment is neither a guess nor a certainty but is based upon evidence the teacher deems valid and reliable.

But judgment also implies uncertainty, especially in the classroom setting. The evidence for assigning a grade is rarely conclusive or complete, consequently teachers are required to make a judgment. Using greater amounts of information can reduce, but rarely eliminate, the need for them to do so. Assessment evidence is always incomplete, thus teachers must be concerned about the validity and reliability of judgments made from it.

To summarize our discussion of purpose, the goal of grading is to obtain enough valid evidence about student accomplishments to make a grading judgment that is fair, communicates the level of a student's academic performance, and can be supported with evidence. Grades should be based mainly on data such as tests, projects, and performance assessments. The concreteness of these evidence types not only helps the teacher to be objective in awarding grades, but also can help to explain or defend a grade that is challenged. Bearing this in mind, there are three main questions to consider when making a **grading system:**

➤ Against what standard shall I compare my students' performance?
➤ What aspects of student performance shall I include in my grades?
➤ How should different kinds of evidence be weighted in assigning grades?

CHAPTER CASE STUDY

Visit the text OLC to read the case of Sarah Hanover, a high school math teacher who is confronted by angry parents about her grading practices.

www.mcgrawhill.ca/college/airasian

Embedded in these three questions are other questions that all teachers must address when grading. Unfortunately, few school boards have explicit grading policies that specify how to answer these questions. Most school boards and even Ministries and Departments of Education have particular grading formats teachers must use (e.g., A, B, C; good, satisfactory, poor), but teachers must work out the specific details of their grading systems for themselves. These factors contribute to the premise that all grades are based on judgment.

FOUR TYPES OF COMPARISON FOR GRADING

Recall the definition of grading as the process of judging the quality of a student's performance by comparing it to some standard of performance. In order to judge the quality of a student's performance, comparison must be involved. Many bases of comparison can be used to assign grades to students. Typically, classroom grading procedures compare a student's performance to:

1. Other students (norm-referenced grading)
2. Predefined performance standards (criterion-referenced grading)
3. A student's own ability
4. A student's prior performance
5. Standards of provincial/territorial assessments

The first two comparisons are most commonly used by teachers in assigning grades (Brookhart, 1999). In general, comparisons based on a student's ability or prior performance are not in common practice. Comparing students against the standards of provincial/territorial assessments will be discussed in Chapter 9.

Norm-Referenced Grading (Comparison with Other Students)

Norm-referenced grading is based upon comparing a student's performance with other students' performance.

A grading curve sets up quotas for each grade.

Assigning grades to students based upon a comparison with other students in the class is referred to as **norm-referenced grading.** In norm-referenced grading, teachers establish a **grading curve** that defines what percentage of the students can get A's, B's, C's, etc. This curve, which varies from teacher to teacher and is established before an assessment is given, sets up quotas for each grade. Following are two examples of grading curves.

A	Top 20 percent of students	A	Top 10 percent of students
B	Next 30 percent of students	B	Next 40 percent of students
C	Next 30 percent of students	C	Next 45 percent of students
D	Next 10 percent of students	D	Last 5 percent of students
F	Last 10 percent of students		

If the curve on the left were applied to grading a unit test, the teacher would administer the test, score it, and arrange the students in order of their scores from highest to lowest. The highest scoring 20 percent of the students (including ties) would get an A grade; the next 30 percent, a B grade; the next 30 percent, a C grade; and so on.

Since the norm-referenced grading system is designed to ensure that there is a distribution of grades across the various grading categories, not all students can get the top grade no matter how well they perform. Conversely, if a student answers only 40 out of 100 test questions correctly, but was the highest scoring student in the class, he or she would receive an "A" grade in norm-referenced grading. As the recommendations of Faculty of Education at University of Lethbridge (2005) point out, norm-referenced grading provides no information about standards and actual student achievement may not be reflected in a score. There is no single best grading curve that should be used in every norm-referenced grading situation. Instead, teacher discretion determines the nature of the grading curve. A grading curve should be fair to the students and represent academic standards that the teacher feels are appropriate and realistic for the students.

The type of comparison that is used to assign grades to students can influence their effort and attitude. For example, norm-referenced grading tends to undermine the learning and effort of students who repeatedly score near the bottom of the class, since they continually receive poor grades. Norm-referenced grading poses a lesser threat to the top scoring students in the class, although it can spur competition among students for the high grades. Competitive, norm-referenced approaches that make a student's success or failure dependent on the performance of classmates can also reduce student cooperation and interdependence, because success for one student reduces the chance of success for other students.

Norm-referenced grading makes a student's grade dependent on the performance of classmates, which can reduce student cooperation.

Criterion-Referenced Grading (Predefined Performance Standards)

Criterion-referenced grading compares a student's performance or achievement to predefined performance standards. **Performance standards** define the level or score that a student must attain to receive a particular grade. All students who reach a predefined level get the same grade, regardless of how many students reach that level. A common example is the test for a driver's licence, which is often a pass-fail example of performance standards. Passing this test has nothing to do with how other

Grading that compares a student's achievement to predefined performance standards is called criterion-referenced grading.

applicants taking the test perform because applicants' scores are not compared to one another. It is possible for all or none of the applicants to pass. Criterion-referenced grading is the most commonly used grading system in schools. The criteria used to determine performance standards can be either performance-based or percentage-based.

Performance-Based Criteria

Criterion-referenced grading is the most commonly used grading system in schools.

Performance-based criteria spell out in detail the specific learning students must demonstrate to receive a particular grade. For example, in some classrooms teachers utilize contract grading in which the student and teacher negotiate the quality and amount of work the student must satisfactorily complete to receive a particular grade. If the student meets the negotiated performance standard in the allotted time, he or she receives the promised grade.

In criterion-referenced grading, there is no limit to the number of students who can receive a particular grade.

Another example of employing performance-based criteria in grading is through the use of a holistic rubric. Performance standards are embedded in a holistic rubric and a student's performance is judged based on how he or she performs in comparison to the standard, not in comparison to other students. See Chapter 7, page 166, for more information on holistic rubrics.

Percentage-Based Criteria

This second, common type of criterion-referenced standard uses cutoff scores based on the percentage of items answered correctly. In the case of report card grading, an overall percentage of mastery across many individual assessments is used. The following cutoff percentages comprise a widely used standard of this type:

90 to 100 percent of items correct = A

80 to 89 percent of items correct = B

70 to 79 percent of items correct = C

60 to 69 percent of items correct = D

Less than 60 percent of items correct = F

Ministries and Departments of Education may also define the percentage-based criteria that are used within their respective provinces or territories. For example, Ontario's Ministry of Education and Training notes in their *Guide to the Provincial Report Card* (*Grades 1–8*; 1998) that the cut-off percentages for report card grades are:

80 to 100 percent = A- to A+

70 to 79 percent = B- to B+

60 to 69 percent = C- to C+

50 to 59 percent = D- to D+

Below 50 percent = R (Remediation is required)

Any student who scores within one of the above performance standards will receive the corresponding grade. There is no limit on the number of students who can receive a particular grade and the teacher does not know what the distribution of grades will be until after the tests are scored or the report card grades are completed. Note that this is not the case in the norm-referenced grading approach.

There also is the reality in that alphanumerical grades (e.g., A, B, C) may have been assigned and teachers find themselves doing reverse conversions in some cases from letters/level to percentages/numbers. For example, assume that you are a Grade 11 teacher in Ontario. You will report students' final grades in percentages, however, throughout the semester you have used other grading systems. Here is an example of converting from one grading system to another for a percentage grade of 74% (O'Connor, 2000):

Letter Grades	Achievement Level (Ontario Ministry of Education, 1999)	Description (Ontario Ministry of Education, 1999)	% Grade Range
B+, B, B–	3	A high level of achievement. Achievement is at the provincial standard.	70–79%

Some teachers devise their own percentage-based cutoff scores. Similar to the grading curve in norm-referenced grading, in some instances, the grading standards used in criterion-referenced grading are based upon a teacher's judgment about what is appropriate for his or her class. The recommendations of Faculty of Education at University of Lethbridge (2005) remind teachers that standards should not be set too low. Standards should be reasonable given the nature of the subject matter and students' abilities.

Interpreting and Adjusting Grades

The focus on content mastery in criterion-referenced grading makes it especially crucial that teachers provide good instruction and develop valid assessments that cover the range of objectives taught. In criterion-referenced grading, getting an invalid or unclear test item wrong can have implications for students' grades. It is important for teachers to examine assessment results that are unusual or unexpected. Typically, unexpectedly low results provoke teachers to ask: do these low scores indicate a problem with the test or instruction, or a problem with the effort students put into preparing for the test? For example, if a test contains items that were not taught as part of the instructional unit, the test scores do not validly reflect students' achievement. As well, before using assessment information to grade students on their report cards, the overall quality of that information should be considered. Grades are only as meaningful as the information on which they are based.

Regardless of whether one employs a norm- or a criterion-referenced grading system (see Table 8.1 for a comparison of norm- and criterion-referenced grading), the grading curve or performance standards should be determined before assessment is carried out. Doing this helps teachers to think about expected performance and allows them to inform students of what will be needed to get high grades. When properly defined, a grading system tells students what constitutes high and low achievement. However, judgments are sometimes incorrect and need to be adjusted. Consequently, once established, performance standards and grading curves need not be set in stone. If, for some reason, a standard or grading curve turns out to be inappropriate or unfair, it can and should be changed before grades are assigned. Fairness means assessing what students were taught, using appropriate assessment procedures, and establishing realistic grading curves or performance standards. This does not mean that the teacher lowers grading curves or selects low performance standards; a practice that could diminish the validity of grades and discourage student effort. The discretion lies with the classroom teacher to make changes in grading curves and standards when he or she judges them to be invalid for some reason. Teacher discretion is at the heart of good grading.

If a grading standard or curve proves to be inappropriate or unfair, it should be changed before grades are assigned.

TABLE 8.1	Comparison of Norm-Referenced and Criterion-Referenced Grading	
	Norm-Referenced	**Criterion-Referenced**
Comparison made	Student to other students.	Student to predefined criteria.
Method of comparison	Grading curve; percentage of students who can get each grade.	Standard of performance; scores students must achieve to get a given grade.
What grade describes	Student's performance compared to others in the class.	Student's percentage mastery of course objectives.
Availability of a particular grade	Limited by grading curve. Not all students can get an A.	No limit on grade availability. All students could get an A.

Comparison to a Student's Own Ability

Teachers frequently make remarks such as "Omar is not working up to his ability," "Tim is not doing as well as he can," or "Raquel continues to achieve much higher grades than I expected she would." When teachers make such statements, they are comparing a student's actual performance to the performance they expect, based on their judgment of the student's ability. The terms "overachiever" and "underachiever" are also used to describe students who do better or worse than teacher judgments of what they should be doing. Many teachers assign grades by comparing a student's actual performance to their perception of the student's ability level.

In this ability-based grading approach, students with high ability who do excellent work would receive high grades, as would students with low ability who the teacher believed were achieving "up to their potential." Even though the actual performance of the low-ability students may be well below that of the high-ability, high-achieving students, each group would receive the same grade if each were perceived to be achieving up to their ability. Conversely, students with high ability who were perceived by their teacher to be underachieving—that is, performing below what the teacher thinks they are capable of performing—would receive low grades. An argument advanced in defence of this grading approach is that it motivates students to do their best while it punishes unmotivated students who do not work up to their perceived ability.

However, grading based on student ability is not recommended for a number of reasons (Kubiszyn & Borich, 2003). First, the approach depends on the teacher having an accurate perception of each student's ability. Teachers do have a general sense of students' abilities from their early assessments and the students' classroom performance, but this information is too imprecise to use as a basis for grading. Formal tests designed to measure ability may not accurately predict a student's capacity for learning. Even for experts, it is difficult to make valid predictions about what a student of a certain general ability level is capable of achieving in any specific subject area.

Even formal tests designed to measure ability are rarely precise enough to accurately predict a student's capacity for learning.

Second, teachers often have a difficult time differentiating a student's ability from other characteristics such as self-assurance, motivation, or responsiveness. This is especially problematic in light of recent constructivist thinking that students have numerous types of abilities or intelligences, not just one (Sternberg, 1997). Given these multiple abilities or intelligences that help students learn and perform in different modalities (e.g., oral, visual, written), which ones should a teacher focus on to judge a student's ability?

Third, grades comparing performance against expectations are confusing to people outside the classroom, especially parents. For example, a high-ability student who attained 80 percent mastery of the instruction might receive a C grade if perceived to be underachieving, while a low-ability student who attained 60 percent mastery might receive an A grade

Teachers should not assign grades by solely comparing a student's actual performance to their perception of the student's ability level.

*There is little
correlation between
grades and student
mastery of course
content in ability-based
grading systems.*

for exceeding expectations. An outsider viewing these two grades would probably think that the low-ability student mastered more of the course, because that student got the higher grade. In short, there is little correlation between grades and student mastery of course content in ability-based grading systems.

These reasons argue strongly against the use of a grading system that compares actual to predicted achievement. Many report cards do allow separate judgments about student achievement and ability. The teacher can record a subject matter grade based on the student's actual achievement, and then, in a separate place on the report card, indicate if he or she thinks the student is working up to expectations. Usually, the teacher writes comments or checks boxes to show whether the student "needs improvement," "is improving," or "is doing his best" relative to his or her ability. Even in this approach, teachers must be cautious about putting too much faith in their estimates of student ability and potential.

Comparison to a Student's Prior Performance

Basing grades on student improvement over time creates problems similar to those of grading estimates of student ability. Student improvement is determined by comparing a student's early performance to his or her later performance. Students who show the most progress or growth get high grades and those who show little progress or growth get low grades. An obvious difficulty with this approach is that students who do well early in the grading period have little opportunity to improve, and thus have little chance to get high grades. Low scorers at the start of the term have the best chance to show improvement, and thus tend to get high grades. It is not surprising that students graded on improvement quickly realize that it is in their best interests to do poorly on early assessments. In this manner, early performance will be low and improvement can be shown easily.

Like comparing actual to predicted performance, grading on the basis of improvement also causes problems with grade interpretation. A student who improves from very low achievement to moderate achievement may get an A, while a student who had high achievement at the start and therefore improved little may get a B or a C, when overall, it was the latter student who mastered more of the subject matter than the student who got the A grade.

*The same grading
system must be applied
to all students in the
class in order to convey
a consistent and
understandable message
about classroom
standards.*

Some teachers recognize this difficulty and propose the following solution: give the students who achieve high standards throughout the term an A grade for their high performance, but also give A grades to students who improve their performance a great deal over time. While this suggestion overcomes the problem noted above, it creates a new problem. In essence, these teachers are proposing to simultaneously use two very different grading systems, one based on high achievement and the other on high student improvement. This approach provides rewards for both groups of students, but confuses the meaning of their grades, since the grades can mean two different things: achievement or improvement. Thus, grading systems based on improvement and ability, and grading systems based on combinations of these two, are not recommended. Grades convey a consistent, understandable message only if the same approach is applied to all students.

DECIDING WHAT TO GRADE

Once the comparative basis for assigning grades is decided on, the teacher must select the students' products and performances that will be used to compile grades. This is a critical decision because the products and performances that are included define what the grades mean. You may find yourself saying, "What do I want my grades to convey about student performance?" and "Do the assessments I've included in the grade reflect what I want to convey?" It is not necessary for teachers to include all available assessment information when assigning grades.

The quantity and nature of assessment information available to a teacher varies depending on the grade level and subject area. For example, in social studies or history, an elementary teacher may have information from quizzes, worksheets, oral reports and portfolios. High school math teachers may have homework papers, class discussion and test results to consider in assigning grades. In addition to these indicators of student achievement, teachers have informal perceptions of students' effort, interest, motivation, cooperation, and behaviour. Grading often covers both academic achievement and affective performances.

Each teacher must decide which of the many formal and informal information sources available to use in determining a report card grade.

Academic Achievement

Grades are usually viewed as an indication of how much students have learned from instruction. Assessments of students' achievement of the course objectives should be the major component of subject matter grades. Note that the more valid the assessments used in grading, the more valid the resulting grades (Brookhart, 1999). Formal subject matter assessments such as teacher-made tests, papers, quizzes, homework, projects, worksheets, and portfolios are the best types of evidence to use in assigning report card grades. They are suitable in two respects. First, they provide information about students' academic performance, which is what grades are intended to describe. Second, as tangible products of students' work, they can be used to explain or defend a grade if the need arises. It is defensible to say to a student, "I gave you a C on your report card because when I compared your test scores, projects, and homework assignments in this marking period to my grading standards, you performed at a C level."

Formal subject matter assessments such as teacher-made tests and homework provide the evidence to explain or defend a grade.

Grading as a process cannot be separated from the quality of the instruction and assessment information teachers collect prior to grading. Just as good instruction can be undermined by invalid assessment, good grading can be undermined by poorly constructed, invalid, and unreliable assessments. Irrelevant, invalid evidence about student achievement will produce irrelevant, invalid grades. The guidelines for constructing valid assessments described in Chapters 5 through 7 should underlie the assessments teachers construct and use in their grades.

Students are given greater opportunity to demonstrate achievement when grades are based on several types of assessment information.

As a final consideration in the process of assessing students' academic achievement, grading should be based upon a varied assortment of valid and reliable evidence. A general rule of grading is to draw on several different types of information rather than a single type, because this gives students the opportunity to show what they can do. Also, since students are required to remember, understand, and apply most subject areas, varied procedures are needed to assess all outcomes of instruction.

Affective Performances

Teachers know their students as individuals, not one-dimensional achievers. Teachers recognize when their students are working hard, when their students are not able to sustain their attention, and when students' home situation affects their school performance. Because of this, teachers often find it difficult to be completely objective and dispassionate dispensers of report card grades. Yet, affective characteristics should not be major factors in report card grades. A common situation in which student motivation, interest, and effort enter into grades is when a teacher awards a B+ to a student whose academic performance places her between a B and a B+ grade. Since the student is motivated, participates in class, and works diligently, the teacher is taking into account more than just formal assessments of achievement.

Teachers may nudge upward the grades they give to conscientious, participating students in order to keep them motivated. Such adjustments distort the intended meaning of a grade, but most teachers do make them based upon their knowledge of a particular student's needs. Grading is a human judgmental process, and it is virtually inevitable that such teacher adjustments will be made. These borderline decisions usually operate for the benefit of the student and the psychic comfort of the teacher.

Students who work hard, are cooperative, and show great motivation and interest deserve to be rewarded, but subject matter grades are not the proper arena for such rewards. Nor should these grades be used to punish students for behavioural problems or late work unless timeliness is part of the performance criteria. Some provinces and territories include categories for grading students' affective performances. In British Columbia, "social responsibility" is a student development characteristic that is graded on report cards. Figure 8.1 is a rubric that teachers can refer to when grading the four different aspects of "social responsibility" (British Columbia Min-

FIGURE 8.1   *Quick Scale: Grades 6 to 8 Social Responsibility.*

This *Quick Scale* presents summary statements from the four categories in a one-page format for ease of use. In most cases, these scales can be used to evaluate student development anytime during the year. In the *Elaborated Scale*, each of the four categories is printed on a separate page.

Aspect	Not Yet Within Expectations	Meets Expectations (Minimal Level)	Fully Meets Expectations	Exceeds Expectations
CONTRIBUTING TO THE CLASSROOM AND SCHOOL COMMUNITY	• often appears to be unfriendly and negative • does not take responsibility or work cooperatively	• usually friendly and, if asked, will include others • with support, will take responsibility, contribute, and work cooperatively	• routinely kind and friendly, and helps and includes others if asked • takes responsibility, contributes, and works cooperatively	• kind, friendly, inclusive, and helpful • voluntarily takes on responsibilities and contributes; effective in groups
SOLVING PROBLEMS IN PEACEFUL WAYS	• unwilling or unable to solve interpersonal problems; may be illogical or blame others, or become violent or sarcastic • tends to view problems in black and white; has difficulty considering more than one perspective, generating strategies, and predicting consequences	• may try to solve interpersonal problems and consider others' feelings, but often needs support; may become frustrated and blame others • can clarify familiar, concrete problems and issues, and propose some strategies; may misinterpret consequences	• tries to solve interpersonal problems calmly; often shows empathy and considers others' perspectives • can clarify an increasing range of problems or issues, generate and compare potential strategies, and anticipate some consequences	• uses a repertoire of strategies to deal with interpersonal problems; tries to be logical and non-judgmental; considers others' feelings and perspectives • can clarify increasingly complex problems and issues, propose and evaluate strategies, and weigh consequences
VALUING DIVERSITY AND DEFENDING HUMAN RIGHTS	• often disrespectful and may avoid or be negative towards those perceived as different in some way	• usually respectful to others and accepting of differences, but may not see the need for action on human rights	• usually treats others fairly and respectfully; tries to be unbiased; shows some support for human rights	• usually treats everyone fairly and respectfully; shows an increasing commitment to correcting injustices
EXERCISING DEMOCRATIC RIGHTS AND RESPONSIBILITIES	• tends to be egocentric or apathetic; may show a sense of power-lessness	• shows some interest in making the world a better place, but ideas tend to be very general and follow-through tends to be incon-sistent	• shows a sense of community and an interest in making the world a better place; tries to follow through on planned actions	• shows a growing sense of altruism and optimism—a commitment to making the world a better place

istry of Education, 2005). Another example is from Sir Wilfrid Laurier School Board (2005) in Quebec. Figure 8.2 is part of the Elementary School Report Card that includes students' affective performances or competencies.

FIGURE 8.2
Excerpt from Sir Wilfrid Laurier School Board Report Card.

CROSS-CURRICULAR COMPETENCIES / COMPÉTENCES TRANSVERSALES

INTELLECTUAL COMPETENCIES / COMPÉTENCES INTELLECTUELLES

➤ uses information / exploite l'information

➤ solves problems / résout des problèmes

➤ exercises critical judgment / exerce un jugement critique

➤ uses creativity / fait preuve de créativité

METHODOLOGICAL COMPETENCIES / COMPÉTENCES MÉTHODOLOGIQUES

➤ adopts effective work habits / se donne des méthodes de travail efficaces

➤ uses information and communication technologies / exploite les technologies de l'information et de la communication

PERSONAL AND SOCIAL COMPETENCIES / COMPÉTENCES PERSONNELLES ET SOCIALES

➤ develops own identity / développe son identité

➤ cooperates with others / coopère avec les autres

COMMUNICATION-RELATED COMPETENCIES / COMPÉTENCE DE L'ORDRE DE LA COMMUNICATION

➤ communicates appropriately / communique de façon appropriée

Students are graded accordingly as "A = very satisfactory," "B = satisfactory," "C = with a few difficulties," "D = with great difficulty," "NR = not reported." Many other Canadian school boards include similar categories for grading effective performances.

SOURCE: Courtesy of the Sir Wilfrid Laurier School Board Educational Services Department, Rosemere, Quebec.

In the last three main sections of this chapter, we have seen that teachers must decide what standards of comparison to use in assigning grades. This means deciding upon either a norm-referenced or a criterion-referenced standard. Once this decision has been made, the teacher must establish a grading curve in the norm-referenced approach or a set of performance standards in the criterion-referenced approach. Next, the teacher must determine what performances will be included in the grades. Because grades are mainly intended to convey information about students' mastery of subject matter, rather than their personal qualities, grades should be based primarily upon assessments of student achievement. Although, teachers' subjective perceptions and insights inevitably influence the grading process to some extent, they should not be allowed to greatly distort the subject matter grade.

SUMMARIZING VARIED TYPES OF ASSESSMENT INFORMATION

Report card grades require teachers to summarize each student's performance on the many individual assessments gathered during the marking period. In some subject areas, summarization across a term is easy and straightforward. In other subject areas, there is a great deal and varying types of data to summarize.

Figure 8.3 shows a page from a Grade 5 teacher's actual grade book for the first five weeks of term two in a Canadian geography unit. At the bottom of the figure is a list of all the assessments the students were expected to complete. Each student is assigned a grade for each of the assessments. Cells that have an empty circle indicate that the student has not yet turned in that assessment. Assessment topics that have no grades listed for all students, such as "Around World in 26 Letters," indicate assessments that are in process but not completed.

At the end of term, teachers must synthesize each student's assessment data. Calculating each student's overall performance has been made easier with the use of spreadsheets and varied computer grading programs. A commonly used spreadsheet program is *Microsoft Office Excel 2003*, which can assist teachers with the organization of assessment data and the calculation of grades. Table 8.2 shows the results of a computer grading program (Class Action Gradebook Software, 2005). The scores for each assessment are shown in the columns labelled "Classwork," "Homework," "Tests." The average of each student's assessments is shown on the left of the table under "Grade." As a function of the initial software set-up, grading standards are entered. Consequently, a letter grade appears to the right of the "Grade" column.

The following is a simple example of summarization of assessment data and grade conversion for report card purposes. Suppose that over the course of a term in a particular subject, you had administered 12 weekly tests, each scored on the basis of 100 points. Since each test is worth the same amount, to arrive at a grade you would sum each student's score on the 12 tests and calculate the mean or average score. (See Appendix C on page 305 for a comparison of mean, median, and mode.) Assume that you were using a criterion-referenced approach with these performance standards: 100% to 90% = A+, 89% to 80% = A, 79% to 70% = B, 69% to 60% = C, and below 60% = D. Each student's percentage grade would be compared to the performance standards and then assigned a corresponding letter grade. However, most grading situations are not as simple as this example. It is important to note that not all teachers would have the same scenario since different performance standards may be in place, a norm-referenced grading system may be employed, and assessment information often varies.

FIGURE 8.3 *Grade 5 Teacher's Mark Book.*

Subject Canadian Geography Unit; Section 02	Assignment		1		+3 2		+2 3		4				+3 5						6	7		Sit Report	8				9		10		
			√		√		√		√				√						√	√	√ Term 2						√		√		
Month . . .		1st week						2nd week						3rd week						4th week						5th week					
Date . . .																						↓									
Students . . .		M	T	W	T	F		M	T	W	T	F		M	T	W	T	F		M	T	W	T	F		M	T	W	T	F	
Abra, G.	1		70		92		79		99		'		91		'		√+		81		60		47		√		80		82		85
Avakian, P.	2		50		95		79		92		'		90		'		√+		100		60		86		√+		100		91		100
Bornstein, E.	3		40		82		47		○		'		74		'				○		80		40		'		80		64		55
Brooks, P.	4		70		76		89		86		'		82		'		√+		93		80		79		√+		90		99		100
Chang, M.	5		54		84		47		(88)	88	'		67		-'10				(39)	39			62				55		(96)		80
Chou, C.	6		60		91		84		100		'		85		'		√+		91		70		87		√		100		100		95
Davis, L.	7		49		67		47		○		'		(55)		'		√+		59		40		58		√				(98)		80
Garcia, G.	8		70		94		89		100		'		86		'		√+		92		40		93		√+		97		100		
Haley, N.	9		69		68		100		83		'		88		'		√+		89		80		87		√+				100		90
Katz, W.	10		(30)		73		74		100		'		99		'		√+		0		20		73				80		77		80
Morgan, J.	11		39		73		47		98		'		(62)				√+		90		70		46				70		100		80
Nguyen, T.	12		70		76		89		92		'		78		'		√+		88		70		67		√		80		99		100
Ortiz, J.	~~13~~																														
Rodriguez, H.	14		68		62		79		81		ab		69		'		√+		31		ab		59		√		70		94		80
Schmitt, O.	15		63		79		74		98		'		79		'		√+		77		80		60		√		95		99		
Vance, N.	16		59		~~34~~	60	58		92		'		75		-'10		(√+)		86		100		67		'				82		80
Winston, D.	17		(71)		87		100		85		'		95		-'10				89		100		59		√+		100		100		75
Zang, E.	18		80		79		100		83		'		74		-'10		√+		6		100		53		√+		95		80		95
	19																														
	20																														
	21																														
	22																														
	23																														
	24																														
	25																														
	26																														
	27																														
	28																														
	29																														
	30																														
	31																														
	32																														
	33																														
	34																														
	35																														
			Weekly Geo #8 (10)		Current Event—Oct		Pictonitions Quiz (19)		Weekly Geo #9 (14)		Around World in 26 letters (25)		Current Event—Nov		Mystery Post Card		Canadian Squares		Weekly Geo #10 (18)		Sec 2 Quiz (10) P26–30		Weekly Geo #11 (15)		December Cities		Around World in 20 cards		Weekly Geo #12 (11)		

Consider a more typical example of a mark book for social studies, shown in Figure 8.4. This set of marks includes many different kinds of assessment information: homework assignments, quizzes, unit tests, and projects. Here different grading formats are used for different assessments such as checkmarks (✓), percentage grades, and letter grades. Converting this assessment information into a single grade is a complicated process. There are additional questions that must be considered in the grading process. You need to ask yourself, "What specific performances or assessment information will be included in the calculation of the final term

TABLE 8.2 Sample Computer Grading Program

Class Action - [A Sample Class - Period One - 2nd Semester 2000]

File Edit Class Grading Attendance Graphs Window Help

Classroom | Grade Summary | Homework | Classwork | Tests | Student Report | Parent Letter | Profi

Student Information | Class Statistics | What If?

Name Class Count: 20	Grade		Homework Wt: 25%	Miss	Classwork Wt: 25%	Miss	Tests Wt: 50%	Miss
Brown, Watson	82.6%	B-	75.0%	1	92.0%		81.7%	
de Oliveria, Miguel	76.1%	C	62.5%		75.0%		83.5%	
del Aguila, Jose	91.8%	A-	87.5%		100.0%		89.9%	
Figg, Ingrid	75.4%	C	68.8%		91.0%		70.9%	
Hubbard, La Vette	86.3%	B	87.5%		100.0%		78.8%	
Jones, Bobbette	82.0%	B-	87.5%		94.0%		73.3%	
Jones, Bobby	86.7%	B	93.8%		94.0%		79.5%	
Le, Hortense	72.2%	C-	71.9%		91.0%		63.0%	
Luong, Woo	89.4%	B+	84.4%		91.0%		91.1%	
Newton, Amber	79.9%	B-	40.6%	3	100.0%		89.4%	
Nguyen, Tran	82.9%	B-	50.0%	2	90.0%		95.8%	
O'Donnell, Johnston	85.9%	B	78.1%	1	91.0%		87.2%	
Ontiveros, Hilda	75.2%	C	56.3%	1	82.0%		81.2%	
Pell, Joquim	88.5%	B+	87.5%		94.0%		86.2%	
Sanford, Tikesha	84.0%	B	93.8%		93.0%		74.6%	
Schmit, Chrisopher	73.7%	C	84.4%		87.0%		61.7%	1
Sledge, Shimika	82.7%	B-	81.3%		78.0%		85.7%	
Valdez, Freddie	87.2%	B	87.5%		100.0%		80.7%	
Williams, MollyBe	90.9%	A-	93.8%		94.0%		87.9%	
Yoshaki, Bill	68.9%	D+	65.6%	1	87.0%		61.5%	

SOURCE: "Class Action—[A Sample Class—Period One—2nd Semester 2000]," Class Action Gradebook, www.classactiongradebook.com.

grade?" "How much will each kind of information count in determining the grade?" These are just some of the considerations that all teachers face when they begin to combine different kinds of assessment information into a single grade. The following sections contain suggestions for answering such questions.

FIGURE 8.4 *Marking Book for Social Studies Assessments.*

	HW #1	HW #2	HW #3	HW #4	quiz	quiz	test unit 1	test unit 2	test unit 3	test unit 4	perf. based task Explor.	proj. New France
Avadis, P.	✓	✓	✓	✓-	85	90	80	85	50	80	B+	B
Babcock, W.	✓	✓	✓	✓-	90	90	85	80	60	80	B	B
Cannata, T.	✓	✓-	✓	✓	80	75	70	70	45	75	C-	C
Farmer, P.	✓+	✓+	✓+	✓	100	95	90	85	70	95	A-	A-
Foster, C.	✓+	✓+	✓	✓	90	80	85	90	65	80	B	B+
Gonzales, E.	✓	✓-	✓-	✓-	70	75	60	70	55	70	C	B-
Grodsky, F.	✓-	✓-	✓-	✓-	65	65	65	60	35	60	C	C
Miarka, S.	✓	✓	✓	✓	80	90	70	85	65	85	C	B
Picardi, O.	✓	✓	✓	✓	75	80	85	75	65	80	B	B_
Ross, O.	✓+	✓	✓	✓	85	80	90	90	75	95	A	A-
Sachar, S.	✓-	✓	✓	✓+	80	85	75	80	40	80	B+	B
Saja, J.	✓	✓	✓	✓	75	80	85	85	50	80	B	B+
Stamos, G.	✓	✓+	✓+	✓	70	60	75	85	50	70	B_	B
Whalem, W.	✓	✓	✓	✓	70	70	50	60	60	70	B_	B_
Yeh, T.	✓+	✓+	✓+	✓+	95	100	95	95	75	95	A	A_

What Should Be Included in a Grade?

As the teacher, if you were summarizing student performance for report card purposes, you would have all of the assessment data that are shown in Figure 8.4 to take into account during the grading process. You should recognize that not all teachers will arrive at the same decisions and there is no best way to assign grades in all classrooms. Here are some points to consider.

Almost all teachers would include the unit tests and the project results in determining their students' grades. These are formal, summative indicators of student achievement that should be reflected in the grade a student receives. Most teachers rightly assign grades based mainly on formal assessments. Still other teachers would also include quiz results and homework, although there would be less unanimity among teachers on this point. Some teachers regard quizzes and homework as practice activities that are more closely tied to instruction than to assessment. Other teachers view homework and quizzes as indicators of how well students have learned their daily lessons and thus include them as part of the student's grade. Others would not count homework because it is never clear who actually does the work. These teachers may reserve comments that relate to homework completion to the anecdotal section of the report card. Some provinces, such as Ontario, include a category such as, "Homework Completion" as one of nine assessed "Learning Skills" (Ministry of Education of Ontario, 1998). Elementary students are graded as "E = Excellent, G = Good, S = Satisfactory, or NI = Needs Improvement."

Some teachers view quizzes and homework as more closely tied to the instructional process than to the grading process.

Let us assume that you have decided to include three types of formal assessment information in your students' social studies grades: tests, projects, and quizzes. Having decided what student performances will be included, you now must determine whether each kind of information will count equally or whether some kinds should be weighted more heavily than others.

Selecting Weights for Assessment Information

An immediate concern in summarizing student performance on different kinds of information is how each should be weighted. In general, teachers should give the more substantial types of student performance (e.g., tests, projects, and portfolios) more weight than short quizzes or homework assignments, since the former provide a more complete, integrated and valid view of students' subject matter learning.

Some Ministries and Departments of Education hold policies with respect to general grade weighting practices. For example, in Ontario secondary schools, the final course grade is 70 percent based on assessment and evaluation conducted throughout the course and 30 percent based on a final evaluation (e.g., examination) that is administered toward the end of the course (Ontario Ministry of Education, 1999). Further, grade weightings should reflect standards, expectations, and learning goals. At the secondary level, for each course, teachers should provide students with a written grading policy that describes how grades are to be weighted (O'Connor, 2002).

Again referring to the example from Figure 8.4, you might decide that unit tests and projects should count equally and that both should count more than quiz results. As a basis for this decision you should be certain that the unit tests reflected the important aspects of content instruction and that the assigned project required students to integrate their knowledge about the topic. You should be certain that the performance-based assessment task (oral presentation on explorers) that utilized a rubric was an opportunity for students to openly demonstrate their knowledge. Finally, you may decide that the two quizzes will count as much as one unit test. Consequently, you have identified seven pieces of information that will be combined to determine your students' report card grades in social studies:

➤ four separate marks for each of the four unit tests

➤ two separate marks for each of the project and performance-based assessment task

➤ one combined mark for the two quizzes

If the report card grade is considered as one whole, the unit tests count as four-sevenths of the grade, the project and performance-based assessment task count as two-sevenths of the grade, and the quiz results count as one-seventh of the grade.

Methods for weighting the various types of assessment information should be kept simple.

Regardless of how a teacher weights each kind of assessment information, it is strongly suggested that the weightings be simple. It is better to weight some things twice as much as others than to weight some five times as much and others seven times as much. In most instances, the final grades arrived at using a simple weighting scheme will not differ greatly from those arrived at using a more complex, cumbersome weighting scheme. Weighting grades is an exercise in professional judgment (O'Connor, 2000).

Combining Different Assessment Information

Figure 8.4 shows that student performance on different assessments often is represented in different ways. As a teacher, it is your job to combine the selected scoring formats into a single summary score that includes performance on tests, projects, and quizzes. Some of the information shown in Figure 8.4 would have to be changed into another format, preferably a numerical one. This means that the project and performance-based task letter grades would have to be converted into numerical scores on a scale of 0 to 100 percent, so that they would correspond to the scores for the quizzes and unit tests. You may decide that for the project grades, the following scale could be used to assign numerical scores to the projects: A+ = 88, A = 85, A- = 82, B+ = 78, B = 75, B- = 72, C+ = 68, C = 65, C- = 62. If, for example, a student got a B- on one of the projects, that students' numerical score on the project would be 72. It is important to note that this is not the only way that the different scores could be put on the same scale, nor is it without limitations. This is, however, one approach to accomplishing your task of converting grades into a numerical format.

Each type of assessment information should be expressed in terms of the same scale so that all can be combined into a composite score.

It is important to stress that all performance indicators should be expressed in terms of the same scale, so that they can be combined meaningfully. As another example, suppose that you gave two tests, one with 50 items and one with 100 items, and that you wanted each test to count equally in determining a student's grade. Now suppose that two students, Gianluca and Marcus, each got a perfect score on one of the tests and a zero score on the other: Marcus got his perfect score on the 50-item test and Gianluca got his on the 100-item test. Because the tests are to count equally, you might think that the students' grades should be the same regardless of the number of items on each test. However, if you calculate the average performance for Marcus and Gianluca using the *number* of items they got right across both tests, the resulting averages will be quite different: Marcus's average would be 25 (50 + 0)/2 = 25) and Gianluca's average would be 50 (0 + 100)/2 = 50). Gianluca would get a higher grade than Marcus, even though they each attained a perfect score on one test and a zero score on another and the tests were to count equally. Clearly, combining raw scores or number of items correct and finding their average does not give equal weight to each test.

The problem in this example is that you did not take into account the difference in the number of items on the two tests; you did not put the two tests on the same scale before computing an average. If you had changed the scores from number of items correct to percentage of items correct *before* averaging, Marcus and Gianluca would have had the same overall performance [Marcus = (100 + 0)/2 = 50; Gianluca = (0 + 100)/2 = 50]. Or if you had expressed performance on both tests in terms of the 100-point test, the averages would have been the same, since Marcus's perfect score on a 50-item test would be worth 100 points on a 100 point scale. Once again, if scores are not expressed in a common scale, student performance will be distorted and grades will not reflect actual achievement. See the Technology and Assessment box for information on computerized grading systems.

Validity of the Information

Before combining assessment information into a grade, the quality of that information must be considered. Grades will be only as meaningful as the information on which they are based. If the project grades were assigned subjectively or with no clear criteria in mind they will not accurately reflect student achievement. If the unit tests did not test a representative sample of what was taught, the scores students attained will not be valid indications of their achievement. In this regard, if you were using the Marking Book in Figure 8.4, you should examine the results of the unit 3 test, since they were much lower than scores on the other unit tests. Do these scores indicate a problem with the test or a problem with the effort students put into preparing for the test? How should this result be handled in grading? These questions have to be answered before information can be combined and used for grading.

You may have noticed the poor performance on the unit 3 test when you scored the test, and no doubt asked yourself why the scores were so low. Normally, questions about the match between an assessment instrument and the things students were taught occur *before* an assessment instrument is used. Sometimes, however, mismatches are overlooked or do not become apparent until after the instrument is administered and scored. Unexpectedly low scores typically provoke teacher concern and attention.

TECHNOLOGY AND ASSESSMENT

Computerized Grading Systems

www.asyluminc.com

Some school boards in Canada have adopted a software program called, "MarkBook" to assist teachers in analyzing student achievement. The program generates report card grades and drafts comments. The software is compatible with palm and pocket PC technology and there is a French version as well.

There are a host of other software products designed for classroom teachers' grading. Find links to these sites along with "MarkBook" on our OLC at

www.mcgrawhill.ca/college/airasian.

Grades are only as meaningful (valid) as the information upon which they are based.

If unexpectedly low scores on some part of a test indicate a mismatch with instruction, then grading adjustments should be made.

You should look over the items in the unit 3 test (a textbook test), and compare the items to the topics and skills that you taught in that unit. If you find that a large number of the test items had come from a section of the textbook that you had decided not to teach, then by oversight you had failed to remove the items. Thus, the match between the unit test and classroom instruction was not good, and your students have been penalized by being asked questions about material they had not been taught. Clearly, the unit 3 test scores do not reflect your students' actual achievement and, if used in grading, would reduce the validity of the grades.

Consequently, you may decide to change the students' scores on the unit 3 test to better reflect their achievement. For example, you might estimate that about 20 to 25 percent of the items on the test were from the section you had not taught. If most students had done poorly on these items, you might decide to increase each student's unit 3 score by 20 percentage points. These increased scores would provide a better indication than the original scores of what students had learned from the instruction provided.

It is important to point out that adjustment of low scores on a test should occur only after reexamining both the test and your instruction. Test scores should be raised so that they will provide a more valid indication of how well students learned from their instruction. Your grades should reflect your students' subject matter mastery. Low assessment scores should not be raised simply because they are low or because you are disappointed with them.

Computing Overall Scores

Having decided on score equivalents for the project assessments and having adjusted scores on the unit 3 test to correct the partial mismatch between instruction and assessment, you are ready to compute your students' social studies grades. To do this, you must (1) weigh each kind of assessment information; (2) sum the scores; and (3) divide by 7, which is the number of assessment items you are using to grade (one overall quiz score, four unit test scores, and two project scores). This computation will provide an average social studies score for each student's marking period. Table 8.3 shows the seven components to be included in each student's grade, their total, and their average.

Consider P. Avadis's scores in the table. This student received a total quiz score of 88, based on the average of two quizzes rounded off to a whole number. The four test scores—with 20 points added to the unit 3 score—are as shown in the table. The two project grades are expressed in terms of the numerical equivalents. Adding these scores gives a total score of 556, which, when divided by 7 (for the seven pieces of information that were combined), gives an average performance of 79. The average for each student gives an indication of the proportion of social studies objectives each student achieved in the marking period. You can now apply your performance standards to award students' grades.

TABLE 8.3	Computation of Students' Social Studies Grades, Social Studies, Term 1								
	Quizzes	Test 1	Test 2	Test 3	Test 4	Proj. 1	Proj. 2	Total Score	Average
Avadis, P.	88	80	85	70	80	78	75	556	79
Babcock, W.	90	85	80	80	80	75	75	565	81
Cannata, T.	78	70	70	65	70	62	65	480	69
Farmer, P.	98	90	85	90	95	82	82	622	89
Foster, C.	85	85	90	85	80	75	78	578	83
Gonzales, E.	73	60	70	75	70	65	72	485	69
Grodsky, F.	65	65	60	55	60	65	65	435	62
Miarka, S.	85	70	85	85	85	65	75	550	79
Picardi, O.	78	85	75	85	80	75	72	550	79
Ross, O.	83	90	90	95	95	85	82	620	89
Sachar, S.	83	75	80	60	80	78	75	531	76
Saja, J.	78	85	85	70	80	75	78	551	79
Stamos, G.	65	75	85	70	70	72	75	512	73
Whalem, W.	70	50	60	80	70	72	72	474	68
Yeh, T.	98	95	95	95	95	85	82	645	92

TWO APPROACHES TO ASSIGNING GRADES

Here we return again to our basic distinction between norm- and criterion-referenced grading.

A Criterion-Referenced Example

You might decide to assign grades based on a criterion-referenced approach because you believe that this approach offers each student an opportunity to get a good grade if he or she has mastered what was taught. At this juncture, some teachers consider students' nonacademic characteristics when it comes time to assign a grade. Some teachers consider how much effort has been put into the class or what effect a high or low grade will have on their students. Teachers are sometimes aware of how much pressure the students get from parents and the reaction that they will have to a particular grade. These teachers are aware of their responsibility to grade students primarily on their academic performance, but they allow for small individual student adjustments. Still other teachers grade strictly by the numbers. These teachers calculate each student's average and assign grades based strictly on that average. They believe that this is the only way to be fair to all students. Opinions will always differ about making such grading adjustments.

The following is an example of performance standards that you could adopt for your social studies grades based on a criterion-referenced approach:

A+	= 88 or higher	A	= 85 to 87	A–	= 82 to 84
B+	= 78 to 81	B	= 75 to 77	B–	= 72 to 74
C+	= 68 to 71	C	= 65 to 67	C–	= 62 to 64
D+	= 58 to 61	D	= 55 to 57	D–	= 52 to 54
F	= less than 52				

Looking at the overall term averages as shown in Table 8.3 you could apply your performance standards to award grades. The grades awarded to each student were as follows:

Name	Average	Grade	Name	Average	Grade
Avadis, P.	79	B+	Picardi, O.	79	B+
Babcock, W.	81	B+	Ross, O.	89	A+
Cannata, T.	69	C+	Sachar, S.	76	B
Farmer, P.	89	A+	Saja, J.	79	B+
Foster, C.	83	A–	Stamos, G.	73	B–
Gonzales, E.	69	C+	Whalem, W.	68	C+
Grodsky, F.	62	C–	Yeh, T.	92	A+
Miarka, S.	79	B+			

Teachers' judgments about nonacademic characteristics often enter into grading when the student is close to reaching the next higher grade level.

Notice that student Babcock, W. is within one point of the performance standard for the next higher grade. It is for students who are close to reaching the next higher grade that teacher judgments about nonacademic characteristics usually enter into grading.

To summarize, you had to make many decisions to arrive at these grades. You had to decide whether to use a norm-referenced or a criterion-referenced grading approach. Having selected the criterion-referenced approach, you had to decide on performance standards for awarding grades. Next you had to decide upon the kinds of assessment information that would be included in your grades and how to weight each kind. You then had to decide how to put all assessment scores on the same scale because some information was expressed in percentage scores and other information as letter grades. Then you had to decide whether to adjust any scores because of faulty instruments. Finally, you had to decide whether to base her grades solely on the students' average academic performance or to alter them slightly because of affective or personal characteristics (Borich, 2003; Tombari & Borich, 1999). Teachers with different students and in different schools likely would have made different decisions, but all would have had to confront the same issues. Key Assessment Tools 8.1 summarizes the steps in the grading process.

A Norm-Referenced Example

To complete this example, consider how you would have assigned grades if you had chosen a norm-referenced grading approach. In this case, you would have decided in advance upon a grading curve that identified the percentage of students that you wanted to receive each grade. Suppose you used a norm-referenced curve that gave the top 20 percent of the students an A, the next 20 percent a B, the next 40 percent a C, and the last 20 percent a D.

In norm-referenced grading, a teacher decides in advance the percentage of students receiving each grade.

To assign grades using this norm-referenced curve, you must first arrange the students from highest to lowest average score. The norm-referenced ordering for your class follows.

Name	Score	Name	Score
Yeh, T.	92	Saja, J.	79
Farmer, P.	89	Sachar, S.	76
Ross, O.	89	Stamos, G.	73
Foster, C.	83	Gonzales, E.	69
Babcock, W.	81	Cannata, T.	69
Avadis, P.	79	Whalem, W.	68
Miarka, S.	79	Grodsky, F.	62
Picardi, O.	79		

KEY ASSESSMENT TOOLS 8.1

Steps in the Grading Process

1. Select a standard of comparison (norm-referenced or criterion-referenced).
2. Select types of performances (tests, projects, etc.).
3. Assign weights for each type of performance.
4. If alphanumerical grades (e.g., A, B, C) have been assigned, convert these marks into numbers.
5. Record the number of points earned out of the total possible points for *each individual performance* graded.
6. Total the points earned for *each type of performance* and divide this by the total number of possible points. This gives a percentage for each type of performance.
7. Multiply each of these percentages by the weights assigned.
8. Sum the totals and apply the chosen standard of comparison to the totals.
9. Review the grades and make adjustments if necessary.

In norm-referenced grading, two students who achieve the same score must receive the same grade, regardless of the curve used.

Because there are 15 pupils in the class, 20 percent of the class is three students. Thus, Yeh, T., Farmer, P., and Ross, O., the three highest-scoring students, received A grades. The next 20 percent of the students—Foster, C., Babcock, W., and Avadis, P.—got B grades. The next 40 percent of the class (six students) should get C grades and the last 20 percent of the class should get D grades. However, in assigning grades by the norm-referenced approach, it is important to bear in mind that students who attain the same score must receive the same grade regardless of the curve being used. Therefore, even though students Miarka, S., Picardi, O., and Saja, J., should get C grades because they were in the middle 40 percent of the class, they will get a B grade because they all got 79 like Avadis, P. Similarly, Cannata, T. should get a D grade, but because Gonzales, E. is getting a C grade and Gonzales, E. and Cannata, T. both attained a score of 69, Cannata, T. will get a C grade, too. Notice the differences in the grade distributions under the norm-referenced and the criterion-referenced approaches. Remember that these differences are mainly the result of decisions made about the grading curve or performance standards that are used. Regardless of the method of grading adopted, it is extremely important for you to be able to explain the grading process to students, parents, and administrators. Key Assessment Tools 8.2 lists the guidelines for grading.

Report Cards

In Canada, report cards have existed for the last 100 years. Neatly printed, uniform report cards came into existence in the early 1900s with the demise of the one-room schoolhouse (Moll, 1998). Report card forms vary from one school system to another and from a grade division to another.

KEY ASSESSMENT TOOLS 8.2

Guidelines for Grading

➤ The chosen grading system is consistent with the purpose of grading.

➤ Data for grading is gathered throughout the grading period.

➤ Varied pieces of data are collected (tests, projects, quizzes, etc.).

➤ Students are informed about the system used to grade them.

➤ The grading system separates subject matter achievements from nonacademic performance (effort, motivation, etc.). Nonacademic performance is evaluated independently of subject matter performance.

➤ Grading is based on valid and reliable assessment evidence.

➤ Important evidence of achievement is weighted more than less important evidence (e.g., tests weighted more than quizzes).

➤ The grading system is applied consistently across all students.

Some of the common forms that school boards and provinces require teachers to record student performance are:

➤ letter grades (e.g., A, A-, B+, B, B-, C+, etc.)
➤ standards-based achievement categories (e.g., E = Excellent, G = Good, F = Fair, P = Poor)
➤ percentage or other numerical grades (e.g., 90, 65, 72, 83)
➤ pass-fail
➤ checklists that are graded individually
➤ written narratives describing students' accomplishments and challenges
➤ student self-evaluation

The most widely used system of recording student performance in Canadian elementary, middle, and high school is letter grades (Moll, 1998). In Kindergarten and the lower elementary grades, standards-based achievement categories and written narratives are often used by teachers to report student performance.

Many school boards and provinces require teachers to write comments about each student's performance on the report card. Still other boards and provinces require teachers to grade performance in both academic subjects and social and learning skill areas. The report card categories that are graded often reflect standards, expectations, or learning goals that are mandated by the provinces/territories and/or the school boards. Ideally, the grades in each of these categories should reflect students' progress and skill development against the given standards, expectations, or learning goals. To quote Canadian author, Ken O'Connor (2002), "What matters is how much learning occurs; teachers need to look at the most recent information to determine grades. In general, the highest most consistent level of performance, not the performance range should be reflected in the report card grade."

There are many different varieties of grading forms. Figure 8.5 is an example of a final report card for Kindergarten (Sir Wilfrid Laurier School Board, 2005) that employs both standards-based achievement categories (1 = exceeds expectations, 2 = meets expectations; 3 = partially meets expectations) as well as student self-evaluation ("I like stories" ☺ ☺ ☹). Note that there are six categories of development that are graded (physical, emotional, social, language, intellectual, work methods). Figure 8.6 is a report card for the first term of an elementary grade (British Columbia Ministry of Education, 2005). A written narrative describing students' social and learning skills precedes the grades. Each of the curricular areas are sub-categorized into expectations and respectively graded using standards-based achievement categories (e.g., 4 = Exceeding Expectations, 3 = Meeting Expectations, 2 = Approaching Expectations, 1 = Not Yet Meeting Expectations). Additionally, teachers offer parents recommendations for support-

FIGURE 8.5   *Example of a Final Report Card for Kindergarten.*

COMMUNICATION 4
YEAR END EVALUATION JUNE 2006
ÉVALUATION DE FIN D'ANNÉE JUIN 2006

AFFIX LABEL HERE

ABSENCES
TOTAL

At the end of the Kindergarten program, your child / *À la fin du programme de la maternelle, votre enfant*
1   exceeds expectations / *dépasse les attentes*
2   meets expectations / *satisfait les attentes*
3   partially meets expectations / *satisfait partiellement les attentes*

PHYSICAL DEVELOPMENT / *DÉVELOPPEMENT PHYSIQUE*

EMOTIONAL DEVELOPMENT / *DÉVELOPPEMENT ÉMOTIF*

SOCIAL DEVELOPMENT / *DÉVELOPPEMENT SOCIAL*

LANGUAGE DEVELOPMENT / *DÉVELOPPEMENT LANGAGIER*   E/F   ↑

INTELLECTUAL DEVELOPMENT / *DÉVELOPPEMENT INTELLECTUEL*

WORK METHODS DEVELOPMENT / *DÉVELOPPEMENT DE MÉTHODES DE TRAVAIL*

Teacher(s) Signatures / *Signature des enseignant(e)s* : _____
_____

Principal's Signature / *Signature de la direction* : _____

AT THE END OF JUNE, WHAT I LIKED ABOUT KINDERGARTEN
À LA FIN DE JUIN, CE QUE J'AI AIMÉ À LA MATERNELLE

I like stories.
J'aime les histoires.

I like writing.
J'aime écrire.

I like working with numbers.
J'aime travailler avec les nombres.

I like art work.
J'aime les arts plastiques.

I like using computers.
J'aime utiliser l'ordinateur.

I like physical activities.
J'aime les activités physiques.

I like music.
J'aime la musique.

I like playing with friends.
J'aime jouer avec des ami(e)s.

_____   _____

SOURCE: Courtesy of the Sir Wilfrid Laurier School Board Educational Resources Department, Rosemere, Quebec.

ing students' learning at home. Finally, Figure 8.7 is a secondary school (Grades 9–12) report card from Ontario (Ontario Ministry of Education, 1999). Here percentage grades and the median for all students taking the course are reported for the first and final reporting period. Additional written narratives are noted in the "Comments" box, which focus on the students' learning strengths, areas for improvement, and next steps or goals. Students' social and learning skills are evaluated with standards-based achievement categories (e.g., E = Excellent, G = Good, S = Satisfactory, N = Needs Improvement). Regardless of the fact that certain boards and provinces have required report forms, the British Columbia Teacher's Federation (BCTF) notes that teachers have the professional autonomy to decide what methods to use to assess and evaluate students' performance. Thus, despite the particular system or report form used, grades are always based on teacher judgments.

GRADING STUDENTS WITH EXCEPTIONALITIES

In earlier chapters, we discussed issues with respect to assessing students with exceptionalities. Grading exceptional students can also present classroom teachers with a variety of challenges. Based on the disparities in academic performance that often occur between some students with exceptionalities and their peers, you may find yourself asking, "How should I assign grades to my students with exceptionalities?"

The Nature of the Challenge

Embedded in the question above, are a host of other questions. For example, who should be primarily responsible for grading a student with an exceptionality: the classroom teacher, a special education teacher, an educational assistant, or these three in combination? Should the same standards be used to assess students with and without exceptionalities? How should the student's Individual Education Plan (IEP) enter into the grading process? What is the best report card form to describe the performance of students with exceptionalities? These and many other questions face the classroom teacher in grading students with exceptionalities (Guskey & Bailey, 2001).

First consider the question of who should be responsible for grading students with exceptionalities. Often the answer to this question is determined by the extent of a student's inclusion in the mainstream classroom. This varies among students from full-time inclusion to part-time inclusion in particular subject areas to complete withdrawal. Generally, the teacher who delivers the instruction in a particular subject area, should be responsible for grading a student in that subject area. For the purposes of this

FIGURE 8.6 *Page 1 of an Example of an Elementary Grade Report Card.*

Primary Progress Report-First Term

Student:
Date: 2006
Grade: 2

Sam has begun Grade 2 with a positive attitude toward his learning. He has made some good friends in his class. Sam has overcome his early shyness and now willingly contributes to class discussions and activities. It is a pleasure to see his confidence build each day.

Learning Outcomes

Progress Levels	4=Exceeding Expectations	2=Approaching Expectations
	3=Meeting Expectations	1=Not Yet Meeting Expectations

Language Arts

Reading Outcomes — Level
- Reads orally with fluency and few errors — 3
- Retells events from a story in proper sequence — 3
- Describe the main idea of a story — 3
- Identifies the main information in pictures — 4
- Reading progress in relation to the learning outcomes — 3

Writing Outcomes
- Identifies misspelling of commonly used words — 2
- Uses punctuation and capitalization properly — 2
- Sorts and organizes information on a specific topic — 2
- Keeps a personal journal of daily events — 2
- Progress in writing in relation to the learning outcomes — 2

Speaking and Listening
- Speaks in turn (puts hand up) — 3
- Follows simple spoken instructions — 4
- Listens to stories and is able to respond to questions about the story — 3
- Progress in speaking and listening in relation to the learning outcomes — 3

Mathematics — Level
- Counts orally by 1's to 30, 2's to 10, 5's to 30, and 10's to 100 — 4
- Can add and subtract numbers up to 1000 — 4
- Identify number and non number patterns and reproduce them — 3
- Estimate the size of objects using standard and non-standard units — 4
- Can collect and organize number information — 3
- Progress in mathematics in relation to the learning outcomes — 4

Science — Level
- Safely carries out simple experiments and procedures — 3
- Describes the characteristics of different plants and animals — 4
- Draws simple conclusions from what is seen — 3
- Identifies the stages in the life cycles of a plant — 2
- Progress in science in relation to the learning outcomes — 3

FIGURE 8.6   *Page 2 of An Example of An Elementary Grade Report Card.*

Social Studies

• Identifies different occupations in the community	4
• Describes how individuals in a community ca help each other	4
• Describes and compares natural and human built environments	2
• Draws a simple map and understands how to use it	3
• Progress in social studies in relation to the learning outcomes	4

Physical Education

• Participates in physical education activities	3
• Understands the safety rules and follows instructions	3
• Understands the rules of soccer and is able to play the game	4
• Demonstrates the ability to throw an object at a target with accuracy	2
• Progress in P.E. in relation to the learning outcomes	3

Fine Arts

• Produces two dimensional drawings that include some detail	2
• Completes art projects in a timely manner	2
• Progress in visual arts in relation to the learning outcomes	2

Personal Planning

• Identifies a number of activities that contribute to a healthy life style	**3**
• Explains how physical activity contributes to health	4
• Understands how eating the right foods can keep a person healthy	3
• Progress in personal planning in relation to the learning outcomes	3

Work Habits

• Shows a positive attitude towards learning	3
• Demonstrates consistent effort	3
• Focuses on tasks	3
• Begins learning activities with little support from the teacher	3
• Progress in work habits relative to expectations	3

Social Responsibility

• Cleans up area when finished using materials	3
• Treats classmates fairly and respectfully	3
• Able to identify simple ways to improve the classroom	4
• Progress in social responsibility	3

Here are some ways to support learning at home

Continue with the scheduled journal writing time with Sam as he now shows a greater willingness to put his ideas on paper. Encourage Sam's interest in books by reading to and with him at least once per day, especially the big machine books that I will continue to provide from our classroom library.

Sam has made a good start to the year. He is a well behaved student who is adapting well to Grade 2 and his new classroom. Sam's development is characteristic of many children in his age group.

Teacher's Signature	Principal's Signature	Parent/ Guardian Copy: Keep this copy for your records. Write your comments on the Report card cover, sign it, and return to your child's teacher.

Note: Attendance information and instructions to parents are on the report cover.

FIGURE 8.7   *Secondary School Report Card.*

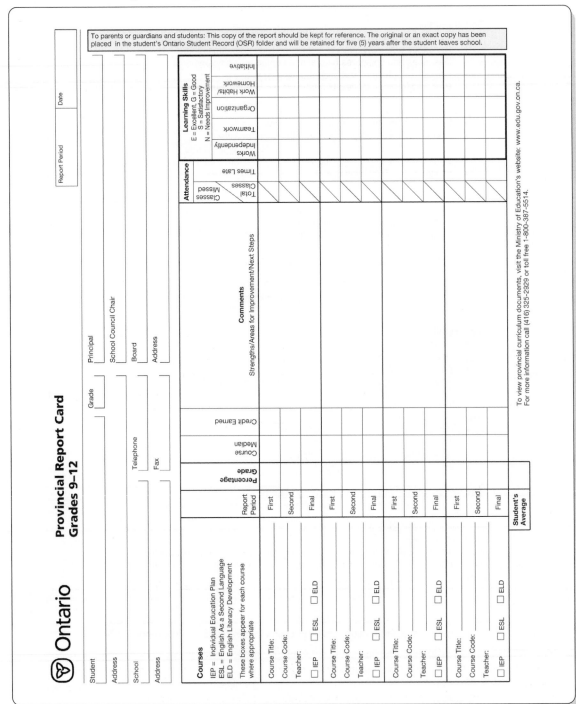

SOURCE: © Queen's Printer for Ontario, 1998. Reproduced with permission.

chapter, discussion will focus on the issues related to grading students with exceptionalities who are either integrated into the regular classroom on a part-time or full-time basis.

The nature of the challenge that teachers face in grading students with exceptionalities is often the disparity in their achievement compared to the achievement of students without exceptionalities. While it is important to understand that not all exceptionalities hamper a student's ability to achieve grade-level expectations, many exceptionalities do pose significant challenges for a student. This prompts teachers to ask the question: Should the same standards be used to assess students with and without exceptionalities?

If the same grading standards are applied to all students in the class, the students with exceptionalities may receive low grades. If the teacher uses different standards for students with and without exceptionalities, the same grade will hold different meanings depending on which grading standard was applied to a certain student. This problem is also apparent when students are moved from segregated special education classrooms to mainstream classrooms where often the grading standards are very different (Valdes, Williamson, & Wagner, 1990).

Some Possible Strategies

It is most likely that the grading approaches for students with exceptionalities will be based on the objectives in the student's IEP. Consequently, teachers ask: How should the student's Individual Education Plan (IEP) enter into the grading process? The IEP represents the recommended instruction and desired student outcomes based on a set of standards unique to each student. The grading strategy can be created by a team that often includes the classroom teacher, resource or special education teacher, the student's parents, and the student (Munk & Bursuck, 2003). The following are some possible strategies for grading students with exceptionalities:

➤ **Contract grading:** The teacher and the student jointly determine the type and quality of work a student will complete in order to receive a particular grade. The contract spells out what amount of work at what level of quality is needed for a student to receive a grade. Different students have different contracts with different terms.

➤ **IEP-based grading:** Students are graded on the percentage of objectives in their IEP that they complete in a term or marking period. The grading standards would be criterion-referenced with different percentages of completion resulting in different grades (i.e., 80 percent or more completion is an A, 70 to 79 percent completion is a B, and so on). This approach is similar to grading a student based on her or his improvement over time.

➤ **Multiple grading:** The student receives different grades for different performances rather than a single, overall grade. For example, a student could receive separate grades for effort, participation, achievement, and progress. Such an approach allows the teacher to make some distinctions in the student's overall performance and to show areas of strength and weakness. A similar approach is to adjust grading weights for different students by, for example, counting effort or projects more than test results.

➤ **Level-based grading:** Students are given grades that indicate both their achievement level and curriculum level. For example, a student who shows B-level achievement in a below grade level curriculum can be graded B(2). The number in parentheses represents the level of the curriculum in which a student is performing on a standards-based achievement scale of 1–4. This is another way of representing a student's ability level in a grade.

➤ **Narrative grading:** The teacher does not assign a grade, but provides a substantial written or oral description of the student's performance, achievements, strengths, and weaknesses based upon the teacher's observations and assessments of the student. Note that this is an informative, but time-consuming, grading approach.

Teachers use some strategies more than others in grading students with exceptionalities. Among the commonly used strategies are IEP-based grading, multiple grading, and contract grading. Teachers are likely to place more grade weighting on the learning process than the product. For students with exceptionalities, teachers are less likely to change their grading standards, pass students just for high effort or pass students no matter what their performance (Bursuck et al., 1996).

It is difficult for teachers to convey the many important messages to the different audiences interested in grades. The most common grading system used in schools, letter grades, limits the information that can be conveyed in a grade because the single letter conveys little of the specifics about what the student can or cannot do and has or has not learned. Reporting systems that allow teachers to provide more information about a student's grade than a single letter or number can help teachers with this dilemma. Systems such as the level-based and narrative grading approaches allow the teacher to provide important information about the meaning of the student's performance. The ability to describe a student's specific learning outcomes, the grade level of student performance, the amount of improvement, the weight given to effort and achievement, the availability of an aide for a student, or other pertinent factors related to student performance helps teachers in grading a student with an exceptionality. Employing such information takes a student's exceptionality into account in the grades a student receives and also provides the desired perspective on the meaning of the grades.

OTHER METHODS OF REPORTING STUDENT PROGRESS

Report card grades are the most common way that students and their parents are kept informed of how things are going in the classroom. But the functionality of grades is limited because they are usually provided infrequently, provide little *specific* information about how a student is performing, and sometimes include information about the teacher's perceptions of a student's effort, motivation, cooperation, and classroom demeanor. Moreover, since report card grades usually reflect student performance on a variety of assessment tasks, it is quite possible for two students to receive the same grade but have performed very differently on the assessments used to determine the grade. Because of these limitations, several approaches for reporting students' school progress are needed and used by teachers.

Grades are the most common device by which students and parents are kept informed about how things are going in the classroom.

To have a complete and specific picture of their child's school performance, parents must receive more than the report card.

Parent-Teacher Conferences

Parent-teacher conferences allow flexible, two-way communication, unlike the one-way communication that grades provide. Conferences permit discussion, elaboration, and explanation of student performance. The teacher can get information from the parents about their concerns and perceptions of their child's school experience. Information can also be obtained about special problems the student is having, from physical and emotional problems to problems of classroom adjustment. Parents can inform the teacher of their concerns and ask questions about their child's classroom behaviour and about the curriculum being taught. Certainly a parent-teacher conference can address a broader range of issues and concerns than a report card grade can.

Unlike grades, parent-teacher conferences provide flexible, two-way communication.

Moreover, parents learn a great deal about their children's performance from parent-teacher conferences. A study by Shepard and Bliem (1995) on a sample of elementary school parents examined the usefulness of report cards, parent-teacher discussions, standardized tests, and graded examples of students' schoolwork for parents' understanding of their child's progress in school. Ninety-four percent of the parents indicated that discussions with teachers were useful or very useful in understanding their child's progress, and 90 percent also said that receiving graded examples of their child's work was useful or very useful. Only 76 percent of the parents felt that report cards were useful or very useful for informing them about their child's school progress. Thirty-six percent cited standardized tests as useful or very useful for informing them about progress. Parents look for information beyond report cards to indicate how their children are performing in school.

It is natural for teachers to feel somewhat uneasy at the prospect of a conference with parents. Because teachers will have certain things they want the parents to know and because there is always an element of uncertainty about the way the conference will go, it is recommended that teachers prepare an agenda of the things they want to cover. For example, most teachers will want to provide a description of the student's academic and social classroom performance. They will also want to ask the parents questions such as, "What does he say about the workload in school?" Certainly teachers will want to give parents the opportunity to ask questions. Parents are most likely to ask questions such as "Is my child at grade level in reading?" "How is my child's behaviour in class?" "Does she get along with her classmates?" or "Why did my son get a C– in math?" Finally, a teacher, in conjunction with the parents, may want to plan a course of action to help the student. The course agreed upon should contain actions on the part of teacher, parents, and student.

Planning conferences is necessary to accomplish such agendas. The individual teacher will want to gather samples of the student's work—perhaps in a portfolio—and identify (with examples) particular behavioural or attitudinal issues that should be raised. If there is a potential problem, the teacher ought to look over the student's official school record file in the school office to see whether the problem surfaced in other grades. All of this preparation should be done before the conference. Teachers may wish to have a counsellor or administrator attend a conference if it is likely to be confrontational.

Finally, the teacher will want to locate a comfortable, private spot to hold the conference. Usually this means before or after school in the teacher's classroom, when students are not present. If this is the case, provide suitable, adult-sized chairs for the parents. Conferences work better when they are private and undisturbed, and when all parties are comfortably situated.

Tips for a Successful Parent-Teacher Conference

The following tips can help the actual parent-teacher conference proceed successfully.

Conferences should be private, undisturbed, and well planned.

1. *Set a proper tone.* This means making parents feel welcome, maintaining a positive attitude, and remembering that a student is not "their" concern or "your" concern, but a mutual concern. If possible, find out what parents want to know before the conference so that you can prepare for their questions. Don't do all the talking; be a good listener and use the conference to find out parents' perceptions and concerns. Talk in terms parents will understand; avoid educational jargon, such as "discovery learning," "rubrics," "higher-order thinking skills," or "prosocial behaviour," that confuses rather than clarifies discussion. Providing examples of student work from portfolios, performance assessments, and scoring rubrics can help parents understand classroom expectations and student performance.

2. *Be frank with parents, but convey both the student's strengths and weaknesses.* Do not hold back unpleasant information because you think the parents will become confrontational. The aim of parent-teacher conferences is for each party to understand and help the student. It is the teacher's responsibility to raise issues with parents that will help the student, even though discussion of those issues might be unpleasant. If you do not know the answer to a question, do not bluff. Tell the parents you do not know the answer, then research it after the conference and follow up by relaying it to the parents.

3. *Do not talk about other students or colleagues by name or by implication.* Never belittle colleagues or the principal in front of parents, no matter what your feelings. Saying things like "last year's teacher did not prepare Rosalie well in math" or "teachers get so little support for their ideas from the principal" is inappropriate. True or not, it is not professional to discuss such issues with parents. Do not compare a child to other students by name or show parents other students' work, test scores, or grades. Teachers are professionals and they have an obligation to act professionally. This means being truthful with parents, not demeaning colleagues in front of parents, concentrating discussion only on the parents' child, and not discussing information from the conference with other teachers. This caution is appropriate for all forms of parent-teacher interaction.

4. *If a course of remedial action for the student seems appropriate, plan the action jointly with the parents.* Make both parties responsible for implementing the plan: "I will try to do these things with Janessa in class, and you will try to do these other things with her at home."

5. *Finally, summarize the conference before the parents leave.* Review the main points and any decisions or courses of action that have been agreed upon.

Teachers must maintain their professional demeanor during parent-teacher conferences.

Parent-teacher conferences can be very useful to both teachers and parents if planned and conducted successfully. They allow the teacher to supplement his or her information about the student and the parents to obtain a broader understanding of their child's school performance. The main drawback to parent-teacher conferences is that they are time-consuming. Many school boards set aside a day or two in the school calendar specifically for parent conferencing. Key Assessment Tools 8.3 reviews these guidelines for parent-teacher conferences.

Additional Reporting Methods

A common method of informing parents about their child's school performance is to either send examples of schoolwork home or to collect it in a portfolio to be examined during a parent-teacher conference or school open house. Periodic newsletters, often written and assembled by students,

KEY ASSESSMENT TOOLS 8.3

Parent-Teacher Conferences

1. Plan in advance of the conference by gathering samples of the student's work and identifying issues to discuss with parents; if possible, find out what parents want to know before the conference.

2. Identify a private, comfortable place for the conference.

3. Set a proper tone by:

   a. Remembering that the student is of mutual concern to you and the parents.

   b. Listening to the parents' perspectives and concerns.

   c. Avoiding educational jargon, yet giving concrete examples.

   d. Being frank with parents when conveying the student's strengths and weaknesses.

4. Admit to not knowing the answer to a question and be willing to find out; do not try to bluff parents.

5. Do not talk about or belittle other colleagues or students by name or implication; do not compare one student to another by name.

6. If a remedial action is agreed upon, plan the action jointly with parents and make each party responsible for part of the plan.

7. Orally review and summarize decisions and planned actions at the end of the conference.

8. Write summary notes of the conference.

can be sent home. If a teacher has developed or selected a scoring rubric, a copy of the rubric with the student's level of performance circled can be used to provide information about an area of the student's learning.

Letters and phone calls to parents are used mainly to inform parents of a special problem that has occurred and, as such, should be used infrequently by teachers. Regular written or phone communication between a teacher and a parent should occur if the parent specifically requests frequent written progress reports. Also consider written or phone communication as a way to share positive feedback about a student's work or effort at school. Parents are usually pleased to receive such reinforcements from you, the teacher. Regardless of the purpose, it is extremely important that your written communication is free of spelling and grammatical errors. Few things can create a poorer impression in a parent's mind than a misspelled, grammatically incorrect letter from their child's teacher.

These are just some of the ways in which teachers can communicate and interact with parents. Each of these forms of communication can provide important supplementary information that rounds out the picture of a student's life at school.

CHAPTER REVIEW

CHAPTER REVIEW

Visit Chapter 8 of the Online Learning Centre at **www.mcgrawhill.ca/ college/airasian** to take chapter quizzes, link to related Web sites, read PowerWeb articles and news feed updates, and access study tools, including the case study referenced in this chapter.

What is grading and what is the objective of grading?

➤ Grading is the process of judging the quality of a student's performance by comparing it to some standards of performance.

➤ The objective of grading is to be fair to all students and to reflect students' learning.

Why is grading regarded as a difficult task for teachers?

➤ teachers have little instruction in the process

➤ judgments are made based on incomplete evidence

➤ students' work habits and behaviour may influence subject matter judgments

➤ there is no single universally accepted grading strategy

➤ grading is complicated

➤ there is a limited research base for grading

➤ when using cooperative learning approaches it is difficult to determine how well individual students understand the processes used in a group-based solution

What purposes do grades serve?

➤ Grades serve administrative, informational, motivational, and guidance functions.

What are the four types of comparison for grading?

➤ Norm-referenced grades compare a student's performance to that of other students in the class. Students with the highest scores receive the designated highest grades. A grading curve sets up quotas for each grade.

➤ Criterion-referenced grades compare a student's performance to a predefined standard of mastery. There is no limit to the number of students who can receive a particular grade.

➤ Grades can be based on comparisons of a student's performance to the student's ability (not recommended).

➤ Grades can be based on a student's prior performance (not recommended).

What should be included in a grade?

➤ Student performances that demonstrate mastery of subject matter should be included in a grade.

➤ Social and learning skills (e.g., effort, motivation, participation, behaviour) should not be included in subject matter grades; however, some school boards expect teachers to report on these skills separately.

➤ Tests and projects should be weighted most heavily in arriving at a grade.

How are grades summarized?

➤ Each type of assessment data needs to be expressed in the same way and on the same scale.
➤ Weightings must be assigned to grades.
➤ Computerized programs can assist teachers in summarizing grades.

What are the two approaches to assigning grades?

➤ The criterion-referenced approach offers each student the opportunity to get a grade in relation to whether he or she has mastered what was taught.
➤ In norm-referenced grading, a teacher decides in advance the percentage of students receiving each grade.

What are report cards?

➤ Report cards communicate information about student achievement.
➤ Report card grades are a representation of a student's performance across a variety of assessments that were completed during a term or grading period.

What are some strategies when grading students with exceptionalities?

➤ Contract grading
➤ IEP-based grading
➤ Multiple grading
➤ Level-based grading
➤ Narrative grading

What are other means of communicating student progress?

➤ Parent-teacher conferences, open houses, phone calls, newsletters, notes, and papers and projects sent home are other forms of communicating student progress.

QUESTIONS FOR DISCUSSION

1. What are the purposes of giving grades to students? How well do different grading formats meet these purposes?
2. What are a teacher's responsibilities to students when assigning grades on a paper, test, or project? What additional responsibilities to students do teachers have when they assign report card grades?

3. Is the task of assigning report card grades the same for elementary and high school teachers? How might the process of assigning grades differ at the two levels?

4. How can the information on report cards be supplemented and made more informative for parents and students?

5. What are possible ways, both good and bad, that grades can impact students? What can be done to lessen the detrimental impact of grades?

6. Think of some proactive strategies to inform parents of their student's progress so that report card grades do not come as a surprise.

ACTIVITY

Table 8A contains information that a teacher accumulated about her students during a marking period. Use this information to assign a report card grade to each student. Answer the questions that follow the table.

TABLE 8A Grading Activity

Student	Test 1	2	3	4	Project	Class Participation	Independent Work	Homework Completion	Cooperation with Others
Malcolm	40	60	55	100	A–	Good	Good	Good	Good
Victoria	90	95	45	85	A	Excellent	Excellent	Excellent	Excellent
Jason	70	65	20	30	C	Excellent	Good	Poor	Poor
Jamal	85	80	50	85	B–	Poor	Poor	Good	Poor
Gretta	70	70	15	65	D	Good	Excellent	Poor	Excellent
Susan	45	75	45	100	C	Excellent	Excellent	Good	Good
Maya	75	80	45	75	B–	Good	Good	Good	Good
Maria	70	75	30	70	A	Excellent	Good	Good	Good
Oscar	80	90	45	85	C	Poor	Poor	Poor	Poor
Angelina	30	40	10	40	D–	Poor	Excellent	Poor	Excellent
Omar	60	60	15	45	D	Poor	Poor	Poor	Poor

1. Will you use a norm-referenced or a criterion-referenced grading approach? Why?

2. Will you include all the information in the table in determining a grade or only some of the information? State what you will and will not include and explain why.

3. Will all the pieces of information you have decided to include count equally, or will some things count more than others?

4. How will you take into account the different representation of student performance on different pieces of information (e.g., percentages, letter grades, excellent-good-poor)? Specifically, how do you convert the "excellent," "good," and "poor" grades?

5. What, if anything, will you do about Test 3?

6. How will you summarize the different pieces of information into a single score or rating?

7. What will be your grading curve (norm-referenced) or performance standards (criterion-referenced) for awarding grades?

8. What grade would each student receive?

9. In what ways is this exercise artificial? That is, would there be a difference between the way you graded these students and the way a teacher who had actually taught them for the marking period would grade them?

10. Overall, is there evidence of student improvement in performance skills? How do you know?

11. If you graded the students in a norm-referenced way, go back and regrade using a criterion-referenced approach. If you graded the students in a criterion-referenced approach, go back and regrade using a norm-referenced approach.

12. What are the strengths and weaknesses of the grading system you have developed?

CHAPTER 9

LARGE-SCALE ASSESSMENT

CHAPTER OBJECTIVES

After reading this chapter, you will be able to:

➤ Define large-scale assessment, standardized achievement tests, curriculum standards, assessment standards, achievement standards

➤ Describe what is going on in the Canadian provinces and territories with regard to large-scale assessment

➤ Explain how large-scale assessments are constructed

➤ Discuss some implications for teachers of large-scale assessment

➤ Outline the problems that exist with standardized testing

➤ State activities that help students prepare for assessments

M r. Li's Grade 10 students are preparing for the provincial literacy test that will take place in one month. He has been providing preparatory activities that focus on reading, writing, and test-taking strategies. Most of the students recall the experience of writing a provincial test from their years in elementary school. Some are eager to participate and be given an opportunity to demonstrate their learning and academic growth. Other students are sick with worry, remembering their anxiety during the previous experiences with large-scale assessment. Mr. Li perceives that some of the students' parents, as well as the school principal, expect that most of the Grade 10 students' scores will be at or higher than the provincial standard. He believes that both his regular instruction and the added review that he has been providing will give his students the opportunity to do well. Nevertheless, like many of his students, Mr. Li is a little anxious about the imminent provincial literacy test.

Provincial testing is a form of large-scale assessment. In general, **large-scale assessment** includes standardized achievement tests that are given to a large number (usually thousands) of students in order to measure their performance as an indicator of what they know and can do at a certain point in time. Large-scale assessment has become a regular feature on the Canadian educational landscape. Based on a call for accountability in education, most provinces and territories have introduced large-scale assessment as a mechanism for determining, equitably and reliably, the degree to which students meet core subject curriculum expectations. Test results can be used to establish benchmarks for educational standards (Skwarchuk, 2004).

The increase in large-scale assessment in education is a phenomenon that is not exclusive to Canada:

> An emphasis on standards, accountability and testing has been a feature of reforms in many countries. Almost everywhere we find more large-scale testing of students and more reporting of the results of these tests than was the case a few years ago. Increasing national assessment is complemented by more and more international assessment and in both cases the results are used more overtly for public comparisons. (Levin, 1998, p. 133)

While ostensibly useful for ensuring school and teacher accountability, large-scale assessment is not without its deficiencies and detractors. The purpose of this chapter is to define and describe large-scale assessment, examine the large-scale assessment programs within each Canadian province or territory, and discuss Canadian involvement in large-scale international assessment programs and studies. This chapter will also provide useful information on how to help students prepare for large-scale assessments.

DEFINING LARGE-SCALE ASSESSMENT

This chapter will present large-scale provincial and national standardized testing. In Chapter 10, there will be a focus on commercially available standardized achievement tests. Both chapters feature standardized tests. **Standardized tests** assess students' performance under uniform conditions. There are structured directions for administration, specific procedures for scoring, and guidelines for interpretation of the results. Thus, standardized tests are administered, scored, and interpreted in a standard way regardless of where or when they are given. It is therefore possible for a student's performance to be compared with the performance of other students at the same age or grade level. Thus, standardized tests have norms and measures of validity and reliability.

Standards are used to assess students, teachers, and schools in a particular province or territory. The standards are intended to guide learning and assessments.

Chapters 9 and 10 are differentiated by the administrative purposes of the standardized tests. Large-scale provincial and national assessments are a mechanism for determining the degree to which students meet core subject curriculum expectations and in order to establish benchmarks for educational standards; whereas commercially available standardized achievement tests provide a measure of a student's performance in an academic subject area as compared to a sample of his or her peers where the student's strengths and weaknesses can be identified.

Large-scale assessment typically takes the form of standardized achievement tests. **Standardized achievement tests** measure students' knowledge and mastered skills and provide information about students' performance in an academic subject area such as reading, writing, mathematics, or science. A student's performance score in any one of the academic subject areas is compared to a sample of their peers. In other words, a standardized achievement test is a test that compares a student's knowledge or skill with that of other students (norm-referenced) and/or against a standard (criterion-referenced).

Wherever large-scale assessment is undertaken, standardized achievement tests are developed by experts from the provincial Ministries or Departments of Education and practicing educators. These tests are piloted and scored by trained evaluators. Large-scale assessment results are usually presented as test scores aggregated at the student, school, district, and provincial levels.

Achievement levels on most provincial and territorial assessments are based on three different, but related standards: curriculum standards, assessment standards, and achievement standards. **Curriculum standards** state what students are expected to know at any given grade level. They are found written as knowledge, skill, and attitude expectations or learning outcomes in provincial curricula. Curriculum standards are written to demonstrate the developmental sequence of different types of knowledge (e.g., declarative and procedural) and cognitive skill acquisition as students move from grade to grade. Instruction and assessment should be coordinated to reflect provincial and territorial curriculum standards. Further, curriculum standards are used to guide activities such as teachers' instructional emphases, textbook selection, and assessment methods. **Assessment standards** are descriptions of what students should know or be able to demonstrate at various grade levels and varying degrees of proficiency. Levels may be designated by a range of terms such as *basic, proficient*, and *advanced* or *acceptable standard* and *standard of excellence*. Figure 9.1 provides an example of mathematics assessment standards for Grade 6 students in Alberta. Finally, **achievement standards** are judgments about the percentage of students who are expected to attain acceptable or high levels of proficiency. For example, in Alberta, 85 percent of students are expected to achieve the acceptable or excellent achievement standards of proficiency on provincial tests (McEwen, 1995).

In most jurisdictions, results of large-scale standardized testing for each district school board and school are made available to the public, usually through the mainstream press. Schools are ranked and subject to comparison, which can leave those schools with low rankings and their teachers subject to criticism. There are many factors, other than poor instructional practice that may mitigate on the performance of students within a school on large-scale standardized achievement tests.

For each school, results are usually reported in a way that indicates the percentage of students, at the grade level being tested, who have achieved at a particular level. These levels refer to the achievement levels such as 1, 2, 3, and 4, which represent a description of the degree of achievement that students have attained within the test. In this example, 1 is the lowest level of achievement and 4 is the highest. It is likely that most provinces would strive to have their students attain a provincial standard of at least 3. Results are also reported in terms of increases and decreases from year-to-year at each of the levels.

LARGE-SCALE ASSESSMENT IN CANADA

Provincial and Territorial Large-Scale Assessment Programs

All Canadian provinces and territories, with the exclusion of Prince Edward Island and Nunavut, have implemented large-scale assessment programs. These programs are designed to measure student achievement of curriculum expectations or learning outcomes in core subject areas. Some large-scale assessment takes the form of high-stakes testing where the results have implications for student promotion, graduation, or the acquisition of scholarships (Agrey, 2004). The following briefly summarizes the state of large-scale assessment in each of the Canadian provinces and territories (also see Figure 9.2 for a summary).

FIGURE 9.1 *Description of Mathematics Assessment Standards.*

The following statements describe what is expected of Grade 6 students in mathematics at the *acceptable standard* or the *standard of excellence*, based on outcomes in Alberta's *Program of Studies*.

Acceptable Standard	Standard of Excellence
Students who meet the *acceptable standard* in Grade 6 Mathematics have a basic understanding of mathematical concepts and related procedural knowledge. They demonstrate their understanding in concrete, pictorial, and symbolic modes and are able to translate from one mode to another. For example, students who meet the *acceptable standard* know that the solution to the number sentence $42 \times 2 = \square$ is 84, and they can demonstrate their understanding in concrete and pictorial ways. They are able to write related number sentences and verify them using manipulatives and diagrams.	Students who meet the *standard of excellence* in Grade 6 Mathematics have a thorough understanding of mathematical concepts and related procedural knowledge. They consistently demonstrate their understanding in concrete, pictorial, and symbolic modes, and easily translate from one mode to another. They are able to create problem situations to illustrate concepts and to analyze and explain relationships among concepts. For example, students who meet the *standard of excellence* can write all number sentences related to $42 \times 2 = \square$, justify them using manipulatives and diagrams, and create problem situations to exemplify the relationship.
Students who meet the *acceptable standard* are able to reflect upon, explain, and defend their ideas, using objects, diagrams, everyday and mathematical terminology, and, when appropriate, technology. They understand mathematical questions presented with objects, diagrams, or symbols in everyday and school settings. Students who meet the *acceptable standard* derive meaning from problem-solving experiences in their world and build on a foundation of previous learning.	Students who meet the *standard of excellence* are able to assess, explain, and defend their ideas clearly, using objects, diagrams, and exact mathematical terminology. They understand mathematical questions presented with objects, diagrams, or symbols in both common and unusual settings. Students who meet the *standard of excellence* derive meaning from problem-solving experiences in familiar and unusual settings and build on a foundation of previous learning.
Students who meet the *acceptable standard* perform the mathematical operations and procedures that are fundamental to mathematics in Grade 6 and apply what they know to solving routine problems in familiar settings. They can describe the steps they used to solve a particular problem and can defend their solution to the problem.	Students who meet the *standard of excellence* perform the mathematical operations and procedures that are fundamental to mathematics in Grade 6 and apply what they know to solving and creating novel problems. They can clearly describe the steps that they or other students used to solve a particular problem, and they can justify the solution as well as suggest alternative solutions and/or strategies.
Students who meet the *acceptable standard* have a positive attitude about mathematics and a sense of personal competence in using mathematics in their daily lives. They demonstrate confidence when using common mathematical procedures and when applying problem-solving strategies in familiar settings.	Students who meet the *standard of excellence* have a positive attitude toward mathematics and show confidence in performing mathematical tasks. They are self-motivated risk-takers who persevere when solving novel problems. They take initiative in trying new methods and are creative in their approach to problem solving.

SOURCE: Government of Alberta—Ministry of Education. (2005a). Retrieved from www.education.gov.ab.ca/k_12/testing/achievement/ bulletins/Gr6_Math/gr6_math_standards.asp.

Alberta

Through its *Achievement Testing Program*, Alberta conducts provincial achievement tests in Grade 3 for language arts and mathematics and in Grades 6 and 9 for language arts, mathematics, science, and social studies. Alberta also has *Diploma Examinations* in core academic courses for Grade 12 students. These examinations are primarily comprised of selected-response test items, and 50 percent of a student's final course grade is derived from these tests. All test results for individual students are available to the students, their parents, teachers, and the administrators in their schools. School, district, and provincial results are reported publicly (Government of Alberta—Ministry of Education, 2005b).

British Columbia

British Columbia has established the *Foundation Skills Assessment*, which is a province-wide assessment of academic skills in numeracy, reading comprehension, and writing for students in Grades 4 and 7. The *Provincial Learning Assessments* are also administered to Grades 4 and 7 students in cross-curricular areas that are not covered by the *Foundation Skills Assessment*. British Columbia also conducts Grade 10 language arts, science, and mathematics, Grades 11/12 social studies, and Grade 12 language arts *Graduation Program Examinations* for the certification of its graduating students. These examinations employ both selected- and constructed-response test items, with 40 percent of the mark on the examinations counting for their overall grade in these subject areas (Government of British Columbia—Ministry of Education, 2005).

Manitoba

In 1999, Manitoba administered the *Provincial Standards Tests* to students in Grades 3, 6, 9, and 12 for mathematics and language arts (or Français for Francophone students). These test scores were used for a proportion of final grades for students in Grades 6, 9, and 12 (20 percent, 25 percent, and 30 percent, respectively). Manitoba continues to carry out a province-wide assessment of critical competencies in reading and numeracy at the beginning of Grade 3 and to assess Grade 12 students in Senior 4 English language arts/Français langue première, Français langue seconde-immersion, and mathematics/mathématiques. Individual districts have the option of testing students at Grades 6 and 9 (Government of Manitoba—Manitoba Education, 2005).

New Brunswick

New Brunswick conducts compulsory large-scale literacy *Provincial Assessments* of students in Grades 2, 5, and 12, and mathematics assessments in

Grades 5 and 8. Anglophone students are tested in English; whereas, French immersion and Francophone students are tested in French. All of these tests employ selected-response test items except the writing literacy test. New Brunswick also employs an *English Language Proficiency Assessment* in Grade 9, which measures language literacy through measures of reading comprehension and writing. Students who do not pass this assessment may apply to be reassessed in Grade 10 (Government of New Brunswick—Department of Education, 2005).

Newfoundland and Labrador

Newfoundland and Labrador are currently collaborating with other Atlantic provinces on the development of provincial assessments for Grades 3, 6, 9, and 12. In the past, Newfoundland and Labrador's *Provincial Assessment Program* have used the *Canadian Test of Basic Skills* (*CTBS*; Nelson, 1998) to measure student achievement provincially, and periodically mandated the assessment of Grades 3 and 6 students in language arts. The *Provincial Assessment Program* last reported assessment results from the 2003–2004 school year. Newfoundland and Labrador also mandate that, in order to graduate, all Grade 12 students must take *Public Examinations* in all of their core subjects including English, math, biology, chemistry, physics, earth systems, world geography, world history, and French. The achievement score from *Public Examinations* contributes 50 percent of the final grade for each of these courses (Government of Newfoundland and Labrador—Department of Education, 2005).

Northwest Territories

Northwest Territories employs the curriculum and large-scale assessment program developed for Alberta students (Government of the Northwest Territories—Department of Education, Culture, and Employment, 2005).

Nova Scotia

In Nova Scotia, provincial assessments are coordinated under the *Program of Learning Assessment* (*PLANS*). These assessments exist for mathematics in Grades 5, 8, and 12, reading literacy in Grade 6, language arts in Grade 9, and chemistry, English, and physics in Grade 12. The assessments at the Grade 12 level are part of the "Nova Scotia Examinations (NSE)" that count for 30 percent of a student's final course mark. The PLANS exists for both Anglophone and Acadian/Francophone students. As part of its "Learning for Life Plan," the province of Nova Scotia also mandates that all Grade 6 students participate in the *Elementary Literacy Assessment*, a program that identifies students with reading and writing deficiencies in order to provide them with additional literacy support (Government of Nova Scotia—Department of Education, 2005).

Nunavut

Nunavut currently has no large-scale assessment program. The Nunavut Department of Education is, however, looking at the large-scale assessment programs in various provinces in order to adopt a framework suitable for its own students with administration in either English or Inuktitut (D'Souza, 2003).

Ontario

In Ontario, provincial assessment is undertaken by the *Education Quality and Accountability Office* (*EQAO*), an agency that is independent of the provincial Ministry of Education. Annually, Grades 3 and 6 students are assessed in reading, writing, and mathematics, and Grade 9 students in mathematics. As well, all Grade 10 students must pass the *Ontario Secondary School Literacy Test* (*OSSLT*) in order to graduate at the end of high school. *EQAO* has also instituted the "Education Quality Indicators Framework," which is designed to provide contextual information such as demographics that assist in fair interpretation of achievement scores (Education Quality and Accountability Office, 2005).

Quebec

Provincial Assessments of students in French and mathematics take place in Grades 6, 9, 11, and 12. As well, each year the Ministère de l'Éducation selects subject areas, including English, physical science, provincial history, and French reading, which will make up the *Uniform Ministry Examinations*. Secondary IV and V students participate in these examinations and the results are factored into the overall final grade that students receive for those subjects (Gouvernement du Québec—Ministère de l'Éducation, Loisir et Sport, 2005).

Saskatchewan

Saskatchewan has developed the *Provincial Learning Assessment Program* as the framework for large-scale assessment of its students. In 2002, Grades 5, 8, and 11 students from 101 randomly selected Saskatchewan schools were tested for their level of critical and creative thinking ability. Prior to this, provincial assessments were conducted in mathematics (2001) and language arts (1998, 1996, and 1994) (Government of Saskatchewan—Department of Learning, 2005).

Yukon Territory

Since 1999, the Department of Education for Yukon Territory has conducted the *Yukon Achievement Tests* (*YAT*), which includes large-scale assessment of Grades 3, 6, and 9 students in language arts and math. Yukon

FIGURE 9.2   *Summary of Provincial and Territorial Large-Scale Assessment.*

Province/Territory	Assessment Programs
Alberta	*Achievement Testing Program* ➤ Grade 3 (language arts and math) ➤ Grade 6 and 9 (language arts, math, science, and social studies) *Diploma Examinations* ➤ Grade 12 (core academic courses)
British Columbia	*Foundation Skills Assessment* ➤ Grades 4 and 7 (numeracy, reading comprehension, and writing) *Provincial Learning Assessments* ➤ Grades 4 and 7 (cross-curricular areas that are not covered by the *Foundation Skills Assessment*) *Provincial Examinations* ➤ Grade 12 (core academic areas)
Manitoba	*Provincial Standards Tests* ➤ Grade 3 (math and language arts) ➤ Optional Grades 6 and 9 (Senior 4 English language arts/ Français langue première, Français langue seconde-immersion, and mathematics/mathématiques)
New Brunswick	*Provincial Assessments* ➤ Grades 2, 5, and 12 (literacy) ➤ Grades 5 and 8 (math) *English Language Proficiency Assessment* ➤ Grade 9 (reading comprehension and writing)
Newfoundland and Labrador	*Provincial Assessment Program* ➤ Grades 3 and 6 (language arts) *Public Examinations* ➤ Grade 12 (English, math, biology, chemistry, physics, earth systems, world geography, world history, and French)
Northwest Territories	*Achievement Testing Program* ➤ Grade 3 (language arts and math) ➤ Grades 6 and 9 (language arts, math, science, and social studies) *Diploma Examinations* ➤ Grade 12 (core academic courses)
Nova Scotia	*Program of Learning Assessment (PLANS)* ➤ Grades 5 and 8 (math) ➤ Grades 6 and 9 (language arts) ➤ Grade 12 (chemistry, English, math, physics) *Elementary Literacy Assessment* ➤ Grade 6 (reading and writing)
Ontario	*Education Quality and Accountability Office (EQAO)* ➤ Grades 3 and 6 (reading, writing, and math) ➤ Grade 9 (math) ➤ Grade 10 (literacy)

(Continued)

FIGURE 9.2   *Summary of Provincial and Territorial Large-Scale Assessment (continued).*

Province/Territory	Assessment Programs
Quebec	*Provincial Assessments* ➤ Grades 6, 9, 11, and 12 (French and math) *Uniform Ministry Examinations* ➤ Secondary IV and V (selected subject areas)
Saskatchewan	*Provincial Learning Assessment Program* ➤ Grades 5, 8, and 11 (critical and creative thinking [2002], math [2001], and language arts [1998, 1996, and 1994])
Yukon Territory	*Yukon Achievement Tests* ➤ Grades 3, 6, and 9 (language arts and math) *Provincial Examinations* (from British Columbia) ➤ Grade 12 (core academic areas)

Territory students and teachers follow the curriculum developed by the British Columbia Ministry of Education. Consequently, all Grade 12 students in Yukon Territory schools must pass the *Provincial Examinations* designed for British Columbia students in order to graduate (Government of Yukon—Department of Education, 2005).

National and International Assessment Programs

School Achievement Indicators Program (SAIP)

The School Achievement Indicators Program (SAIP), a national assessment program conceived in 1989 by the Council of Ministers of Education, Canada (CMEC), provides data on the mathematics, reading/writing, and science literacy of students within all provinces and territories across Canada. Each year since 1993, 13- and 16-year-old students have been tested in one of these areas of literacy according to a schedule that follows a cyclical pattern: mathematics content and problem solving (1993, 1997, and 2001), reading/writing (1994, 1998, and 2002), and science (1996, 1999, and 2004). Results from SAIP are designed to complement those from provincial and territorial assessment programs and are thus used by Ministers of Education to help inform decisions about the quality of curricula and schooling within each of their jurisdictions.

As an example, in the spring of 2004, over 25,000 English- and French-speaking 13- and 16-year-old students participated in the SAIP Science III Assessment. Representatives from 17 educational jurisdictions across Canada designed, developed, and reviewed a paper-and-pencil science assessment instrument that was used as the measure of science literacy for the SAIP Science III Assessment. The questions on the instrument were constructed to examine scientific conceptual and procedural knowledge and the ability to use science to solve problems (Council of Ministers of Education, Canada, 2004). This assessment protocol differed from the two previous SAIP Science Assessments, which also included a hands-on practical task component.

As with all SAIP assessments, student achievement for the SAIP Science III Assessment was measured using a five-level curriculum framework: Level 1 performance is considered low, Level 2 or above is the expected performance of 13-year-old students, Level 3 or above is the expected performance of 16-year-old students, and Levels 4 and 5 denote higher levels of performance. For example, a Level 3 student can typically perform the following:

> use chemical properties to compare and classify substances;
> know that some life forms are unicellular and others are multicellular, and that life forms are involved in the transfer of energy;
> compare gravitational and electrical forces;
> compare distances from the Earth to the Moon, the Sun, and other stars;
> analyze experiments and judge their validity;
> identify areas where science knowledge and technology address societal problems (Council of Ministers of Education Canada, 2004).

The results of the SAIP Science III Assessment demonstrated that over 70 percent of 13-year-old students attained Level 2 or higher and 40 percent reached Level 3. For the 16-year-old students, 64 percent attained Level 3 or above and 20 percent performed at Level 4 or 5 (Council of Ministers of Education Canada, 2004a).

Starting in 2007, SAIP will be replaced by the Pan-Canadian Assessment Program (PCAP), which will assess the performance of 13-year-old students across Canada in reading, mathematics, and science. Assessment of second languages, information and communications technologies, and the arts is expected to be included as part of PCAP's mandate once the program has been established.

Programme for International Student Assessment (PISA)

In 2000 and 2003, approximately 30,000 15-year-old students from over 1,000 schools across Canada participated in the Programme for International Student Assessment (PISA). PISA is a project of the Organization for Economic Co-operation and Development (OECD), with the mandate to assess the skills and knowledge of the participants in reading (2000), mathematics (2003), and science (2006) across 41 countries.

One of the principal aims of PISA is to determine how well secondary school graduates are prepared to enter into society as contributing members. To this end, PISA data are used to answer the following questions (Government of Canada, 2005):

➤ How well are young adults prepared to meet the challenges of the future?
➤ Are they able to analyze, reason, and communicate their ideas effectively?
➤ Do they have the capacity to continue learning throughout life?
➤ Are some kinds of teaching and school organization more effective than others?

Results from the 2003 PISA mathematics assessment demonstrated that students from only two countries outperformed Canadian students: Hong Kong-China and Finland. Comparison among provinces across Canada showed that students in Alberta, British Columbia, and Quebec performed as well as the top-performing countries. As well, Alberta's performance was above the Canadian average, while Newfoundland and Labrador, Prince Edward Island, New Brunswick, Nova Scotia, and Saskatchewan performed below the national average (Council of Ministers of Education Canada, 2004b). For the 2000 PISA reading assessment, Canadian students placed third behind Finland and Korea (Council of Ministers of Education Canada, 2001).

IMPLICATIONS OF LARGE-SCALE ASSESSMENT

It is not clear yet that large-scale assessment is an effective way to increase student motivation to learn and actual learning, but it is affecting teachers' classroom work, including what they focus on and how they allocate time.

Proponents of large-scale assessment are quick to suggest that province- or territory-wide standardized achievement testing is a valuable mechanism for improving the quality of teaching and learning within schools. Through student achievement scores, districts, schools, and teachers are forced to provide evidence of the quality of teaching and learning that is taking place within our schools. Large-scale assessment indirectly applies pressure on educators to increase the number of students who achieve a targeted standard of achievement. But there are some negative implications associated with large-scale assessment. This section of the text will outline some of these implications.

The Impact on Teachers and Teaching

Teachers' attitudes towards large-scale, province-wide standardized assessment have been studied in Manitoba (Skwarchuk, 2004) and Ontario (Lam & Bordignon, 2001). In her study with Manitoba teachers, Skwarchuk found that two-thirds of the teachers polled disagreed with the use of standardized tests for assessing student achievement. As one teacher pointed out, "if it is our belief that learning is developmental, then administering one test to everybody discriminates against learning styles and readiness of students for those tasks" (Skwarchuk, p. 265). Teachers also indicated that these tests were often stressful for teachers and students alike and that uncontrolled variables, insufficient test time, and "unscrupulous testing practices" (Skwarchuk, p. 265) made the test results unreliable and invalid. To sum up the feelings of many teachers, it could be said that they felt as if provincial testing is a "colossal waste of resources" (Skwarchuk, p. 266) and "that the money would be better spent on professional development" (Lam & Bordignon, 2001, p. 138). According to Lam and Bordignon, a high percentage of Ontario English teachers expressed that the Grade 9 province-wide literacy test (last administered in the 1999–2000 school year) "did not tell them more than what they already knew about their students...did not adequately measure what they taught in the classroom and how they taught it...and that the test results did not reflect the schooling's effectiveness" (Lam & Bordignon, p. 137).

Lam and Bordignon (2001) were also interested in determining whether teachers believed that large-scale assessment enhanced student motivation to learn and increased actual student learning. Accordingly, Lam and Bordignon found that teachers perceived that large-scale assessment did not improve students' attitude toward English, their motivation toward reading or writing, or their literacy learning.

Skwarchuk (2004) also found that teachers, who were responsible for conducting standardized tests as part of provincial assessments, used a number of strategies to prepare their students. These included, "covering a wide variety of course topics in the curriculum, covering curriculum material in depth, reviewing old exam questions, and developing practice tests that were similar to the testing format" (Skwarchuk, p. 268). It may be the case that teachers may feel the pressure to engage in instructional practices that are more test-like and focused on memorization as opposed to thinking (Earl, 1999). This may be at the expense of good instructional pedagogy. Teachers must recognize that the ultimate test-taking strategy is good teaching.

Problems and Limitations of Large-Scale Assessment

While large-scale assessment may be regarded as useful for ensuring school and teacher accountability and for measuring the attainment of expectations or learning outcomes, it is limited and problematic in a number of ways. Large-scale assessments are unable to measure some very important student characteristics such as "sense of citizenship, ethics, confidence/self-esteem, aesthetic appreciation, respect for others, self-discipline, social competence, and desire to learn" (Froese-Germain, 1999, p. 5). Without this important information about students, large-scale assessment paints an incomplete picture of the nature of the educative experience that exists for students within their classrooms. It evaluates teacher and school performance using an incomplete data set.

Another concern with large-scale assessment is that it draws conclusions about the quality of teachers and learning in schools without taking important non-school parameters into account. As noted by Froese-Germain (1999), "A student's capacity to learn is affected by a host of factors including: the impact of poverty; parents' educational level; mental, physical, and emotional health; the effect of racial and other forms of discrimination; and language of origin" (p. 6). It is definitely unfair to hold teachers and schools accountable when these factors are not considered. Further, it is egregiously unfair to compare schools and teachers, in terms of student achievement and school effectiveness, when these factors are not considered as part of the equation.

A joint position statement with respect to provincial testing has been published by the Canadian Psychological Association and the Canadian Association of School Psychologists (Simner, 2000). There is a collective concern that the public tends to compare schools based on the outcomes of mandated tests. There is a failure to recognize that other factors influence students' test performance including motivation and absenteeism (Simner, 2000). It is the concern of the Canadian Psychological Association and the Canadian Association of School Psychologists that making schools solely responsible for students' test performances places pressure on teachers, administrators, and students (Simner, 2000).

A summary of issues associated with the nature and use of large-scale assessments is presented in Table 9.1. Some of the issues are addressed by some provinces that include performance assessment measures in their large-scale assessments.

Reconsidering Large-Scale Assessment

Gallagher (2004) sees a great danger when top-down accountability programs, in the guise of large-scale assessment programs, cause teachers to feel disempowered. He believes that teachers are the key to genuine change and he urges them to "turn the tables" by publicly asking crucial questions and letting voters and policymakers know what is educationally best for their students. He offers 10 questions for teachers to raise about systems of accountability:

1. Any accountability system should regard classroom teachers as *leaders*. Does this one?
2. Does the system focus on building capacity, or merely on control?
3. Does the system foster commitment, or merely compliance?
4. Does the system promote an integration of accountability with actual school improvement?

TABLE 9.1 Summary of Issues with Large-Scale Assessments

➤ To permit machine scoring, standardized tests are limited to multiple-choice items which, in turn, limits what can be tested. For example, you can test language skills (e.g., punctuation) but not writing ability or how students use language.

➤ To ensure that test scores are comparable over time, few substantive changes are made over the years; this discourages curricula updates.

➤ Although advocated as a means to carry out international comparisons of student learning and performance, these tests are not sensitive to differences in curricula for particular ages and grades in different countries (nor can they be made so).

➤ Because each question is assigned the same score value, the student who answers more of the difficult (and/or important from the program standpoint) questions is judged the equal of the student who gets only the easy ones.

➤ In order to achieve a proper dispersion in the scores (to facilitate making comparisons), questions that are almost always answered correctly or incorrectly tend to be avoided. Aspects of performance that should be tested may therefore not be represented at all because they make no contribution to score dispersion. This leads to overtesting of minutiae and undertesting of important conventions.

➤ Large-scale assessments stress the product of learning, not the process. They measure a student's ability to recall facts, define words, and perform routine calculations, not higher learning processes such as analyzing, synthesizing, forming hypotheses, and exploring alternative ways of solving problems.

➤ More critically, large-scale assessments have nothing to do with performance standards but only measure relative standards.

➤ Large-scale assessments do not serve as a useful diagnostic tool because they do not show students where they went wrong; corrected tests are never returned, excluding the process of feedback that is at the core of learning and education.

➤ Large-scale assessments systematically rule out students' independent creativity and criticism by eliminating the need to construct answers for themselves.

➤ Rather than increasing accountability, large-scale assessments merely shift it from teachers and school authorities to anonymous government officials or corporate bureaucrats who cannot be confronted or held accountable if tests are poorly constructed, administered, or marked.

➤ Many studies have shown that standardized tests are biased against socioeconomic, racial, and ethnic minority groups.

SOURCE: *Standardized testing: Undermining equity in education*, Froese-Germain, 1999. Report prepared for the National Issues in Education Initiative. Ottawa, Canada: Canadian Teachers' Federation. pp. 53–54.

5. Does it risk the complexity that is an inherent part of education, rather than demand simplicity?

6. Does it include all students or merely those on the margins?

7. Does it engage all teachers?

8. Does it engage all other relevant stakeholders?

9. Does it keep pedagogy at its centre?

10. Does it encourage *high-impact* assessment that truly benefits students and teachers, or simply *high-stakes* assessment that merely punishes them?

Motivating Students and Teachers for Large-Scale Assessment

In addition to becoming aware of provincial/territorial standards and building them into their classroom teaching in a balanced way, how can teachers motivate students to do their best on these tests? Table 9.2 lists strategies that could be used to motivate students to study for large-scale assessments.

Staying Focused on Quality in the Classroom

Coping with the pressures of large-scale assessment and other mandates may be easiest for the teacher who has clear personal and professional standards for the proper role of assessment in the classroom. Reiterating

TABLE 9.2	Strategies to Motivate Students to Study for Large-Scale Assessments
Discuss importance of good performance	Link performance to eligibility in extracurricular activities
Hold assemblies to motivate students	Require/recommend summer school
Publicly recognize students for good performance	Use scores for assigning grades
Schedule special activities (e.g., pizza party, field trips)	Place students in classes
	Exempt students who do well from required course work

SOURCE: J. Pedulla, L. M. Abrams, G. F. Madaus, et al. (2003), *Perceived Effects of State Mandated Testing Programs on Teaching and Learning: Findings from a National Survey of Teachers* (Boston: National Board on Educational Testing and Public Policy).

earlier themes from this book, here are five basic questions with which to judge the soundness of one's own approach to assessment (Popham, 2003):

➤ Do my classroom assessments measure genuinely worthwhile skills and knowledge?

➤ Will I be able to promote my students' mastery of what is measured in my classroom assessments?

➤ Can I describe what skills and knowledge my classroom tests measure in language that is clear enough for my own instructional planning?

➤ Do my classroom assessments yield results that allow me to tell which parts of my instruction were effective or ineffective?

➤ Do my classroom tests take too much time away from my instruction?

PREPARING STUDENTS FOR LARGE-SCALE ASSESSMENTS

The rest of this chapter discusses how to prepare students for testing. Many of these practices may appear to be practices that all teachers would perform. However, such is not the case. It is remarkable how often these practices are ignored or overlooked. Failure to carry out these activities can jeopardize the validity of tests.

Issues of Test Preparation

We use tests and other assessments to help make decisions about students' learning in some content area. A student's performance on a test or assessment is meant to represent the student's mastery of a broader body of knowledge and skills than just the specific examples included on the test or assessment. Tests and other assessments gather a sample of a student's behaviour and use that sample to generalize how the student is likely to perform if confronted with similar tasks or items. For example, the performance of a student who scores 90 percent on a test of poetry analysis, chemical equation balancing, or capitalization rules is interpreted as indicating that the student has mastered about 90 percent of the general content domain he or she was taught and tested on. The specific tasks or test items are selected to represent the larger group of similar tasks and items.

Expectations or learning outcomes, instruction, and the test *should* all be related to each other. After all, the purpose of large-scale assessment is to determine how well students have learned what they were taught. By definition, an assessment must be related to instruction, and instruction is, amongst other things, preparation for the test. The important question, however, is: when does the relationship between expectations or learning outcomes, instruction, and the test become so close that it is inappropriate or unethical?

Large-scale assessments should give information about how well a student can answer questions similar but not identical to those taught in class.

There is an important difference between teaching to the test and teaching the test itself.

There is an important ethical difference between teaching to the test and teaching the test itself. Teaching to the test involves teaching students the general skills, knowledge, and processes that they need to answer the questions on a test. This is an appropriate and valid practice. It is what good teaching and testing are all about. But teaching the test itself—that is, teaching students the answers to specific questions that will appear on the test—is neither appropriate nor ethical. It produces a distorted, invalid picture of student achievement. Such a test will give information about how well students can remember the specific items they were taught, but it will not tell how well they can do on questions that are similar, but not identical, to the ones they have been taught. Teachers have an educational and ethical responsibility not to corrupt the validity of students' large-scale assessment performance by literally teaching them the exact items that will be on the test.

Another problematic practice difficult to classify is teachers' limiting instruction to overly narrow objectives that sometimes accompany a test. When working with a predetermined curriculum, it is appropriate for teachers to confine their instruction to the expectations or learning outcomes that will be tested, so long as they do not prepare the students for the specific test items that will be used to measure these objectives. However, it is improper for teachers to consciously exclude important expectations or learning outcomes from their instruction solely because they are not on the test.

Mel Levine, MD, professor of pediatrics at the University of North Carolina Medical School in Chapel Hill, suggests a "do no harm" approach to assessment practices that states some important and useful strategies. See Key Assessment Tools 9.1.

The following sections describe other actions that teachers should carry out to prepare their students for large-scale assessments. As you read these sections, bear in mind the preceding list of inappropriate practices. Also bear in mind that concern about test preparation is not confined to paper-and-pencil tests, but also includes other assessment strategies and tasks.

Provide Good Instruction

Good instruction is the most important preparation for formal large-scale testing.

The single most important thing a teacher can do to prepare students for formal large-scale assessments is to provide them with good instruction. Earlier it was noted that good teaching includes activities such as providing a review at the start of a new lesson, setting an appropriate difficulty level for instruction, emphasizing important points during instruction, giving students practice on the expectations or learning outcomes they are expected to learn, and maintaining an orderly classroom learning environment. These practices will prepare students for testing better than anything else a teacher might do. A primary ethical responsibility of teaching, therefore, is to provide the best instruction possible, without corrupting the

KEY ASSESSMENT TOOLS 9.1

"Do No Harm" Assessment Practices

1. Assessment can help elevate education standards, but not if it creates larger numbers of students who are written off as unsuccessful. When a student does poorly, determine which link in the learning chain is uncoupled. Testing should not be an end in itself, but rather a call to action.

2. Not all students can demonstrate their strengths in the same manner. Beyond the large-scale assessment, students have opportunities to demonstrate their learning differently, using the means of their choice (portfolios, expert papers, oral presentations, and projects, as well as multiple-choice tests).

3. Some students who excel on tests might develop a false sense of security and confidence, failing to realize that adult careers tap many abilities that no test can elicit. Take care to nurture vital capacities that are not testable.

4. Avoid the hazard of teachers' teaching to the tests because your work or school is being judged largely on the basis of assessment results. Teachers should never have their students rehearse or explicitly prepare for tests. Good results on such tests should be the product of the regular, undisturbed curriculum.

Source: Adapted from Levine, 2003.

large-scale assessment in the ways described above. In the absence of good instruction, all aspects of assessment are greatly diminished.

Review Before Testing

Throughout the school year, many expectations or learning outcomes are introduced, some early and others at the end of the year. Because the topics students most remember are the ones most recently taught, it is good practice to provide students with a review prior to large-scale assessment. The review can take many forms: a question and answer session, a written or oral summary of main ideas, or administration of a review test. The review serves many purposes: to refresh students on expectations or learning outcomes taught early in the unit, to provide one last chance to practise important behaviours and skills, and to afford an opportunity to ask questions about things that are unclear. Often, the review exercise itself provokes questions that help students grasp partially understood ideas.

Test reviews often provoke questions that help students grasp partially understood ideas.

Ensure Familiarity with Question Formats

If students are not familiar with the types of questions used on an assessment, the assessment does not produce a valid assessment of what they have learned.

If a large-scale assessment will contain questions that use an unfamiliar format, students should be given practice with that format prior to testing. The need for such practice is especially important in the elementary grades where students first encounter matching, multiple-choice, true-false, short-answer, and essay questions. Students must learn what is expected of them for each type of question, and how to record their answer. One opportune time to familiarize students with question formats is during the review exercises prior to the chapter or unit test. Pretest practice with new types of question and response formats can reduce anxiety and permit a more valid assessment of student learning. In addition to familiarizing students with new types of questions and response formats, there is a general set of test-taking guidelines that can help students do their best on tests. These guidelines will not enable students to overcome the handicaps of poor teaching and lack of study, but they can help focus students during testing. Table 9.3 lists some advice that you may want to give students before a large-scale assessment (Ebel & Frisbie, 1991).

Another set of skills, called **testwise skills,** help students identify unintended clues to the correct answer. For example, when responding to multiple-choice questions, the testwise student applies the following probabilities:

To be testwise is to be able to identify unintended clues to the correct answers.

➤ If the words "some," "often," or similar vague words are used in one of the options, it is likely to be the correct option.

➤ The option that is longest or most precisely stated is likely to be the correct one.

➤ Any choice that has grammatical or spelling errors is not likely to be the correct one.

➤ Choices that do not attach smoothly to the stem of the question are not likely to be correct.

Scheduling the Test

If you as the test administrator have some latitude with respect to when you can schedule administration of a large-scale assessment, you should consider the times when students are most likely to show their best performance. For example, if testing were to occur the day of the school's championship basketball game, the period after an assembly or lunch, or on the first day after a school vacation, it is likely that students would give a subpar test performance. Likewise, a teacher should not schedule a test on a day that he or she will be away just so the supply teacher will have something to keep the students busy. The supply teacher may not be able to answer students' questions about the assessment protocols. Furthermore, if it is an elementary classroom, the presence of a stranger in the

TABLE 9.3	Common Test-Taking Strategy Advice for Students

➤ Read test directions carefully.

➤ Find out how questions will be scored. Will all questions count equally? Will points be taken off for spelling, grammar, neatness?

➤ Pace yourself to ensure that you can complete the test.

➤ Plan and organize essay questions before writing.

➤ Attempt to answer all questions. If guessing is not penalized, guess when you don't know the answer.

➤ When using a separate answer sheet, check often to make certain that you are marking your responses in the correct space.

➤ Be in good physical and mental condition at the time of testing.

classroom may make the students uncomfortable and unable to do their best.

In the elementary school there may be more flexibility in scheduling large-scale assessments than in high school, where rotary means that students must be in certain places at certain times. The math teacher who has a class immediately after lunch has no choice but to test students then. While no teacher has complete control over scheduling a large-scale assessment, it is useful to bear in mind that there are some times when students are able to perform better on tests than others, when given the latitude in scheduling assessment administration.

Giving Students Information about the Assessment

It is a good idea to let students know when the assessment will be given, what areas will be covered, what types of questions it will contain, how much it counts, and how long it will take. By providing this information, the teacher can help reduce some of the anxiety that inevitably accompanies the announcement of a large-scale assessment. The hardest assessment for students to prepare for is the first one they take in a class. Even if a teacher provides detailed information about topics to be covered, types of items, number of questions, and the like, students always have some uncertainty about the assessment. Of course, it is impossible for a teacher to provide the pretest information students need to prepare for the assessment. The specifics of test content, types of questions, and test length need to be considered well before the assessment is given. Simply ensure that you have not focused mainly on memorization skills and that you have covered a representative sample of the skills.

CHAPTER REVIEW

CHAPTER REVIEW

Visit Chapter 9 of the Online Learning Centre at **www.mcgrawhill.ca/ college/airasian** to take chapter quizzes, link to related Web sites, and read PowerWeb articles and news feed updates.

What is large-scale assessment?

➤ Large-scale assessment includes standardized achievement tests that are given to a large number (usually thousands) of students in order to measure their performance as an indicator of what they know and can do at a certain point in time.

What is a standardized achievement test?

➤ A standardized achievement test measures students' knowledge and mastered skills and provides information about students' performance in an academic subject area. A standardized achievement test compares a student's knowledge or skill with that of other students (norm-referenced) and/or against a standard (criterion-referenced).

What are curriculum standards?

➤ Curriculum standards are the statements about what students are expected to know at any given grade level. They are found written as knowledge, skill, and attitude expectations or learning outcomes in provincial curricula.

What are assessment standards?

➤ Assessment standards are descriptions of what students should know or be able to do at various grade levels and/or various levels of proficiency. Levels may be designated by a range of terms such as *basic, proficient,* and *advanced* or *acceptable standard* and *standard of excellence.*

What are achievement standards?

➤ Achievement standards are judgments about the percentage of students who are expected to attain acceptable or higher levels of proficiency.

What is SAIP?

➤ SAIP is the acronym for the School Achievement Indicators Program, a national assessment program that provides data on the mathematics, reading/writing, and science literacy of 13- and 16-year-old students.

What is PISA?

➤ PISA is the acronym for the Programme for International Student Assessment, a project of the Organization for Economic Co-operation and Development that was created to compare the skills and knowledge of 15-year-old students in reading, mathematics, and science across 41 countries.

What are some strategies that may be used to motivate students to study for large-scale assessment?

➤ Discuss importance of good performance
➤ Hold assemblies to motivate students
➤ Publicly recognize students for good performance
➤ Schedule special activities (e.g., pizza party, field trips)
➤ Link performance to eligibility in extracurricular activities
➤ Require/recommend summer school
➤ Use scores for assigning grades
➤ Place students in classes
➤ Exempt students who do well from required coursework

What is the difference between "teaching to the test" and "teaching the test"?

➤ "Teaching to the test" is an appropriate and valid practice that involves teaching students the general skills, knowledge, and processes that they need to answer questions on a test. "Teaching the test" is an unethical practice that involves teaching students the answers to specific questions that will appear on the test.

QUESTIONS FOR DISCUSSION

1. For a particular grade level and subject, what is the evidence of provincial or territorial curriculum, assessment, and achievement standards? How do these influence instruction and evaluation at the classroom level?

2. What are some good and bad effects of large-scale assessment on teachers and students at different levels of education?

3. What kinds of concerns, efforts, and influences are shaping province-wide and territory-wide testing? Is it good that these efforts are often viewed as "high stakes"?

4. What are some issues of validity and reliability with respect to large-scale assessment?

5. What are the benefits and demerits of using performance assessment tasks as part of large-scale assessment?

6. What is your opinion about each of the strategies for motivating students to study for large-scale assessments listed in Table 9.2?

ACTIVITIES

1. Research two large-scale assessment programs that exist within the province or territory in which you wish to teach. Collect sample assessment items from each. Select a grade and compare the items for that grade with curriculum learning outcomes or expectations for that province or territory.

2. Find out what "campus-wide standards" exist for student performance and assessment at your college or university. Write a brief plan for improving existing standards or for creating new ones.

3. Using publicly available information on SAIP or PISA results, draw some conclusions about the level of language, math, or science literacy of students within the province or territory in which you intend to teach as compared with students from other provinces, territories, or countries.

CHAPTER 10

STANDARDIZED ACHIEVEMENT TESTS

CHAPTER OBJECTIVES

After reading this chapter, you will be able to:

➤ Define terms related to standardized testing

➤ Distinguish between teacher-made, provincial, and standardized tests in terms of objectives, construction, and scoring

➤ Understand the need for administration protocols with standardized tests

➤ Interpret standardized achievement test results

➤ Identify factors that influence the validity and reliability of standardized tests

➤ Understand the use of standardized tests in identifying students with exceptionalities

➤ Cite suggestions for reporting standardized test results to parents

U zair Qureshi is in his first full year of teaching. As a Grade 5 teacher, he is required by his school board to test his students in the fall term on the *Canadian Test of Basic Skills* (*CTBS*; Nelson, 1998). A week prior to the scheduled testing date, the test booklets and examiner's manual arrive at the school. Uzair takes some time to preview the materials and the scripted administration directions. The testing occurs over the course of three days and during this time Uzair follows the administration protocols verbatim. Three months pass and the results are returned to the school along with individual student performance reports for parents. These reports are sent home and Uzair begins to receive numerous phone calls and email messages from parents requiring information to help them interpret their children's scores.

Standardized tests are administered, scored, and interpreted the same way no matter where or when given.

Some of the assessments that students complete are not created by their teachers. In addition to the provincial and national large-scale assessments that were discussed in Chapter 9, commercially available standardized achievement tests are another example of assessments that are devised by individuals other than classroom teachers. Recall from Chapter 9 that **standardized tests** assess students' performance under uniform conditions. There are structured directions for administration, specific procedures for scoring, and guidelines for interpretation of the results. Thus, standardized tests are administered, scored, and interpreted in a standard way regardless where or when given. It is therefore possible for a student's performance to be compared with the performance of other students at the same age or grade level. Standardized tests have norms, and measures of validity and reliability.

Educators who recommend the administration of standardized tests include school administrators and resource teachers, the local school board, or the provincial or territorial Ministry/Department of Education. Educators vary in their decisions about the use of these tests and the grade levels that are tested, but in general, standardized tests are administered for one or more of the following purposes:

1. to provide evidence for student placement in programs;
2. to document developmental information about student achievement over time;
3. to evaluate program effectiveness;
4. to compare the performance of local students to a national sample of peers;
5. to contribute to overall educational accountability.

Standardized tests may be individually administered to a student by an examiner in a one-on-one setting, or group administered tests are delivered to a whole class or cohort of students at the same time.

Standardized aptitude tests predict a student's ability to learn a skill.

There are two types of standardized tests: aptitude and achievement. **Standardized aptitude tests** attempt to predict a student's ability to learn a skill or accomplish a level of complexity. Tests of cognitive abilities and intelligence tests are examples of standard aptitude tests. In Canada, the *Canadian Cognitive Abilities Test* (*CCAT*; Nelson, 1998) is a commonly used cognitive abilities test. This test is designed to assess the pattern and level of students' development in reasoning and problem solving with verbal, quantitative, and spatial symbols (see Figure 10.4 for a description of the subtests). The *Wechsler Intelligence Scale for Children* (*WISC-IV*; Harcourt Canada, 2003) is a measure of general intellectual functioning. There are a series of assessments that are divided into verbally-mediated subtests and visually-oriented subtests. This assessment is time sensitive and includes Canadian norming data. The *WISC-IV* is administered by trained and certified psychometrists.

Standardized achievement tests measure students' knowledge and mastered skills and provide information about student performance in the academic subject areas such as reading, writing, spelling, mathematics, science, and study skills. A student's performance score in any one of the academic subject areas is compared to a sample of his or her peers and the student's strengths and weaknesses are identified. Here are some examples of commercially available achievement tests used in Canada:

Standardized achievement tests provide information about students' academic performance as compared to their peers and identify strengths and weaknesses.

➤ *Canadian Test of Basic Skills* (*CTBS*; Nelson, 1998)
➤ *Canadian Achievement Test* (*CAT-3*; Canadian Test Centre, 2001)
➤ *Gates-MacGinitie Reading Tests* (*GMRT*; Nelson, 1992)
➤ *Canada Quick Individual Achievement Test* (*C-QUIET*; Canadian Edumetrics, 1990)

It is important to note that decisions about students should never be made on the basis of a single standardized test but rather on the basis of information gathered from a variety of assessments. In particular, the results of standardized achievement tests tell the teacher what the students have/have not learned and the skills that they can/cannot perform under certain conditions. Standardized achievement tests should not be interpreted without also considering information about the students' daily classroom performance.

Note that Chapters 9 and 10 are differentiated by the administrative purposes of the standardized tests. Large-scale provincial and national standardized tests (see Chapter 9) are a mechanism for determining the degree to which students meet core subject curriculum expectations and in order to establish benchmarks for educational standards. This chapter will focus on the use, administration, interpretation, application, and reporting of commercially available standardized achievement tests. Table 10.1 compares these standardized achievement tests with teacher-made and provincial tests.

Many teachers have mixed reactions to standardized tests. Some teachers believe that these tests are inappropriate for their class because the curriculum might not cover some of the test content. Often parents put too

TABLE 10.1 Comparison of Teacher-Made, Provincial, and Standardized Achievement Tests

	Teacher-Made	Provincial	Standardized Achievement
Content and/or objectives	Specific to class instruction; picked or developed by the teacher; narrow range of content tested, usually one unit or chapter of instruction in a subject	Topics commonly taught or desired to be taught in schools of a province or territory; broad range of content covered in a subject area, often covering many years of instruction in a subject	Topics commonly taught in many schools across Canada; broad range of content covering a year of instruction in a subject
Item construction	Written or selected by the classroom teacher	Professional item writers	Professional item writers
Item types	Various	Multiple-choice and performance	Mainly multiple-choice
Item selection	Teacher picks or writes items as needed for test	Many items written and then screened; best items chosen for test	Many items written and then screened and tried out on students before few best items chosen for test
Scoring	Teacher	Machine and scorers	Machine and scorers
Scores reported	Number correct, percent correct	Usually percent correct or level for individuals; percent or proportion of mastery for groups	Percentile rank, stanine, grade-equivalent scores
Interpreting scores	Norm- or criterion-referenced, depending on classroom teacher's preference	Criterion-referenced	Norm-referenced and developmental

much emphasis on these measures and discount the teacher's judgment that is based on months of observing their child in school. Teachers perceive that they have a good sense of how their students are doing and therefore the results of standardized tests only corroborate what they already know about their students.

Most teachers do not think standardized tests are important to the day-to-day functioning of their classrooms, but parents often view the results with great seriousness.

The reality is that these standardized tests aren't created to serve the immediate needs of the classroom teacher. They're more for the use of administrators and curriculum planners. But they do contribute to the quality of the school system and thus indirectly to the student's education. In addition, the information the tests provide about an individual student can be useful as a check on the teacher's own evaluation based on classroom assessment. Therefore, it is important that teachers and students take these standardized tests seriously.

This chapter will acquaint you with how such tests are constructed and standardized, equip you to administer them, and prepare you to interpret them for your own knowledge and for explaining them to parents. We will also discuss issues of validity.

HOW STANDARDIZED ACHIEVEMENT TESTS ARE CREATED

There are two key points to remember about standardized achievement tests: (1) they are usually norm referenced and (2) their main function is to compare a student's performance to that of a national group of similar students. The tests make possible statements such as "Jondalar scored higher than 87 percent of Grade 7 students in Canada in math"; "Maria is in Grade 3, but her grade equivalent score on the standardized test was sixth grade, third month"; "Ayla scored above average in science compared to Grade 8s in the nation"; and "Compared to other Grade 2 students, Giuseppe was in the bottom quarter in reading." In each case, a student's test performance was obtained by comparing it to a group of similar students across the country. Standardized achievement tests are used in schools mainly because they provide comparisons of student achievement beyond the confines of their classroom. Such comparisons are not possible based on teacher-made tests.

Standardized achievement tests are usually norm referenced.

The most commonly used standardized achievement tests are published in the form of test batteries. A **test battery** is a collection of tests in many different subject areas that are administered together. Rather than constructing one test for math, a totally separate test for reading, and yet another for writing, most test publishers construct a single test battery that contains many different subject area tests. For example, the *Canadian Achievement Test* (*CAT-3*; Canadian Test Centre, 2001) includes reading/language and mathematics tests ranging across Grades 1 through 12. The subject area tests for reading/language include comprehension, vocabulary, and mechanics and expression. The mathematics test includes problem-solving tasks that require students to apply mathematics skills and concepts. There are supplemental tests of word analysis, spelling, language/writing conventions, computations, and numerical estimation.

A student gets a separate score on each subject area test, or subtest. The entire battery consists of 150–200 items that take approximately 3½ hours to complete. The main advantages of a test battery are that (1) its broad content coverage provides a general picture of a student's school achievement and (2) a student's score on one subtest can be compared to his or her score on other subtests.

A test battery provides a general picture of a student's school performance and compares performance across subject areas.

Test Construction

Since the information obtained from a standardized achievement test differs from that obtained from a teacher-made, textbook, or provincial test, it should not be surprising to learn that the standardized test is constructed differently as well. A well-constructed standardized achievement test has three characteristics: (1) it is carefully constructed, with item tryouts, analysis, and revision occurring before the final version of the test is completed; (2) there are written directions and procedures for administering and scoring the test; and (3) score interpretation is based on the test having been administered to a carefully selected sample of students from across Canada. The performance of this national sample, or **norm group,** is what local student performance is compared to. (See Appendix C on page 305 for a discussion of normal distribution and standard deviation of scores.) Figure 10.1 compares the steps in constructing a teacher-made achievement test with the steps in constructing a standardized achievement test.

FIGURE 10.1

Steps in constructing Teacher-Made and Standardized Achievement Tests.

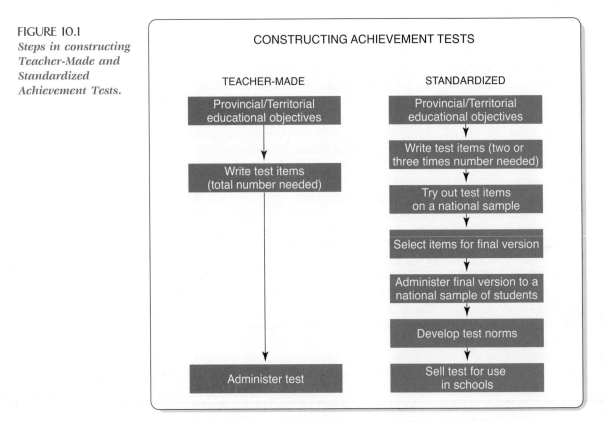

Choosing Objectives

A teacher-made test and a national standardized achievement test both start with educational objectives. In the teacher-made test, the objectives that have been emphasized during instruction are assessed. The standardized test constructor, on the other hand, seeks to assess only objectives that are commonly taught across the nation in all classrooms at a particular grade level. These objectives are found by examining widely used textbooks and board curriculum guidelines. The objectives and skills that are *common* across textbooks and guidelines are selected for inclusion in the test. This means that some objectives a particular classroom teacher emphasizes may not be assessed by a standardized achievement test.

Standardized tests try to assess objectives that are taught nationally in classrooms at a particular grade level.

Writing and Reviewing Items

Once the objectives are identified, the standardized test publisher, like the classroom teacher, must construct or select test items. Unlike the classroom teacher, who writes just as many items as are needed for a test, the standardized test publisher generates two or three times more items than are needed on the final test. A staff of professional item writers, most of them experienced teachers, research and write items and passages to be tried out.

Standardized test items are reviewed and edited for content, style, and validity, as well as for ethnic, cultural, racial, and gender bias.

The selected items go through several cycles of review and revision before being accepted for use. Curriculum specialists study the items to be sure they assess the intended objectives. Test construction specialists review them to be sure they are well written, without ambiguity or clues to test items. Other groups review the items to determine whether they are biased in favour of particular student groups. The following quote exemplifies the test item screening process:

> All items were reviewed for appropriateness of content for students from different socioeconomic backgrounds and from different racial and ethnic groups. Items that survived these editorial reviews were placed in a pool of test items to be tried out in appropriate grade groups. The pool of items for each subtest was twice the number required for the subtest. The results of these initial tryouts were used to select the items for the original form of the test. These items were further refined by a team of Canadian reviewers. (Teacher's Handbook; *CCAT*; Nelson, 1998, p. 3)

Trying Out Items

All the test items are tried out and the more valid and reliable ones are selected for the final version of the test. Since no test constructor—classroom teacher or standardized test publisher—knows how well any item will work until it actually is tried on a group of students, the publisher tries out the items on a sample of students similar to those for whom the final test is intended. The communities chosen for these tryouts represent different sizes, geographical locations, and socioeconomic levels. The trial test forms look like the final test form and are administered by classroom teachers so that the administrative situation during the tryout is as similar as possible to the way that the final, published test will be administered.

There are two reasons for trying out test items before finalizing the test. First, the test constructor wants to make sure that all the items are clearly written and understood by students. By examining student responses after the tryout, unclear items can be identified, revised, or discarded. Second, test items that ensure a spread of test scores among the test takers must be selected. After the tryout, the statistical properties of each item are analyzed to make certain the final test contains items that differentiate among test takers. This permits the desired norm-referenced comparisons in the standardized achievement tests.

Two important indices for judging test items are difficulty and discrimination. The **difficulty index** of a test item indicates the proportion of test takers who answered the item correctly. Thus, a difficulty of 90 means that 90 percent of the students answered the item correctly, while an item with a difficulty of 15 was answered correctly by only 15 percent of the test takers. The **discrimination index** indicates how well students who scored high on the test as a whole scored on a particular item. An item that discriminates well among test takers is one that high test scorers get correct, but low test scorers get incorrect. That is, the item discriminates between students in the same way as the whole test. (See Appendix C on page 305 for elaboration on these indices.)

The test constructor's purpose is to differentiate among students according to their levels of achievement. The test constructor is not likely to select final items for the test that all students got right or wrong in the tryout, because these items do not help differentiate high from low achievers. To accomplish the desired norm referencing among test takers, the test must consist of items that about half the students get correct and half get incorrect and that discriminate among students in the same way as the test as a whole. Only then does the test differentiate students across the possible scoring range and permit the desired norm-referenced comparisons among test takers. The item tryout provides the information needed to select items for the final test version.

The preceding steps accomplish three important aims: (1) they identify test objectives that reflect what most teachers across the nation are teaching; (2) they produce test items that assess these objectives; and (3) they identify a final group of items that will produce the desired norm-referenced comparisons among test takers. The final version of the test, including the selected test items, directions for administration, separate answer sheets, and established time limits, must then be "normed."

After tests are tried out, standardized test items are statistically analyzed to ensure that they provide the spread among scores that are needed on norm-referenced tests.

Difficulty index indicates the proportion of test takers who answered the item correctly.

Discrimination index compares overall test scores on a particular item.

To differentiate among students, commercial tests contain many items that approximately one-half of the test takers get right and one-half get wrong.

Norming the Test

In order to provide information that allows comparison of an individual student's performance to that of a Canadian sample of similar students, the final version of the test must be given to a sample of students from across the nation. This process is called norming the test. **Test norms** describe how a national sample of students who took the test actually performed on it. Different test norms are developed for tests in the fall and the spring, so that students who are tested in the fall can be compared to the fall norming group and students who take the test in the spring can be compared to the spring norming group. This is done because the time of the year that a student takes a standardized test makes a considerable difference in his or her performance level; the more instruction the student has had, the higher his or her scores should be.

Test norms describe how a national sample of students who are representative of the general population perform on the test.

Suppose that a standardized test publisher wishes to norm the final version of an achievement test for Grade 5 students. To do this, the publisher needs to obtain information about how Grade 5 students across Canada perform on the test. The publisher (1) selects a representative sample of Grade 5 students from across the country, (2) administers the test to this sample, (3) scores the test, and (4) uses the scores of the sample to represent the performance of all Grade 5 students across the country. Assuming the sample of Grade 5 students was well chosen, the scores made by the sample are a good indication of how all Grade 5 students would perform on the test.

Obviously, the representativeness of the sample determines how much confidence a teacher can have in the comparisons made between individual students and the "national average." The development of norms is a critical aspect of constructing these tests. Standardized test publishers recognize this and strive to select samples that are representative of the group for whom a test is intended. One publisher describes the test development procedures with respect to norming the standardized achievement test:

> Norms for CAT-2 were developed from a Canada-wide norming study involving 88 school jurisdictions...to ensure representativeness by region, district size, and degree of urbanization...The target population to which CAT-2 norms are intended to apply includes all schools in Canada in which English is the language of instruction...The sample comprised over 50,000 students from Grades 2 through 12 that were drawn by stratified random sampling procedures from the national public, separate, private and native school populations. (Handbook for Test Coordinators, *CAT-2*; Canadian Test Centre, 1992, pp. 11–12)

Four criteria are used to judge the adequacy of the test norms: sample size, representativeness, recentness, and description of procedures. (Popham, 2000). In general, a large sample of students in the norm group is preferable to a small sample; in other words, a norming sample of 10,000 to one of 1,000 Grade 5 students. But sample size alone does not guarantee representativeness. If the 10,000 students in the norming sample were all

If we assume a norming sample is representative of the general population, a large sample is preferred to a small one.

from private schools in the same province, the sample would not provide a good representation of the performance of students across Canada. There must be evidence that the norming sample is representative of the national group for whom the test is intended.

School curricula change over time. New topics are added and others are dropped. Thus, it is important to renorm standardized norm-referenced tests about every seven to nine years to keep up with these changes. It is unfair to compare today's students to a norm group that was taught a different curriculum.

The final criterion for judging the adequacy of standardized test norms is the clarity of the procedures used to produce them. The clearer and more detailed the description of the procedures followed in test construction, the better the test user can judge the appropriateness of the test. Publishers provide different kinds of manuals outlining procedures to accompany their tests. A *technical manual,* for example, provides information about the construction of the test, including objective selection, item writing and review, item tryout, and norming. A *teacher's manual* provides a description of the areas tested, as well as guidelines for interpreting and using the results of the test. These manuals are accessible to classroom teachers to help them understand and use the test results. Another source of information about published tests is *The Sixteenth Mental Measurements Yearbook* (Spies & Plake, 2005), which provides reviews written by experts in the field.

Standardized test manuals provide information about test construction and interpretation.

It is worth noting that standardized achievement tests may be norm-referenced, criterion-referenced, or both. Recall that in criterion-referenced scoring an individual's score is compared to a predetermined standard or level of performance. A standardized achievement test that is both norm-referenced and criterion-referenced is one that compares the performance of an individual to his/her peers and evaluates how much material the individual has learned according to a set standard (Aiken, 2000).

ADMINISTERING THE TEST

Once a test is normed, it is ready to be sold to school systems. School boards usually base their selection of a particular test on the judgment of a research/assessment administrator or a joint administrator-teacher committee. Once the test battery is selected, other decisions have to be made. In what grades will students be tested? Will all subtests of the achievement battery be administered? What types of score reports are needed? Should students be tested at the start of the school year or at the end of the year? Different school systems answer these questions differently. Whatever the ultimate decisions, it is usually the classroom teacher who is given the task of administering the tests.

The Need for Consistent Administration

A standardized test is meant to be administered to all students under the same conditions whenever and wherever it is given. The reason for standardizing administrative conditions is to allow valid comparisons between local scores and those of the national norm group. If a student takes the test under conditions different than the national norm group, then comparisons of the student's performance to the norm group are misleading. It is not fair to compare the performance of a student who was given 40 minutes to complete a test to others who were given only 30 minutes. It is not fair to compare a student who received teacher assistance during testing to students who did not. Thus, every national standardized test comes with very specific and detailed directions to follow during test administration.

The directions spell out in great detail how a teacher should prepare for testing, how the room should be set up, what to do while the students are taking the test, how to distribute the tests and answer sheets, and how to time the tests. In addition, the directions suggest ways to prepare students for taking the test. Finally, the directions provide a script for the teacher to read when administering the test.

Standardized tests must always be administered under the same conditions in order for there to be valid comparisons between local scores and those of the national norm group.

Every teacher who administers a standardized test is expected to use its accompanying script and not deviate from it. If the conditions of administration vary from the directions provided by the test publisher, comparisons with the norming sample and interpretations of students' performances may be invalid.

INTERPRETING SCORES

Several weeks after test administration, results are returned to the school. It is important to remember that the tests usually are norm-referenced and compare a student's performance to those of a reference group of students. The most common comparisons are of a student against a national sample of students in the same grade or of a student against his or her own performance in different subtest areas. However, these are not the only comparisons that can be made from a standardized achievement test.

A school board may also compare its students to a narrower sample than students in the same grade nationwide. For example, suppose a school is in an urban sector and serves a large, multi-racial, multi-ethnic population. The information sought for this school is likely to be how students compare to a national sample drawn from similar urban sector schools. Most standardized test publishers can provide such a comparison.

Suppose that a school is in an affluent suburban area. Past experience has shown that when students in this school are compared to a representative national sample, they generally do very well. Here the information sought is likely to be how students in the school do in comparison to similar students in other affluent suburban schools. Once again, standardized test publishers can usually provide such a comparison.

Although national norms are the most commonly reported and used, most standardized test publishers can provide more specific standardized test norms according to geographic location, type of community (rural, suburban, urban), type of school (public, private), and particular school system. A student's test performance may appear quite different depending on the choice of norm group to which he or she is compared: a representative national sample, a sample of students in urban schools, a sample of students in suburban schools, or a sample of students from his or her own school board.

Standardized achievement tests provide the classroom teacher with many different kinds of scores. In interpreting these tests, the number of items a student got correct, called the **raw score,** is not useful in itself. The teacher needs to know how that raw score compares to the chosen norm group, and special types of scores provide this information. Since there are so many types of scores available, discussion here is confined to the three most common types: percentile rank, stanine, and grade equivalent score. If there is a question about the meaning and interpretation of scores not discussed here, the teacher's manual that accompanies a test contains the desired explanation.

Percentile Rank Scores

Probably the most commonly used score is the **percentile rank.** Percentile ranks range from 1 to 99 and indicate what percentage of the norm group the student scored above. If Tawon, a seventh grader, has a percentile rank of 91 on a standardized math test, she scored higher on the test than 91 percent of the national sample of Grade 7 students who made up the norm group. If Josh has a percentile rank of 23 in reading, he scored higher on the reading test than only 23 percent of the students in the norm group. Percentiles do not refer to the percentage of items a student answered correctly; they refer to the percentage of students in the norm group who scored *below* a given student.

The composition of the norm group defines the comparison that can be made. Thus, Tawon's percentile rank of 91 based upon local norms means that she did better than 91 percent of the Grade 7 students in her own school board. This does not necessarily mean that she would have a percentile rank of 91 if compared to Grade 7 students nationally. A student's percentile rank can vary depending on the group to which he or she is compared.

One of the main advantages of standardized test batteries is that they are normed on a single group. This allows the teacher to compare a student's performance across the many subtests and to identify strengths and weaknesses. Thus, a teacher can make statements about how a given student performs in math compared to writing, reading, vocabulary, and other tested areas.

Stanine Scores

The **stanine** is a second type of standardized test score. Stanines are distributed on a nine-point scale, with a stanine of 1 representing the lowest
performance and a stanine of 9 the highest. These nine numbers are the
only possible stanine scores a student can receive. Like a percentile rank,
stanines are designed to indicate a student's performance in comparison to
a larger norming sample. Table 10.2 shows the approximate relationship
between stanines, percentile ranks, and the percentage of students that are
represented by each statistic.

*Stanines are a nine-
point scale with 1
representing the lowest
category and 9 the
highest.*

Although there is comparability between stanine scores and percentile
rank scores, most teachers use stanines to represent general achievement
categories, with stanine scores of 1, 2, and 3 considered below average,
4, 5, and 6 considered average, and 7, 8, and 9 considered above average. While stanines are not as precise as percentile ranks, they are easier
to work with and interpret, which is a major reason for their popularity
among teachers and test publishers. As with the percentile rank, a student's stanine score in one subject can be compared to his or her stanine
performance in another subject on the same test battery to identify strong
and weak areas of the student's achievement.

Grade Equivalent Scores

While stanines and percentile ranks provide information about a student's
performance compared to the norm group, other types of standardized test
scores seek to identify a student's development across grade levels. They
are intended to compare student performance to a series of reference
groups that vary developmentally. The most common developmental scale

TABLE 10.2 Approximate Percentile Ranks Corresponding to Stanine Scores

Stanine Score	Approximate Percentile Rank	Percent of Students
9	96–99	4%
8	90–95	7%
7	78–89	12%
6	60–77	17%
5	41–59	20%
4	23–40	17%
3	11–22	12%
2	5–10	7%
1	1–4	4%

A grade equivalent score is an estimate of a student's development level but is not indicative of the grade in which a student should be placed.

is the **grade equivalent score,** which is intended to represent students' achievement in terms of a scale based upon grade and month in school. It is important to note that the month of September is considered to be "grade.0" of a given school year, October is "grade.1," November is "grade.2," and so on. Since the school year is 10 months long (September through June), the numbers that denote the months range from "0" to "9." A grade equivalent score of 7.5 stands for Grade 7, fifth month of school (i.e., February). A grade equivalent score of 11.0 stands for the beginning of Grade 11 (i.e., September). On some tests, the decimal point is omitted in grade equivalent scores, in which case a grade equivalent score of 43 stands for Grade 4, third month and a score of 108 stands for Grade 10, eighth month.

Grade equivalent scores are easily misinterpreted. A scoring scale that is organized in terms of grade and month in school is so familiar to most teachers that it can seduce them into making incorrect interpretations of scores. Consider Luisa, who took a standardized achievement test battery at the start of Grade 5. When her teacher received the results he saw that Luisa's grade equivalent score in mathematics was 7.5. What does this score indicate about Luisa's mathematics achievement?

If we asked 100 teachers to explain what they believed Luisa's grade equivalent score in math meant, the great majority of them would give one of the following *incorrect* intepretations.

➤ Luisa does as well in mathematics as a Grade 7 student in the fifth month of school.
➤ Luisa can do the mathematics work of a Grade 7 student.
➤ Luisa's score indicates that she can succeed in a Grade 7 mathematics curriculum.

However, except under very rare conditions, each of these interpretations is incorrect or unsubstantiated. Remember, Luisa took a *Grade 5* mathematics test, which contains mathematics items commonly taught in Grade 5. Luisa did not take a Grade 7 mathematics test, so we have no way of knowing how she would do on Grade 7 math material. Certainly she wouldn't have had the benefit of math normally taught in Grade 6. All we know is how Luisa performed on a Grade 5 test, and this tells us nothing about how she might perform on tests for a higher grade level.

If all of the preceding interpretations are inappropriate, what is the correct interpretation of Luisa's grade equivalent score of 7.5? The most appropriate interpretation is that *compared to other Grade 5 students,* Luisa is well above the national average in Grade 5 mathematics. Developmentally, she is ahead of the "typical" Grade 5 students in mathematics achievement. Caution must be exercised when interpreting grade equivalent scores more than one grade level above or below that of the student. Standardized test publishers warn against misinterpretations of grade equivalent scores in their manuals.

Another use of the grade equivalent score is to assess a student's academic development over time. The change in a student's grade equivalent score over time is often used as an indication of whether the student is making "normal progress" in his or her learning. For example, if a student's grade equivalent score is 8.2 when tested in Grade 8, one might expect the student's grade equivalent to be around 9.2 if tested at the same time in Grade 9. However, it is important to recognize that development is an irregular process, which may jump ahead greatly at certain times but remain static at others. Thus, small deviations from so-called normal growth of one grade equivalent per year should not be interpreted as representing a problem. Table 10.3 compares the characteristics of percentile rank, stanine, and grade equivalent scores.

For more discussion of the terms and concepts in this section, as well as other terms such as, "normal distribution" and "standard deviation," see Appendix C, "Statistical Applications for Classroom Assessment" on page 305.

CHAPTER CASE STUDY

Visit the text OLC to read the case of Melinda Grant, a first-year elementary school teacher who worries about being held accountable for her students' year-end standardized test scores.

www.mcgrawhill.ca/ college/airasian

EXAMPLES OF STANDARDIZED TESTS

The following will provide some authentic examples of students' questions on standardized tests, profiles for teachers to interpret standardized tests, and summaries of students' standardized test scores. It should be noted that these are provided here as merely examples, several other batteries and reports exist on the standardized test market.

TABLE 10.3 Comparison of Three Common Standardized Test Scores			
	Percentile Rank	Stanine	Grade Equivalent Score
Format of score	Percentage	Whole number	Grade and month in school
Possible scores	1 to 99 in whole numbers	1 to 9 in whole numbers	Prekindergarten to 12.9 in monthly increments
Interpretation	Percent of students a given student did better than	1 to 3 below average; 4 to 6 average; 7 to 9 above average	Above average, average, below average compared to students in the same grade
Special issues	Small differences often overinterpreted	Broad index of student achievement	Frequently misinterpreted and misunderstood

Example 1: Practice Test

Figure 10.2 (pp. 279–281) is the "Levels 14 to 16 Practice Test" from the *Canadian Achievement Test-3* (*CAT-3*; Canadian Test Centre, 2001). This example is administered to students in Grade 4, 5, or 6 prior to the official administration of the *CAT-3*. The "Practice Test" allows students the opportunity to become familiar with the testing procedures and question formats. The teacher provides the following introduction, "This test is just for practice, so that you can get used to doing this kind of test." This example includes a Sample A and a Sample B. The teacher reads these directions to the students, "First, you will practise answering questions in reading and language. Turn to Page 2 and find Sample A. Read Sample A and find the correct answer. Mark an answer by filling in the circle that goes with the answer you choose for the item." After this question has been completed by all students, the teacher then says, "Read Sample B and find the correct answer. Find the circles for Sample B in the box labelled 'Answer Sheet' and fill in the circle that goes with the answer you choose." Then students independently read the passage found on Pages 2 and 3 of the "Practice Test" and answer the three comprehension questions on Page 3. After completing this exercise, students read the boxed passage on the bottom of Page 3 and choose the best sentence to complete the blank. Students are instructed to score their responses for questions 1–4 in the box at the top of Page 2 labelled, "Answer Sheet." Finally, Page 4 includes three Mathematics problems that are to be scored on the top of Page 4.

Example 2: Student Diagnostic Profile

Figure 10.3 (pp. 282 and 283) is a "Level 18 Student Diagnostic Profile" and is designed for the teacher to record a Grade 8 or 9 student's test results from the *Canadian Achievement Test-3* (*CAT-3*; Canadian Test Centre, 2001). Once complete, this profile may be used by a teacher to plan instructional activities to reinforce specific objectives. First, the scorer or teacher crosses out the question item numbers that the student answers incorrectly. Then the student's **raw score** (number of correct responses) is added up for each subtest in Reading, Language, Mathematics, Vocabulary, Spelling, Language/ Writing Conventions, and Computation and Numerical Estimation. The column labelled, "Performance Criteria," ranks the student's number of correct responses as "L = low," "C = competent," or "P = proficient." The total number of "competent" and "proficient" objectives are noted at the bottom of each subtest summary. For the objectives that are identified as "low," the teacher may choose to address through instruction or remediation. However, one caution should be noted in using this profile information; in most cases, any single skill area is assessed with a limited number of items. This may not provide reliable enough information for curriculum planning or decision making. Rather, teachers should follow up the skill area information with additional information collected through other assessment measures.

Example 3: Overview of Standardized Tests

The tables in Figure 10.4 (p. 284) offer an overview of two Canadian standardized tests. The *Canadian Test of Basic Skills* (*CTBS*; Nelson, 1998) is a battery of tests that is designed to assess students' development in the academic foundation skills. The subtests address the curriculum areas of Vocabulary, Reading, Language, Sources of Information, Mathematics, Science, and Maps and Diagrams. Students in primary, elementary, and high school (Kindergarten to Grade 12) can be tested on the various **forms** (versions of the test) of these standardized achievement measures. All questions are in a multiple-choice format and students mark their answer choices on an answer sheet. By contrast, the *Canadian Cognitive Abilities Test* (*CCAT*; Nelson, 1998) is a series of tests that provides information on the level of development of general and specific cognitive skills of students. These skills are correlated with learning and problem solving. This aptitude test assesses three ability areas: Verbal, Quantitative, and Nonverbal. These ability area tests are scored separately and also as a composite to identify strong and weak areas of specific cognitive skills. Educators can then capitalize on a student's strongest areas for instruction while building up weaker areas. Test forms exist for students at the primary and elementary/high school levels.

Example 4: Student List Report

The sample "Student List Report" from the *Canadian Test of Basic Skills* (*CTBS*; Nelson, 1998) found in Figure 10.5 (p. 285) has been generated for 10 students in a Grade 3 class. The students' names, genders, and ages at the time of the test are noted in the far left hand column. In the column labelled, "Scores," four statistics are provided: "SS" is a developmental standard score (an arbitrary score used for conversion on many standardized tests); "GE" is the grade equivalent; "NPR" stands for the national (i.e., Canadian) percentile rank; and, to the right of this statistic is an "S," which is the stanine. Students' scores are listed for each of the Reading (Vocabulary, Reading subtests), Language (Spelling, Capitals, Punctuation, Usage/Expression subtests), and Mathematics (Concepts/Estimation, Problem Solving/Data, Computations subtests) measures. The "Composite" column is a single score that represents students' overall performance on the tests. Additionally, the bottom of the "Student List Report" provides averages for each column based on this total class sample of 24 students.

Example 5: Student Performance Chart

Figure 10.6 (p. 286) is a computer-generated chart from the *Canadian Test of Basic Skills* (*CTBS*; Nelson, 1998) that graphs an individual student's performance on all the subtests of the *CTBS*. Each bar graph represents a subtest and plots this student's percentile rank scores. Note that percentile ranks are not on an equal interval scale and that a score is in the average range if it falls between the 16th and the 84th percentile rank. This chart may be retained in the student's official school record and shared with parents during a parent-teacher conference. On this particular report, this student's performance is not compared to other students in the class, but against the Canadian norming population. Other reports can be generated to provide comparisons of an individual student within a school and/or within a school board. Each test publisher presents the results of standardized tests in slightly different formats, but the basic information and its interpretation do not vary much from publisher to publisher.

THE VALIDITY OF STANDARDIZED ACHIEVEMENT TESTS

A great deal of time, expertise, and expense are put into the construction of standardized achievement tests. The most widely used tests are technically strong, with well-written items, an attractive format, statistically sophisticated norms, and reliable, consistent student scores. More care, concern, and expertise are put into producing a standardized achievement test than are typically put into constructing a teacher-prepared or textbook test.

It is still appropriate, however, to raise the question of whether a standardized achievement test provides the information needed to make valid decisions about student achievement. Teacher-prepared and textbook tests are judged mainly in terms of whether they provide a fair assessment of how well students have learned the things they were taught. Standardized achievement tests are judged on this basis too, but on other bases as well. Regardless of the test, if it does not provide the desired information about student achievement it is not valid and therefore not useful for decision making. For standardized achievement tests, four factors influence validity and reliability: (1) the appropriateness of the content and objectives tested, (2) the representativeness of the norming sample, (3) the conditions under which the test is administered, and (4) misinterpretations of test results. This section examines these issues and their potential effect on the validity of standardized achievement tests.

Appropriate Coverage

Standardized tests are designed to assess the core objectives that most classroom teachers at that grade level cover in their instruction.

Standardized tests are not constructed to assess every classroom teacher's unique instructional objectives. Rather they are designed to assess the core objectives that *most* classroom teachers cover in their instruction. By selecting a common set of objectives, test constructors seek to ensure that

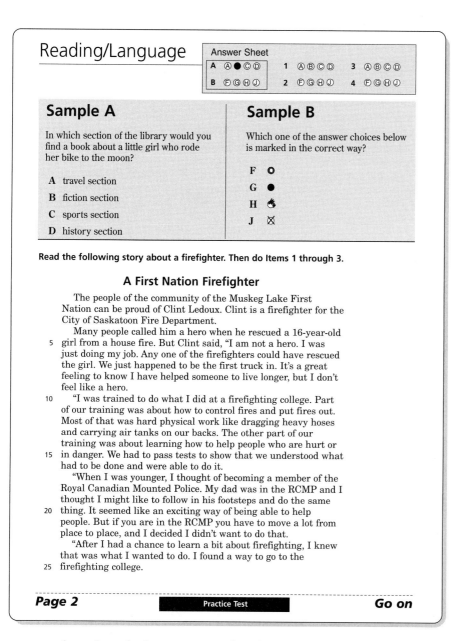

FIGURE 10.2

Example 1: Practice Test. (Page 2)

most students have had exposure to the objectives tested. Of course, this does not mean that every standardized test is equally relevant to the curriculum in a given classroom where some of the topics taught are not included on standardized tests.

While most classroom teachers find that the objectives tested on standardized achievement tests reflect their own instruction, few teachers find *all* of the topics they included in standardized tests. Teachers whose classroom instruction deviates greatly from the text or who consistently introduce unusual materials and concepts often find that the topics covered by

A standardized test cannot be valid for a particular class if it does not match the instruction given in that class.

FIGURE 10.2

Example 1: Practice Test. (Page 3)

"Being a firefighter is a wonderful job. It is hard, but it is also exciting, and you get to meet a lot of great people. If you have any dreams of one day becoming a firefighter, go for it! Follow your dreams. And if you have any questions about this job, just
30 drop in to any fire hall and I'm sure the guys there will be very happy to answer them."

1   Clint does not think he was a hero for rescuing the 16-year-old girl because

    A the girl is recovering.

    B he was trained to do that job.

    C he was following his dreams.

    D the other firefighters rescued the girl.

2   The words "follow in his footsteps" (line 19) mean

    F stay behind him.

    G stay in his tracks.

    H do the same thing.

    J go to the same places.

3   What is the main reason Clint Ledoux became a firefighter?

    A It is hard work.

    B It is dangerous.

    C It is a way of helping people.

    D It is a way of meeting people.

Read the following paragraph and then do Item 4.

> Matthew and Grandma arrived at the lake early. They didn't catch a fish all morning. At noon they ate a picnic lunch. _____

4   Which of the following sentences is the best closing sentence for the paragraph?

    F By noon they were getting hungry.

    G The sun was just rising over the lake.

    H They counted the fish they had caught.

    J They could see the dock and the boat through the trees.

Page 3   Practice Test   *Stop*

the national tests are different from those they have been teaching. The time of year when testing takes place and the teacher's sequencing of topics also influence students' opportunities to learn the objectives being assessed.

Finally, virtually all standardized achievement tests rely heavily on multiple-choice test items. Restricting items to the multiple-choice format means that some topics or objectives may be tested differently than they were taught or tested in the classroom. For example, to assess spelling, most teachers give a weekly spelling test in which students have to spell

FIGURE 10.2

Example 1: Practice Test. (Page 4)

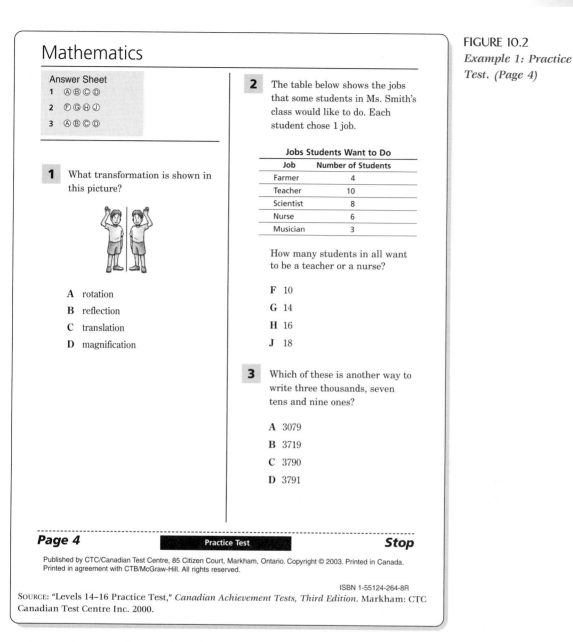

Mathematics

Answer Sheet

1 Ⓐ Ⓑ Ⓒ Ⓓ
2 Ⓕ Ⓖ Ⓗ Ⓙ
3 Ⓐ Ⓑ Ⓒ Ⓓ

1 What transformation is shown in this picture?

A rotation

B reflection

C translation

D magnification

2 The table below shows the jobs that some students in Ms. Smith's class would like to do. Each student chose 1 job.

Jobs Students Want to Do

Job	Number of Students
Farmer	4
Teacher	10
Scientist	8
Nurse	6
Musician	3

How many students in all want to be a teacher or a nurse?

F 10

G 14

H 16

J 18

3 Which of these is another way to write three thousands, seven tens and nine ones?

A 3079

B 3719

C 3790

D 3791

Page 4   Practice Test   **Stop**

Source: "Levels 14–16 Practice Test," *Canadian Achievement Tests, Third Edition*. Markham: CTC Canadian Test Centre Inc. 2000.

each word correctly. In standardized achievement tests, spelling is assessed by presenting students with four or five words and asking them to identify the one that is spelled incorrectly. Most students are not taught spelling this way. This and the preceding factors discussed can reduce the match between the content of a standardized achievement test and the content of classroom instruction, thus lowering validity.

It is the responsibility of each local school board to determine if the content of a standardized achievement test is valid for students in that board. If, after inspecting the test items and the publisher's description of what is

Each school or board must decide if the content of a standardized achievement test matches its own objectives.

FIGURE 10.3

Example 2: Student Diagnostic Profile. (Page 1)

Part 2

Objective Competency Summary

1. Find the column labelled Item Numbers. In the column, cross out the item number for each incorrect or invalid response. (For Reading, an Item Number may appear twice among the objectives.)

2. Look at the column labelled # Correct. For each objective, count the number of items <u>not</u> crossed out and record the total on the line.

3. Find the column labelled Performance Criteria.

The "L" in this column represents low performance, the "C" competent performance and the "P" proficient performance. Circle the letter that corresponds to the number of items answered correctly.

4. For each test, count the number of objectives for which Cs or Ps were circled and enter the total in the box.

Review the Objective Competency Summary and plan instructional activities to teach or review those objectives not competently performed by individual students and/or your class as a whole. Refer to the *Teacher Resource Manual* for planning information and suggested instructional activities.

Basic Battery

Reading	Item Numbers	# Correct	Performance Criteria
Fiction	1 2 3 4 5 6 7 8 9 58 59 60 61 62	___ / 14	L 0-7 C 8-13 P 14
Non-Fiction	30 31 32 33 48 49 50 51 52 53	___ / 10	L 0-4 C 5-9 P 10
Poetry	12 13 14 15 16 17 18 19 34 35 36 37	___ / 12	L 0-6 C 7-11 P 12
Words/Phrases in Context	3 13 17 30 32 35 36	___ / 7	L 0-3 C 4-6 P 7
Stated Information	2 15 16 48 49 50 58 60	___ / 8	L 0-3 C 4-7 P 8
Visual Materials	1 12 34 39 40 41	___ / 6	L 0-4 C 5 P 6
Central Thought	9 19 33 37 42 53	___ / 6	L 0-2 C 3-5 P 6
Analysis of Text	4 6 7 14 18 59 61	___ / 7	L 0-2 C 3-6 P 7
Critical Assessment	5 8 31 51 52 62	___ / 6	L 0-2 C 3-5 P 6

Total Number of Cs and Ps ☐

Language	Item Numbers	# Correct	Performance Criteria
Sentence Structure	10 11 20 21 22 23 24 54	___ / 8	L 0-3 C 4-7 P 8
Writing Conventions	38 43 44 45 46 47	___ / 6	L 0-2 C 3-5 P 6
Paragraph Structure	25 26 27 55 56 57	___ / 6	L 0-2 C 3-5 P 6
Information Management	28 29 63 64 65 66	___ / 6	L 0-2 C 3-5 P 6

Total Number of Cs and Ps ☐

Mathematics	Item Numbers	# Correct	Performance Criteria
Number Concepts	2 3 4 5 7 8 9 15 27 31 32 33	___ / 12	L 0-6 C 7-11 P 12
Measurement	6 16 34 35 36 38 39 40	___ / 8	L 0-3 C 4-7 P 8
Patterns	10 13 17 18 26 30	___ / 6	L 0-2 C 3-5 P 6
Data Analysis and Probability	11 22 23 24 25 28 37	___ / 7	L 0-2 C 3-6 P 7
Geometry and Spatial Sense	1 12 14 19 20 21 29	___ / 7	L 0-2 C 3-6 P 7

Total Number of Cs and Ps ☐

tested, the test content appears to be different from what students were taught, judgments about students' achievement may not be valid and should be made with caution.

Representative Norms

Standardized test publishers strive to obtain norming samples that are representative of national groups of students. However, there are some impor-

Supplemental Tests

Vocabulary

	Item Numbers	# Correct	Performance Criteria
Word Meaning	1 2 3 4 5 6 7 8	___ / 8	L 0-3 C 4-7 P 8
Multi-meaning Words	19 20 21 22 23 24	___ / 6	L 0-2 C 3-5 P 6
Words in Context (modified cloze)	9 10 11 12 13 14 15 16 17 18	___ / 10	L 0-3 C 4-9 P 10

Total Number of Cs and Ps ☐

Spelling

		# Correct	Performance Criteria
Consonants	9 10 11 12 15 18 19 20 22	___ / 9	L 0-3 C 4-8 P 9
Vowels	2 5 6 7 8 13 14 17 23	___ / 9	L 0-3 C 4-8 P 9
Structural Units	1 3 4 16 21 24	___ / 6	L 0-2 C 3-5 P 6

Total Number of Cs and Ps ☐

Dictation

		# Correct	Performance Criteria
Spelling	all items	___ / 24	L 0-10 C 11-22 P 23-24

Total Number of Cs and Ps ☐

Language/Writing Conventions

		# Correct	Performance Criteria
Sentences/Phrases/Clauses	7 8 9 10 12 14 15 16	___ / 8	L 0-3 C 4-7 P 8
Writing Mechanics	1 2 3 4 5 6 11 13	___ / 8	L 0-4 C 5-7 P 8
Editing Skills	17 18 19 20 21 22 23 24	___ / 8	L 0-3 C 4-7 P 8

Total Number of Cs and Ps ☐

Computation and Numerical Estimation

		# Correct	Performance Criteria
Add/Subtract Whole Numbers	1 2 3 5 8 11	___ / 6	L 0-2 C 3-5 P 6
Multiply/Divide Whole Numbers	9 14 17 18 21 22	___ / 6	L 0-2 C 3-5 P 6
Decimal Operations	6 7 10 12 23 24 25 26	___ / 8	L 0-3 C 4-7 P 8
Estimation Strategies	4 13 15 16 19 20	___ / 6	L 0-2 C 3-5 P 6

Total Number of Cs and Ps ☐

SOURCE: Canadian Test Centre: "Level 18 Student Diagnostic Profile," *Canadian Achievement Tests, Third Edition*. Markham: CTC/Canadian Test Centre Inc. 2000.

FIGURE 10.3
Example 2: Student Diagnostic Profile.
(Page 2)

tant factors that can undermine the appropriateness of test norms and thereby test validity: (1) norms go out of date; (2) the curriculum in a subject area changes; (3) textbooks are revised and new instructional materials appear; and (4) the same test is often administered in a school board over a number of years so teachers and students become familiar with its content and items. Inappropriate or out-of-date test norms reduce the validity of comparisons and decisions made from standardized achievement tests. While there is no hard-and-fast period within which standardized achievement test norms should be revised, seven to nine years is a

FIGURE 10.4　*Example 3: Overview of Standardized Tests.*

Overview: Canadian Tests of Basic Skills

		Primary Form K				Elementary Form K						Elementary Form L (Survey)						High School Form K		
Curriculum Area	Grade	Fall K–Midyear 1	Spring K–Spring 1	Midyear 1–Midyear 2	Midyear 2–Midyear 3	3	4	5	6	7	8	3	4	5	6	7	8	9	10	11–12
	Level	5	6	7	8	9	10	11	12	13	14	9	10	11	12	13	14	15	16	17/18
Vocabulary		Vocabulary				Vocabulary												Vocabulary		
Reading		Word Analysis				Reading Comprehension						Vocabulary Comprehension						Reading Comprehension		
				Reading																
Language		Listening																		
		Language				Spelling						Integrated Language						Correctness and Appropriateness of Expression		
						Capitalization														
						Punctuation														
						Usage and Expression														
Sources of Information				Sources of Information		Reference Materials												Use of Sources of Information		
Mathematics		Mathematics		Math Concepts		Math Concepts and Estimation						Concepts						Ability to Do Quantitative Thinking		
				Math Problems		Math Problem Solving and Data Interpretation						Estimation								
												Problem Solving								
				Math Computation		Math Computation						Data Interpretation								
Science		Science				Science												Analysis of Science Materials		
Maps and Diagrams						Maps and Diagrams														

Overview: Canadian Cognitive Abilities Test

		PRIMARY			LEVELS A–H						
Ability Area	Grade	Fall K–Midyear 1	Spring 1–Spring 2	Spring 2–Spring 3	4	5	6	7	8–9	10–11	12
	Level	1	2	A	B	C	D	E	F	G	H
Verbal		Verbal Reasoning Oral Vocabulary					Verbal Classification Sentence Completion Verbal Analogies				
Quantitative		Relational Concepts Quantitative Concepts					Quantitative Relations Number Series Equation Building				
Nonverbal		Relational Concepts Quantitative Concepts					Figure Classification Figure Analogies Figure Analysis				

NOTE: The shaded areas indicate the tests that are included in the different batteries and levels. Grade/level designations are for typical cognitive/achievement levels. Out-of-level testing is described in the *Teacher's* and/or *Assessment Coordinator's Handbook*.

Source: "Overview: Canadian Tests of Basic Skills" and "Overview: Canadian Cognitive Abilities Test," *Canadian Test of Basic Skills*, Nelson, 1998.

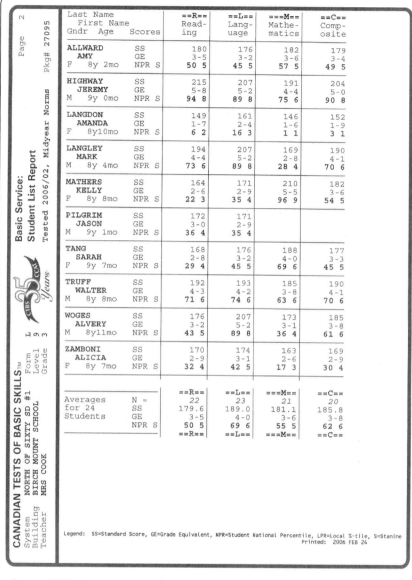

FIGURE 10.5

Example 4: Student List Report.

Page 2 Pkg# 27095

Tested 2006/02, Midyear Norms

Basic Service: Student List Report

CANADIAN TESTS OF BASIC SKILLS™ Form L 9, Level 9, Grade 3

System: NORTH OF SIXTY SD #1
Building: BIRCH MOUNT SCHOOL
Teacher: MRS COOK

For use and interpretation of score reports, refer to Teacher's Handbook

Last Name First Name Gndr Age	Scores	==R== Read-ing	==L== Lang-uage	===M== Mathe-matics	==C== Comp-osite
ALLWARD **AMY** F 8y 2mo	SS GE NPR S	180 3-5 50 5	176 3-2 45 5	182 3-6 57 5	179 3-4 49 5
HIGHWAY **JEREMY** M 9y 0mo	SS GE NPR S	215 5-8 94 8	207 5-2 89 8	191 4-4 75 6	204 5-0 90 8
LANGDON **AMANDA** F 8y10mo	SS GE NPR S	149 1-7 6 2	161 2-4 16 3	146 1-6 1 1	152 1-9 3 1
LANGLEY **MARK** M 8y 4mo	SS GE NPR S	194 4-4 73 6	207 5-2 89 8	169 2-8 28 4	190 4-1 70 6
MATHERS **KELLY** F 8y 8mo	SS GE NPR S	164 2-6 22 3	171 2-9 35 4	210 5-5 96 9	182 3-6 54 5
PILGRIM **JASON** M 9y 1mo	SS GE NPR S	172 3-0 36 4	171 2-9 35 4		
TANG **SARAH** F 9y 7mo	SS GE NPR S	168 2-8 29 4	176 3-2 45 5	188 4-0 69 6	177 3-3 45 5
TRUFF **WALTER** M 8y 8mo	SS GE NPR S	192 4-3 71 6	193 4-2 74 6	185 3-8 63 6	190 4-1 70 6
WOGES **ALVERY** M 8y11mo	SS GE NPR S	176 3-2 43 5	207 5-2 89 8	173 3-1 36 4	185 3-8 61 6
ZAMBONI **ALICIA** F 8y 7mo	SS GE NPR S	170 2-9 32 4	174 3-1 42 5	163 2-6 17 3	169 2-9 30 4

Averages for 24 Students		==R==	==L==	===M==	==C==
	N =	22	23	21	20
	SS	179.6	189.0	181.1	185.8
	GE	3-5	4-0	3-6	3-8
	NPR S	50 5	69 6	55 5	62 6
		==R==	==L==	===M==	==C==

Legend: SS=Standard Score, GE=Grade Equivalent, NPR=Student National Percentile, LPR=Local %-tile, S=Stanine
Printed: 2006 FEB 24

THOMSON NELSON

SOURCE: CTBS Forms K & L Teacher's Handbook, Levels 9–14 (Grades 3–8) by NELSON. © 1998. Reprinted with permission of Nelson, a division of Thomson Learning: www.thomsonrights.com. Fax 800-730-2215.

generally accepted time period used by the publishers of the most widely used standardized tests. Obviously, the older the test norms, the less representative they are of instructional content and national student performance. Specific information about test norming procedures and the age of the norms should be provided in the publisher's test manual.

When standardized test norms do not match the characteristics of the local students, valid decisions cannot be made from the test results.

FIGURE 10.6 *Example 5: Student Performance Chart.*

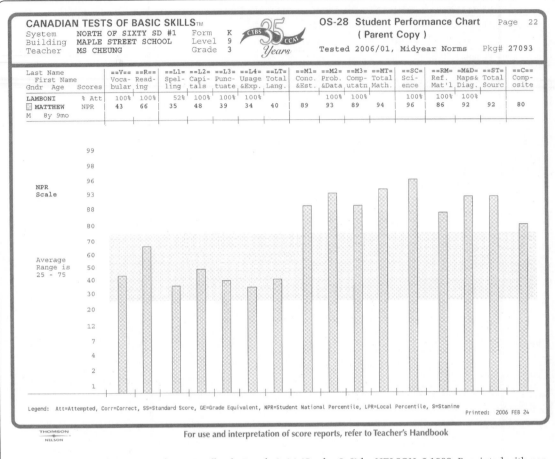

CANADIAN TESTS OF BASIC SKILLS™

				OS-28	Student Performance Chart	Page 22
System	NORTH OF SIXTY SD #1	Form	K		(Parent Copy)	
Building	MAPLE STREET SCHOOL	Level	9			
Teacher	MS CHEUNG	Grade	3		Tested 2006/01, Midyear Norms	Pkg# 27093

Last Name First Name Gndr Age	Scores	==V== Voca- bular	==R== Read- ing	==L1== Spel- ling	==L2== Capi- tals	==L3== Punc- tuate	==L4== Usage &Exp.	==LT== Total Lang.	==M1== Conc. &Est.	==M2== Prob. &Data	==M3== Comp- utatn	==MT== Total Math.	==SC== Sci- ence	==RM== Ref. Mat'l	==M&D== Maps& Diag.	==ST== Total Sourc	==C== Comp- osite
LAMBONI	% Att	100%	100%	52%	100%	100%	100%			100%	100%		100%	100%	100%		
☒ MATTHEW	NPR	43	66	35	48	39	34	40	89	93	89	94	96	86	92	92	80
M 8y 9mo																	

Legend: Att=Attempted, Corr=Correct, SS=Standard Score, GE=Grade Equivalent, NPR=Student National Percentile, LPR=Local Percentile, S=Stanine

Printed: 2006 FEB 24

THOMSON
NELSON

For use and interpretation of score reports, refer to Teacher's Handbook

SOURCE: CTBS Forms K & L Teacher's Handbook, Levels 9–14 (Grades 3–8) by NELSON. © 1998. Reprinted with permission of Nelson, a division of Thomson Learning: www.thomsonrights.com. Fax 800-730-2215.

Conditions of Administration

Deviating from test administration directions reduces the validity of test results.

It was emphasized earlier that valid interpretations of students' standardized test performance depend on students taking the test under the conditions recommended by the test publisher. Deviations from the test administration directions—allowing students more time than specified, helping students while they are taking the test, coaching students before the test on specific items they will be asked, and generally not following the directions provided—all reduce the validity of the test results and the decisions based on those results.

Of course, students who require accommodations in testing should be provided with the appropriate resources. These accommodations are noted in the student's Individualized Educational Plan under the recommendations (see page 288, "Standardized Tests and Students with Exceptionalities"). Typically, when the scores of students who receive accommodations are reported, they are flagged to indicate the test was not taken under standard conditions.

Potential Misinterpretations

There are two common problems in interpreting standardized test scores: misinterpretation and overinterpretation. Because the types of scores that are used to describe student performance on standardized achievement tests are different from those teachers commonly use, the likelihood of misinterpretation is heightened. The most common misinterpretations involve the percentile rank, which is mistaken for the percentage of items a student answered correctly, and the grade equivalent score, which is mistakenly thought to indicate the curriculum level at which a student is performing in a subject area. As previously mentioned, percentile ranks indicate the percentage of students in the norm group that a student scored above. Grade equivalent scores indicate how well a student performs on grade-level objectives compared to other students in that grade.

The main problem in interpreting standardized test scores is *overinterpretation*, not misinterpretation. Because standardized tests are constructed by professionals, tried out on nationwide samples of students, and provide numerical indices that describe a student's performance compared to students nationwide, there is a widespread belief that they give precise, accurate descriptions of student achievement. Certainly parents and the public at large put more faith in standardized test results than in teacher-made assessments gathered over time in the day-to-day classroom setting. But while the information provided by the 40 or so multiple-choice items found in a typical standardized subtest is useful, it can never match the information a teacher accumulates through daily instruction and assessment of students. As one publisher has stated:

> Though standardized achievement scores cannot and should not replace teacher observations and classroom assessment information, they can provide unique supplementary information that bears on decisions about selecting learning objectives and procedures, designing or choosing instructional materials, and creating an effective learning environment. (Teacher's Handbook; *CTBS*; Nelson, 1998, p. 2)

Even when there are no problems with test content, norms, and administration, standardized test scores still are overinterpreted. For example, it is common for teachers and parents to treat small differences in standardized test scores as if they are significant and indicate real performance differences. A percentile rank difference of 6 to 8 points or a 2- to 5-month grade equivalent difference between students rarely indicates important or meaningful differences in their achievement or development. There is suf-

The main problem in interpreting standardized test scores is overinterpretation.

Information gained from standardized tests may not be as revealing as information gathered through daily instruction and assessment by the classroom teacher.

Teachers should guard against treating small differences in standardized test scores as if they were reliable indicators of real differences among students.

**TECHNOLOGY
AND ASSESSMENT**

**Resources for
Standardized Tests**

www.ets.org

Educational Testing
Service (ETS) assists
teachers to measure the
educational and
intellectual progress of
their children. The ETS
Test Collection includes
information on more than
25,000 tests. The link to
this site will offer
teachers reviews on tests
from a variety of
Canadian, U.S., and
foreign publishers.

Find a direct link to these
tests on our OLC at

www.mcgrawhill.ca/
college/airasian.

*Information from
standardized
achievement tests
usually corroborates a
teacher's perceptions of
students.*

ficient unreliability in any test score, whether standardized or teacher-made, to make small scoring differences indicators of true differences among students. Standardized test constructors try to defeat overinterpretation of small score differences by warning against them in their test manuals and by presenting scores as percentile or stanine bands (see Table 10.1), but they are not always successful. In short, teachers should guard against treating small score differences as if they are meaningful.

Finally, the smaller the number of items that make up a test, the less reliable its results and the less trustworthy its score. This can be a particular problem in standardized achievement tests that include a few performance-based, open-ended items. While performance-based items can assess areas not tested by multiple-choice items, one must interpret performance-based items cautiously because there are relatively few such items. Normally, the subtest scores on standardized test batteries are quite reliable and consistent. However, when a subtest is further broken down into specific topics, skills, or objectives, with separate scores given for each, one must be cautious about how much one reads into the scores. Often such information is used to diagnose a student's strengths and weaknesses, and while such information may provide a basis for further exploration of student performance, it should be reviewed critically because of the very few items on which it is typically based.

While standardized achievement tests can give teachers useful assessment information that they cannot gather for themselves, such information should be used in conjunction with information gathered from their own assessments. For the most part, the information from standardized achievement tests corroborates perceptions the teacher has already formed about students. When the two types of evidence do not corroborate each other, the teacher should look again at his or her perceptions to be sure the student is not being misjudged.

STANDARDIZED TESTS AND STUDENTS WITH EXCEPTIONALITIES

Students who have been identified with an exceptionality are likely to have a great degree of experience with standardized tests. In Canada, when educators suspect that a student is encountering academic challenge, a psychoeducational assessment is completed. A **psychoeducational assessment** is comprised of both *aptitude* and *achievement* tests and is designed to identify a student's cognitive strengths and weaknesses. The batteries are administered by a registered psychologist who is either appointed by the school board or is in private professional practice (Canadian Psychological Association, 1996). Based on the results of the tests, the student's exceptionality is designated citing the *Diagnostic and Statistical Manual of Mental Disorders* (*DSM-IV-TR, 2000*).

A **psychoeducational report** includes information about the student, assessment measures, findings, and conclusions. It is completed to provide recommendations with respect to school placement and academic instruction. The psychoeducational report also makes recommendations with respect to how educators can take advantage of a student's natural strengths and talents while compensating for his or her weaknesses. Instructional placement and resources are addressed as part of the student's Individualized Educational Plan. Copies of the psychoeducational report are given to both the parents and all educators who will work with the student. This confidential document is retained in the student's official school records.

REPORTING RESULTS TO PARENTS

At times teachers are expected to provide information to parents about students' performance on standardized tests. If the test has been administered to an entire class(es) of students, a teacher might hold a meeting to discuss and explain test scores to all parents. You should remember that parents are not likely to be testing experts and will basically want to know how their children performed. A representative from the school board or district could also be available to talk to parents who want a more detailed explanation of statistics (McEwan, 1998).

It is more often the case that a parent-teacher conference is booked to discuss an individual student's test performance. Parents should be provided with a written copy of the scores prior to the meeting. You should begin the conference with general information about the test and its purpose. Explicitly distinguish between a standardized test and a classroom test or assessment. Begin to refer to scores by first describing the student's overall performance and then identify the student's strengths and weaknesses based on specific test results.

To interpret the scores, focus on one subtest such as reading, and explain the meaning of the student's score. It is easier to explain stanines or percentile rank scores than grade equivalents. Be aware that parents also misinterpret percentile rank scores unless they are provided with a brief explanation of the differentiation between percentile rank scores and percentages. Percentages are the percentage of items answered correctly on a test, whereas, a percentile rank score between 16 and 84 is within an "average" range of scores (see page 272 for more information on percentile rank scores). To emphasize these distinctions, provide parents with visual aids such as graphs and charts when describing these statistics.

Make your interpretations brief, but accurate. Bear in mind that you do not need to interpret every bit of information in the test report. You should interpret the student's test scores in the context of general classroom performance to help the parents fully understand the student's achievement.

Do not patronize the parent and avoid comments like, "This has probably been difficult for you as a parent to understand."

To summarize, standardized achievement test batteries can be used to compare an individual student's performance to that of a larger group of students beyond the local classroom or board, usually a national sample of students in the same grade. They can also provide information about a student's areas of strength and weakness. Because such comparisons are sought, standardized achievement test constructors must go through a complicated test construction process to develop their tests. They must identify content and objectives that are commonly taught at a particular grade level in classrooms across the country. Then they must write and try out items that assess these common objectives. From this trial assessment a final set of items is selected based upon content appropriateness and a desired statistical range. The final version of the test, with its directions, answer sheets, and test booklets, is then administered to a large sample of students who are thought to represent students across the country. The purpose of this test "norming" is to provide information about the performance of a national sample of students against which the performance of future test takers can be compared.

Student performance on standardized achievement tests is described mainly through scores that indicate how a student compares to other students. The most commonly used scores are (1) percentile ranks that describe what percentage of the norming sample the student scored above; (2) stanines that, scoring on a scale of 1 to 9, roughly divide students into below average, average, and above average categories; and (3) grade equivalent scores that are developmentally based scores indicating how well a student compares to a national sample of peers in his or her grade. Other kinds of scores are sometimes provided with standardized tests, but they are used less than these three.

IN CONCLUSION

Standardized achievement test results should be interpreted in conjunction with what teachers know about students from their own classroom assessments. Further, interpretations of standardized test results should be based on knowledge of the test objectives, the representativeness and age of the test norms, and the conditions under which the test was administered to students. A mismatch between test and classroom objectives, old or nonrepresentative norms, or not following prescribed administrative conditions can reduce the validity of decisions based on the test results. Finally, test users must be cautious about assuming that standardized test scores are error-free. Small score differences should not be overinterpreted, because they rarely indicate meaningful performance differences.

CHAPTER REVIEW

CHAPTER REVIEW

Visit Chapter 10 of the Online Learning Centre at **www.mcgrawhill.ca/ college/airasian** to take chapter quizzes, link to related Web sites, and read PowerWeb articles and news feed updates, and access study tools, including the case study referenced in this chapter.

What are standardized tests?

➤ Standardized tests assess students' performance under uniform conditions. There are structured directions for administration, specific procedures for scoring, and guidelines for interpretation of the results.

What is the difference between standardized aptitude and standardized achievement tests?

➤ Standardized aptitude tests attempt to predict a student's ability to learn a skill or accomplish a level of complexity.

➤ Standardized achievement tests provide information about student performance in the academic domains and identify the student's strengths and weaknesses.

What purposes do standardized tests serve?

➤ provide evidence for student placement in programs;

➤ document developmental information about student achievement over time;

➤ evaluate program effectiveness;

➤ compare the performance of local students to a national sample of peers;

➤ contribute to overall educational accountability.

What are the characteristics of a well-constructed standardized achievement test?

➤ Is carefully constructed, with item tryouts, analysis, and revision occurring before the final version of the test is completed;

➤ Has written directions and procedures for administering and scoring the test;

➤ Has score interpretation based on the test having been administered to a carefully selected sample of students from across Canada.

What are test norms?

➤ Test norms describe how a national sample of students who took the test actually performed on the test.

➤ Different test norms are developed for tests in the fall and the spring.

➤ Four criteria to judge the adequacy of test norms are: sample size, representativeness, recentness, and description of procedures.

What is the difference between a difficulty index and a discrimination index?

➤ Difficulty index of a test item indicates the proportion of test takers who answered the item correctly.

➤ Discrimination index indicates how well students who scored high on a test, scored on a particular item.

How are test scores interpreted?

➤ Raw scores are the number of items answered correctly on a test.

➤ Percentile rank is the percentage of the norm group a student scored above.

➤ Stanine scores describe students' performance on a 9-point scale with 1 representing the lowest category and 9 the highest.

➤ A grade-equivalent score is an estimate of a student's development level but is not indicative of the grade in which a student should be placed. Since the school year is 10 months long (September through June), the numbers that denote the months range from "0" to "9."

What are some considerations to ensure that standardized tests are valid?

➤ Appropriate coverage: A standardized test should match the instruction given in a class.

➤ Representative norms: Standardized test norms should match the characteristics of the local students.

➤ Conditions of administration: Test administration directions must be strictly adhered to.

➤ Potential misinterpretations: Test scores should not be overinterpreted and information should be gathered from daily instruction.

What is a psychoeducational assessment and a psychoeducational report?

➤ A psychoeducational assessment is comprised of both *aptitude* and *achievement* tests and is designed to identify a student's cognitive strengths and weaknesses.

➤ A psychoeducational report includes information about the student, assessment measures, findings, and conclusions. It is completed to provide recommendations with respect to school placement and academic instruction.

What are good strategies for communicating test results to parents?

➤ Hold a meeting to discuss and explain test scores to all parents.

➤ Provide parents with a written copy of the scores prior to the meeting.

➤ Begin the conference with general information about the test and its purpose.

➤ Distinguish between a standardized test and a classroom test or assessment.

➤ Describe the student's overall performance and then identify the student's strengths and weaknesses based on specific test results.

➤ Explain stanines or percentile rank scores and be aware that parents also misinterpret percentile rank scores.

➤ Interpret the student's test scores in the context of general classroom performance to help the parents fully understand the student's achievement.

What do teachers need to remember about using standardized test results?

➤ Standardized test results have value in providing comparability information, but they are only part of the assessment picture and they do have limits.

➤ Standardized test results should not be evaluated in isolation from other information such as a student's classroom performance.

QUESTIONS FOR DISCUSSION

1. Are standardized tests fair to all students? Why or why not? What personal characteristics could influence how a student does on a standardized test? Would these same characteristics influence how he or she performs on a teacher-prepared test? Why?

2. What can a teacher do to help make students less anxious about taking standardized tests? Would the same actions help students when they take teacher-prepared tests?

3. If you could select only one scoring format from a norm-referenced standardized test to explain to parents, which would you choose? Why? What are the limitations of your choice?

4. What factors should influence the use of standardized achievement test results for assessment by classroom teachers?

5. What are the differences in the information provided by a norm-referenced and a criterion-referenced standardized test?

6. What are some validity issues concerning standardized tests?

7. How should results be communicated to parents?

8. Cite one misinterpretation of standardized test scores and what you could do as a teacher to ensure that you do not misinterpret scores in this fashion.

9. How does the media analyze and use the results of standardized tests to persuade audiences about school boards?

ACTIVITIES

Refer to the Student Performance Chart for Matthew in Figure 10.6 for the following activities.

1. Review the bar graphs of Matthew's chart. In your own words, interpret what the chart is saying about Matthew's performance on each subtest. On which subtest does Matthew score the highest percentile rank? Why are some stanines the same? What does the pattern of scores suggest about Matthew? What does this information tell you about how Matthew performs in his Grade 3 class?

2. Write a one-page letter to Matthew's parents explaining the results of his performance on the *Canadian Test of Basic Skills*. You should seek to identify the most important information and convey it in a way that parents can understand. Provide Matthew's parents with some information about the subtests and a basic definition of a percentile rank. You should interpret the information about Matthew's performance scores for his parents. Indicate what Matthew's parents should do if they have any questions.

EPILOGUE
Summing Up Classroom Assessment

As a way of summing up this book, let's revisit its central idea: that assessment is not an end in itself. It is a means to an end: classroom decision making. The decision-making process itself is made up of three steps: (1) collecting information, (2) interpreting information, and (3) making a decision based upon the interpretation. The validity of decisions depends upon both the quality of the information collected and the quality of the interpretation. Information is the raw material of classroom decision making, and meaning is added to this raw material when the teacher answers the question, "What is this information telling me?" Because the decisions that teachers make can affect both students and teachers in important ways, teachers are responsible for the quality of the assessment information they collect and the interpretations they make from that information.

Collecting Assessment Information

Good decisions are based upon good information, and three factors determine the quality of assessment information:

1. The conditions under which information is collected, including the physical and emotional context during assessment, the opportunity provided to students to show their typical behaviour, and the quality of instruction provided prior to assessing achievement.
2. The quality of the instruments used to collect the information, including factors such as the clarity of test items or performance criteria, the relationship of an assessment procedure to the characteristic being assessed, and the appropriateness of the language level of items.
3. The objectivity of the information, including unbiased scoring.

If efforts are not made to ensure the quality of the assessment information, teachers' decision making will be seriously flawed. Consider, for example, the things that can lower the validity and reliability of the report card grades a teacher assigns.

➤ Portions of a teacher's achievement tests might assess things the students were not taught. (validity lowered)
➤ The items a teacher writes might be ambiguous, poorly written, or too complex for the students. (validity lowered)

➤ The sample of behaviour observed might be too small to provide information about the students' typical behaviour. (reliability lowered)

➤ Scoring of the assessment information might be careless and subjective. (validity and reliability lowered)

➤ Informal information about student interest, motivation, and attitude might be based on inappropriate indicators. (validity lowered)

Most teachers will interpret whatever information they have as if it were valid and reliable. If it is not, decisions will be faulty, and the grades will not be a valid indication of student learning.

Interpreting Assessment Information: Five Guidelines

The second step in decision making is interpreting the available assessment information. It is not until information is interpreted that decisions about classroom organization, planning, teaching, learning, and grading can be made. Although it is not reasonable to expect teachers to always interpret information correctly, it is reasonable to expect them to improve their interpretations as a result of conscientious practice.

Teachers are most likely to misinterpret assessment information early in the school year, when a student's behaviour changes abruptly, or when new information about the student becomes available. In general, the less a teacher knows about a student, the more interpretation is required, and the more likely that subsequent interpretations will tend to be based upon earlier ones.

There are five general principles that should guide interpretation of classroom assessment information. These principles cut across all assessment purposes and types that have been discussed.

1. *Assessment information describes students' learned behaviours and their present status.* The behaviours and performances observed during assessment represent what students have learned to do, think, feel, and say. For a variety of reasons (e.g., cultural, societal, economic, familial), some students learn more, retain more, and have more opportunities to learn than others. Whatever the cause of these learning differences, the information provided by classroom assessment should tell only about what students have learned to do.

   Assessment also describes how students currently perform, not necessarily how they will perform in the future. Students have sudden developmental spurts, become more interested in some things and less interested in others, and reach a point when they "bloom" academically after many years of low performance or "hit the wall" and experience a decline in academic performance. Thus, when teachers or parents use words like *potential* and *capacity* to describe students, they are making assumptions that assessments do not always support. Discussion of a student's "capacity" suggests a fixed amount of ability, interest, or motivation that places a limit on a student's performance. Assessments cannot gauge such limits, and interpretations along these lines should be avoided. Interpretations focused on "potential" and "capacity" can be especially damaging to students from low socio-economic families who often have had fewer opportunities to learn than other students, but who often perform quite well given the opportunity and practice.

But isn't assessment information used to predict student success? Don't the grades students receive in one school year often predict the grades they receive in future years? Aren't students who struggle to read in Grade 1 usually still struggling at the end of elementary school? Although these examples seem to suggest that assessments can provide information about students' potential or capacity, such a conclusion is faulty.

The chief reason that many students maintain the same subject grades or reading group placement over time has less to do with their "potential" or "capacity" than with the stability of their school and classroom environment. If we take a student at the start of Grade 1, place him or her in the lowest reading group, and provide objectives and instruction that are less challenging than those for other groups, we should not be surprised if the student fails to move out of that reading group by the end of the school year. This is an example of a self-fulfilling prophecy. It suggests that the reason assessments often remain stable over time has more to do with the nature of classroom expectations and instruction than with our ability to assess students' potential or capacity. Thus, assessment information should be interpreted as indicating a student's current level of performance; and this level of performance can change.

2. *Assessment information provides an estimate, not an exact indication, of student performance.* Under no condition should assessment information be treated as if it were infallible or exact. There are always numerous sources of error that can influence students' performances. A single observation or test result has limited meaning and provides, at best, an approximation of a student's performance. Standardized achievement test publishers explicitly recognize this fact and use score bands to indicate the range of scores within which the student's true performance is likely to fall if tested many times. In all assessments, small differences or changes in students' performances should not be interpreted as real or significant. For example, placing students in reading instruction groups based upon a 3- or 4-point test score difference in reading performance is an overinterpretation of the assessment information.

Although informal assessments are rarely expressed numerically, they too are best treated as estimates of student performance. Individual assessments should always be interpreted with the above cautions in mind. The larger the sample of behaviour obtained and the more varied the assessments used, the more confident a teacher can be when interpreting the information. In all cases, however, it is best to interpret assessments as if they provided an estimate of performance, not an exact indication of it.

3. *Single assessments are a poor basis for making important decisions about students.* Many teacher decisions can substantially affect the lives and opportunities of students. Consequently, such decisions should not be based on a single assessment. At times, when teachers make decisions based on a single assessment, there is the tendency to ignore additional information about students that might contribute to improving the validity of important decisions.

   Unfortunately, in the current milieu of educational accountability, there is strong pressure to rely upon the results of a single assessment when making decisions. The growing use of scores from provincial/territorial tests to determine who will be promoted, receive a high school diploma, and require remedial education is one example of this pressure. Using a single score or rating seems objective and fair to people who do not understand the limitations of assessment information. Although reliance on single assessments makes decision making quicker and easier than collecting more broadly based information, it also increases the likelihood of making invalid decisions. Most teachers are sensitive to this danger and collect varied kinds of assessment information before making a grading, promotion, or placement decision about a student.

4. *Valid interpretations should be made from assessment information.* First, teachers need to take care to collect assessment information that is pertinent to the characteristics/criteria that need to be assessed. Once this assessment information is gathered, interpretations and evaluations can be made. Other aspects of student performance that were not intended to be assessed must not influence these interpretations. For example, if a teacher is assessing a student's homework assignment and it is returned messy and disorganized, the teacher should not globally describe the student as "unmotivated." At times, a student's behaviour or work habits cloud a teacher's judgment. It is very important that a teacher use only assessment information that is a valid indicator of a student's work, otherwise invalid interpretations may result.

5. *Assessment information describes performance; it does not explain the reasons for it.* An assessment describes student performance at a particular point in time: Lisa performed poorly on the math test, Bart's oral speech was not well prepared, Ming's social studies project was the best in the class. But, when a teacher assesses a student, it is difficult to ignore the fact that the teacher *knows* the student. In other words, the teacher may know the underlying reasons why a student has performed in a certain manner. However, background information that a teacher knows about a student should not influence the assessment. Using Bart as an example, his teacher might

know that Bart has no interest in public speaking, but this information should not be used to influence the assessment. Teachers should not use underlying causes to explain what they have seen during the assessment process.

It is rarely possible to determine with reasonable certainty why students performed as they did just by examining the assessment itself. To explain student performance, teachers must look beyond the immediate assessment information. Furthermore, teachers must be cautious when interpreting explanations of student performance because, more often than not, failure to look beyond the assessment information at hand leads to incorrect interpretations about students and their characteristics.

This caution is especially appropriate for English as a Second Language students who may have limited out-of-school opportunities or cultural practices different from those of the majority group. When a student is confronted by an unfamiliar language, new situations, or expectations that are alien to his or her culture, the underlying causes of that student's performance may be very different from those that underlie performance among majority group students. Teachers must be sensitive to such differences when interpreting students' performances. The following is a list of some specific do's and do not's for interpreting assessment information:

INTERPRETING ASSESSMENT INFORMATION: DO'S AND DO NOT'S

DO...	DO NOT...
...base interpretations on multiple sources of evidence	...treat small score or rating differences as if they were meaningful and important
...recognize the cultural and educational factors that influence and explain student performance	...use assessment results to draw conclusions about a student's capacity or potential
...determine whether the information collected provides a valid description of a student's characteristics	...rely upon a single assessment when making a decision that has important consequences for students
...recognize that any single assessment provides an estimate of a student's present status, which can change with changes in the environment and through experience	...confuse information provided by an assessment with explanations of what caused the performance; explanations must be sought outside the bounds of the original assessment information
...consider contextual factors that might provide alternative explanations for student behaviour or performance	...uncritically assume that an assessment measure provides valid information about the desired characteristic

Assessment: A Tool Used Wisely

Assessment is a chain of many links that imposes numerous responsibilities on teachers because it is such an integral part of what goes on in classrooms. It is not expected that teachers will always assess correctly, interpret information appropriately, and decide infallibly. However, it is expected that teachers will recognize their responsibilities in these areas and strive to carry them out as best they can. Remember, how teachers collect, interpret, and use assessment information has many important consequences for their students.

An analogy is an appropriate way to conclude. The automobile is a device that enables us to accomplish a great many activities. When operated properly and with an understanding of its dangers and limitations, it saves much time and energy. However, if operated carelessly and improperly, the automobile also has the potential to inflict serious injury. When it was time for you to apply for your driver's licence, your parents were apprehensive about the prospect of your driving. They knew the advantages of obtaining a licence, but they also knew the dangers. They did not deny you the privilege of driving despite the dangers, but they probably explained to you both its benefits and its dangers. They also no doubt impressed on you the responsibility that accompanies being in control of an automobile. This analogy applies for your use of classroom assessment.

Principles for Fair Student Assessment Practices for Education in Canada

The *Principles for Fair Student Assessment Practices for Education in Canada (1993)* contains a set of principles and related guidelines accepted by professional organizations as indicative of fair assessment practice within the Canadian educational context. Assessments depend on professional judgement; the principles and related guidelines presented in this document identify the issues to consider in exercising this professional judgement and in striving for the fair and equitable assessment of all students.

Assessment practice is broadly defined in the *Principles* as the process of collecting and interpreting information that can be used: (i) to provide feedback to students, and to their parents/guardians where applicable, about the progress they are making toward attaining the knowledge, skills, attitudes, and behaviours to be learned or acquired, and (ii) to inform the

The *Principles of Fair Student Assessment Practices for Education in Canada* was developed by a Working Group guided by a Joint Advisory Committee. The Joint Advisory Committee included two representatives appointed by each of the following professional organizations: Canadian Education Association, Canadian School Boards Association, Canadian Association for School Administrators, Canadian Teachers' Federation, Canadian Guidance Counselling Association, Canadian Association of School Psychologists, Canadian Council for Exceptional Children, Canadian Psychological Association, and Canadian Society for the Study of Education. In addition, the Joint Advisory Committee included a representative of the Provincial and Territorial Ministries and Departments of Education.

Financial support for the development and dissemination of the *Principles* was provided principally by the Walter and Duncan Gordon Charitable Foundation, with additional support provided by various Faculties, Institutes, and Colleges of Education and Provincial and Territorial Ministries and Departments of Education in Canada. This support is gratefully acknowledged.

The Joint Advisory Committee invites users to share their experiences in working with the *Principles* and to submit any suggestions that could be used to revise and improve the *Principles*. Comments and suggestions should be sent to the Joint Advisory Committee at the address shown below.

The *Principles for Fair Student Assessment Practices for Education in Canada* is not copyrighted. Reproduction and dissemination are encouraged. *Principles* reproduced in this document with permission. Please cite the Principles as follows:

Principles for Fair Student Assessment Practices for Education in Canada. (1993). Edmonton, Alberta: Joint Advisory Committee (Mailing address: Joint Advisory Committee, Centre for Research in Applied Measurement and Evaluation, 3-104 Education Building North, University of Alberta, Edmonton, Alberta, T6G 2G5).

various educational decisions (instructional, diagnostic, placement, promotion, graduation, curriculum planning, program development, policy) that are made with reference to students. Principles and related guidelines are set out for both developers and users of assessments. Developers include people who construct assessment methods and people who set policies for particular assessment programs. Users include people who select and administer assessment methods, commission assessment development services, or make decision on the basis of assessment results and findings. The roles may overlap, as when a teacher or instructor develops and administers an assessment instrument and then scores and interprets the students' responses, or when a ministry or department of education or local school system commissions the development and implementation of an assessment program and scoring services and makes decisions on the basis of the assessment results.

The *Principles for Fair Student Assessment Practices for Education in Canada* is the product of a comprehensive effort to reach consensus on what constitutes sound principles to guide the fair assessment of students. The principles and their related guidelines should be considered neither exhaustive nor mandatory; however, organizations, institutions, and individual professionals who endorse them are committing themselves *to endeavour to follow their intent and spirit* so as to achieve fair and equitable assessments of students.

Organization and Use of the Principles

The *Principles* and their related guidelines are organized in two parts. Part A is directed at assessments carried out by teachers at the elementary and secondary school levels. Part A is also applicable at the post-secondary level with some modifications, particularly with respect to whom assessment results are reported. Part B is directed at standardized assessments developed external to the classroom by commercial test publishers, provincial and territorial ministries and departments of education, and local school jurisdictions.[1]

Five general principles of fair assessment practices are provided in each Part. Each principle is followed by a series of guidelines for practice. In the case of Part A where no prior sets of standards for fair practice exist, a brief comment accompanies each guideline to help clarify and illuminate the guideline and its application.

The Joint Advisory Committee recognizes that in the field of assessment some terms are defined or used differently by different groups of people. To maintain as much consistency in terminology as possible, an attempt has been made to employ generic terms in the *Principles*.

---

[1] Boards, boroughs, counties, and school districts.

Part A: Classroom Assessments

Part A is directed toward the development and selection of assessment methods and their use in the classroom by teachers. It is organized around five interrelated themes:

I. **Developing and Choosing Methods for Assessment**
II. **Collecting Assessment Information**
III. **Judging and Scoring Student Performance**
IV. **Summarizing and Interpreting Results**
V. **Reporting Assessment Findings**

Part B: Assessments Produced External to the Classroom

Part B applies to the development and use of standardized assessment methods used in student admissions, placement, certification, and educational diagnosis, and in curriculum and program evaluation. These methods are primarily developed by commercial test publishers, ministries and departments of education, and local school systems.

The *Principles* and accompanying guidelines are organized in terms of four areas:

I. **Developing and Selecting Methods for Assessment**
II. **Collecting and Interpreting Assessment Information**
III. **Informing Students Being Assessed**
IV. **Implementing Mandated Assessment Programs**

See the full *Principles* at www.education.ualberta.ca/educ/psych/crame/files/eng_prin.pdf.

APPENDIX B
Taxonomy of Educational Objectives: Major Categories

Major Categories in the Cognitive Domain[1]	Major Categories in the Affective Domain[2]	Major Categories in the Psychomotor Domain[3]
1. Knowledge	1. Receiving	1. Perception
2. Comprehension	2. Responding	2. Set
3. Application	3. Valuing	3. Guided Response
4. Analysis	4. Organization	4. Mechanism
5. Synthesis	5. Characterization by a Value or Value Complex	5. Complex Overt Response
6. Evaluation		6. Adaptation
		7. Origination

[1]From Benjamin S. Bloom et al., *Taxonomy of Educational Objectives: Book 1, Cognitive Domain.* Published by Allyn & Bacon, Boston, MA copyright © 1999 by Pearson Education.
[2]From David R. Krathwohl, Benjamin S. Bloom, & Bertram B. Masia, *Taxonomy of Educational Objectives: Book 2, Affective Domain.* Published by Allyn & Bacon, Boston, MA. Copyright
© 1984 by Pearson Education.
[3]From *The Classification of Educational Objectives in the Psychomotor Domain,* by E. J. Simpson, 1972, Washington, DC: Gryphon House.

Statistical Applications for Classroom Assessment

This appendix describes some of the basic statistical information classroom teachers can use in scoring and interpreting their students' test performance. It contains a basic introduction to four areas: (1) raw scores and score distributions, (2) the mean and standard deviation, (3) item difficulty and discrimination, and (4) the normal distribution and standardized test scores.

Raw Scores and Score Distributions

A *raw score* indicates the number of points a student got on a test. For example, Jason took a 70-item multiple-choice test and got 42 items correct. If 1 point is given for each correct answer, his raw score is 42. Caitlyn took a 20-item short-answer test on which each item counted 5 points. She got 17 items correct and thus received a raw score of 85 (17 items × 5 points each). Most frequently, raw scores are converted to percentage scores using the formula: raw score/highest possible score × 100 = percentage score. Thus Jason's percentage score is 60 (42/70 × 100 = 60), and Caitlyn's percentage score is 85 (85/100 × 100 = 85).

Either raw or percentage scores can be arranged into a **test score distribution** that shows how the class as a whole performed. The raw and percentage scores for a class of 15 students who took a math test that had 10 problems worth 5 points each appear in Table C.1.

The performance of this class can be represented in a test score distribution by listing scores from highest to lowest. Test score distributions can be based on either raw scores or percentage scores. To construct a distribution, start by listing the possible scores students could have earned. For example, the class above took a 10-item test on which each item counted 5 points. Thus, the only raw scores possible ranged from 50 to 0 in 5-point increments (i.e., 50, 45, 40, 35, . . ., 15, 10, 5, 0). Similarly, since percentage scores are based on a 100-point scale, the only percentage scores possible on the 10-item test ranged from 100 to 0 in 10-point increments (i.e., 100, 90, 80, . . ., 20, 10, 0). The test score distributions in Table C.2 show how the class did. "Number" indicates the number of students who got a particular score; for example, three students got a raw score of 50, four got 40, and none got 10.

The two test score distributions show the same information on two different scales. The raw score scale is based on the total number of points on the test, 50, while the percentage score scale is based on a test of 100 total points. Teachers often transform the raw score distribution into a percent-

TABLE C.1

Name	Raw Score (Number Right × 5)	Percentage Score (Raw Score/50 × 100)
Lloyd	25	50
Chris	35	70
Jennifer	50	100
Kristen	40	80
Gail	25	50
Marta	35	70
Marita	40	80
David	40	80
Juan	45	90
Mike	20	40
Ted	30	60
Charles	50	100
Christina	35	70
Heather	40	80
Sara	50	100

TABLE C.2

Raw Score Distribution		Percentage Score Distribution	
Raw Score	Number	Percentage Score	Number
50	3	100	3
45	1	90	1
40	4	80	4
35	3	70	3
30	1	60	1
25	2	50	2
20	1	40	1
15	0	30	0
10	0	20	0
5	0	10	0
0	0	0	0

age score distribution to keep all of their tests on a 100-point scale. Recall this strategy from Chapter 8 when test, quiz, and project scores were converted so there would be comparability across them. Notice also that the above example is intended to be mathematically simple to convey the basic ideas of test score distributions.

Summarizing Test Scores

The Mean

Test score distributions are useful, but often teachers want to summarize the information they provide into a single score that represents the performance of the class. There are many ways to summarize scores, but the most common is the **mean.** The mean, also commonly called the **average,** is calculated by adding together each student's test score and dividing the total by the number of students. One can calculate the mean of either raw scores or percentage scores.

The original raw and percentage scores for our hypothetical class appear in Table C.3. Recall that the maximum raw score would be 50. The sums of the raw and percentage scores are shown at the bottom of the table. If these sums are divided by the total number of students, 15, the raw and percentage score means are 37.33 and 74.67, respectively. These means provide a single-number description of the class's performance. The mean raw score for the class is 37.33 out of 50, and the mean percentage score is 74.67 out of 100.

Two additional, though less frequently used, indices of the average performance of a class are the median and the mode. The **median** is the middle score in the test score distribution, after the scores have been arranged in order from highest to lowest. The **mode** is the score that more students

TABLE C.3		
Name	Raw Score	Percentage Score
Lloyd	25	50
Chris	35	70
Jennifer	50	100
Kristen	40	80
Gail	25	50
Marta	35	70
Marita	40	80
David	40	80
Juan	45	90
Mike	20	40
Ted	30	60
Charles	50	100
Christina	35	70
Heather	40	80
Sara	50	100
Sum of scores	560	1120

got than any other. Medians and modes are best determined after constructing a test score distribution. For example, consider the raw score distribution in Table C.2.

The median is the middle score in the distribution. Because there are 15 students who took the test, the middle score is the eighth from the top. Three students had raw scores of 50, one had a raw score of 45, and four had a score of 40. Thus, the eighth score from the top is a 40, and this is the median. Note that if there is an even number of scores in the distribution, the median would be determined by taking the average of the two middle scores. The mode is the score (or scores, as there can be more than one mode) that more student received than any other. The distribution shows that the score more students got than any other was 40, so the mode is 40. In this case, the median and the mode were the same, although this is not always the case.

The Standard Deviation

Suppose that two classes were tested with the same test and that the mean percentage score in each class was 74. Could we conclude that performance in the two classes was identical? No, we could not, because the mean does not tell us how the scores of the two classes are distributed from high to low. Table C.4 compares the scores of students in two classes, each of which has a mean of 74. Based on your observation of these two percentage score distributions, would you say that the performance in the two classes was identical?

Comparing the performance of the two classes indicates that the students in class A performed much more alike than the students in class B. The

TABLE C.4

Student	Class A	Class B
1	72	74
2	76	64
3	74	84
4	75	50
5	73	98
6	74	60
7	77	88
8	71	59
9	72	89
10	76	74
Sum	740	740
Mean	74	74

range, or the difference between the highest and lowest score, was 6 (77–71) in class A and 48 (98–50) in class B. In other words, students in class A were much more similar, or homogeneous, in their performance than students in class B, who were quite heterogeneous. The mean score for each class, though the same, does not indicate how similar or dissimilar the scores within the classes were. Note how a sense of the spread of scores could be obtained by examining the score distribution for each class.

When we describe a test score distribution, we also must consider the extent to which the scores are spread out around the mean. To find out about this characteristic of scores, we use another statistic called the **standard deviation.** The standard deviation provides information about score variability—that is, how similar or dissimilar a class's test scores are. Usually, test scores are described by both their mean and standard deviation. The mean tells about the average performance of a class, and the standard deviation tells about how homogeneous or heterogeneous scores were within the class.

Mathematically, the standard deviation (σ) is represented as:

$$\sigma \text{ (Standard deviation)} = \sqrt{\frac{\text{sum of } (x^2)}{n}}$$

where x is the difference of a student's score from the mean (score minus the mean) and n is the number of students who were tested. Calculating the standard deviation for class A's scores would be done as shown in Table C.5, given that the mean score for class A was 74. Adding up the squared difference of each student's score from the mean equals 36. Thus, according to the formula, the standard deviation of the scores in class A is equal to the square root of 36 divided by 10 (the number of students who were tested), or 3.6. The square root of 3.6 is equal to 1.89, which is the standard deviation for class A. When you calculate the standard deviation for class

TABLE C.5		
Student	**Class A**	**(Student's Score – Mean Score)^2**
1	72	$(72 - 74)^2 = 4$
2	76	$(76 - 74)^2 = 4$
3	74	$(74 - 74)^2 = 0$
4	75	$(75 - 74)^2 = 1$
5	73	$(73 - 74)^2 = 1$
6	74	$(74 - 74)^2 = 0$
7	77	$(77 - 74)^2 = 9$
8	71	$(71 - 74)^2 = 9$
9	72	$(72 - 74)^2 = 4$
10	76	$(76 - 74)^2 = 4$

B, which also has a mean of 74, you should get a standard deviation of 14.81 [square root of (2194/10) = 14.81]. Notice that the larger the standard deviation, the more spread out the scores are around the mean. Although class A and class B had the same mean score, the standard deviation of class B was much larger than that of class A, indicating greater heterogeneity in class B.

Item Difficulty and Discrimination

As we noted in Chapter 10, the difficulty index of a test item is indicated by the proportion or percentage of students who got the item correct. Thus, if 20 out of 25 students in a class answered an item correctly, the difficulty of that item would be (20/25) × 100 = 80 percent. Thus, somewhat confusingly, the higher the "difficulty," the easier the item.

The difficulty of test items is related to the spread of test scores. If all items on a test are very easy, most students will get high scores and there will be few differences among students. The same is true if all the test items are very difficult, except that all students will get low scores. When the difficulty of test items is around 50 percent, meaning that about half the students pass and half fail each item, the resulting test scores will be maximally spread out from low to high. This is an important result for the construction of commercial standardized *norm-referenced* tests, which are intended to compare the relative achievement of students. The more students' scores differ, the better for making comparisons and distinctions among them. Thus, in standardized norm-referenced test construction, it is necessary to have items that have difficulties in the middle (35 to 65 percent) range to ensure a spread of scores.

In classroom assessment, which is generally *criterion-referenced* and focuses on individual student mastery (not differentiation among students), item difficulty is not a major concern. Classroom assessment items usually have higher difficulties (i.e., are easier) than standardized, norm-referenced test items. This would be expected as long as classroom tests reflect classroom instruction.

Also as we noted in Chapter 10, a test item's discrimination index compares the difference in performance of high and low test scores on an item. An item is said to have **positive discrimination** if more students who do well on the test as a whole answer it correctly than students who do poorly on the test as a whole. Thus, if 85 percent of the class with the highest overall test scores got an item correct compared to only 55 percent of those with the lowest overall test scores, the item discrimination would be 85 percent – 55 percent = 30 percent. In determining item discrimination, the lower group's percentage is always subtracted from that of the higher group. The higher the discrimination, the greater the difference between the high and low test scorers on that item. Notice that it is possible to get **negative discriminations.** For example, if 40 percent of the top scorers and 60 percent of the bottom scorers got the item correct, the discrimination index would be 40 percent – 60 percent = –20 percent. In such a case, one might want to check the scoring key or look at the options in the item to try to identify the ones that the top group is selecting incorrectly.

Item discrimination, like item difficulty, is important in the construction of commercial standardized tests. It is necessary that each item in such tests have high positive discrimination. While it is also desirable for classroom tests to have items with positive discrimination, it is less important than for commercial tests because classroom tests are usually scored in a criterion-referenced way and their higher item difficulties reduce the differences between high and low scorers.

Normal Distributions

The *normal distribution* is the familiar "bell-shaped" curve shown in Figure C.1. This curve is extremely important in commercial standardized achievement testing because norms such as the percentile rank and stanine are derived from it.

Normal distributions can be used to describe scores when a large group of people take a well-designed standardized test. As indicated along the bottom of the curve, the lowest possible scores correspond to the far left portion of the curve, while the highest possible scores correspond to the far right portion. Other scores fall at regular increments between the two extremes. The height of the distribution at any given point represents the number of students who got the score that corresponds to that point. Notice that the distribution is highest in the middle and lowest at the two ends,

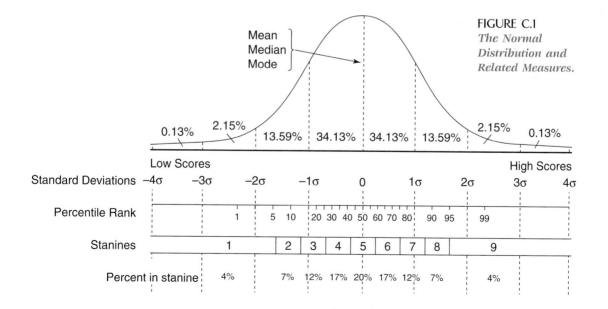

FIGURE C.1
The Normal Distribution and Related Measures.

indicating that most test takers score near the middle and very few score at either end. As Figure C.1 shows, the normal distribution has three important properties:

➤ The mean score is exactly in the middle of the distribution, and half of all scores fall above it and half below it.

➤ The median and mode scores are the same as the mean.

➤ The standard deviation divides the normal distribution into sections as follows:

1. About 68 percent of all the students' scores fall between 1 standard deviation below the mean and 1 standard deviation above the mean.

2. About 95 percent of all the students' scores fall between 2 standard deviations below the mean and 2 standard deviations above the mean.

3. Almost 100 percent of all the students' scores fall between 3 standard deviations below the mean and 3 standard deviations above the mean.

The following is a concrete illustration of these properties and how they are used in obtaining norm-referenced scores on standardized achievement tests. Assume you are a standardized test constructor who has produced a 30-item norm-referenced mathematics computation test for Grade 7 students. To do this, you followed the steps described in Chapter 10: select common objectives, write items to assess these objectives, and try the items out on many Grade 7 students to identify the items with moderate difficulties and high discriminations to include on the final test version. You have identified the 30 items for your test and have but one additional step to complete: administering the test to a representative sample of 10,000 Grade 7 students from across Canada in order to develop test norms. These norms will be the comparative scores that will be used to interpret future test takers' performance.

You administer the test to the 10,000 Grade 7 students who are meant to represent all Grade 7 students across the country, and you score each student's test. You now have 10,000 scores. Because you selected items of moderate difficulty and high discrimination and because you tried out the final version of the test on a large number of Grade 7 students, the distribution of scores on your test will be similar to the normal curve; many students will score near the middle of the score range and few will score very low or very high. Because 10,000 individual scores is a large number to deal with, you decide to summarize them by calculating the mean and standard deviation, using the procedures described previously. Let's assume that when your computer finishes these calculations on the math computation test scores, the mean score is 13 and the standard deviation is 3. You have a normal distribution with a mean score of 13 and a standard deviation of 3. This distribution is shown in Figure C.2.

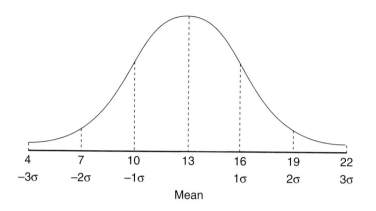

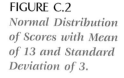

FIGURE C.2
Normal Distribution of Scores with Mean of 13 and Standard Deviation of 3.

Notice that the score of 13, which is the mean score for the group, is at the centre of the distribution. Note also how the standard deviation has been used to mark off other score points on the distribution. The scores that correspond to 1 standard deviation below the mean, 10 (13 − 3 = 10), and to 1 standard deviation above the mean, 16 (13 + 3 = 16), are shown, along with the scores corresponding to 2 standard deviations below (13 − 6 = 7) and above (13 + 6 = 19) the mean and 3 standard deviations below (13 − 9 = 4) and above (13 + 9 = 22) the mean.

The distribution shown in Figure C.2 is an example designed to illustrate how the normal curve is used to compare raw scores to standardized norm-referenced test performances. Further information on the interpretation of the normal distribution of scores can be found in most introductory statistics books.

GLOSSARY

A

Ability What one has learned over a period of time from both school and nonschool sources; one's general capability for performing tasks.

Achievement What one has learned from formal instruction, usually in school.

Achievement standards Judgments about the percentage of students who are expected to attain acceptable or higher levels of proficiency.

Affective domain Assessments that involve feelings, attitudes, interests, preferences, values, and emotions.

Analytic scoring Essay scoring method in which separate scores are given for specific aspects of the essay (e.g., organization, factual accuracy, and spelling).

Anecdotal record A short, written report of an individual's behaviour in a specific situation or circumstance.

Aptitude One's capability for performing a particular task or skill; usually involves a narrower skill than ability (e.g., mathematics aptitude or foreign language aptitude).

Assessment The broad process of collecting, synthesizing, and interpreting information to aid classroom decision making; includes information gathered about students, instruction, and classroom climate.

Assessment standards Descriptions of what students should know or be able to do at various grade levels and/or various levels of proficiency.

Average The number derived by adding up all the test scores and dividing the total by the number of students who took the test.

B

Bias A situation in which assessment information produces results that give one group an advantage or disadvantage over other groups because of problems in the content, procedures, or interpretations of the assessment information; a distortion or misrepresentation of performance.

C

Checklist A written list of performance criteria associated with a particular activity or product on which an observer marks the student's performance on each criterion using a scale that has only two choices.

Cognitive domain Intellectual activities such as memorizing, interpreting, applying, problem solving, reasoning, analyzing, and thinking critically.

Constructed response item A test item to which the student responds by writing or constructing his/her own answer; short answer, completion, essay.

Convergent question A question that has one correct answer.

Criterion-referenced grading Determining the quality of a student's performance by comparing it to preestablished standards of mastery.

Curriculum The skills, performances, attitudes, and values students are expected to learn from schooling; includes statements of desired student outcomes, descriptions of materials, and the planned sequence that will be used to teach students.

Curriculum standards Statements about what students are expected to know at any given grade level.

D

Diagnostic assessment The process of collecting, synthesizing, and interpreting information for the purpose of improving student learning; assessment takes place at the beginning of the school year or before a unit of instruction.

Difficulty index Indicates the proportion or percentage of students who answered a test item correctly.

Discrimination index Indicates the extent to which students who get a particular test item correct are also likely to get a high score on the entire test.

Distractor A wrong choice in a selection test item.

Divergent question A question that has more than one acceptable answer.

E

Educate To change the behaviour of students; to teach students to do things they could not previously do.

Educational objectives Statements that describe a student accomplishment that will result from instruction—specifically, the behaviour the student will learn to perform and the content on which it will be performed.

Evaluation Process of judging the quality or value of a performance or a course of action.

F

Form The particular version of a commercial test that has more than one equivalent version.

Formative assessment The process of collecting, synthesizing, and interpreting information for the purpose of improving student learning while instruction is taking place; assessment for improvement, not grading.

G

Global objectives Very broad statements of intended learning that require years to accomplish.

Grade equivalent score A standardized test score that describes a student's performance on a scale based upon grade in school and month in grade; most commonly misinterpreted score; indicates student's level of performance relative to students in his/her own grade.

Grading The process of judging the quality of a student's performance.

Grading curve Method used in norm-referenced grading to set up quotas for each grade.

H

Higher-level cognitive behaviour Cognitive behaviour that involves more than rote memorization or recall.

Higher-level question A question that begins with action words such as *explain*, *predict*, *distinguish*, and *solve*.

Holistic scoring Essay scoring method in which a single score is given to represent the overall quality of the essay across all dimensions.

I

Instruction The methods and processes by which students' behaviours are changed.

Instructional objectives Specific objectives used to plan daily lessons.

Items Questions or problems on an assessment instrument.

K

Key A list of correct answers for a test.

L

Large-scale assessment Use of standardized achievement tests that are given to a large number of students in order to measure their performance.

Logical error The use of invalid or irrelevant assessment information to judge a student's status or performance.

Lower-level cognitive behaviour Cognitive behavior that involves rote memorization and recall.

Lower-level question A question that generally begins with words such as *who, what,* and *when.*

M

Mean The average of a group of scores.

Measurement The process of assigning numbers or categories to performance according to rules and standards (e.g., scoring a test).

Median The middle score of when all scores are listed from lowest to highest.

Mode The score that is obtained by more students in a group than any other; there can be more than one mode in group of scores.

N

Negative discrimination When a test item is answered incorrectly more frequently for high scorers on the test than for low scorers; the item discriminates in a different direction than the total score of the test.

Nonstandardized assessment An assessment approach intended to assess a single group of students, such as a class.

Norm group The group of students who were tested to produce the norms for a test.

Norm-referenced grading Determining the quality of a student's performance by comparing it to the performance of other students.

Numerical summarization Use of numbers to describe performance on an assessment.

O

Objective Agreement among independent judges, scorers, or observers.

Observation Technique used to collect assessment data by watching or listening to student activities and student products.

Options Choices available to select from when answering a multiple-choice test item.

P

Percentile rank A standardized test score that describes the percentage of students a given student scored higher than (e.g., an 89th percentile rank means that a student scored higher than 89 percent of the students in the norm group).

Performance assessment Observing and judging a student's skill in actually carrying out a physical activity (e.g., giving a speech) or producing a product (e.g., building a birdhouse).

Performance criteria The aspects of a performance or product that are observed and judged in performance assessment.

Performance standards The levels of achievement students must reach to receive particular grades in a criterion-referenced grading system (e.g., higher than 90 receives an A, between 80 and 90 receives a B, etc.).

Portfolio A well-defined collection of student products or performances that shows student achievement of particular skills over time.

Positive discrimination When a test item is answered correctly more frequently for high scorers on the test than for low scorers; the item discriminates in the same direction of the total score of the test.

Practical knowledge The beliefs, prior experiences, and strategies that enable a teacher to carry out classroom duties and activities.

Prejudgment Inability to make a fair and objective assessment of another person because of interfering prior knowledge, first impressions, or stereotypes.

Premise The stem or question part of a matching item.

Psychoeducational assessment Assessment comprised of both aptitude and achievement tests and is designed to identify a student's cognitive strengths and weaknesses.

Psychoeducational report Report that includes information about the student, assessment measures, findings, and conclusions.

Psychomotor domain Physical and manipulative activities such as holding a pencil, buttoning buttons, serving a tennis ball, playing the piano, and cutting with scissors.

R

Range The difference between the highest and lowest test scores in a group; obtained by subtracting the highest test score from the lowest test score.

Rating scale A written list of performance criteria associated with a particular activity or product on which an observer marks a student's performance on each criterion in terms of its quality using a scale that has more than two choices.

Raw score The number of items correct or the total score a student obtained on an assessment.

Reliability The extent to which an assessment consistently assesses whatever it is assessing; if an assessment is reliable, it will yield the same or nearly the same information on retesting.

Response The answer choices given for a matching item.

S

Scores Symbols or numbers used by teachers to represent a student's achievement in a subject area.

Scoring Method that provides a numerical description of performance that is used to represent a student's performance.

Scoring rubric A rating scale based upon written descriptions of varied levels of achievement in a performance assessment; also called a descriptive rating scale.

Selected response item A test item to which the student responds by selecting the answer from choices given; multiple-choice, true-false, and matching items.

Self-fulfilling prophecy The process in which teachers form perceptions about student characteristics, treat students as if the perceptions are correct, and students respond as if they actually have the characteristics, even though they might not have originally had them; an expectation becomes a reality.

Specific determiners Words that give clues to true-false items; *all*, *always*, *never*, and *none* indicate false statements, while *some*, *sometimes*, and *may* indicate true statements.

Standard deviation A measure of the variability or spread of scores for a group of test takers.

Standardized achievement test Test used to measure students' knowledge and mastered skills and provides information about students' performance in an academic subject area.

Standardized aptitude test Test used to attempt to predict a student's ability to learn a skill or accomplish a level of complexity.

Standardized assessment An assessment that is administered, scored, and interpreted the same for all students taking the test, no matter when and where it is used.

Standardized test Test used to assess students' performance under uniform conditions.

Stanine A standardized test score that describes student performance on a 9-point scale. Scores of 1, 2, and 3 are often interpreted as being below average; 4, 5, and 6 as being average; and 7, 8, and 9 as being above average.

Stem The part of a multiple-choice item that states the question to be answered.

Subjective Lack of agreement among judges, scorers, or observers.

Summative assessment The process of collecting, synthesizing, and interpreting information for the purposes of determining student learning and assigning grades; assessments made at the end of instruction or teaching.

Supply question A test item requiring the student to write or construct an answer: short answer, completion, essay.

T

Test A formal, systematic, often paper-and-pencil procedure used to gather information about students performance; the results of a test are used to make generalizations about how students would perform on similar but untested performances.

Test battery A group of subtests, each assessing a different subject area but all normed on the same sample; designed to be administered to the same group of test takers.

Test norms Describes how a national sample of students who took the test actually performed on the test.

Test score distribution The listing of test scores from lowest to highest; the spread of students' scores.

Testwise skills The test taker's ability to identify flaws in test questions that give away the correct answers; used during tests to outwit poor item writers.

V

Validity The extent to which assessment information is appropriate for making the desired decision about students, instruction, or classroom climate; the degree to which assessment information permits correct interpretations of the desired kind; the most important characteristic of assessment information.

REFERENCES

CHAPTER ONE

Canadian Achievement Test 3 (CAT-3). **(2001).** Markham, Canada: Canadian Test Centre, Inc.

Canadian Test of Basic Skills. **(1998).** Scarborough, Canada: Nelson.

Gates-MacGinitie Reading Tests. **(1992).** Scarborough, Canada: Nelson.

Linn, R. L. (1997). Evaluating the validity of assessments: The consequences of use. *Educational Measurement: Issues and Practices, 16*(2), 14–16.

McMillan, J. H. (2000). *Essential assessment concepts for teachers and administrators.* Thousand Oaks, CA: Corwin Press.

Moss, P. A. (2003). Reconceptualizing validity for the classroom. *Educational Measurement: Issues and Practices, 22*(4), 13–25.

Wechsler intelligence scale for children (4th Ed.: Canadian). **(2003).** Toronto, Canada: Harcourt Assessment Canada.

CHAPTER TWO

Delpit, L. (1995). *Other people's children: Cultural conflict in the classroom.* New York: The New Press.

Hargreaves, A., Earl, L., & Ryan, J. (1996). *Schooling for change: Reinventing education for early adolescents.* London: Falmer Press.

Katz, S., Earl, L., & Olson, D. (2001). The paradox of classroom assessment: A challenge for the 21st century. *McGill Journal of Education, 36* (1), 13–26.

Ladson-Billings, G. (1994). *The dreamkeepers.* San Francisco: Jossey-Bass.

Manitoba Education and Youth (2003). *Independent Together—Supporting the Multilevel Learning Community.* www.edu.gov.mb.ca/ks4/cur/multilevel/blms/blm_5a.doc. Reproduced by permission of Manitoba Education Citizenship and Youth, from *Independent Together: Supporting the Multilevel Learning Community.* Copyright © 2003 Manitoba Education and Youth. All rights reserved.

Shulha, L. M. (1999). Understanding novice teachers' thinking about student assessment. *Alberta Journal of Educational Research, 45* (3), 288–297.

Trouilloud, D. O., Sarrazin, P. G., Martinek, T. J., & Guillet, E. (2002). The influence of teacher expectations on student achievement in physical education classes: Pygmalion revisited. *European Journal of Social Psychology, 32,* 591–607.

Wilson, R. J., & Martinussen, R. L. (1999). Factors affecting the assessment of student achievement. *Alberta Journal of Educational Research, 45* (3), 267–276.

Wilson, R. J. (1990). Classroom practices in evaluating student achievement. *Alberta Journal of Educational Research, 36,* 4–17.

Wiseman, D. L., Cooner, D.D., & Knight, S.L. (1999). *Becoming a teacher in a field-based setting.* Belmont, CA: Wadsworth.

CHAPTER THREE

Anderson, L. W. (Ed.), Krathwohl, D. R. (Ed.), Airasian, P. W., Cruikshank, K. A., Mayer, R. E., Pintrich, P. R., Raths, J., & Wittrock, M. C. (2001). *A taxonomy for learning, teaching, and assessing: A revision of Bloom's taxonomy of educational objectives.* New York: Longman.

Bloom. B. S. (Ed.), Engelhart, M. D., Furst, E. J., Hill, W. H., & Krathwohl, D. R. (1956). *Taxonomy of educational objectives: The classification of educational goals. Handbook I: Cognitive domain.* New York: David McKay.

Canadian Achievement Test 3 (CAT-3). Markham, Canada: Canadian Test Centre.

Canadian Charter of Rights and Freedoms. (1982). *Constitution Act, 1982* (79).

Daniels, H, & Zemelman, S. (2004). Out with textbooks, in with learning. *Educational Leadership, 61*(4), 36–40.

Dworet, D, & Bennett, S. (2002). A view from the north: Canadian policies and issues in special education. *Teaching Exceptional Children, 34*(5), 22–27.

Gardner, H. (1995). Reflections of multiple intelligences: Myths and messages. *Phi Delta Kappan.* Nov., 200–207.

Gates-MacGinite Reading Tests, 3rd Edition (GMRT-3). Itasca, IL: Riverside Publishing Company.

Hannah, L. S., & Michaels, J. U. (1977). *A comprehensive framework for instructional objectives: A guide to systematic planning and evaluation.* Reading, MA: Addison-Wesley.

Harrow, A. H. (1972). *A taxonomy of the psychomotor domain.* New York: David McKay.

Hunter, M. (1982). *Mastery learning.* El Segundo, CA: TIP Publications.

Krathwohl, D. R., Bloom, B. S., & Masia, B. B. (1964). *Taxonomy of educational objectives: Handbook II: Affective domain.* New York: Longman.

Krathwohl, D. R., & Payne, D. A. (1971). Defining and assessing educational objectives. In R. L. Thorndike (Ed.), *Educational measurement* (pp. 17–41). Washington, DC: American Council on Education.

Marzano, R. C., Pickering, D., & McTighe, J. (1993). *Assessing student outcomes: Performance assessment using the dimension of learning model.* Alexandria, VA: Association for Supervision and Curriculum Development.

Slavin, R. (2003). *Educational psychology: Theory and practice,* 7th edition. Boston, MA: Allyn and Bacon.

Wiggins, G., & McTighe, J. (1998). *Understanding by design.* Alexandria, VA: Association for Supervision and Curriculum Development.

Woodcock Reading Mastery Tests (WRMT-R). Circle Pines, MN: AGS Publishing.

CHAPTER FOUR

Bell, B., & Cowie, B. (2001). The characteristics of formative assessment in science education. *Science Education, 85,* 536–553.

Black, P., & Wiliam, D. (1998). Inside the black box. *Phi Delta Kappan.* pp. 139–148. Retrieved from www.pdkintl.org/kappan/kbla9810.htm.

Boston, C. (2002). The concept of formative assessment. *Practical Assessment, Research & Evaluation, 8*(9). Retrieved from http://PAREonline.net/getvn.asp?v=8&n=9.

Canadian Association of Second Language Teachers (2005). The CASLT assessment toolkit: Formative assessment instruments for second language learning. Retrieved from: www.caslt.org/research/assessment.htm.

Chin, C. (2004). Questioning students in ways that encourage thinking. *Teaching Science, 50*(4), 16–21.

Chappuis, S., & Stiggins, R. (2002). Classroom assessment for learning. *Educational Leadership, 60,* 40–43.

Christensen, C.R. (1991). The discussion teacher in action: Questioning, listening, and response. In C.R. Christensen, D.A. Garvin, and A. Sweet, *Education for Judgment.* Boston: Harvard Business School Press.

Earl, L., & Cousins, J. B. (1996). *Classroom assessment: Changing the face; facing the change.* Ontario Public School Teachers' Federation.

Earl, L., & Katz, S. (2000). The paradox of classroom assessment. *Orbit, 30*(4), 8–10.

Green, S., & Mantz, M. (2002). Classroom assessment practices: Examining impact on student learning. Paper presented at the Annual Meeting of the American Educational Research Association (New Orleans, LA, April 1–5, 2002).

The Joint Committee on Standards for Educational Evaluation (2003). *The student evaluation standards: How to improve evaluations of students.* Thousand Oaks, CA: Corwin Press.

Leung, C., & Mohan, B. (2004). Teacher formative assessment and talk in classroom contexts: assessment as discourse and assessment discourse. *Language Testing, 21*(3), 335–359.

Morgan, N., & Saxton, J. (1991). *Teaching, questioning, and learning.* New York: Routledge.

The Saskatoon Public School Division (2004). Instructional strategies online: Questioning. Retrieved from: http://olc.spsd.sk.ca/DE/PD/instr/questioning.html.

Wiggins, G., & McTighe, J. (1998). *Understanding by design.* Alexandria, VA: Association for Supervision and Curriculum Development.

CHAPTER FIVE

Cranton, P. (2000). *Planning instruction for adult learners* (2nd ed.). Toronto, Canada: Wall & Emerson Inc.

Curry, C. (2003). Universal design accessibility for all learners. *Educational Leadership, 61*(2), 55–60.

Frisbie, D. A. (1992). The multiple true-false item format: A status review. *Educational Measurement: Issues and Practice, 11*(4), 21–26.

Joint Advisory Committee, Centre for Research in Applied Measurement and Evaluation (2002). *Principles for fair student assessment practices for education in Canada.* Edmonton, Canada: University of Alberta. www.2Learn.ca/Projects/Together/fair.html.

Marso, R. N., & Pigge, F. L. (1989). Elementary classroom teachers' testing needs and proficiencies: Multiple assessments and inservice training priorities. *Educational Review, 13,* 1–17.

Marso, R. N., & Pigge, F. L. (1991). The analysis of teacher-made tests: Testing practices, cognitive demands and item construction errors. *Contemporary Educational Psychology, 16,* 279–286.

CHAPTER SIX

Cizek, G. (1999). *Cheating on tests: How to do it, detect it, and prevent it.* Mahwah, NJ: Lawrence Erlbaum Associates.

Ebel, R. L., & Frisbie, D. A. (1991). *Essentials of educational measurement,* (5th ed.) Englewood Cliffs, NJ: Prentice-Hall.

Frances Kelsey Secondary School Cheating Policy. Retrieved on August 9, 2005 from www.fkss.ca/community/CheatPolicy.html.

Gentile, J. R. (2000). An exercise in unreliability. *Teaching of Psychology. 27*(3), 210–221.

Kubiszyn, T., & Borich, G. (2003). *Educational testing and measurement,* 7th edition. Glenview, IL: Scott, Foresman.

Levine, M. (2003). Celebrating diverse minds. *Educational Leadership, 61*(2), 12–18.

Manitoba Teachers' Society. Retrieved February 3, 2005 from www.mbteach.org/studassess.htm.

Ontario Secondary School Teachers' Federation. Retrieved February 3, 2005 from www.osstf.on.ca/www/issues/studenttesting/10wayseffective.html.

Personnel Psychology Centre. Public Service Commission of Canada. Retrieved August 9, 2005 from www.psc-cfp.gc.ca/ppc/assessment_cp4_e.htm.

Queen's University Instructional Development Centre. Retrieved August 11, 2005 from www.queensu.ca/idc/idcresources/handouts/Guide_Scoring_Essay.htm.

Runté, R. (2002). *Managing Assessment in Inquiry-Driven Courses.* Retrieved November 30, 2005 from www.mcmaster.ca/cll/stlhe2002new/HTML/notes/runte2.html.

Seaman, P. (2003). Multiple choice testing: Will it work for me? *Teaching Voices, 35.* Retrieved August 11, 2005 from www.lib.unb.ca/Texts/Teaching/bin/get12.cgi?directory = JAN03/&filename = seaman.htm.

Starch, D., & Elliott, E. (1912). Reliability of the grading of high-school work in English. *School Review, 20,* 442–457.

Starch, D., & Elliott, E. (1913). Reliability of grading work in mathematics. *School Review, 21,* 254–259.

Summergrad, D. (1999). Calling it what it is. *Education Week,* August 4, p. 46.

CHAPTER SEVEN

Bartz, D, Anderson-Robinson, S., & Hillman, L. (1994). Performance assessment: Make them show what they know. *Principal, 73,* 11–14.

Forgette-Giroux, R. & Simon, M. (2000). Organizational issues related to portfolio assessment implementation in the classroom. *Practical Assessment, Research & Evaluation, 7*(4). Retrieved January 15, 2006 from http://PAREonline.net/getvn.asp?v = 7&n = 4.

Goodrich, H. (1997). Understanding rubrics. *Educational Leadership 54*(4), 14–17.

Herbert, E. A. (1992). Portfolios invite reflection from both students and staff. *Educational Leadership, 49*(8), 58–61.

McTighe, J. (1996). Performance-based assessment in the classroom: A planning framework. In R. Blum & J. Arter (eds.), *Student performance assessment in an era of restructuring.* Alexandria, VA: Association for Supervision and Curriculum Development.

Mehrens, W. A., Popham, W. J., & Ryan, J. M. (1998). How to prepare students for performance assessments. *Educational Measurement: Issues and Practice, 17*(1), 18–22.

Quality Counts '99. Rewarding results, punishing failure. *Education Week* (January 11, 1999).

Ryan, J., & Miyasaka, J. (1995). Current practices in teaching and assessment: What is driving the change? *NAASP Bulletin, 79,* 1–10.

Tierney, R, & Simon, M. (2004). What's still wrong with rubrics: Focusing on the consistency of performance criteria across scale levels. *Practical Assessment, Research & Evaluation, 9*(2). Retrieved January 15, 2006 from http://PAREonline.net/getvn.asp?v=9&n=2.

Wiggins, G. (1992). Creating tests worth taking. *Educational Leadership, 44*(8), 26–33.

Wiggins, G., & McTighe, J. (1998). *Understanding by design.* Alexandria, VA: Association for Supervision and Curriculum Development.

CHAPTER EIGHT

Alberta Assessment Consortium (2002). *Emerging data: More than just number crunching.* Retrieved September 13, 2005 from www.aac.ab.ca/smerg02.html.

Borich, G.D. (2003). *Effective teaching methods,* 5th edition. Englewood Cliffs, NJ: Prentice-Hall.

British Columbia Ministry of Education (2005). *B.C. Performance Standards.* Retrieved September 13, 2005 from www.bced.gov.bc.ca/perf_stands/.

British Columbia Ministry of Education (2005). *Primary Report Card Sample.* Retrieved September 13, 2005 from www.bced.gov.bc.ca/reportcards/examples/example3.pdf.

Brookhart, S.M. (1999). Teaching about communicating assessment results and grading. *Educational Measurement: Issues and Practice, 18*(1), 5–13.

Bursuck, W.D., Polloway, E.A., Plante, L., Epstein, M.H., Jayanthi, M., & McConeghy, J. (1996). Report card grading adaptations: A national survey of classroom practices. *Exceptional Children, 62*(4), 301–318.

Guskey, T.R., & Bailey, J.M. (2001). *Developing grading and reporting systems for student learning.* Thousand Oaks, CA: Corwin Press.

Hubelbank, J.H. (1994). *Meaning of elementary school teachers' grades.* Unpublished dissertation, Boston College, Chestnut Hill, MA.

Katz, S., & Earl, L. (2000). The paradox of classroom assessment. *Orbit, 30,* 8–10.

Kubiszyn, T., & Borich, G. (2003). *Educational testing and measurement,* 7th edition. New York: John Wiley & Sons, Inc.

Ministry of Education and Training of Ontario (1998). *Guide to the Provincial Report Card (Grades 1–8).* Retrieved February 18, 2005 from www.edu.gov.on.ca.

Ministry of Education and Training of Ontario (1999). *Guide to the Provincial Report Card (Grades 9–12).* Retrieved February 18, 2005 from www.edu.gov.on.ca.

Moll, M. (1998). The history of grading in three minutes. Retrieved February 18, 2005 from www.ctf-fce.ca/en/press/1998/pr30.htm.

Munk, D.D., & Bursuck, W.D. (2003). Grading students with disabilities. *Educational Leadership, 61*(2), 38–43.

O'Connor, K. (2000). Grading—An exercise in professional judgment. *Orbit, 30,* 40–42.

O'Connor, K. (2002). *How to grade for learning: Linking grades to standards* (2nd Ed). Glenview, IL: Pearson Professional Development.

Salend, S., & Duhaney, L. (2002). Grading students in inclusive settings. *Teaching exceptional children, 34* (3), 8–15.

Shepard, L., & Bliem, C. (1995). Parents' thinking about standardized tests and performamce assessment. *Educational Researcher, 24,* 25–32.

Sir Wilfred Laurier School Board (2005). *Kindergarten year end evaluation.* Retrieved February 18, 2005 from www.swlauriersb.qc.ca/english/edservices/pedresources/workshops/report_cards03/cycle_1.pdf.

Sir Wilfrid Laurier School Board (2005). *Kindergarten year end evaluation.* Retrieved February 18, 2005 from www.swlauriersb.qc.ca/english/edservices/pedresources/workshops/report_cards03/kindergarten.pdf.

Sternberg, R. (1997). What does it mean to be smart? *Educational Leadership, 54*(6), 20–24.

Tombari, M., & Borich, G. (1999). *Authentic assessment in the classroom.* Upper Saddle River, NJ: Prentice-Hall.

University of Lethbridge (2005). Faculty of Education. *Norm-versus criterion-referenced grading.* Retrieved September 13, 2005 from http://people.uleth.ca/~runte/inflation/norm.htm.

Valdes, K.A., Williamson, C.L., & Wagner, M.M. (1990). *The national longitudinal transition study of special education students,* Vol. 1. Menlo Park, CA: SRI International.

CHAPTER NINE

Agrey, L. (2004). The pressure cooker in education: Standardized assessment and high-stakes. *Canadian Social Studies, 38*(3). Retrieved October 16, 2005 from www.quasar.ualberta.ca/css/ Css_38_3/ARagrey_pressure_cooker_education.htm.

***Canadian Test of Basic Skills.* (1998).** Scarborough, Canada: Nelson.

Council of Ministers of Education, Canada. (2001). *Measuring up: The performance of Canada's youth in reading, mathematics and science.* Retrieved October 18, 2005 from www.cmec.ca/pisa/2000/CanadaReport.en.pdf.

Council of Ministers of Education, Canada. (2004a). *Science in Canadian schools— 2004.* Retrieved October 18, 2005 from www.cmec.ca/ saip/science3/public/highlights.en.pdf.

Council of Ministers of Education, Canada. (2004b). *Measuring up: Canadian results of the OECD PISA Study.* Retrieved October 18, 2005 from www.cmec.ca/pisa/2003/highlights.en.pdf.

D'Souza, P. (2003). Alberta has no deal with Nunavut, spokesperson says. Retrieved October 16, 2005 from www.nunatsiaq.com/archives/nunavut030307/news/iqaluit/30307_02.html.

Earl, L. M. (1999). Assessment and accountability in education: Improvement or surveillance? *Education Canada, 39*(3), 4–6.

Ebel, R. L., & Frisbie, D. A. (1991). *Essentials of educational measurement,* 5th edition. Englewood Cliffs, NJ: Prentice-Hall.

Education Quality and Accountability Office (2005). *Assessments for learning.* Retrieved October 17, 2005 from www.eqao.com/categories/home.aspx?Lang=E.

Froese-Germain, B. (1999). *Standardized testing: Undermining equity in education.* Report prepared for the National Issues in Education Initiative. Ottawa, Canada: Canadian Teachers' Federation.

Gallagher, C. W. (2004). Training the accountability tables: Ten progressive lessons from one "backward" state. *Phi Delta Kappan, 85*(5), 352–360.

Gouvernement du Québec—Ministère de l'Éducation, Loisir et Sport. (2005). Éducation préscolaire, enseignement primaire et secondaire. Retrieved October 17, 2005 from www.mels.gouv.qc.ca/EPPS-org.htm.

Government of Alberta—Ministry of Education. (2005a). *Description of mathematics assessment standards.* Retrieved October 17, 2005 from www.education.gov.ab.ca/k_12/testing/achievement/bulletins/Gr6_Math/gr6_math_standards.asp.

Government of Alberta—Ministry of Education. (2005b). *Achievement tests.* Retrieved October 17, 2005 from www.education.gov.ab.ca/k_12/testing/achievement/default.asp. Reproduced with the permission of the Minister of Education, Province of Alberta, Canada, 2006.

Government of British Columbia—Ministry of Education. (2005). *Provincial student assessment program.* Retrieved October 17, 2005 from www.bced.gov.bc.ca/assessment.

Government of Canada. (2005). *Programme for International Student Assessment.* Retrieved October 18, 2005 from www.pisa.gc.ca/what_pisa.shtml.

Government of Manitoba—Manitoba Education. (2005). *Assessment and evaluation.* Retrieved October 17, 2005 from www.edu.gov.mb.ca/ks4/k-s4map.html#assess.

Government of New Brunswick—Department of Education. (2005). *K-12.* Retrieved October 17, 2005 from www.gnb.ca/0000/anglophone-e.asp#e.

Government of Newfoundland and Labrador—Department of Education. (2005). *Evaluation and research division.* Retrieved October 17, 2005 from www.ed.gov.nl.ca/edu/dept/er.htm.

Government of the Northwest Territories—Department of Education, Culture, and Employment. (2005). *Assessment and evalua-*

tion. Retrieved October 17, 2005 from www.ece. gov.nt.ca/Divisions/kindergarten_g12/ indexK12.htm.

Government of Nova Scotia—Department of Education. (2005). *About PLANS.* Retrieved October 17, 2005 from http://plans.ednet.ns.ca/about.shtml.

Government of Saskatchewan—Department of Learning. (2005). *Welcome to assessment for learning & system information & accountability units.* Retrieved October 17, 2005 from www.sasked.gov.sk.ca/branches/cap_building_ acct/afl/aflindex.html.

Government of the Yukon. (2005). *Yukon students continue trend for success on achievement tests.* Retrieved October 17, 2005 from www.gov.yk.ca/news/2005/05-258.html.

Lam, T. C. M., & Bordignon, C. (2001). An examination of English teachers' opinions about the Ontario grade 9 reading and writing test. *Interchange, 32*(2), 131–145.

Levin, B. (1998). An epidemic of education policy: (What) can we learn from each other? *Comparative Education, 34*(2), 131–141.

Levine, M. (2003). Celebrating diverse minds. *Educational Leadership, 61*(2), 12–18.

McEwen, N. (1995). Accountability in Alberta. *Canadian Journal of Education, 20*(1), 27–44.

Pedulla, J. J., Abrams, L. M., Madaus, G. F., Russell, M. K., Ramos, M. A., & Miao, J. (2003). *Perceived effects of state mandated testing programs on teaching and learning: Findings from a national survey of teachers.* Boston: National Board on Educational Testing and Public Policy.

Popham, W. J. (2003). The seductive allure of data. *Educational Leadership, 60*(5), 48–51.

Simner, M. L. (2000). *A joint position statement by the Canadian Psychological Association of School Psychologists on the Canadian Press Coverage of the Province-wide Achievement Test Results.* Retrieved from http://cpa.ca/documents/ joint_position.html.

Skwarchuk, S.-L. (2004). Teachers' attitudes toward government-mandated provincial testing in Manitoba. *Alberta Journal of Educational Research, 50*(3), 252–282.

CHAPTER TEN

Aiken, L. R. (2000). *Psychological testing and assessment* (10th Ed.). Boston: Allyn & Bacon.

American Psychiatric Association. (2000). *Diagnostic and statistical manual of mental disorders—Fourth Edition (DSM-IV-TR).* Washington, DC.

Canadian Achievement Test-2. Handbook for Test Coordinators. (1992). Markham, Canada: CTB Macmillan/McGraw-Hill.

Canadian Achievement Test-3. (2001). Markham, Canada: Canadian Test Centre, Inc.

Canadian Cognitive Abilities Test. (1998). Scarborough, Canada: Nelson.

Canadian Cognitive Abilities Test—Teacher's Handbook. (1998). Scarborough, Canada: Nelson.

Canadian Psychological Association. (1996). *CPA accredited programmes.* Retrieved December 7, 2002 from www.cpa.ca/accredlist.htm.

Canadian Test of Basic Skills. (1998). Scarborough, ON: Nelson.

Canadian Test of Basic Skills—Teacher's Handbook. (1998). Scarborough, ON: Nelson.

MacGinitie, W. H., & MacGinitie, R. L. (1992). *Gates-MacGinitie reading tests.* Scarborough, Canada: Nelson.

McEwan, E. K. (1998). *How to deal with parents who are angry, troubled, afraid or just plain crazy.* Thousand Oaks, CA: Corwin Press, Inc.

Spies, R. A., & Plake, B. S. (2005). *The sixteenth mental measurements yearbook.* Lincoln, NE: Buros Institute of Mental Measurements, University of Nebraska Press.

Popham, W.J. (2000). *Modern educational measurement: Practical guidelines for educational leaders,* 3rd edition. Boston, MA: Allyn & Bacon. Englewood Cliffs, NJ: Prentice-Hall.

PsychCorp. (2003). *Wechsler intelligence scale for children* (4th Ed. Canadian). Toronto, Canada: Harcourt Assessment Canada.

Wormeli, C. T., & Carter, D. E. (1990) *Canada quick individual achievement test.* White Rock, Canada: Canadian Edumetrics.

CREDITS

SUBJECT INDEX

Ability
   defined,   39
   grading and,   203, 204, 228
   multiple types of,   203
Abuse,   23
Academic achievement. *See also* Achievement
   grade equivalent scoring and,   275
   grading and,   205–206, 219
   parent-teacher conferences and,   230
Academic environment,   21
Accountability,   238
Accuracy and instructional assessment,   80
Achievement
   ability vs.,   203
   defined,   39
   grading and,   202–206, 228
   performance assessment and,   152, 182, 184
   process vs.,   228
   report cards and,   204
   valid indicators of,   99
Achievement standards,   240
Achievement Testing Program (Alberta),   242,
      245
Achievement Testing Program (Northwest
      Territories),   245
Achievement tests. *See also* Test(s)
   commercial. *See also* Commercial standardized
      achievement tests
   national,   8
   preparation for,   253–257
   problems with,   253–257
Achievement-ability comparison,   277, 288
Action questions,   76
Activities
   follow-up,   204
   objectives and,   55–56, 60
   observation of,   6
Affective domain,   52–53, 62
   grading and,   206, 207–208, 219
Alternative assessments,   148
Analytic scoring,   136, 159
   rubics and,   166–167
   rubrics and,   171–172
Anecdotal records,   159

Answer key,   133
Aptitude,   40
Assessment standards,   240
Assessment(s),   2
   accuracy of,   29–33
   alternative,   148
   authentic,   148
   bias,   295
   capacity,   296
   classroom equilibrium, for,   3
   comparison of various types of,   149, 150
   data collection for,   5–7
      See also Data/information collection
   defined,   2
   diagnostic,   3
   disabilities and,   62
      See also Disabilities; Pupil accommodations
   early. *See* Diagnostic assessment; Early
      assessment
   ethics and,   13–14, 29–33
   evaluation and,   2, 5
   example of,   2–3, 8–10
   fairness of,   13–14, 123, 159
   feedback and incentives, for,   4
   formal. *See* Formal observation/assessment
   formative,   4, 89, 152
   good,   8–13
      See also Reliability; Validity
   grading and,   5, 202
      See also Grading; Scoring
   group,   8
   IEP and,   62
      See also Individual Education Program (IEP)
   informal. *See* Informal observation/assessment
   instruction. *See* Instructional assessment
   interpreting, five guidelines,   296–299
   measurement and,   2, 5
      See also Measurement
   multidisciplinary,   15
   multiple,   159, 184
   nonstandardized,   8
   objectives in,   48–59, 60
      See also Teaching objectives
   objectivity,   295

observation for. *See* Observation

performance. *See* Performance assessments

planning and, 3, 59–61
   See also Planning

portfolio. *See* Portfolios

potential, 296

preplacement, 62

product, 149, 150

provincial and territorial, 240–246

pupil placement, for, 4

purpose of, 3–4, 152, 184

reliability, 295

self. *See* Pupils, self-assessment by; Teachers,
   self-assessment by

standardized, 7, 8, 262
   See also Commercial standardized
      achievement tests; Standardized
      assessments

summarizing various types of, 209–217

summative. *See* Summative assessment

summing up, 295–300

tasks during instruction, 69

tests for, 2, 5
   See also Test(s)

third step in instruction, as, 40, 41

types of, 4–5

validity, 295

Authentic assessments, 148

Benchmarks, 238

Bias, 13, 182–183
   assessment, 295
   commercial standardized tests and, 268
   defined, 183

Bloom's Taxonomy, 51–52, 55–56, 76
   examples relating to, 77

Braille, 142

Canadian Achievement Test (CAT-3), 3, 8, 51,
   263, 265, 276

Canadian Cognitive Abilities Test (CCAT), 263,
   277

Canadian Council for Exceptional Children
   (CCEC), 143

Canadian Quick Individual Achievement Test (C-
   QUIET), 263

Canadian Test of Basic Skills (CTBS), 3, 8, 243,
   262–263, 277

"Carryover" effect, 136

CAT-3. *See* Canadian Achievement Tests (CAT-3)

Challenge questions, 76

Charter of Rights and Freedoms, 62

Cheating, 129–131

Checklists, 159–162, 180, 182
   multiple grading and, 228

Classroom assessment, 2
   See also Assessment(s)

Classroom context, 23, 42

Classroom equilibrium, 3

Classroom society/environment, 3, 4
   See also Social environment
   basic realities of, 21
   early assessment and, 25
   rules/routines for, 23

Cognitive domain, 50, 53, 62

Cognitive Taxonomy, 51–52

Commercial standardized achievement tests,
   262–290
   administering, 270–271, 281, 286
   coverage, 278–282
   creation of, 265–270
   defined, 263
   manuals for, 270
   pupil accommodations for, 288–289
   purposes of, 263
   reporting results of, to parents, 289–290
   teacher-made vs., 264, 266, 267, 279–282
   teachers' reactions to, 264
   textbook tests vs., 279–282
   validity of, 278–288

Communication
   between parents and teachers, 229–230, 231
   early assessment and, 24
   objectives and, 55–56
   personal, 24
   rules for classroom, 21

Completion items, 92
   after-test review of, 139
   scoring of, 131, 133–134

Computer grading program, 209

Computer-based testing as pupil accommodation,
   116

Computer/Internet resources, 116
   regarding norm-and criterion-referenced
     grading, 215
   standardized tests, for, 288

Constructed response items, 6, 90, 91

Content
  commercial standardized tests and, 268, 281
  grading and, 202, 203, 204
Contract grading, 227, 228
Convergent questions, 76
Cooperation, 204
Cooperative learning, 196
Cooperative teacher practice, 176, 184
Council of Ministers of Education, Canada
    (CMEC), 246
Criterion-referenced grading, 199–202, 218–219
  disabilities and, 227, 228
  essay questions and, 136
  norm-vs., 221
  performance assessment, for, 152, 199–200
    See also Performance criteria
  websites regarding, 215
Culture, 13, 23, 62
  differences vs. deficits and, 31
Curriculum
  achievement tests, 263
  commercial standardized tests and, 265, 267,
    279–282, 281
  defined, 39
  grading and, 228
  large-scale assessment, 254
  portfolios and, 174
  rubrics and, 166
  standardized achievement tests, 239
  test preparation and, 123, 124
Curriculum standards, 239
  large-scale assessment, 240
  provincial and territorial, 240

Data/information collection, 5–7
  during instruction, 69–72
  early assessment and, 21–33
  ethics and, 13
Descriptive rating scales, 162, 164, 166
    See also Scoring rubrics
Diagnostic assessment, 3, 5, 20, 23, 68, 89
  guidelines, 26–28
  planning, 60
Diagnostic questions, 76
Difficulty index, 139, 268
Diploma Examinations (Alberta), 242, 245
Disabilities, 4, 14–15, 23
    See also Pupil accommodations
  grading and, 223–228

legal issues on, 62–63
  planning and, 61–63
  range of, 62
Discrimination index, 139, 268
    See also Summary indexes
Divergent questions, 76
"Do no harm" approach, 254, 255

Early assessment, 5, 20–33
    See also Diagnostic assessment
  accuracy of, 29–33
  characteristics of, 26–28
  ethics and, 29–33
  gathering information for, 21–23
  planning and, 44, 59–60
  pupil descriptions and, 25–26
  reliability and, 24–25, 30, 32–33, 59–60
  source of information for, 24–25
  validity and, 24–25, 30–32, 59–60
Educate (defined), 39
Education Quality and Accountability Office
    (EQAO) (Ontario), 244, 245
Educational objectives, 49, 50, 54
    See also Objectives
  disabilities and, 62
  examples of, 57–58
  matching strategies and assessments with, 60
  questions asked about, 58–59
Elementary Literacy Assessment (Nova Scotia),
    243
English Language Proficiency Assessment (New
    Brunswick), 243
Essay questions, 92, 94, 95
  scoring, 131, 134–137
Ethics, 13–14, 21, 29–33
  large-scale assessment, 254
Evaluation, 2, 5, 8, 192
Expectations, 40, 48
Extension questions, 76

Feedback, 4
  performance assessment and, 152
Focused observation form, 21–22
Follow-up activities, 204
Follow-up questions, 79
Form (of test), 277
Formal observation/assessment, 6
  capacity for learning, and, 204

disabilities and,   62
early assessment, for,   24–25
grading and,   205
performance assessment as,   149, 158–159
supplement informal, to,   73
Formative assessment,   4, 5, 68, 89, 152
  formal/informal,   73–74
  guidelines,   73–74
  lower/higher level,   73–74
Foundation Skills Assessment (British Columbia),
    242, 245
Frances Kelsey Secondary School Cheating Policy,
    130

Gates-MacGinitie Reading Tests (GMRT),   3, 8,
    263
Gates-MacGinitie Reading Tests 2nd Edition
    (GMRT-2),   51
Generalization (in assessment),   184
Generalization questions,   76
Global objectives,   48–49, 50, 54
Global questions,   78
Goals,   48, 74
  See also Objectives
Grade equivalent score,   273–275, 277
  misinterpretation and,   287
Grades
  defined,   192
  what should be included in,   212–213, 219
Grading,   5, 159, 192–232
  See also Report cards; Scoring/score
  academic achievement and,   205–206
  co-operative learning,   196
  comparisons for,   198–205
  computer,   209
  computing overall scores for,   216–217
  contract,   227, 228
  cooperative learning, for,   196
  criterion-referenced,   217–219
      See also Criterion-referenced grading
  defined,   192
  different countries (website), in,   215
  difficulties in,   194–195
  disabilities and,   223–228
  fairness in,   194–195, 202
  forms of,   192, 228
  group-based learning,   196
  guidelines for,   220

interpretation/adjustment in,   201–202, 209,
    219, 228
      See also Scoring/score; interpreting
  level-based,   228
  multiple,   228
  narrative,   228
  norm-referenced,   219–220
      See also Norm-referenced grading
  purposes of,   193
  rationale for,   193–194
  steps in,   219
  validity and,   202, 205, 215–216
  websites regarding,   215
  weighting information for,   213–214, 219
Grading curve,   198, 202, 221
Grading system,   197–198
Graduation Program Examinations (British
    Columbia),   242
Graphic rating scales,   162, 164
Groups,   4, 8
  See also Cooperative learning
  elementary school,   23
  high school,   23

Higher level affective behaviour,   53
Higher level cognitive behaviour,   51
Higher level objectives,   58–59, 60
Higher level questions,   77, 78, 90, 91, 92, 94–97
Higher level/order thinking,   51, 150
Higher order thinking skills (HOTS),   58
Holistic scoring,   136, 159
  rubrics and,   166–167, 169–170, 171–172
Home reports,   289–290
HOTS. See Higher order thinking skills

IEP. See Individual Education Program
Incentives,   4
Individual Education Program (IEP),   14–15
  commercial standardized tests and,   289
  description of,   62
  grading and,   223, 227, 228
  testing and,   142, 143
Informal observation/assessment,   6, 27
  affective domain and,   53
  during instruction,   71
  early assessment, for,   24–25, 27
  grading and,   205
  group,   8

supplemented with formal,   73
Information. *See also* Data/information collection
    combining different assessment,   214–215
    commercial standardized tests and,   264, 265
    grading and,   202
    weighting of,   213–214, 219
Information questions,   76
Instruction
    commercial standardized tests and,   279–282
    conduction of,   4
    defined,   39
    disabilities and,   62, 82–83
    grading and,   202
    IEP and,   62
    interruptions to,   69
    objectives and,   49, 55–56
    performance assessment and,   182
    planning of,   23
        See also Planning
    process of. *See* Process
    questioning during,   7
    resources for. *See* Resources
    test items and,   99, 100
Instructional assessment,   4, 5, 68–83
    accuracy,   80
    improving,   74
    incompleteness,   81
    indicators during,   71
    objectivity,   80
    planning and,   69–72
    practical knowledge and,   72–73
    pupil accommodation and,   82–83
    reliability in,   73–74, 81
    steps in,   70–71
    tasks in,   69–73
    validity,   80
    validity in,   71, 74
Instructional objectives,   49, 50, 54
    scoring and,   137
Intelligences, multiple,   203
Interpretive exercises,   95–97
Interventions,   82
Items,   88
    See also Test items
Judgment,   2, 5, 27, 152, 182
    grading as,   192, 197–198, 202, 218–219
    holistic vs. analytic scoring and,   159
    portfolios, of,   175, 177, 180
    rating scales and,   162
    students, by,   175, 180

Key, answer,   133

Labeling,   27, 32
Ladson-Billings, G.,   31
Language,   23
    native,   62
Language disabilities,   143
Large-scale assessment,   238
    Alberta,   242, 245
    British Columbia,   242, 245
    classroom quality,   252
    curriculum,   254
    defined,   239
    description of mathematics standards,   241
    ethics,   254
    expectations,   253
    familiarity with question format,   256
    implications,   248–253
    information about the test,   257
    instruction,   254–255
    international programs,   246–248
    limitations,   249–250
    Manitoba,   242, 245
    motivation,   252
    national programs,   246–248
    New Brunswick,   242–243, 245
    Newfoundland and Labrador,   243, 245
    Northwest Territories,   243, 245
    Nova Scotia,   243, 245
    Nunavut,   240
    Ontario,   244, 245
    Prince Edward Island,   240
    problems,   249–250
    provincial and territorial,   240–246
    provincial and territorial curriculum,   240
    Quebec,   244, 246
    reconsidering,   250–252
    reporting of, to schools,   240
    review before testing,   255
    Saskatchewan,   244, 246
    scheduling the test,   256–257
    student preparation,   253–257
    teachers and,   248–249
    test preparation,   253–254
    validity,   256
    Yukon Territory,   244–246, 246
LDA. *See* Learning Disabilities Association of
    Canada

Learning
  capacity for,   204
  cooperative,   196
  difficulty in,   159
  grading and,   202
  objectives and,   54
  portfolios for,   174, 175, 180
  rubrics and,   166
  self-assessment of,   74
Learning Disabilities Association of Canada (LDA),
  143
Learning environment,   3, 21
Lesson plans. *See also* Planning
  early assessment and,   59–60
  guidelines for,   61
  varied strategies/activities in,   60
Level (of test),   277
Level-based grading,   228
Levels of tolerance,   71
Listening,   79
Logical error,   31–32
Lower level affective behaviour,   53
Lower level cognitive behaviour,   51
Lower level objectives,   58–59, 60
Lower level questions,   76–77, 91

Matching items,   91
Means/end statements,   60
Measurement,   2, 5, 192
    defined,   131
Modeling, of self-assessment,   74
Monitoring,   70
  cheating, for,   130
  disabilities and,   143
Moral environment,   21
Multidisciplinary assessment,   15, 62
Multiple choice items,   90
Multiple grading,   228
Multiple intelligences,   203
Multiple observations/assessments,   159, 184
Multiple-choice items/questions,   90–91, 279–282,
  288
  after-test review of,   138–140
  interpretive exercise as form of,   95–97

Narrative grading,   228
National achievement tests,   8
Nationality,   13

Newsletters,   231
Nonstandardized assessments,   8
Norm-referenced grading,   198–199, 202, 219–220
  commercial standardized tests, for,   266, 268,
    269
  criterion vs.,   221
  disabilities and,   227, 228
  websites regarding,   215
Normal curve equivalents,   277
Nova Scotia Examinations (NSE),   243
Numerical rating scales,   162–165, 164
Numerical summarization,   163, 166

Objective scoring,   133, 184, 194–195
  scoring rubrics for,   136
  steps to ensure,   136–139
Objectives. *See also* Educational objectives;
    Teaching objectives
  activities and,   55–56, 60
  affective,   52–53, 54
  cognitive,   45, 49, 50
  commercial standardized tests and,   267–268,
    269, 279–282
  criteria for successful,   58
  extended,   58–59
  global,   48–49, 50, 54
  higher vs. lower level,   58–59, 60
  IEP and,   62
  instructional,   49, 50, 54, 137
  psychomotor,   53
  questioning and,   78, 78–79
  writing/critiquing tests, and,   97, 99
Objectivity
  assessment,   295
  instructional assessment,   80
Observation,   6
  affective domain and,   53
  informal vs. formal,   6, 27
    See also Formal *or* Informal observation/
      assessment
  multiple,   159, 184
  performance assessment, for,   156–158, 182
  psychomotor domain and,   53
Official assessments,   5
  "do no harm" practices in,   123, 124
  grading as,   193
    See also Grading
  preparing pupils for,   253–254

Ontario Secondary School Literacy Test (OSSLT), 244
Open-ended test items, 76, 288
Options (for question answers), 90
Oral questioning, 7, 71
　bias and, 183
　cognitive domain and, 53
　pupil accommodation, as, 116
　strategies for, 78–79
Orderliness, 3, 25
Organization for Economic Co-operation and Development (OECD), 247
Outcomes, 40, 48

Pan-Canadian Assessment Program (PCAP), 247
Paper-and-pencil tests, 5, 6
　administering, 128–129
　cheating on, 129–131
　cognitive domain and, 53
　disabilities and, 115–116, 141–143
　group assessment, for, 8
　guidelines for writing/critiquing, 97–115
　higher-level questions on, 94–97
　keeping track of time during, 129, 142
　performance assessments and, 148–149, 199
　physical setting for, 128, 142–143
　psychological setting for, 128–129
　scoring of, 131–137
Parent-teacher conferences, 192, 229–231, 232, 289
Parents
　grading and, 192
　information from, 5
　legal issues and, 62
　reporting to, 231, 289–290
Percentage-based criteria, 200–201
Percentile rank, 272, 273, 275, 289–290
　misinterpretation and, 287
Performance assessments, 5, 6, 148–185
　See also Assessment(s); Test(s)
　advantages/disadvantages of, 181
　anecdotal records for, 159
　checklists for, 159–162, 180
　commercial standardized tests for, 262, 265, 266, 271–275, 288, 289–290
　compared with other assessments, 149, 150
　criteria for, 152–156
　developing, 151–159
　general role of, 148–149
　main source of error in, 182

paper-and-pencil tests and, 148–149, 199
portfolios for, 173–180
　See also Portfolios
purpose of, 152, 184
rating scales for, 162–166, 180
reliability of, 159, 163, 180–182, 184–185
rubrics for, 163, 166–173
　See also Scoring rubrics
schools, in, 149–150
setting for, 158–159
specificity vs. practicality in, 155–156
validity of, 159, 180–183
Performance criteria, 152–156
　See also Scoring rubrics
examples, 153
holistic vs. analytic, 166–167
　See also Analytic scoring; Holistic scoring
informing pupils about, 171–172, 173, 182
portfolios, for, 176–177, 180
rating scales, in, 162–166
reliability and, 184
Performance standards, 199, 202, 218–219, 221
Performance-based criteria, 200
Performance-based test items, 288
Personal beliefs/feelings, 31, 31–32
Personal communication, 24
Plagarism, 131
Planning, 3, 23, 39–62
　See also Lesson plans
assessment and, 59–61
early assessment and, 59–60
first step in instruction, as, 40, 41
guidelines for, 61
IEP and, 62–63
instructional assessment and, 69–72
objectives in, 48–59
　See also Teaching objectives
observation, of, 6
parent-teacher conferences, of, 230–231
pupil disabilities and, 61–63, 82–83
role of, in teaching, 39–40
test items, 109–112
time allocation in, 47
Portfolios, 28, 173–180
advantages/disadvantages of, 181
defined, 173
parent-teacher conferences and, 230
purpose of, 175
scoring of, 177–180
setting for, 176
Poverty, 23

Practical knowledge,   72–73

Practice,   123, 125

Practice test,   276

Predefined standards,   199

Predication questions,   76

Pregnancy,   23

Prejudgment,   30–31

Premises (for questions),   91

Preplacement assessment,   62

Pretests,   24

Principles for Fair Student Assessment Practices,   301–302

Problem solving,   150, 204

Process,   40–41
   cooperative learning and,   196
   grading and,   228
   observation of,   6
   performance criteria for,   154, 173, 176
   portfolios and,   176
   product vs.,   154, 228
   scoring rubrics and,   170–172

Process decisions,   3

Product assessment/observation,   6, 149, 150
   advantages/disadvantages of,   181
   criteria for,   154, 173, 176
   grading and,   228
   portfolios and,   176

Production items,   6

Program of Learning Assessments (PLANS) (Nova Scotia),   243, 245

Programme for International Student Assessment (PISA),   247

Provincial Assessment Program (Newfoundland and Labrador),   243, 245

Provincial assessments,   262
   See also Assessment(s); Test items; Test(s)
   commercial standardized tests and,   264

Provincial Assessments (New Brunswick),   242, 245

Provincial Assessments (Quebec),   244, 246

Provincial Examinations (British Columbia),   245

Provincial Examinations (Yukon Tereritory),   246

Provincial Learning Assessment Program (Saskatchewan),   244, 246

Provincial Learning Assessments (British Columbia),   242, 245

Provincial standards,   240

Provincial Standards Test (Manitoba),   242, 245

Provincial testing,   238

Psychoeducational assessment,   288

Psychoeducational report,   289

Psychomotor domain,   53, 62

Public Examinations (Newfoundland and Labrador),   243

"Pull-out" programs,   62

Pupil accommodations,   4, 15
   commercial standardized tests, for,   288–289
   deafness, for,   143
   during instruction,   82–83
   planning and,   61–63
   tests, for,   115–116, 141–143, 288–289

Pupil behaviour
   assessing normal/abnormal,   71
   reliability and typical,   32–33

Pupil characteristics,   21, 25–29
   grading and,   194, 203, 219
   performance assessment and,   183
   planning and,   43–44, 59–60
   validity and,   30–32, 183

Pupil improvement,   204

Pupil involvement,   74, 78, 182
   portfolios, in,   175, 180
   use of rubrics, in,   172–173, 173

Pupil placement,   4

Pupils,   74
   descriptions of,   25–26
   diagnosing problems/disabilities of,   4
    See also Disabilities
   discussing test results with,   142
   grading and,   192
   motivating,   192, 193, 203
   pairing/grouping of,   4
    See also Groups
   preparing,   182, 271
   self-assessment by,   74, 204
    See also Judgment, by students
   source of learning about,   24–25
   with special needs. See Special needs

Questioning/questions,   75–76
   See also Test items
   oral. See Oral questioning
   purposes and types of,   75–76, 125
   strategies for,   78–79
   student self-assessment, for,   74
   written tests, on. See Test items

Questionnaires, affective domain and,   53

Race,   13, 31, 62
Rating scales,   162–166, 180, 182
   multiple grading and,   228
Raw score,   276, 277
   defined,   272
Reading, portfolio for,   174
Real-world problem solving,   150
Reliability,   8, 11–13
   assessment information,   295
   commercial tests, of,   279–282, 287
   early assessment and,   24–25, 30, 32–33, 59–60
   ethics and,   13, 29
   grading and,   205
   improving,   123
   instructional assessment,   81
   instructional assessment, in,   73–74
   number of test items, and,   127–128
   performance assessment, of,   159, 163,
      180–182, 184–185
   test scores, of,   287
   threats to,   30, 32–33
Religion,   13
Report cards,   192, 205, 209, 220
   achievement vs. ability, and,   203
   limitations of,   229, 230
   multiple grading on,   228
Reporting methods,   231
   See also Parents, reporting to
Resources,   44–47
   See also Computer/Internet resources
Responses (to questions),   91
Rubrics. *See* Scoring rubrics

Sample,   9
Scaled scores,   277
School Achievement Indicators Program (SAIP),
   51, 246–247
School administrators
   commercial standardized tests and,   265, 270
   grading and,   192
   parent-teacher conferences and,   230
School counselors,   230
School district/system and commercial
   standardized tests,   264, 265, 270, 272, 281
School staff, information from,   5, 6
Science assessment,   246–247
Scores,   192
Scoring,   192

Scoring rubrics,   136, 163, 166–173
   devising,   168–172
   involving pupils in use of,   172–173
   learning curve for,   173
   portfolios, for,   180
   reliability of,   184
   reporting method, as,   231
   steps in preparing and using,   170
Scoring/score,   131–137
   commercial standardized tests, for,   271–275
   criterion-referenced. *See* Criterion-referenced
      grading
   fairness in,   159
   grade equivalent,   273–275, 277, 287
   guidelines for,   137
   holistic vs. analytic,   136, 159
   interpreting,   271–275
      See also Test interpretation
   norm-referenced. *See* Norm-referenced grading
   objective vs. subjective,   133
      See also Objective scoring; Subjective scoring
   percentile rank. *See* Percentile rank
   performance assessment, in,   152, 159, 182
   portfolios, of,   177–180
   raw,   272, 277
   stanine. *See* Stanine
   subjective,   133, 134–135, 202, 209
   unexpected answers, of,   133
Selected response items,   6, 90
Selection items/questions,   90–91, 94
   See also Test items
   objectives and,   125
   scoring of,   131–133
Self-assessment
   students, by,   74
   teachers, by,   60–61
Self-fulfilling prophecy,   29
"Self-help" skills,   53
Sequence questions,   76
Short-answer questions,   92
   after-test review of,   139
   scoring,   131, 133–134
Social environment,   3
   See also Classroom society/environment
   classroom rules/routines for,   21
   oral questioning and,   79
Social responsibility,   206–207
Social skills,   230
Socialization,   23
Socioeconomic background,   23

Special education, 62
See also Special needs
computer resources regarding, 143
grading and, 223, 227
Special needs, 14–15
See also Disabilities; Pupil accommodations;
Special education
computer resources regarding, 143
IEP and, 62
psychomotor domain and, 53
Speech-to-text software, 116
Standard(s)
ethical, 13–14
performance. See Performance standards
reading, 24–25
teacher competence in student assessment,
for, 248
writing, 24–25
Standardized achievement tests, 239, 263
achievement standards, 240
assessment standard, 240
criterion-referenced, 239
curriculum, 239
norm-referenced, 239
Standardized aptitude tests, 262
Standardized assessments, 7, 8
See also Commercial standardized achievement
tests
Standardized tests, 239, 262
Stanine, 273, 275, 277
misinterpretation and, 287
Stem (of question), 90
stereotyping, 13, 31
Stereotyping, 31
Strategies, 60, 61
deter cheating, to, 130–131
grading, for, 195, 204, 227–228
oral questioning, for, 78–79
test-taking, 126
Student diagnostic profile, 276
Subject matter grades, 205–206
Subjective scoring, 133, 134–135, 202, 209
Subtests, 265, 272, 277
Summary reports for parents, 289–290
Summative assessment, 5, 88–89, 166
performance assessment as, 52
portfolios, of, 177–180
Supply items/questions, 90, 92, 94
objectives and, 125

Targets. See Educational objectives
Taxonomy. See also Bloom's Taxonomy
cognitive, 51–52
Teacher's manual, 270
Teacher-made tests
commercial vs., 264, 266, 267, 279–282, 287
textbook vs., 112
Teachers
accountability of. See Accountability
assessment by, 2–3, 5, 152
See also Assessment(s)
characteristics of, 44
commercial standardized tests and, 262, 264
competencies of, 13, 248
cooperative practice by, 176, 184
disabilities identified by, 62
ethics and, 13–14, 21
grading and, 192, 194–198, 202
See also Grading
information from other, 5, 6
judgments by. See Judgment
mark book of, 210–212
marking book of, 210–212
parents and. See Parent-teacher conferences
responsibilities of, 13–14, 21, 59–60, 62, 223
rewards for, 41, 42
self-assessment by, 60–61
standards for assessment competence of, 248
Teaching objectives. See also Educational
objectives; Objectives
domains of, 50–54
levels of, 48–50, 54–55
planning a test, and, 122–123
portfolios and, 174, 176
stating, 54–59
"Teaching to the test", 123
Technical manuals, 270
Test anxiety, 128–129, 129
Test batteries, 265, 272, 273
Test interpretation. See also Grading,
interpretation; Scoring/score, interpreting
misinterpretations and, 279–282, 287
overinterpretation and, 287, 288
student performance report, 277
summary reports for parents, 289–290
Test items, 6, 88–93
See also Questioning/questions
assembling, 113
assessment, 111
commercial standardized tests, on, 267–269

difficulty of. *See* Difficulty index
  guidelines for writing/critiquing, 97–115
  instruction and, 99, 100
  performance-based, 288
  planning, 109–112
  reliability and number of, 127–128, 288
  time, 111–112
  validity and, 100, 137–140
  writing, 110
Test norms, 269–270, 271, 272, 282
Test reviews
  after testing, 138–140
  before testing, 108–109, 123, 124
Test(s). *See also* Achievement tests; Official
    assessments
  commercial. *See* Commercial standardized
    achievement tests
  decisions in planning, 122–123
  defined, 2
  disabilities and, 62
  form of, 277
  level of, 277
  national achievement, 8
  nonstandardized, 8
  paper-and-pencil. *See* Paper-and-pencil tests
  preparation for, 122–123, 271
  provincial. *See* Provincial assessments
  pupil accommodations for, 115–116
  question formats, 125
  scheduling, 125, 125–126
  standardized. *See* Standardized assessments
  strategies for taking, 126, 127
  subject matter pre-, 24–25
  teacher-made, 112, 264
  "teaching to the", 123
  textbook, 112
  unintended clues in, 127
Testwise skills, 124, 256
Textbook tests, 112
  commercial vs., 266
Textbooks
  commercial standardized tests and, 267, 283
  planning and, 45, 59–60
True-false items, 91

Uniform Ministry Examinations (Quebec), 244,
    246

Validity, 8, 10–11, 13, 363
  assessment information, 295
  commercial achievement tests, of, 278–288
  disabilities and, 62
  early assessment and, 24–25, 30–32, 59–60
  ethics and, 13, 29
  grading and, 202, 205, 215–216
  improving, 123
  instructional assessment, 80
  instructional assessment, in, 71, 74
  large-scale assessment, 256
  official assessments, of, 80, 123, 127
  performance assessments, of, 159, 180–183
  portfolio assessment, of, 176
  test items and, 99, 137–140
  test preparation and, 122, 254
  threats to, 30–32
Violence, 23

Wechsler Intelligence Scale for Children
    (WISC-IV), 8, 263
Woodcock Reading Mastery Tests (WRMT-R), 51
Writing, portfolio for, 174, 179

Yukon Achievement Tests (YAT), 244, 246